THE ILLUSTRATED

SELF-CARE BIBLE

Maintaining positive self-care, including physical health, emotional wellness, and life-balance

GENERAL EDITOR: RACHEL NEWCOMBE

HarperCollinsPublishers
1 London Bridge Street
London SE1 9GF

www.harpercollins.co.uk

10 9 8 7 6 5 4 3 2 1

Published by HarperCollinsPublishers in 2020

General Editor: Rachel Newcombe
Authors: Rachel Newcombe, Barbara Currie, Christina Feldman,
C. Norman Shealy, Anthea Courtenay, Lesley Ackland, and Stewart Mitchell
Cover and interior designer: Peter Clayman
Picture researcher: Peter Clayman
Proofreaders: Catherine Brereton and Helena Caldon
Indexer: Ben Murphy

Library of Congress Cataloging-in-Publication Data has been applied for.

ISBN: 978-0-00-841755-0

Printed and bound in China

Note from the Publisher
Any information given in this book is not intended to be taken as a replacement for medical advice. Any person with a condition requiring medical attention should consult a qualified practitioner or therapist

FSC www.fsc.org
MIX
Paper from responsible sources
FSC™ C007454

This book is produced from independently certified FSC™ paper to ensure responsible forest management.

For more information visit: www.harpercollins.co.uk/green

THE ILLUSTRATED
SELF-CARE BIBLE

Maintaining positive self-care, including physical health, emotional wellness, and life-balance

Harper
Collins

CONTENTS

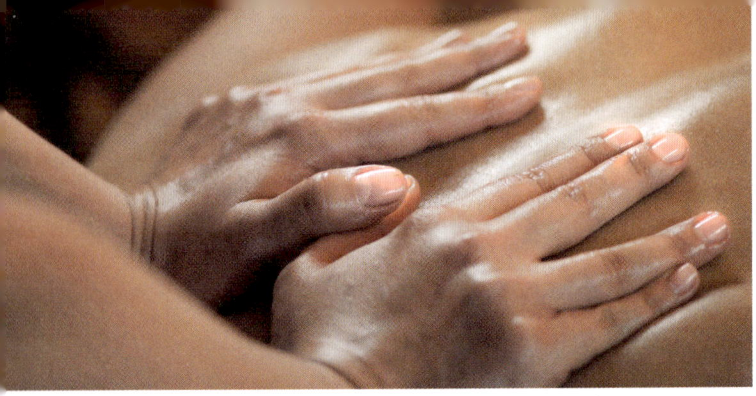

FOREWORD

When life is busy and you're juggling multiple demands, you may often be the last person you take care of. There's no doubt that other people's needs and demands matter, but it's important to look after your own health and well-being, too.

The *Self-Care Bible* helps put the emphasis back on you, so that self-care becomes an essential part of your everyday life. It outlines exactly why your health and well-being is crucial and the reasons why you should focus on it regularly, not occasionally or when you happen to remember.

The book explores three key areas of self-care—physical, emotional, and social/life-balance—and offers practical advice, tried-and-tested techniques, and ideas for incorporating self-care habits into your daily routine.

There's a wealth of information about wellness and how you can nurture yourself to a healthier, more balanced life. Emphasizing the power of natural health, this guide gives step-by-step exercises and advice on healing remedies, massage, meditation, yoga, Pilates, and nutrition.

The emotional wellness section offers insight into common struggles, including better ways of coping with stress, developing emotional resilience, learning to be kinder and more compassionate, and to practice forgiveness. Social wellness topics covered include developing support systems, setting boundaries, and workplace wellness, plus the all-important issue of knowing how and when to ask for help.

Use this book to help nourish, inspire, encourage, and motivate you to live a healthier, fuller life. Whether you read it from start to finish, or dip into it when you feel the need, enjoy the variety of ideas and inspiration it contains and take pride in giving yourself the self-care you deserve. The templates and checklists at the back of the book will help you plan out and put these new ideas into action.

Enjoy exploring the information at your fingertips and, most of all, enjoy developing your own regular self-care habits.

RACHEL NEWCOMBE, GENERAL EDITOR

INTRODUCTION THERAPIES

WHAT IS SELF-CARE?

Self-care isn't a new concept. However, it has become a lot more popular in the mainstream in recent years, and rightly so. It's a buzzword that you may have seen on social media and in magazines, but it's about more than just looking and feeling good. Put simply, self-care is the act of looking after and nurturing yourself—physically, emotionally, and socially.

Discovering and focusing on self-care will allow you to live your best life.

In today's hectic and often stressful world, it's easy to forget to focus on yourself and to look after your needs. When life is busy, it's only natural to get caught up in work, taking care of children, rushing from one place to another, and enjoying an active social life. With so many commitments to juggle, it's no wonder that looking after yourself can get overlooked.

It's often only when things "catch up" with you, when physical or mental health problems occur, that you realize you matter, too, and you need to stop putting yourself last.

That's why self-care is so important. When you learn to focus on self-care, you can integrate it into your daily life to form part of your regular routine. Self-care is about achieving a better balance in your life and knowing when to give in, stop, and look after you. It's learning about your needs, how you cope best in certain situations, and how you can manage difficult issues better. And it's about finding things that you enjoy doing and including them in your life as much as possible.

Ultimately, discovering self-care involves learning to look after and love yourself so that you can experience optimum wellness physically, mentally, and emotionally, allowing you to live your life as the best version of yourself.

SELF-CARE IS NOT . . .

—

Self-care is not about being selfish. It is not a selfish act to focus on yourself and to take time to look after you; it's actually it's a self-respectful act. The more you take time to look after yourself and keep your physical, emotional, and social wellness in check, the more energy you'll have for focusing on your work, friends, loved ones, and the commitments and activities in your life. By developing regular self-care practices, you're taking control and empowering yourself.

Keeping active and looking after your physical wellness is a key part of self-care.

ELEMENTS OF SELF-CARE

—

The art of developing self-care habits doesn't involve one single act. Instead, there are multiple elements involved, from improving areas of your physical wellness routine and looking after your emotional health, to taking care of your life balance and achieving a better social wellness. It is incremental and holistic.

PHYSICAL SELF-CARE

—

Physical self-care involves taking care of your body in order to improve your physical wellness. One of the key elements of keeping your body moving and maintaining the energy you need to get through the day is to ensure that you get a good night's sleep. It is also important to learn how to truly relax and develop healthy night-time routines, giving yourself the best chance for your body to unwind and find deep and restorative sleep.

What you choose to eat and drink plays a major role in your physical wellness. This involves making healthy choices about the foods and drinks that will make you feel good and give you the right balance of the energy and nutrition you need.

Exercising is a vital element of physical self-care, too, and it helps if you can find forms of exercise that not only meet your body's exercise needs, but that you enjoy doing and can incorporate into your daily life.

EMOTIONAL SELF-CARE

—

Mental health plays an equally important role to physical health, yet it is often overlooked. Emotional self-care practices involve finding ways to take care of your mind, from managing stress and developing emotional resilience, to learning to meditate and exploring new ideas for creative pursuits.

Emotional self-care also involves finding out more about your true self and developing skills such as kindness, compassion, and improved communication to help you cope better with challenging situations at home or work.

Making healthy choices about the food you eat is an important part of achieving physical wellness.

SOCIAL SELF-CARE

—

Social self-care involves taking care of your life balance and improving your social wellness. How you live, the support systems you have, and how you communicate with other people can all affect you. So too can your work and home life factors, such as how you deal with money and time management. Focusing on ways to improve your social habits and develop healthy social relationships can boost and re-balance your social self-care needs, allowing for deeper and more nurturing relationships.

Incorporating self-care into your life will help you toward a happier, healthier you.

Developing a self-care routine won't happen overnight. It's a gradual process of finding what works best for you and the areas you most need to focus on, then applying those to your own life. The more you practice self-care, the more it will become second-nature, and the happier and healthier you can be.

THE SELF-CARE CONTINUUM

Self-care plays an important role in all areas of your physical, emotional, and social wellness. While it is good to focus on what you can do to help yourself, it's also important to acknowledge that there are times when you might not be able to manage your health entirely on your own. In fact, asking for and accepting help and advice when you need it is a key component of positive and successful self-care.

Health professionals view the concept of self-care as a continuum. This means that there are situations in which you are fully responsible as an individual for your health and can consciously help yourself and make your own choices. But there are also times when other people should play a part and be professionally responsible by providing you with pure medical care.

The self-care continuum is like a sliding scale. On one side there is you, the individual providing yourself with pure self-care, and on the other side there are health or medical professionals providing you with pure medical care. In between there's a gradual changing scale of scenarios on the continuum where the level of your own involvement and that of other people evolves as required. An example of this "in between" are the situations where you need advice or guidance from other people, but can apply their advice to your self-care, without requiring pure medical care.

PURE SELF-CARE

Pure self-care means that you are responsible as an individual for looking after and managing your health and well-being . This affects the daily choices you make, your lifestyle decisions, and how you self-manage minor ailments and cope with long-term health conditions.

Daily choices are the actions over which you have complete control. This includes the choices you make about things on a daily basis, such as what you eat and drink, what time you get up in the morning, what time you go to bed, and how you manage your hygiene.

Lifestyle choices are the decisions you make about what you do in your free time, as well as in your work. Examples include whether or not you smoke, how often you exercise, what type of diet you follow, what type of job you choose to do, what hobbies and interests you have, etc.

If you experience minor ailments, such as a sore throat, cough, insect bite, cuts, or bruises, then in many cases you're able to use your existing knowledge to make decisions about how to manage these issues yourself. Or you may need to seek help and advice from a natural health practitioner or pharmacist and use their guidance to help you self-manage the ailment.

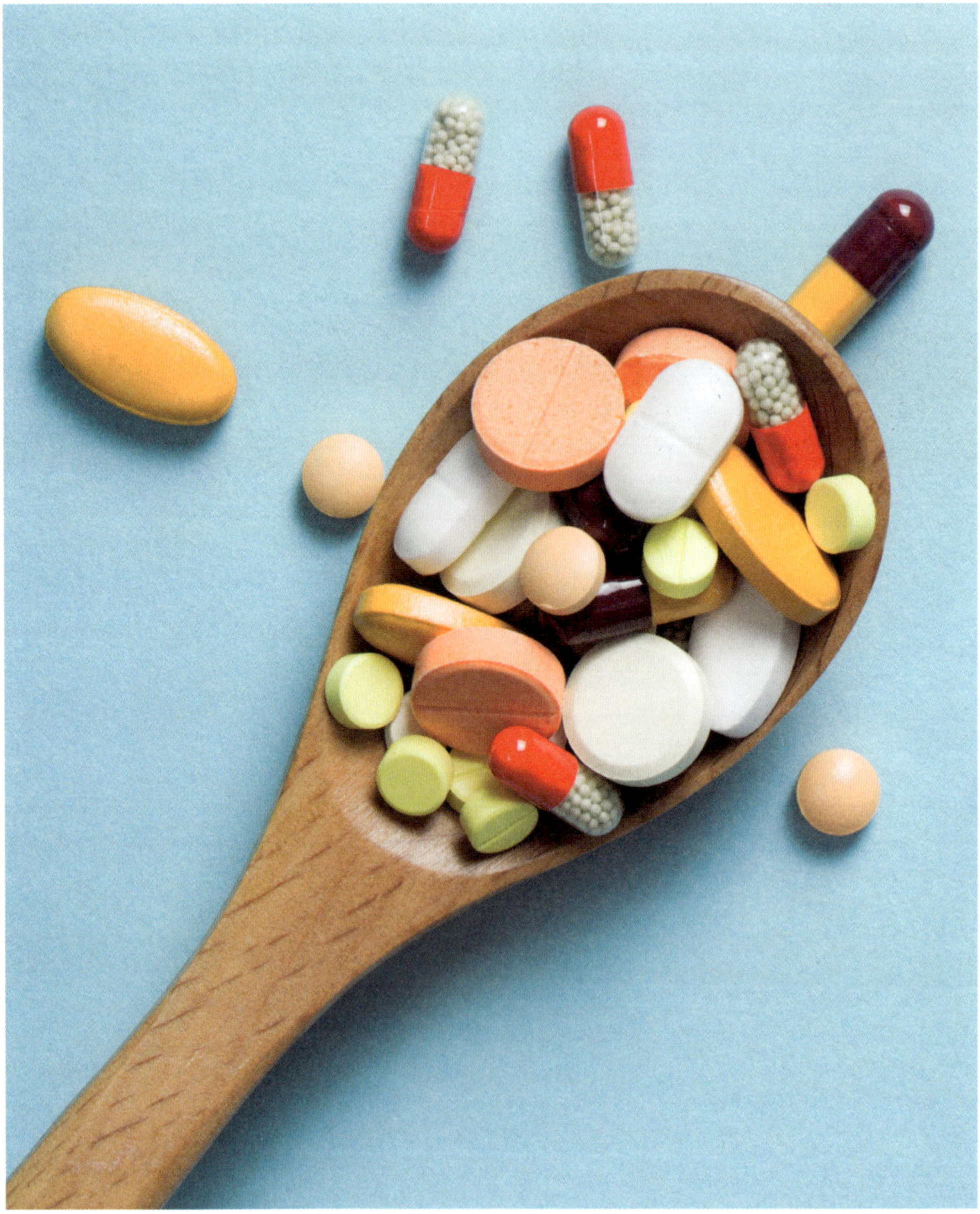

Pure medical self-care can be necessary in the cases of severe or sudden health concerns.

In many cases, if you have a long-term health condition you can often learn to self-manage it without the need to constantly see a health professional, unless a change occurs. For example, in the case of asthma you can manage your health by using inhalers as prescribed, or if you have anxiety, you can take care of yourself by taking prescription medicine or having treatments as advised.

PURE MEDICAL CARE

—

At the other end of the self-care continuum is pure medical care. These are the situations and circumstances where you require help beyond pure self-care. This is where you put yourself in the hands of health and medical professionals who become responsible for supporting your health.

Pure medical care becomes essential if you have a sudden, unexpected accident or illness, have major mental health problems, or suffer from major trauma.

Acute conditions are those that suddenly and unexpectedly happen, such as a stroke, heart attack, an accident at work, or being involved in a car crash. These are situations where you need to turn to medical professionals for help and care (and where it would be damaging to your health and well-being if you did not).

While long-term mental health issues, such as depression, can be successfully managed through self-care (often with guidance and intermittent support), if you experience sudden, acute major mental health problems, then in-hospital psychiatric care may become necessary. In such cases, medical professionals become responsible for looking after you in the best way possible.

Some situations cannot be solved by self-care alone and need the help of health professionals.

In situations where major trauma occurs, such as experiencing severe injuries or a serious car accidents, pure medical care is essential. In these cases, the responsibility for looking after your health and well-being lies with healthcare professionals.

Pure medical care continues until you recover and you can then resume the process of self-care again.

THE BENEFITS OF SELF-CARE

There are numerous benefits to be gained from maintaining self-care. As you begin to regularly incorporate self-care practices into your daily life, you'll notice positive changes occurring—physically, emotionally, and socially—and you'll begin to feel happier and healthier.

Small changes can have a big impact, and that's certainly true for self-care. Self-care involves consciously choosing to do things that nourish or improve your wellness. The more you practice self-care and integrate the habits into your everyday routine, the more benefits you'll gain.

Looking after yourself will make you feel stronger, more positive, empowered, in control, and better equipped to face life's ups and downs head on. Self-care can help reduce stress and enable you to sleep better and deal with difficult emotions. The benefits aren't just personal—they can impact on all areas of your life, from your relationships and lifestyle, to your work and productivity.

From a practical point of view, self-care isn't hard to do, nor is it time-consuming to work on. It has the benefit of being accessible to anyone, and there are plenty of ways to incorporate elements of self-care into your life without spending money.

Here's an insight into just some of the many benefits you could unlock from taking time to focus on yourself and working on your self-care strategy.

MORE ENERGY

—

Regularly practicing self-care, such as eating heathier meals, knocking insomnia on its head, and engaging in exercise you enjoy can result in increased energy. In turn, having more energy helps put the zest back in your life and has many positive benefits, as outlined below.

IMPROVED SELF-CONFIDENCE AND SELF-ESTEEM

—

Taking positive actions to nurture yourself through self-care boosts self-confidence and self-esteem. Self-care can make you feel happier and healthier, more confident in your own self-knowledge, and more mentally connected and in control—even when life throws you a curveball.

BETTER DIET AND NUTRITION

—

Physically, your body will benefit from having a healthier, more nutritionally balanced diet and from getting a better range of vitamins and minerals. Expanding your diet and exploring new food options will mean you're eating a better variety of nutrients, boosting your energy and, in turn, helping your overall physical health.

A balanced diet means a better intake of nutrients.

GAIN A BETTER UNDERSTANDING OF YOURSELF

—

Taking time to focus on yourself gives you the opportunity for introspection. Sometimes it might be hard to face reality and bring up old wounds and worries. But working through these issues can result in gaining a far better understanding of yourself and how to find reserves of strength and coping mechanisms for the next of take over knocks.

IMPROVED SELF-COMPASSION

—

The more you learn to take care of yourself, the better you feel. As you practice self-care, you'll find that your levels of self-compassion will increase, you'll be less critical about yourself, and you'll feel more positive and understanding.

IMPROVED ABILITY TO RELAX

—

You might think you know how to relax, but not all forms of relaxation are equal. If your previous relaxation attempts simply involved slumping in front of the TV at the end of the day, self-care techniques could be a revelation. You'll gain an improved ability to relax, both for short periods during the day and at the day's end, and be able to put them into practice to help you feel healthier and more energized. Plus, self-care activities that help you relax can help reduce stress and anxiety, too.

The benefits of self-care can impact your relationships and your way of living at any stage of your life.

FEELING MORE SOCIALLY CONNECTED

—

As you focus more on your social self-care needs, you'll feel more socially connected. You'll nurture the social connections that are most important to you, identify ones that aren't, and develop a stronger support system.

IMPROVED PRODUCTIVITY

—

When you slow down and focus on the things that matter, rather than trying to juggle anything and everything, your productivity improves. Self-care can involve learning to say "no" to non-essentials—whether that be extra work or additional social commitments—and focusing more on the things you want to do. When you're no longer exhausted by trying to do everything, you'll find that you're more productive with what you choose to do.

DOING MORE OF THE THINGS YOU ENJOY

—

Self-care is all about focusing on the things that help you feel good, whether that's a particular exercise you enjoy or finding new ways to express yourself or get creative. There are so many benefits to be gained for doing more of the things you enjoy, whether it's on a daily or weekly basis.

Taking time to relax can help reduce stress and anxiety in a busy life.

KNOWING HOW TO LOOK AFTER YOURSELF

—

By regularly practicing self-care, you'll get to know yourself so much more and feel re-connected to the true you. There are bound to be times when you feel out of alignment, but once you've learned positive and achievable self-care techniques and are confident about what works for you, you'll be well equipped to look after yourself and handle situations with care.

HOW TO USE THIS BOOK

This book offers a comprehensive guide to the physical, emotional, and social elements of self-care and acts as a bible for everything you need in order to nurture yourself and gain a healthier balance in your home, work, and social life.

The book is designed so that it can be read cover-to-cover or dipped into, allowing you to focus on the areas that are most relevant to you at any one time.

There are helpful resources, practical tips, inspiring techniques, and ideas to try, as well as foods to eat, skills to learn, and exercise routines to adopt. You can take it at your own pace and try things gradually, or dive right in and devour it all. But above all, be open to new ideas, have fun exploring the variety of options available, and enjoy developing a happier, healthier you!

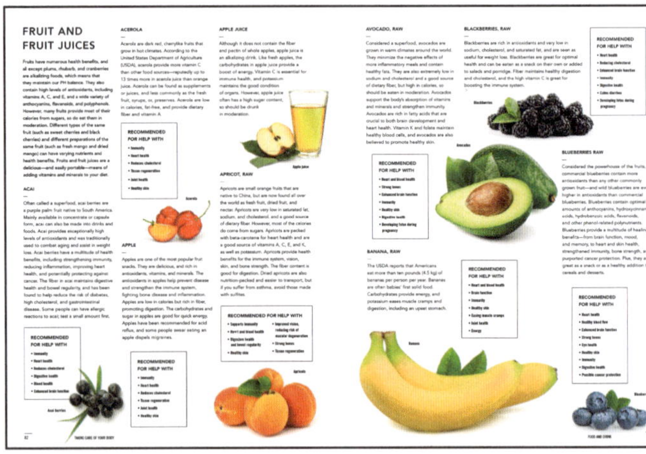

PART ONE: TAKING CARE OF YOUR BODY

Part One focuses on maintaining your body and looking after your physical wellness.

The Sleep and Rest chapter guides you through learning to relax more effectively and developing a healthier night-time routine. There are ideas for beating insomnia and meditation techniques to help you find a greater sense of calm and connection.

The Food and Drink chapter offers a comprehensive guide to improving physical wellness through diet and nutrition. There are extensive guides to different types of foods, the benefits these nutrients have, and how they can build a stronger you. Use these to be inspired to broaden your diet and experiment with new ingredients.

Finding a type of exercise that you enjoy is key to creating a regular routine, so in the Exercise chapter you'll discover lots of ideas for beneficial exercises. Use these to try out new ways to improve your aerobic exercise, posture, balance, and toning.

You can also take care of your physical wellness through therapeutic massage, and in the Massage chapter you'll discover lots of ways to self-massage your body and limbs. Use these ideas to treat your body, relax your muscles, and unwind.

PART TWO: TAKING CARE OF YOUR MIND

Part Two looks at taking care of your mind and your emotional wellness needs.

In the Healing the Mind chapter, you'll find lots of information about mental health issues, such as the effects of stress, learning forgiveness, and why emotional resilience is important. There are ideas and tips to use and apply to your life, including learning meditation and mindful breathing.

In the Self and Selflessness chapter, you can discover more about your own unique identity and how to awaken your true self. There are techniques to use to enhance and develop kindness and compassion, as well as practical ways to connect with nature. Use these ideas to boost and re-balance your emotional self-care.

PART THREE: TAKING CARE OF YOUR LIFE BALANCE

—

Part Three focuses on your social wellness and how you can take steps to improve the balance in your life.

The Friends and Home chapter contains practical advice about developing healthy support systems, learning to set boundaries, improving different forms of communication, and learning when and how to ask for help. Having a safe, secure, clean, and organized home environment is crucial to your health and wellness, so there are some ideas you can put to practical use on how to improve your spatial wellness for greater calm and productivity.

COMMUNICATION

Communication allows you to express yourself and listen to other people. In order to build social relationships, share your experiences, and enhance your support systems, clear communication is crucial.

Good communication is a skill that can be built on and developed. Being able to communicate more effectively can boost your self-confidence, improve your relationships, and help you feel better about yourself. It's a form of self-care, as sharing your true feelings can help release bottled-up feelings and emotions.

As well as just spoken words, good communication involves body language, facial expressions, and posture, from all parties involved.

HOW TO EXPRESS YOURSELF

It's not always easy or straightforward to express yourself, especially if you've not been used to talking about yourself. But when you've got someone on your team or in your support system who cares and will take time to listen to you, it's well worth trying. It can really help lift burdens and boost your emotional wellness.

Here are some tips to help you learn to express yourself effectively:

- Be assertive—be calm and relaxed and try to have positive body posture.
- Explain things as clearly as you can.
- Think before you speak—consider how someone else might take what you say.
- Express your emotions appropriately—don't get angry or confrontational.
- Don't get defensive if the other person expresses a view or opinion that's different to yours.

LISTENING TO OTHER PEOPLE

Communication is a two-way process—it involves talking and listening. In the same way that you'd like people to listen to you, other people in your support network will appreciate you listening to them too. Listening will help build and strengthen your relationship.

You can improve your listening skills by:

- Being patient—let someone else take their time speaking and don't interrupt them.
- Giving them 100 percent attention—turn off your cell phone and focus on the other person.
- Being neutral and open to listening—don't be judgmental about someone else's views or experiences, even if they differ from yours.
- Being prepared to just listen—sometimes a person might simply need someone else to listen to them, without having your advice or input.
- Showing empathy—show that you're listening, and you care, by using verbal and non-verbal acknowledgements.
- Acknowledging their feelings—if someone has strong feelings, acknowledge them so they know you're listening and taking them seriously.
- Being encouraging—if someone else is feeling low or down, be encouraging towards them; it's not always easy to open up and talk.

ONLINE COMMUNICATION

These days, a lot of communication is conducted online. Although some people find it easier to type emails or messages rather than talk to someone, this form of communication comes with its ups and downs.

When you're communicating online, you lose the ability to see each other's facial reactions, posture, and body language. This can sometimes make it tricky to convey a true picture of how you're feeling and the real meaning behind some words and sentences can be misread, misjudged, or lost completely.

Of course, emojis can go some way to express how words are intended, but they still don't replace the ability to actually see an individual's body language or reaction. It's important to bear such issues in mind when you're communicating online and try to be even clearer in the language you use and the way you express yourself with the written word. For example, if you're telling someone about how you feel, you may have to write this down more explicitly, explaining exactly how something or someone made you feel.

COPING WITH CONFLICT

If your communication breaks down and conflict occurs, it can trigger strong emotions, disappointment, and hurt feelings. If handled inappropriately, the conflict can rage on and cause ongoing resentment and fractured relationships. However, by learning to cope with conflict more effectively, you can help to resolve it.

Communication is key when you're dealing with conflict. As much as you may feel hurt, annoyed, or upset, try to remain as calm as possible. Being calm will help you to understand someone else's verbal and non-verbal communication more effectively. Being in control of your emotions also helps you communicate with the other person without intimidating or challenging them.

It's hard to remain calm in the face of conflict, but it's a very useful skill to learn. If necessary, you can save and offload your true emotions later, either to someone else that you trust or to yourself through techniques such as journaling.

Sometimes conflict can also be eased by adding a degree of humor into the situation. It's important that you judge the situation first, though, as when used inappropriately this could escalate things.

Being able to resolve conflict provides an opportunity for growth. You can learn from your experiences, feel confident in your actions, and build a stronger relationship with the person concerned.

In the Finances and Work chapter, you'll find ideas and advice for working on skills such as money management, setting goals, time management, and workplace wellness. Use this information to help you become better informed and to address what's important for your social self-care.

PART FOUR: REFERENCES AND RESOURCES

—

In Part Four you'll find some practical advice and useful tools to use to put everything you've learned about self-care into real and tangible action.

The checklist on page 326 highlights all the key points and goals involved in self-care so that you can remind yourself at a glance.

There are templates to use to help you set yourself goals, develop exercise routines, adopt healthy eating patterns, and learn to budget more successfully. Use these, and you'll be well on your way to achieving all-around self-care success.

There is also a glossary of terms, a list of useful resources—such as websites and organizations you might like to contact— further reading ideas.

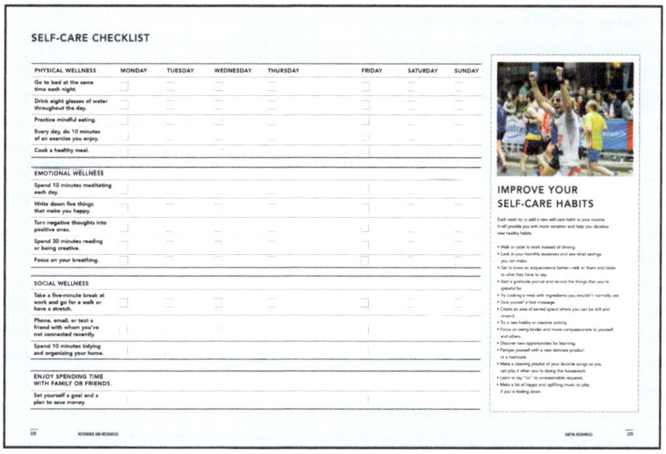

SELF-CARE CHECKLIST

PHYSICAL WELLNESS	MONDAY	TUESDAY	WEDNESDAY	THURSDAY	FRIDAY	SATURDAY	SUNDAY
Go to bed at the same time each night.							
Drink eight glasses of water throughout the day.							
Practice mindful eating.							
Every day, do 10 minutes of an exercise you enjoy.							
Cook a healthy meal.							
EMOTIONAL WELLNESS							
Spend 10 minutes meditating each day.							
Write down five things that make you happy.							
Turn negative thoughts into positive ones.							
Spend 30 minutes reading or being creative.							
Focus on your breathing.							
SOCIAL WELLNESS							
Take a five-minute break at work and go for a walk or have a stretch.							
Phone, email, or text a friend with whom you've not connected recently.							
Spend 10 minutes tidying and organizing your home.							
ENJOY SPENDING TIME WITH FAMILY OR FRIENDS.							
Set yourself a goal and a plan to save money.							

IMPROVE YOUR SELF-CARE HABITS

Each week try to add a new self-care habit to your routine. It will provide you with more variation and help you develop new healthy habits.

- Walk or cycle to work instead of driving.
- Look at your monthly expenses and see what savings you can make.
- Get to know an acquaintance better—talk to them and listen to what they have to say.
- Start a gratitude journal and record the things that you're grateful for.
- Try cooking a meal with ingredients you wouldn't normally use.
- Give yourself a foot massage.
- Create an area of sacred space where you can be still and unwind.
- Try a new hobby or creative activity.
- Focus on being kinder and more compassionate to yourself and others.
- Discover new opportunities for learning.
- Pamper yourself with a new skincare product or a manicure.
- Make a cleaning playlist of your favorite songs so you can play it when you're doing the housework.
- Learn to say "no" to unreasonable requests.
- Make a list of happy and uplifting music to play if you're feeling down.

TAKING CARE OF YOUR BODY

PHYSICAL WELLNESS

PART ONE

SLEEP AND REST

CHAPTER ONE

WHAT IS SLEEP?

A good, undisturbed night's sleep is one of the most enjoyable and totally natural pleasures available to us, yet for many people sleep is hard to come by. This in turn affects the quality of their waking life.

Sleep and dreams are as much a part of life as being busy and active; they unwind the body and mind, restoring our energies to face the next day. Yet how many people regularly wake feeling really refreshed? It has been estimated that at some time half the population will be affected by insomnia. And many people, while not long-term insomniacs, experience times when the quality of their sleep is not all it could be.

Whether you suffer from long-term insomnia, full-blown insomnia, or poor sleeping patterns, this chapter is for you. It will help you to break out of poor sleep habits and bring your whole life into balance. Find out how natural medicine such as herbalism and aromatherapy can help, as well as self-help methods such as exercise, relaxation, and adopting a change of lifestyle. Use this positive, easy-to-follow guide and your sleep problems will be a thing of the past.

THE MYSTERY OF SLEEP

It is an extraordinary fact that something that occupies up to a third of our lives is still a mystery. Of course, we all know that sleep gives us rest: without it we feel tired and irritable and don't function as well as we'd like. Since 1952, sleep research laboratories attached to universities have been studying sleep patterns, with the help of human guinea pigs. They have made numerous investigations not just into how we sleep but why, and no one has yet come up with a complete answer.

If you are beset by insomnia, you might wonder what use such investigations are. Whatever sleep is for, you know you need it and feel rotten without it. But the results of many of these investigations can offer some reassurance to the non-sleeper. They have, for instance, blown away the myth that everyone needs eight hours a night. Some of them suggest that most of us could get by on less sleep than we have without coming to harm. And some have come up with ideas for improving sleep.

SLEEP STATES

In sleep the brain goes through four main stages, each characterized by different types of brainwave—the electrical impulses emitted by the brain.

STAGE 1

—

This first stage, the lightest, is the transition from wakefulness to drowsiness; as we enter it our muscles relax, the blood pressure drops, and the heart rate and digestion slow down. The brain begins to produce hormones such as serotonin and melatonin, which are associated with sleep and sleepiness (whether they actually *cause* sleep is under debate). At the same time, there is an increase in alpha waves—brainwaves of 7–14 cycles per second—which are typical of relaxed wakefulness; alpha waves also appear in people who are meditating, or under hypnosis. This stage lasts between 1–10 minutes in the normal sleeper; although we return to it at intervals during the night, it usually occupies only about 5 percent of our sleep.

STAGE 2

—

This stage starts quite soon after falling asleep and occupies about 45 percent of human sleep. It contains a mixture of deeper, slower brainwaves: theta brainwaves (3.5–7.5 cycles per second) typical of drowsiness and light sleep, and slow delta waves (under 3.5 cycles per second), during which we are really unconscious.

STAGE 3

—

Stage 3, which occupies only about 7 percent of sleep in young adults, is another transition phase to deeper sleep; as delta wave activity increases, we are taken fairly rapidly to Stage 4.

STAGE 4

—

Stage 4 is the deepest form of sleep, with delta brainwaves predominating; it makes us about 13 percent of sleep in young adults. We stay in Stage 4 for quite long periods before surfacing again to REM and Stage 1 several times during the night.

REM SLEEP

—

Rapid Eye Movement sleep is so called because the sleeper's eyes move, indicating that they are dreaming. It occurs during Stage 1 sleep, and increases in quantity later on in the night. It has now been found that we also dream during deeper stages of sleep. It used to be thought that REM sleep was the part of sleep essential to us; it was believed that these periods were needed for brain rest, and that people deprived of them would develop psychosis. This last theory has been disproved, though deprivation of REM sleep does produce irritability and difficulties in concentration, and affects the ability to retain information learned the day before. People totally deprived of REM for more than three days have started having waking dreams, in the form of hallucinations. Others have been found to become less inhibited and conscientious.

Sleep is important for physical wellness for all ages, but particularly important in growing children.

The amount of sleep you need varies from person to person, and age to age.

CORE SLEEP

—

In his book, *Why We Sleep* (OUP, 1988), sleep research expert Dr. Jim Horne proposes that the really essential part of sleep consists of Stages 3 and 4, which he calls collectively Slow Wave Sleep (SWS). During these stages the brain is in what he calls an "off-line" state: it is the only time during which this hard-working organ is totally at rest. SWS occurs largely during the first three cycles, that is, during the first half of a night's sleep.

When people are deprived of sleep by staying up all night, it has been found that they don't need to catch up with all the sleep they've lost. They recover no extra light sleep, and only a fraction of REM sleep. But they do recover all the lost deep sleep, which suggests that it is the sleep that is really essential.

In people who naturally need less sleep than the average, the same pattern is followed during the first few hours as in average sleepers. Although these people sleep for fewer hours, says Dr. Horne, they are getting the essential Slow Wave Sleep: "It is as though these short sleepers have somehow done away with what seems to be the flexible non-restorative sleep—the latter hours of sleep."

He defines Core Sleep as consisting of Slow Wave Sleep and some REM sleep. His conclusion is that so long as we get our ration of Core Sleep, the brain will recover from its waking wear and tear. The rest he calls "optional sleep," which has no essential purpose but "fills the tedious hours of darkness until sunrise, maintaining sleep beyond the point where core sleep declines," and it may in fact not be really necessary.

Good sleep is about quality, not quantity; achieving Stages 3 and 4 of the sleep cycle will support physical and mental wellness.

HOW MUCH SLEEP?

The amount of sleep needed, or taken, by individual people varies enormously. There's a standard belief that eight hours is the norm, but we all know of people who need much less. Former British Prime Minister Lady Thatcher was said to thrive on four or five, and there have been a number of other famous short sleepers, including Winston Churchill and Napoleon (both of whom catnapped during the day), Voltaire, who only needed three hours, and Dostoyevsky, who wrote his books between 3 P.M. and 5 or 6 the next morning.

It's important for couples to realize that these variations are real; a short sleeper married to a long sleeper can make their partner's life quite difficult if they insist on banging around at six in the morning, or interpret the other's genuine needs as laziness.

Short and long sleepers have been found by and large to have different personalities. Short sleepers tend to be hard-working, ambitious, and rather obsessive, as well as extrovert and efficient. Long sleepers worry more, are less self-assured, and value their sleep, which they may use as an escape. They are also often creative people—and creative people are said to dream more and to have more vivid and adventurous dreams than other people. Einstein was a long sleeper.

THE AGES OF SLEEP

—

The amount of sleep we need also varies with age. The "average" 7.5 hours applies to adults between 16 and 50. Most small babies sleep about 16–18 hours a day, and toddlers still need a lot more sleep than adults. However, some older children may actually need less than adults, something which parents don't always recognize. With adolescence, the picture changes: some teenagers will sleep up to 15 hours a night. They are not necessarily being lazy, and will grow out of it. However, parents should note that longer sleeping hours are also a symptom of depression, which can hit teenagers quite badly. At about the age of 16 we reach the "normal" adult pattern—that is, whatever is normal for us.

Older children may need less sleep than adults, until they reach the sleepy teenage years.

As we approach middle age, sleep becomes lighter and more disrupted.

From the age of 40 in men and 50 in women, the pattern alters again. In some women menopause temporarily disrupts sleeping patterns. But in everyone, as they grow older, night-time sleep becomes lighter and more broken, with fewer dreams. In addition, many older people take naps during the day, so needing less sleep at night. Including catnaps, the average sleep for 70-year-olds is about 6 hours in 24. It's important to realize this, since many old people ask their doctors for help with their "insomnia" when in fact they are sleeping quite normally for their age.

YOUR BODY CLOCK CIRCADIAN RHYTHMS

—

The functioning of our bodies is governed by a biological inner clock, known as the circadian rhythm (from the Latin *circa diem*, meaning "about a day"). This regulates the times when various organs become more or less active and when the production of various hormones peaks and tails off. The length of the circadian day is normally between 24 and 25 hours; some people have sleep problems because their body clocks are out of timing with the norm, or disturbed by things like shift work and jet lag.

The siesta, traditional in hot southern European countries such as Spain, is in decline as Mediterranean businesses come into line with the rest of Europe. Yet it could be much more natural than the worldwide norm. The circadian rhythm is set to bring on sleep twice a day, mainly at night, but also in the early afternoon, which is why many people feel sleepy after lunch.

The circadian rhythm also varies with age. Babies sleep regularly during the day, at first at around 3 hourly intervals, tailing off to a morning and an afternoon sleep; by the age of about two and a half they are sleeping in the afternoon only. In the elderly, the need for an afternoon sleep usually returns.

It appears to be the circadian rhythm which is responsible for some people being "owls," finding it hard to wake in the morning but lively at night, while others are "larks," leaping out of bed first thing and drooping by ten in the evening. Interestingly, these differences seem to lessen as people age.

Night-time sleep can shorten in older people, as they can take advantage of retirement to nap during the day.

INSOMNIA

Insomnia is defined by sleep experts as difficulty in initiating and maintaining sleep, which has continued for at least three weeks. Chronic insomnia can last for years, while intermittent insomnia can be triggered by particular anxieties or crises. People experience insomnia in different ways: for some it's the tossing and turning for what feels like hours before they drop off; others wake up at intervals and feel they never get a good night; and others wake early in the morning, and can't get off to sleep again.

Insomnia can't be measured by the number of hours you sleep, since people's needs vary so much. It's been found in sleep laboratories that some insomniacs actually sleep longer than"normal" sleepers: if you need 10 hours and only sleep for 8, then you won't feel as refreshed as the good sleeper who needs 7.

Different types of insomnia have traditionally been related to different states of mind; it's often said that not being able to get off to sleep at night is a symptom of anxiety, while waking early is a sign of depression. In fact, it's not as simple as that. Some anxious and depressed people can actually sleep more, sometimes in an effort to escape from their feelings. Some depressed people can't get off to sleep, and some anxious people fall asleep normally, but wake in the small hours.

A number of sleep experts believe that anger and resentment are more frequent causes of insomnia than anxiety and depression. Others suggest that the overactive, churning mind may not be a cause of insomnia, but a result. In addition, there is often more than one factor involved; an overactive mind may be related to an underactive body, for example. And as you can see from the checklist opposite, the causes are not always emotional.

QUALITY VERSUS QUANTITY

Insomnia is unpleasant. It is boring and uncomfortable in itself, and it can affect your daily activities, work, and relationships. However, it may not be quite as damaging as some insomniacs fear. Sleep research laboratories have shown that people who normally sleep for 7 to 8 hours can adapt over time to as much as 2 hours less sleep daily without impairing their mental or physical ability. And when people have been totally deprived of sleep for between eight and eleven days (the longest times so far studied) most of the body's organs, except for the brain, continue to function remarkably well. While the brain does need rest, Dr. Horne stresses that "everything else from the neck down seems to cope very well, without sleep, provided you get regular rest and regular food."

Nevertheless, too little sleep can and does affect us, both because of genuine fatigue, but also because we believe that shortened sleep will cause us suffering. Our beliefs about how things should be have a major effect on how we react to them.

So, how much sleep do we really need? Dr. Horne believes that around 6 hours is more than adequate for mental health; any sleep after that comes into his category of "optional sleep." If his theory is correct, what the brain needs is Core Sleep. This should provide some reassurance to insomniacs: Core Sleep predominates during the first sleep cycles, so even if you only sleep for a few hours, you will be getting a period of this important mixture of deep and REM sleep.

Conditions in sleep laboratories, of course, where the human guinea pigs are fed and rested, and have chosen to lose sleep, are quite different from those of the person tossing and turning in the lonely small hours—even if they end up getting the same amount of sleep. EEG readings which record brain activity show that most insomniacs actually sleep much more than they claim to: quite often people who feel they have only slept an hour or two have actually slept for several. It appears that people's perception of their insomnia can cause as much stress as the insomnia itself, and it may well be that worrying about insomnia can make you just as stressed and tired as not sleeping. It will also contribute to keeping you awake.

TYPE OF PROBLEM	POSSIBLE CAUSES OR CONTRIBUTORY FACTORS
Taking a long time to get to sleep (most common in people under 30 and women)	Habit Emotional stress: anxiety, depression, unhappiness, anger, guilt, etc Unsolved problems Obsessive thinking Psychiatric disturbances Dietary factors: too many junk foods, stimulating foods and drinks, and eating heavy meals late at night Digestive problems Smoking, especially in the evenings Lack of regular exercise Stress (at home or work) Major life changes: moving house, divorce, changing jobs, etc Certain medical conditions Neurological problems Needing less sleep than you think you do Napping during the day Jet lag, working night shifts and other body clock disturbances External disturbances such as noise
Waking during the night (more common in older people and men)	High degrees of anger and irritability Heavy alcohol consumption Withdrawal from alcohol or drugs (medical or otherwise) Nightmares Fear of nightmares (waking just before you are about to dream) Not being fully extended during the day
Waking early and not going back to sleep	Severe depression Sleeping pill dependency Alcoholism
Getting "enough" sleep but still feeling tired	Sleep apnea (a respiratory disorder) Depression Narcolepsy

So, if you are insomniac, there are three important things to remember. Firstly, you may be getting more sleep than you think. Secondly, so long as you get some sleep and can relax your body, you will not come to long-term harm. Thirdly, your attitude towards your sleep has a lot to do with the quality of the sleep you get. The first step towards beating insomnia is not to worry about it.

Insomnia can be debilitating, but sometimes worrying about poor sleep can make the situation worse.

Only when you drink from the river of silence shall you indeed sing.

Kahlil Gibran

BREAKING THE INSOMNIA HABIT

Human beings are odd creatures: most of us like to think we are independent, free-thinking spirits. Yet a surprising amount of our behavior is totally conditioned, starting when we are very young. Much of our conditioning is helpful and life-supporting: it would be very inconvenient if every time you crossed a road you had to relearn the desirability of looking both ways, or what red, yellow, and green lights mean. Unfortunately, the mechanical part of our brain absorbs other, less helpful lessons, such as associating bed with lying awake.

It's common these days for the brain to be likened to a computer—a computer more vast and complex than any yet built, and of course with a capacity for original thought, but nonetheless a machine which obediently reproduces whatever programming is fed into it.

SELF-TALK

—

The best way to break unhelpful habits is to start exchanging them for helpful ones. The first thing is to recognize in what particular ways your habitual thinking or behavior is keeping you in that sleepless groove. How do you talk to yourself and others about sleep? If you label yourself "insomniac" and tell yourself every time you head for bed that it'll take you ages to get to sleep, you are simply reinforcing the programming that keeps you awake. You can change some of that thinking now, by telling yourself that you are now on the way to improving your sleep, and by no longer telling other people that you suffer from insomnia.

Be honest with yourself about this. Lots of people "enjoy" their ailments. In some cases this can be an excuse for avoiding things they don't want to do, or even living a more fulfilled life. I would stress that this kind of pattern is very rarely deliberate: it's often another conditioned response, perhaps going back to a time when being ill got a child more of its mother's love and attention than when they were was well. Never sleeping well may prevent people like this from facing up to other problems, or taking on new ventures which would mean change. That doesn't mean they are purposefully choosing not to sleep, but it's possible that lack of sleep has secondary advantages, such as making their families feel sorry for them.

Could this apply to you? And if it does, do you really want to be someone others feel sorry for? Close your eyes and imagine for a moment telling your spouse or workmates, "I slept wonderfully last night!" How does it feel? Probably uncomfortable at this moment, because it isn't true. How comfortable would it feel if it were true?

Start noticing your habitual thoughts about insomnia. In particular, look out for sentences beginning "I always ..." or "I never ..." or "I know ..."For example: "I always take hours to get to sleep" or "I always wake up for hours in the middle of the night." These statements may not actually be true, although they feel true to you. As we've seen, most insomniacs overestimate how long they take to get to sleep or lie awake during the night. You could make a start by recognizing that your perception of the amount of sleep you get may be inaccurate.

"I'm never going to get to sleep tonight" is another habitual statement which is an excellent way of programming your brain to stay awake.

"I know I'll feel dreadful if I can't get to sleep." Of course, lack of sleep makes you tired, but you can also talk yourself into feeling worse. There are alternatives, such as telling yourself that even though you'd like more sleep, your body is still getting all the rest it needs.

Make a game of catching these kinds of thoughts. It may help you to write them down. Then try replacing your negative statements with positive ones; a good start might be: "I'm now learning how to sleep better." Make your positive statements ones you can believe. Telling yourself "I am going to sleep perfectly tonight" may not work, because at this point you probably won't believe it, and trying to convince yourself will set up further tension. But you could try: "I will take tonight as it comes." You may be surprised by the results.

Starting to change your self-talk can be a way of opening up other possibilities. Once you realize that you don't have to be a victim of your own thinking and reactions, all kinds of barriers can begin to crumble.

CHANGING THE PATTERN

—

A popular way of treating insomnia today is a behavioral psychology method called stimulus-control, which consists of retraining yourself to sleep by learning to associate bed and bedtime with sleep, and sleep alone. This is the routine:

1. Use your bed and bedroom for sleep only. Don't watch television, listen to the radio, read, work, smoke, scroll social media, surf the internet or eat in bed. Making love is permitted, and can actually help you sleep.

2. Always get up at the same time, including weekends and vacations. Lie-ins may be tempting, but if you take more sleep than you need on Sunday morning it'll be harder to get to sleep on Sunday night. If you find waking up really difficult, place your alarm clock at the other side of the room so that you have to get up to turn it off. Put the light on straight away, as light can stimulate wakefulness.

3. Don't take naps during the day. You can overcome post-lunch sleepiness with some deep breathing, or a quick walk round the block.

4. Don't go to bed until you are really sleepy.

5. If you don't fall asleep within 10 minutes, get up and do something else in another room. Don't go back to bed until you are ready to fall asleep.

There are further sleep-assisting habits you can develop:

1. Deal with specific anxieties during the day or early evening.

2. Avoid stimulating foods and drinks in the evening. These include coffee, tea, and alcohol. Smoking is also a stimulant; if you can't give it up immediately, at least cut down, especially in the evening.

3. Avoid stimulating activities late at night, including strenuous exercise, work and arguments.

4. Establish a winding-down routine before you go to bed. Spend the last hour before bedtime preparing for sleep, including some relaxation and a warm bath.

5. Make sure your bedroom is both well-aired and of a comfortable temperature.

A crucial part of tackling insomnia is mind over matter—tell yourself that you are in control of your sleep.

SELF-HYPNOSIS AND VISUALIZATION

—

The imagination can have a direct effect on the body, for good or ill. When you imagine or remember a disaster, your pulse can start racing and your breathing can become more shallow, as the body's stress system starts revving up. It doesn't matter that the disaster isn't real: your body and nervous system react as though it is. Similarly, when you imagine yourself healthy and happy, your body starts to feel healthier and stronger.

In a relaxed, day-dreaming state, you can mentally picture the outcome that you want, whether it's better sleep, or confidently taking and passing your driving test. It's important to believe and expect that what you visualize will come about. In so doing, you are using an in-depth way of reprogramming your mental computer.

Visualization techniques may not be right for everyone: if you are an anxious striver, you may put too much effort into what should be effortless, or make yourself worse by focusing on symptoms rather than health. But even if you don't use specific techniques, you are using the power of thought and imagination throughout the day, both mentally and verbally. All the more reason to exchange depressing thoughts about your life and your sleep for positive ideas about what you really want.

For successful self-hypnosis, the first, essential step is to be able to relax deeply. If you are normally tense, you may need some help in learning to relax sufficiently. (See "Healing the Mind," pages 210–251.) Some people have successfully taught themselves to visualize from books; there are also some good downloads on the market which can start you off, though it's not a good idea to rely on them for the rest of your life. For most people it's easier initially to be taught by someone else.

THE CHURNING MIND

—

Probably the most common complaint among poor sleepers is difficulty in getting off to sleep. It's almost always related to a mind that won't switch itself off. Your thoughts go round and round, you toss and turn, and an hour later you're tired, twitchy, and wide awake.

The churning mind may be caused by anxiety about something specific—an exam, a job interview, a work project, a partner's illness, or the state of your finances.

Possibly even more often it is caused by resentment or anger, brooding over unpleasant events, sometimes from the recent past, sometimes from way back. You relive the scenes, inventing scenarios in which you find just the right words to put down that person who insulted you yesterday, or even years ago. Or you may be feeling depressed and lonely, wishing your life were different, blaming yourself or others because it isn't, and replaying past regrets, missed opportunities, or lost happiness.

A great deal of night-time churning is connected with unfinished business, something that computer in your head can't stand. It chugs away looking for solutions, and won't shut up. Or it allows you to get to sleep, and then wakes you up with a bad dream to remind you of a problem, or to tell you, "Hey, we really must do some worrying about this!"

One of the most common causes of disrupted sleep is a busy and churning mind.

Regularly waking with nightmares or bad dreams can make you anxious about going to bed in the first place: usually these, too, concern unfinished business. Night terrors—suddenly waking from non-dreaming sleep with a sense of fear and doom—are often the result of past traumas. Recurring dreams, too, may stem from traumatic past events—car crashes, an abusive partner, or an assault—which the conscious mind has tried to forget. But the unconscious mind is still trying to cope with these traumas in the only way it knows how. In such cases it is important to seek professional help from a counselor, psychotherapist, or hypnotherapist who can help you to heal your fears, so that they no longer fester and cause you misery. Some people aren't particularly worried about anything, but just have very active minds. Many of them accept this, often creative people who come up with creative ideas as they lie awake. But if your thoughts are unpleasant, sad, or anxious, they are crying out to be dealt with. Bed is not the place to deal with them.

WHO'S IN THE DRIVING SEAT?

—

Rushing round all day and going to bed with a mind that's exhausted but awake is all too common these days. Modern life doesn't encourage natural rhythms. We start work at the same time all year round, whether it's dark or light; commuter travel is uncomfortable and frustrating. Office atmospheres are often unhealthy as well as fraught: lunch may be a snatched sandwich or hamburger. For many people "relaxation" takes place in the artificial atmosphere and noise of bars and clubs.

Small wonder that rushers-round can't sleep. The whole physical and nervous system becomes jangled and out of gear. There is no breathing space to look at problems—or just to breathe! Body and mind are poorly nourished. And underlying this frantic rush, an anxious little voice is often sending anxious little messages that we don't want to hear—"Am I good enough?"—"Is this all there is to life?"—"Why aren't I happy?"

If your life is anything like this, and it has resulted in insomnia, ask yourself what you are truly getting out of it. OK, so modern life is like that. But does that mean yours has to be? What or who is driving you to overwork, eat badly, maybe drink too much, or work until all hours so that by bedtime your brain is buzzing?

Listen to your thoughts and worries and be kind to yourself to alleviate sleep-robbing stress.

Much of our busy-busy behaviour is due to conditioning by other people, and our beliefs about how life should be lived may be nothing to do with what we really need. The work ethic says we mustn't waste a moment; societal standards say we must have a "good time" and be successful. We must also be seen to be successful by buying and owning more and more goodies for ourselves and our families; to keep the merry-go-round turning we have to work even harder. Yet when you were a child, was this what you wanted from life? Who programmed your computer?

Our beliefs come from a number of different sources, which is why they often conflict. Some psychotherapists point out that we all have multiple personalities, often referred to as sub-personalities or "voices." For example, most people have an inner critic sitting in judgement on their every action; at the same time there's an inner child, made to feel small by the critic's remarks. Many of us have an inner saboteur, doing its best to make us make a mess of things. But there are other parts of us which often don't get addressed—for example, a wise self, a peaceful self, and a creative child who wants to play.

So, try listening to the thoughts and voices underlying your daily rush. Who's driving you on? Are you responding to other people's programming—perhaps a critical father demanding that you prove your worth, or a perfectionist mother setting you impossibly high standards? Do you have to believe those voices from the past? What does the real you need and want from life, and are you getting it?

We are all influenced by the people around us; but take stock and consider, is this what I want from life?

A HEALTHY BEDROOM

Ideally, your bedroom should be associated with sleep, and not with other activities. It should also be warm and welcoming, with a peaceful and healthy atmosphere; some bedrooms, can actually damage your health.

Choose cool, calming colors to help soothe you to sleep.

COLORS

—

Colors have an influence not only on our visual sense but on our nervous system; they radiate at different wavelengths, some of which are stimulating, and some calming. Calming colors for bedrooms are soft blues, greens, pastel pinks, and peaches; neutral colors like beige and cream are also appropriate. Avoid vivid colors, particularly in a child's bedroom—they might seem cheerful but can be overstimulating.

THE BED

—

Your bed should obviously be comfortable, ideally with a firm but not over-hard mattress. People's tastes in mattresses vary, and if you're happy with a squashy one, that's fine. But soft mattresses are not good for your back in the long run.

It's best to sleep with a single pillow, which keeps your neck at a natural angle. A stiff neck is often greatly improved when two or three pillows are replaced with a single one. (It's been suggested, incidentally, that if you sleep badly in strange houses, taking a familiar pillow with you will provide the link with home that will allow sleep to come.) Some people find hop- or herb-filled pillows help them to sleep; you can get them at herbalists and some health food stores. Make sure you like the smell before buying.

FRESH, CLEAN AIR

—

Fresh air is important, provided it doesn't make the room too cold. If you don't like sleeping with an open window, consider getting an ioniser. Ionisers replace negative ions in the atmosphere. These are electrically charged molecules that are found in abundance in mountain air and around waterfalls, and that keep the air healthy and clean.

Keep the air in your bedroom fresh and clean for a restful night.

CRYSTALS AND NATURAL MATERIALS

—

Crystals are very popular as aids to healing, meditation, and clearing the atmosphere. If the idea appeals to you, rose quartz and amethyst are both considered suitable stones for sleep; keep one by your bedside. When you buy a crystal, it should be thoroughly cleansed before you use it, since crystals absorb energies from the atmosphere around them. Soak it for several hours in a bowl of salt water, rinse it under the cold faucet, don't wipe it with a cloth but place it to dry on a sunny windowsill.

Over the last few years complaints of headaches, skin rashes, nausea, lethargy, depression, stress, and fatigue have been related to "sick building syndrome." The health of workers in modern buildings has been affected by factors such as artificial lighting, static electricity from synthetic furniture and fabrics, low frequency electromagnetic radiation from electronic machinery, and airborne particles. Air-conditioning and windows that can't be opened further deplete the atmosphere of negative ions.

We don't hear too much about "sick bedrooms," but some of these factors can also affect your home, particularly if you are sensitive to them. It is increasingly likely that bedrooms have devices such as a computer, smartphone, or tablet. An increasing number of synthetic fabrics are used in furnishings, bedlinen, and nightwear, while harmful gas can be given off by insulation materials, lacquers, glues, and vinyls. There is also increasing evidence that radiation from electric pylons can affect the health of people living near them.

So, use natural fabrics for your bedroom furnishings, linen, and nightwear; and don't have a TV set in there. Although individual items of electrical and electronic equipment are said to give off safe levels of radiation, we are increasingly exposed to radiation of all kinds, and the accumulation from various sources can ultimately get to us. It's also best not to use an electric blanket; if you do, switch it off and unplug it before going to bed.

LOOKING AFTER YOUR BODY

Anxiety, depression, and obsessive thinking all have a strong physical component, since they trigger the production of stress hormones which create further anxiety, depression, and obsessive thinking. Breaking the cycle by looking after your body will have a positive feedback effect on your emotions. Stress hormones are actually produced to gear us up for action. If you start taking regular exercise you will get rid of these hormones healthily. You have to make a commitment, says my "super-anxiety" friend; part of her strategy was to go swimming every day. She had to force herself to go to the pool for the first few days, but it was worth it—feeling physically relaxed and well helped her to get back in control.

EVENING EXERCISE

A word of caution: avoid taking exercise late at night, as it overstimulates the body. One man who sought help for insomnia was found to be running several miles late every night. The simple answer was to schedule his exercise earlier in the day. While a gentle walk around the block to unwind last thing is fine, for sleeping purposes, the best times for strenuous exercise are the afternoon and early evening.

LEARNING TO RELAX

The onset of normal sleep is a drowsy, relaxed state, a state of peaceful letting go. We should be able to drift into this naturally, yet in this busy, stressed age, many people have simply lost the art of relaxation, and have to relearn it.

MEDITATION

—

Watching television, going to the cinema, socializing, and other off-duty activities all have their place, but they are not really relaxing. True relaxation involves switching off the active left brain, and also the part of the nervous system that gears us up for action. It reverses the process of building up tension by bringing into play the parasympathetic nervous system, which counteracts the effects of stress, and helps to strengthen the immune system. Regular relaxation can actually alter body chemistry, and deep states of relaxation can help the brain to produce endorphins—hormones that have been called "the body's own morphine," which have the effects of lifting the mood and relieving pain.

Meditation has many similar effects. Though relaxation is aimed chiefly at the body, and meditation at the mind and spirit, both slow down and rebalance the body–mind system. Many people who meditate regularly find they need less sleep than before, because during their meditation periods they are giving their systems deep rest. Both meditation and relaxation require us, and also enable us, to let go of worry and tension and focus on the present moment. Some people are quite scared of letting go; they feel they must hang on and stay in control. This is partly because many of us have been brought up with the idea that "doing nothing" is a waste of precious time, possibly even sinful; partly because of a not always conscious fear that something terrible will happen if we let go. The most vivid example of this I ever saw was on a plane journey with a friend who was scared of flying: she sat rigid in her seat clutching the armrests, and I suddenly realized that she was actually trying to hold the plane up.

Letting go is a normal part of life's rhythm; hanging on to control builds up physical tensions which go to bed with you. A tense mind is less able to solve problems than a relaxed one: if you learn to relax you will find that it will not make you less efficient, but better able to cope, and have more control over your waking and sleeping patterns.

In 1985 a small study was carried out by the Sleep Laboratory at Leeds University, with a group of airline pilots. Pilots have such irregular hours and routines that they often have to take sleeping pills to get their rest, a far from ideal situation. Ten pilots were taught a mixture of muscle relaxation and mental meditational techniques, which enabled them to get to sleep whenever they needed to, in unusual environments, even on long taxi rides. Eight months later, seven of them were still using these techniques; of the remaining three, one had been practicing his own form of meditation before the study.

Most people in these tense days could benefit from regular relaxation or meditation. Build it into your day: give yourself a space to practice for 20 minutes at least once a day.

RELAXATION TECHNIQUES

—

Although there are some excellent books on relaxation, if you are under severe tension there is nothing to beat personal tuition, in a group or class where you can get individual attention. If you want to make a start on your own, choose a time and a place where you will be peaceful and undisturbed. Tell yourself that you are going to devote the next 20 minutes to completely letting go. (The airplane won't fall down!) Sit comfortably with your back supported and your feet flat on the floor, your hands loose in your lap and your eyes closed. Or lie down, with your head and knees supported by cushions. There are several relaxation techniques favored by experts. Here are two.

Progressive relaxation consists of alternately tensing and relaxing all the muscles in your body, from toe to head, or head to toe, in turn. Take it slowly. When you've been through all the muscles, notice if there are any tense spots left, and let them go. The jaw is often a tension site; clench it and then let it drop. Make sure your tongue is relaxed too. Then enjoy the sense of relaxation until your 20 minutes are up. Come out of your relaxation position slowly; if you jump up you may find yourself slightly giddy.

Another method is to start sitting or lying, stretch the whole body, and let it go, like a cat. Then simply sense that waves of relaxation are flowing through your body as you breathe in, while more and more tension is leaving you with every out-breath. Relaxation can be aided by using mental imagery: as you let go physically, imagine that you are floating on a pool float in the sunlit sea; or that you are a cat, totally relaxed and oblivious of your surroundings; or a heavy sackful of sand; or a balloon floating in a blue sky. (Images of lightness and heaviness both seem to aid relaxation equally well.)

CDs and downloads can also help you learn to relax on your own—there are a number of good ones on the market. Don't, however, become dependent on one product. What you are aiming for is the ability to relax whenever you want to—not just at special relaxation times.

Taking time out to clear the mind is time well spent, for your health and productivity.

GUIDED MEDITATION

CALMING THE MIND

• For this meditation choose something that will serve as your meditation object. It can be a flower, a candle, a stone or leaf, or an object that symbolizes serenity and calmness for you. In the beginning it is best not to select anything that is overly complex or emotionally charged for you.

• Place the object on the ground in front of your meditation place. Let your body settle into a posture of calm alertness.

• Gently close your eyes.

• Take a few moments to soften your body, noticing the points where it connects with the ground, cushion, or chair. Take a few slightly fuller breaths to establish your attention in the moment. Now open your eyes and let your gaze rest gently on the meditation object in front of you.

• Take a few moments to familiarize yourself with the object, noticing its textures, color, and shape.

• Let your eyes rest gently on the object, not wandering the room to notice anything else. Whatever other sensations or thoughts appear, give them minimal attention, bringing a dedicated attention to connect with your meditation object.

• Explore your object fully with your eyes and attention. Cultivate a patient intimacy with it. Notice its textures, color, and shape. Explore all the subtleties of it.

• Now close your eyes and see if you can bring an image of that object to life in your attention. See if you are able to hold a visual impression of your object in your mind, sensing the same detail of shape, color, and texture.

• Initially you may only be able to do this for a few moments. If the image begins to blur or fade in your mind, don't struggle to maintain it, simply open your eyes to visually connect with the object once more.

• You may need to shift your attention from the inner impression to the visual object a number of times before you find yourself able to sustain the impression in your attention for longer periods of time.

• As your attention deepens, you will find a greater ease in accessing the visual imprint of the object in your attention. The image will become increasingly clear in its detail and vividness.

• Let your attention rest within it, fully connected with it. Sense the calmness that begins to emerge with the deepening attention.

• Let your attention be absorbed into the image so that it fills the whole of your consciousness.

• If your attention becomes distracted, know that you can simply open your eyes and renew your connection visually with the object in front of you. Then close your eyes once more, recalling that image and resting within it.

• When you are ready, open your eyes and move out of your meditation posture.

FOOD AND SLEEP

It's impossible to get a really healthy balance in life without including nutrition. Food and drink have a direct chemical influence on our bodies, nervous system, and moods. Overindulgence in junk food, coffee, or alcohol—all of which often accompany a stressed lifestyle—affects your well-being, simultaneously overstimulating the adrenal glands and nervous system and depleting the body of essential vitamins and minerals. In addition, some foods are more stimulating and some more sedative in their own right.

We get many contradictory messages these days about what's good for us and what isn't. And of course individual needs differ: while more and more people are becoming vegetarian, for instance, there are others whose systems really seem to need meat. If you're any doubt, consult a naturopath or nutritionist about your needs. Meanwhile, here are some general guidelines which hold good for everyone who wants to sleep better.

A WORD ABOUT ALCOHOL

- It's true that a small amount of alcohol is a relaxant, and can blur the edges of anxiety. But there are both disadvantages and risks in the alcoholic nightcap.

- Alcohol is a drug; it's possible for one glass to turn into two, or more … and before you know it you have developed a dependency. And even if it helps you to get off to sleep initially, alcohol can actually cause insomnia. To digest it, your liver and kidneys have to work extra hard, and your body has to provide extra adrenaline—which is, of course, a stimulant. It has been found that after alcohol intake, sleep is more disturbed with more awakenings; alcohol also reduces REM sleep.

- Drinking large amounts of alcohol regularly can lead to alcohol addiction—alcoholism, in other words—which affects your body, your work, and your relationships, and your sleep.

- So, ideally, stick to no more than a glass or two of wine, two or three days a week; you'll feel better for it all round. If you feel hardworking deprived on non-alcohol days, boost your morale by telling yourself you're giving your body—especially your hardworking liver—a nice rest!

FOODS AND DRINKS TO GO FOR

Choose plenty of fresh fruit and salads, dried fruits, green and root vegetables, live yogurt, whole grains (brown rice, oats, wholemeal bread, and flour), pulses (lentils and dried beans), fish and free-range chicken rather than red meats, and a moderate amount of fats, eggs, cheese, and dairy products. Among these foods, the more stimulating are raw vegetables, salads, and fruits; so naturopaths recommend fruit and/or dried fruit with breakfast and a large raw salad with lunch.

Root vegetables are believed to be more sedative than those growing above ground; also sedative are the unrefined carbohydrates—potatoes, and wholegrain bread, pasta, and rice, so these are best eaten with the evening meal.

Processed foods are not only lacking in nutrients but can detrimentally affect sleep, too.

Many foods, when combined with carbohydrates, lead to the production of an amino acid called tryptophan, the main building block for serotonin, a neurochemical which is produced as a precursor to sleep. These include milk, eggs, meat, nuts, fish, hard cheeses, bananas, and pulses.

Drink herbal teas, spring water, and pure fruit juices, or some of the non-caffeinated drinks you can buy in health food stores, such as dandelion coffee (made from the dried root rather than powder), or cereal drinks.

FOODS AND DRINKS TO AVOID

Steer clear of refined carbohydrates (white flour and sugar), which fill you up and overwork the digestive system without giving your body any real fuel.

Avoid processed foods. We have been made aware of the dangers of chemical additives, especially to the allergy-prone, but many processed foods still contain additives to which some people have an adverse reaction without always realizing it. In particular, tartrazine (E102, a yellow food coloring), and monosodium glutamate can upset people's sleeping patterns, especially if eaten in the evening.

High-fat foods also put a strain on the digestive system when eaten in the evening—so there may be some truth in the suggestion that cheese can give you bad dreams!

Caffeine, found not just in coffee, but in tea, cola, and chocolate, doesn't only affect you late at night. It can contribute to nervousness and depression at any time.

Excess salt raises the blood pressure and puts the body into overdrive.

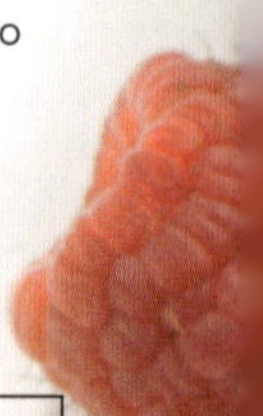

SMOKING

Nicotine is also a stimulant, which can exacerbate sleeplessness, particularly as you grow older. Non-insomniac smokers have been found to take longer to go to sleep than non-smokers and wake up more often during the night. In a trial at Pennsylvania State University, when eight heavy smokers gave up abruptly, the time they took to get to sleep dropped from an average 52 minutes to 18 on the first two nights, and this pattern continued in four of them who continued without smoking for two weeks.

- Initially, giving up may cause a short-term increase in tension, and if you are under a lot of stress at the moment this may not be the best time to stop. But do cut down, especially in the evenings, and try not to smoke during the last hour before going to bed. One way of cutting down is to tell yourself, every time you reach for a cigarette, that you'll have it later. If you make a real commitment to stop, this could improve your sleep quite rapidly.

- You can get many forms of help and support from a number of natural therapies which will help to calm your nervous system and support you during the withdrawal phase. These include a choice of acupuncture, homoeopathy, herbalism, hypnotherapy, kinesiology, and relaxation.

Fresh and dried fruits, live yogurt, nuts, and oats make up a good sleep diet.

BEDTIME

The hour or two leading up to bedtime should be a time of slowly winding down, letting go of the day and its busyness. If you need to have a family discussion (or even an argument), get it over early, and leave matters as resolved as they can be. Write down anything unresolved, and make a definite appointment with yourself and anyone else involved to continue it another time, not in bed.

The same goes for anything else that might be worrying you. Early in the evening, write it down, write down any decisions you have made about dealing with it, and then say goodbye to it for today. You have done all you can.

Keep your bedtime as regular as possible; while you are retraining your body-mind system, late nights are not a good idea. Although scientifically it's not been proven that the hours before midnight are best for sleep, some natural practitioners believe that they are. Around 10 P.M. our body clocks begin to slow down and gear themselves for sleep.

Try to observe your own natural rhythm, and don't stay up beyond the time when you naturally feel sleepy, even if that means forgoing the end of an interesting TV program. Some experts recommend that you don't watch television during the hours before bedtime, since the flickering image can stimulate the nervous system. However, I think this must depend on both the person and the program. A cheering or funny program may help you go to bed in a good mood. But don't fall asleep while you're watching it: you'll have to wake up again in order to go to bed—very confusing to your body clock and making it hard to get to sleep again. The same goes for reading in bed. While the stimulus-control program described previously says the bedroom is only for sleep, some people do find reading in bed a good way to switch their mind away from the worries of the day. This too must be your own choice. But don't waver between systems: if you've chosen to adopt the stimulus-control program, stick to it for the whole 3 weeks.

BEDTIME DRINKS

—

A hot bedtime drink can be soothing and comforting—but bear in mind that it will reach your bladder in the small hours. This might seem obvious, but I've come across more than one elderly person complaining of having to get up to go to the bathroom, without connecting it with their late-night cup of tea! As we get older our kidneys become more active during the night, so the amount an elderly person can comfortably drink before bed will be less than in their younger days. If your bladder is a problem, try having your bedtime drink no later than an hour before bedtime.

The tradition of having a hot milky drink at bedtime is probably based on the fact that milk contains both tryptophan and calcium, which is a muscle relaxant and soothing to the nervous system. A cup of hot milk accompanied by a couple of dolomite tablets (containing calcium and magnesium) can help you get off to sleep, and helps some sufferers from restless legs. Not all proprietary milky drinks are actually good for sleep: chocolate, for instance, has a high caffeine content. Best is plain hot milk, with maybe a teaspoon of honey, or a malted milk. A sprinkling of grated nutmeg on top is also sleep-inducing. If your sleeplessness is related to indigestion, you could try a drink made from slippery elm.

Some people find milk hard to digest, and as it is a food in its own right dietary purists would not recommend it last thing at night. This also applies to late-night snacks, of course. Some people recommend eating a snack of foods containing tryptophan last thing at night—a bowl of cereal, a banana, or a lettuce sandwich for instance. As discussed previously, this is the time when the body should be geared for sleep, not digesting food—and food eaten last thing is more likely to end up as stored fat.

A cup of hot milk in the evening can be soothing and help you drift off to sleep.

However, this is a choice you must make for yourself: if a late-night snack suits you and helps you sleep, that may be the most important factor while you recover your sleep pattern.

Some people find cider vinegar and honey helps them to sleep; the mixture contains a good supply of trace elements, including calcium. Take a teaspoonful of each in a small cup of boiling water.

CHAMOMILE FOR RELAXATION AND SLEEP

- **Chamomile is a small perennial herb with daisy-like white flowers and feathery leaves. In herbalism, chamomile may be taken freely, except during early pregnancy.**

- **As a sedative, make a double-strength tea, using 2 teaspoons of flowers or 1 tea bag. Use a covered vessel, so the steam does not escape. Linden flowers, chamomile, and four cloves make an effective drink before bed, relaxing the body and the mind, and bringing satisfying sleep.**

- **For times of severe stress, make a mixture of three parts chamomile to two parts sage and one part basil (a pinch of ginger powder is optional). Take twice a day to reduce tension and conserve your resources.**

A very pleasant late-night drink is Norfolk Punch, a non-alcoholic blend of herbs and spices found in health food shops and recommended as a relaxant. Some people find that it loses its efficacy if drunk every night—have it as a treat after a particularly fraught day.

Chamomile has long since been brewed into a soothing tea, to relax the mind and body.

BATH TIME

Wash off any remaining stresses of the day by having a bath before bed, and make it sleep-inducing with the help of herbal or aromatherapy preparations. Enjoy your bath as a relaxing treatment; make it warm but not too hot, and give yourself time to soak in the oils or herbs so that you get the full, soothing benefit.

Suitable aromatherapy oils include lavender (used regularly it has the advantage of boosting your immune system, but go easy on it if you are pregnant), chamomile and orange blossom (both rather expensive), meadowsweet, geranium, and hops. Use no more than four to six drops of oil or oils altogether, using the smaller amount if your skin is very sensitive. Agitate the water so that the oil spreads evenly and reaches your whole body. Allow yourself time to soak, relax, and absorb the oil both through your skin and by inhaling the vapor.

Herbs can also be used in the bath by making an extra strong infusion, strained and poured into your bath water. Lime flowers are good; so are hops: pour a cup of boiling water over three crushed heads and steep, covered, for 10 minutes. You can also use lavender, or a mixture of herbs: fill a muslin bag with the heads and tie it to the faucet, so that the hot water runs through it. Before getting into the bath, add a strained infusion of the same herbs. Herbal baths are also soothing for babies. Herbalist Michael McIntyre says: "Chamomile herb is a very suitable way to get your baby to sleep. You can give your baby a chamomile bath. Make a strong tea using an ounce to two pints of water, strain it, and add it to the water in the baby bath." And herbalist Barbara Griggs quotes the French herbalist Maurice Messegué who "recalls being put in a bath of Lime Flowers and Leaves as a child when he couldn't sleep—with magical results ..."

MUSTARD FOOT BATH

Mustard is an annual plant cultivated as a spice all over the world. It has been used for centuries as a pungent condiment and healing herb, by the Greeks, Ayurvedics, and folk practitioners. Mustard's strong taste develops only after the seeds are crushed and come into contact with water or saliva. Large amounts of mustard can cause irritation and inflammation. Avoid contact with the mucous membranes, and with sensitive skin. For a warming mustard foot bath, put one-quarter of a cup of mustard seed in a small cloth bag or a large tea strainer. Steep in hot water for 5 minutes. Soak the feet until the water cools.

MELISSA MIND AND BODY SOOTHER

For frazzled nerves, irritability, and exhaustion, dilute 3 drops Melissa essential oil, 2 drops chamomile oil, and 2 drops bergamot oil in 1 teaspoon of sweet almond oil and add to your bath water.

HYPNOTHERAPY

• Hypnotherapy is not a simple process of telling you that you will sleep well, or stop smoking, or eat less. A good hypnotherapist will need to know why you are not sleeping, and will help you to tackle the problems underlying your insomnia, before going on to help you make inner changes to achieve more control over your own behavior.

• Under hypnosis you reach that relaxed, dreamy (but not usually unconscious) state in which suggestions can be more readily received by your right brain, bypassing the disbelieving left brain. It has sometimes had remarkable results in healing the physical body, and can be very helpful in the relief of pain. But your mind will only receive those suggestions it is willing to receive.

• Hypnotherapists work in a variety of ways, but will normally start by taking your case history and discussing your current problems. They have their own favorite methods of helping you to relax, perhaps by counting down slowly from ten to one, or by asking you to take yourself in imagination to a peaceful, pleasant place—perhaps a country scene, or the seaside, imagining the sights, colors, scents, and sounds. In this relaxed state, with the logical brain on hold, the therapist can help you review your anxieties and fears in a safe atmosphere. They may help you to discover those other, more helpful parts of yourself that have been repressed, and explore ways of making changes in your life. This can be quite an enjoyable game, in which you imagine new scenarios with yourself as both actor and director.

• Hypnotherapy can be very useful if you suffer from recurrent bad dreams or nightmares. A hypnotherapist can help you to discover what those dreams are trying to tell you, and resolve the tension that keeps them recurring. It is also possible to learn to take an active part in one's dreams and so gain some control over them. Challenging and overcoming a fearful figure or event in a dream can have a big spin-off effect on your self-esteem and ability to control your own destiny.

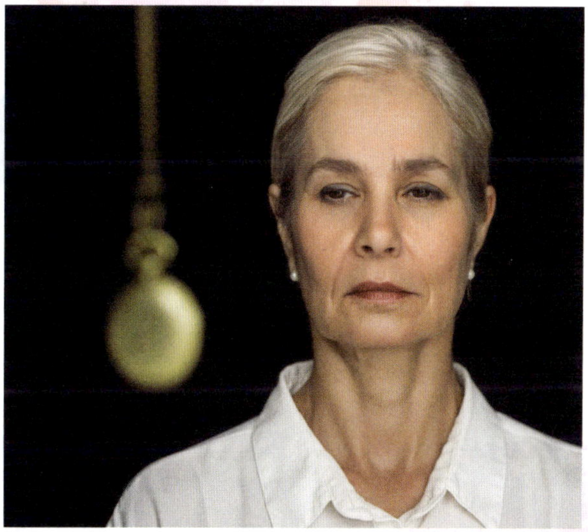

A WORD ABOUT NAPS

For good sleepers, daytime naps can be beneficial and restorative; as we've seen, the human body clock actually seems to be built for sleep twice a day. However, while you are recovering a normal sleep pattern, naps are best avoided. The exception here would be parents of new babies, who are not technically insomniac, but are getting broken nights. If you are elderly and the need for a daytime nap becomes overpowering, take it but remember to allow for less sleep at night.

GOING TO BED

—

After your bath, if you have a partner who is willing to gently massage your neck and shoulders or feet, do encourage this. If you're on your own, gently massage the bits you can reach, and do some gentle stretching and yawning before you get into bed.

Go to bed in cotton nightwear rather than artificial fibers. Some people find it helpful to put a few drops of an essential oil on the pillow—lavender is particularly good. But don't put the drops where your face will come into direct contact with them; undiluted essential oils are quite powerful and can cause skin reactions.

Some people find it helpful just before or just after getting into bed to review the day, and then say a firm goodbye to it. Try it: note particularly the things you have enjoyed, however small, and say thank you for them.

Once in bed, relax and let go. Allow your body to be as comfortable as possible, and know that your mind will soon be taking you into sleep. Don't try to get to sleep: rather, think of sleep as a friend for whom you have made all the right preparations, and who will arrive in their own good time. Remember that the normal person takes 15–20 minutes to get to sleep, so there's no rush. Only a few happy souls hit sleep when their heads hit the pillow.

Once you are in bed, let go of the day and allow your mind and body to relax.

If you are still awake after 20 minutes, you have a choice. The stimulus-control program recommends that you get up and do something, in a different room. Have a hot drink, or read, or write a letter, until you feel sleepy enough to return to bed. The same rule applies if you wake up in the middle of the night.

The alternative is to stay in bed, but allowing yourself to think of pleasant things. Don't lie there worrying or brooding. Whichever system you opt for, commit yourself to it for at least 3 weeks.

MASSAGE BLEND FOR IRRITABILITY

Add 3 drops lavender oil, 3 drops chamomile, and 2 drops neroli to 3 teaspoons grapeseed or sweet almond oil for a soothing massage. Alternatively, add the lavender, chamomile, and neroli to your bath then stir with your hand.

NEROLI MASSAGE BLEND FOR RELAXATION

The blossoms of the bitter orange tree yield neroli oil, also called orange blossom, which has an exquisite fragrance. Neroli is named after an Italian princess, Anne-Marie of Nerola, who used it as a perfume. In folk traditions, orange flowers were included in bridal bouquets as a symbol of innocence and fertility, and to calm nervous couples on their wedding night. Used in a massage blend, it may relieve anxiety, depression, nervous tension, and stress-related problems. Add 3 drops neroli, 3 drops celery, 4 drops rose to 1fl oz or 1fl oz grapeseed or other vegetable oil. Use for gentle massage.

NIGHT THOUGHTS

If your body is relaxed but your mind still active, either before going to sleep or after waking up in the small hours, you can train yourself not to focus on anxiety and worry by concentrating on something else.

One method is to play mental games which will keep your mind occupied and possibly rather bored until you drop off. These include things like counting backward from 100–1, or listing in alphabetical order the names of your friends, or countries, or flowers. You could consider learning a verse or two of a poem before turning in, and reciting it to yourself in bed. Or just pick a harmonious line of poetry, and mentally repeat it to yourself over and over.

Listening to the radio has been the resort of many insomniacs, as you will probably have discovered for yourself, but it has the disadvantage that if there's a really interesting program, you may stay awake to hear it to the end.

If worrying thoughts come into your head, let them go, with the knowledge that you will deal with them at the proper time. As you breathe in, think of peace, tranquility, and calmness entering your system: breathe the worry away.

Another way of dealing with negative or anxious thoughts is not to fight them, but to listen to them in a detached manner as if they were a rather boring radio program, without trying to find solutions to them. Mind games can include images that help to activate the alpha waves that precede sleep: you could take yourself on an imaginary or remembered walk in the country or by the sea. Or take yourself through a film you have really enjoyed.

The more pleasant your thoughts, the more likely you are to relax and go off to sleep. Remember the image of your mind energy: negative thoughts press down on you, while happy ones lift depression away from you. So do thoughts that are not focused on yourself. I discovered accidentally one wakeful night that praying for other people sent me off in no time. Obviously, the purpose of prayer is not to send you to sleep, nor do I assume that everyone believes in prayer. But if you find your mind returning to your own problems, it may help you to switch your attention to a friend or friends who would benefit from a healing thought from you. If they are ill, don't focus on their illness, but visualize them well and happy, or imagine a stream of healing white or gold light going from your heart to surround them. If you don't visualize clearly, this is not important: simply send them well-wishing thoughts.

If someone pops into your mind who has hurt, insulted, irritated, or angered you, send them a healing thought too—they probably need it.

And if you're one of those people who lies awake worrying about the environment, try sending healing thoughts to the planet, to animals, trees, and nature—this will do both you and the environment much more good than if you lie there worrying about it.

FLOWER ESSENCES FOR NIGHT THOUGHTS

The scent of these essences may help to dissipate night thoughts:

Worrying thoughts and mental arguments might respond to white chestnut.

Indecision can be treated with scleranthus.

Stress, strain, frustration, and inability to relax might respond to vervain or rock water, vine, elm, beech, or impatiens.

SELF MASSAGE FOR INSOMNIA

If you are unable to fall asleep, then tossing and turning and furiously rubbing your head only succeeds in increasing the blood supply to your brain. Instead, try this hydrotherapy massage, which harmlessly reduces blood flow to the head and helps the brain naturally switch off.

1 Go to the sink and turn on the cold water. Place each wrist under the flow of water for one minute. Your wrists should feel cooled but not chilled.

2 Use a towel to mop the water from your hands rather than fully drying them. Then go back to bed.

3 Lie on your side so you can insert your hands beneath your underarms. Breathe deeply and assume a sleepy attitude by pretending to be already fast asleep.

4 Almost immediately, you will be aware of increasing warmth in your hands. While this is happening, the blood supply to your brain is reduced. The first time you use this hydrotherapy, you will imagine that you must be dreaming, by which time ...

Don't take your worries to bed with you; acknowledge them, then let them go.

When I let go of what I am.
I become what I might be.

Lao-Tzu

FOOD AND DRINK

CHAPTER TWO

NUTRITION

The use of nutrition for health, or nutritional therapy, can help with almost anything, since food is the basic fuel of all the chemical processes that take place in the body. Almost all ill health of body and mind can have a basis in nutritional elements that are missing or insubstantial within the diet—or in unhealthy additions to our diet, such as large quantities of saturated fat, sugar, and salt. All the systems in the body will be improved by a healthy diet. In a fit state, you are much more likely to fight off infection and deal efficiently with any health problems or injury.

A HEALTHY DIET

Our diet should be made up of complex carbohydrates (5–9 portions per day), fruits and vegetables (4–9 portions), proteins (3–5 portions), and fat (under 1oz/25g) per day is recommended for a healthy diet). We also need to drink plenty of fluids, particularly water. But eating the right foods doesn't necessarily mean that you are getting enough nutrients. Refining and processing foods takes out much of the nutritional value, and pesticides and other agents used in the growing process place extra demands on our bodies. Before our food ever reaches the grocery store it may be nutritionally deficient. Therefore, take extra steps to preserve the nutritional content of your food whenever possible:

- Eat the skins of vegetables.
- Don't cut, wash, or soak fruit and vegetables until you are ready to eat them. Exposing their cut surfaces to air destroys many nutrients.
- Choose brown, unpolished rice and whole grains.
- Choose fresh fruit and vegetables first, but remember that nutritional value decreases with age. Frozen is a better option if you aren't going to eat the food immediately. Eat raw whenever possible; if cooking, use as little water as possible. If you do boil fruit or vegetables, use the water remaining after cooking in your sauces or gravy.
- Eat organic food whenever possible. It may be more expensive, but you can be sure that the food you are eating has been grown without the use of pesticides and ther chemicals.

DIETARY FIBER

Dietary fiber, also known as bulk and roughage, is an essential element in the diet, even though it provides no nutrients. It consists of plant cellulose and other indigestible materials in foods, along with pectin and gum. Chewing it stimulates saliva flow, and the bulk it adds in the stomach and intestines during digestion provides more time for absorption of nutrients. A diet with sufficient fiber produces softer, bulkier stools, and helps to promote bowel regularity and avoid constipation and disorders such as diverticulosis. Other health benefits of fiber include:

- Reduces the production of cholesterol in the body.
- May protect against some coronary diseases.
- Helps to control diabetes.
- Helps to control weight.
- Protects against cancers of the colon.

Fruits and vegetables should make up at least one-third of the food we eat. People who eat five portions a day have a lower risk of heart disease, stroke, and some cancers.

Complex carbohydrates, such as wholegrain cereals, potatoes, and pulses, should make up one-third of our daily diet. They are good sources of energy, fiber, vitamins, and minerals.

Low-fat dairy products, meat, fish, eggs, beans, and pulses are good sources of protein.

The best sources of fiber are fruit and vegetables, wholegrain breads and cereals, and products made from nuts and legumes. An intake of 0.7–2oz. (20–60g.) of fiber per day is ideal. But be aware that a diet too abundant in dietary fiber can reduce the absorption of important trace minerals during digestion. Take a good multivitamin and mineral tablet if you increase your fiber intake significantly.

FOODS TO AVOID

—

Aim to reduce the amount of saturated fat, sugar, and salt in your diet. We all need to consume some fat, yet we need to pay attention to the amount and type of fat we eat. There are two main types of fat: saturated and unsaturated. Too much saturated fat can increase the cholesterol in your blood, which increases your risk of heart disease. Saturated fat is found in foods such as cakes, cookies, French fries, butter, cream, cheese, and fatty meats. Replace these foods with those that contain unsaturated fats, such as oily fish (including tuna, salmon, mackerel, and trout), avocado, and vegetable oils. Trim the fat off meat, drink skimmed milk, replace cream and ice cream with low-fat yogurt, and spread your bread with a reduced-fat spread.

Eating too many foods and drinks high in sugar increases your risk of obesity and related conditions. Swap drinks high in sugars for lower-calorie options. For example, swap a sugary soda for sparkling water with a slice of lemon. Reduce your alcohol intake. Avoid sugary breakfast cereals, cakes, biscuits, and pastries. Check the labels of packaged sauces and meals to make sure they are not high in sugar.

Too much salt in your diet can raise your blood pressure, which leaves you at greater risk of heart disease or stroke. Even if you do not add salt to your food, there are high levels of salt in many food products, such as breads, chips, cereals, soups, and sauces. Check food labels to help you reduce your salt intake.

DRINKS

Water is the most common substance on the Earth's surface, covering more than 70 percent of the planet and present in the atmosphere as water vapor or steam. Human beings are comprised of about 75 percent water. Water is necessary for maintaining the correct osmotic pressure in cells, and is needed for many other body processes, such as transporting nutrients and waste products around the body in the blood (blood is about 80 percent water). Water that has been cooled or heated to form ice, hot water, or steam can be used to treat minor complaints.

Although not harmful in small amounts—approximately one drink per day for adults—there is no nutritional need for alcohol. Other healthy beverages include many herbal teas, green tea, and one or two cups of coffee or black tea daily. Soda "fizzy" drinks and energy drinks are non-essential and, in the case of energy drinks, may be harmful.

HERBAL DRINKS

Herbal teas are becoming increasingly popular as replacements for caffeine-containing drinks. There is a good variety of herbal tea bags available, some of them specially blended to help you relax or sleep. They can be quite expensive; it's often cheaper to buy loose herbs from a herbalist or health food shop and experiment with single herbs or mixtures. Herbs can lose their efficacy over time, so buy them in small quantities, keep them in air-tight jars, and use them promptly.

HERBAL INFUSIONS

Herbal infusions are slightly stronger than teas, and can be taken medicinally three times a day. You can make up an infusion of one or more herbs, using 1–2 heaped teaspoonfuls of dried leaves or flowers to a cup of water. Use a herbal infuser or small teapot, and pour the water onto the herbs when just on the boil. Leave to stand, covered, for at least 5–10 minutes before drinking, or up to 20 minutes if you are taking them medicinally.

Chamomile is one of the best-known herbs for calming the nerves, and for settling the digestion. It is said to have cumulative effects, becoming more effective over a period of time. However, some people find the flavor rather bland, and it has the disadvantage of being mildly diuretic. Lime flower (linden) makes a very effective and pleasant flavored nightcap and is good for headaches, nervous tension, and restlessness.

Somerset scullcap flower

Scullcap is a tonic as well as a sedative, high in magnesium and calcium, which help to strengthen the nervous system. It is not always easy to obtain, and what is often sold as scullcap is another herb called teucrium (wood sage). So get the genuine article, *Scutellaria laterifolia*, from a reputable herbalist.

Passiflora

Passiflora (passion flower) is another good soporific, a constituent of many herbal sleeping pills. Valerian root is well known as a sedative. It tastes like old socks (and smells worse) but a quantity of it can be mixed with more pleasant-flavored herbs.

Valerian has a more "druggy" effect than most herbs, and some people find it gives them headaches if drunk in large quantities; so (unless prescribed by a herbalist) don't take it consecutively for more than a week or two.

Valerian

Hawthorn flowers are good for people who don't sleep because they have heart palpitations. Mint is good for soothing the digestion. Lemon balm and vervain are good for depression.

Hawthorn

TIMING OF MEALS

Far less well publicized than what we eat is the importance of when we eat. The old adage, "breakfast like a king, lunch like a lord, and dine like a pauper," is supported by naturopaths and other natural practitioners, who recommend a hearty breakfast, a moderate lunch, and a light supper, eaten if possible no later than 6 P.M.

There are very good biological reasons for this: the human digestive system functions best in the morning, when it produces a good supply of enzymes for the quick and efficient absorption of nutrients. The digestive process gets slower throughout the day, really starting to slow down around 6 P.M.; by 9 P.M. it is very sluggish indeed. You may feel sleepy after a heavy meal, because the blood goes from the head to the stomach, but still find it difficult to get to sleep because your body has been given an extra task when it should be resting—you wouldn't like to start work at bedtime either! In addition, digestion takes place most efficiently when the body is upright.

Although people's body clocks differ, this slowing down of digestion throughout the day seems to be true for everyone. This means that food eaten late in the evening is liable to remain in the stomach half-digested and putrefying all night, affecting both sleep and our enthusiasm for breakfast in the morning. In some cases it can actually cause a build-up of toxins, leading to ill health.

If you habitually sleep badly, a large breakfast may well be the last thing you feel like in the morning. But remember that you are now changing your habits to encourage your body to relax and sleep; how you start the day will affect how you end it. If you try for a three-week period having a good lunch and an early, light supper, you'll soon find yourself much keener on breakfast.

A hearty and balanced breakfast will set you up for the day ahead–and a good night's sleep.

A hearty and healthy breakfast could include porridge, an oat-based muesli (oats are excellent nerve strengtheners) with yogurt and dried or fresh fruit, wholemeal toast with honey, or cheese if you like it. Unfortunately, our social system is not geared to our body clocks and for the rest of the day you may have to do some adaptation. The lordly lunch accompanied by a large salad may not be available where you work, and if you have a long journey home, the early, light supper may present difficulties. Experiment with packed lunches; raw carrots, celery, and apples need scarcely any preparation. If possible, finish your evening meal by 8 P.M. at the latest.

If you are going straight from work to an evening class, have your hot meal at lunchtime and a sandwich or baked potato before the class. And if you're invited out for a late, delicious dinner—keep the portions down (and the alcohol), relax, and enjoy it! Eating happily is possibly as important as what you eat.

Allergies can range from uncomfortable to fatal; if in doubt, get professional advice.

ALLERGIES AND SENSITIVITIES

If you suffer severely from a food allergy you will probably already be aware of it. But degrees of allergic reaction vary; some people are sensitive to particular foods without having an out-and-out allergy. Their degree of sensitivity can also vary, with reactions worse at particularly stressful times and unnoticeable at others.

The substances most commonly causing allergic reactions or intolerance are wheat, eggs, dairy products, sugar and caffeine, as well as certain chemicals and additives. Very often, people are unaware that something they've been enjoying for years is affecting them badly. This is a common phenomenon known as a masked allergy, when sufferers are actually addicted to the substance that is doing them harm.

It's worth observing your reactions to foods and drinks, particularly those you crave for or consume every day.If you notice that you regularly feel extra hyped up or depressed after any of these, try cutting them out of your diet for a week or two and see whether this makes a difference. If you are suffering from a masked allergy you may get slight withdrawal symptoms; people giving up caffeine, for instance, sometimes experience headaches and fuzziness for a few days. If this happens to you, tell yourself it's actually a good sign, showing that your system is cleansing itself of something that was doing it harm. Drink plenty of spring water to help the process along.

MINDFUL EATING

Our life and well-being rely upon the nourishment we receive. Every mouthful of food we eat is the result of the efforts of the numerous people involved in its growth and the benevolence of nature. For the countless people in our world who face daily deprivation, every meal is a blessing and a lifeline to survival.

For those of us who live with greater abundance and security, food is often taken for granted or has assumed layers of emotional overtone. Moments of mindful eating may be rare in our lives. When we are rushed, food is consumed in haste, something used solely to subdue the distraction of our body's hunger. When our minds are overly full of preoccupation, meals are often eaten habitually, something to get over so we can resume the obsessive thinking we are more interested in.

Eating mindfully will bring your focus to what you are eating, and how much you consume.

When we are bored, food can become a primary means of distraction. In the midst of distress, food is frequently turned to as a source of comfort. Food can become a substitute for the seemingly impossible task of understanding the source of inner turmoil. Learning to approach eating with care and sensitivity is a direct way of cultivating appreciation and nurturing moments of calm in our days.

Approaching meals with intentional awareness cultivates a deeper sense of connection with all life and an appreciation of how precious is our well-being. Learning to stop when we eat, to be fully attentive, is a powerful way of introducing moments of stillness and calm into our day. It can be helpful to approach at least one meal a day with the intention of focusing fully upon it, sitting down to eat, and consciously unhooking from telephones, television, or reading.

Approach this as a time of letting go of haste and busyness. Many people find it useful to have one meal a day in silence, allowing their minds and bodies a time of renewal and ease.

GUIDED MEDITATION

EATING

- **As you sit down with your food, take a few moments just to consciously relax your body and sit quietly.**
- **Sense the space around you, listen to the sounds around you, feel the contact of your body with the chair and the touch of your feet on the ground.**
- **Calmly pass your eyes over the food on your plate. Sense the different textures, shapes, smells, and colors of the food.**
- **As you move to pick up your fork or spoon, be present within the movement of your arms and hands. Be aware of the sensation of your hand taking hold of your cutlery.**
- **As you put the food in your mouth, notice the taste as the food contacts your taste buds.**
- **Chew mindfully, savoring the taste of the food. Notice the moments when your mind is already focused on the next bite, and gently bring your attention back to savor the food you are eating now. You might even experiment with putting your spoon or fork down after each mouthful.**
- **As you swallow and move to take up the next mouthful of food, stay clearly present with that movement.**
- **Let the meal from beginning to end be a time of appreciation and sensitivity.**
- **Notice the changing sensations in your body as they shift from hunger to satisfaction.**
- **Let the whole time of your meal be a dedicated time of calmness and mindfulness.**
- **Sense within your body when you have eaten enough, and stop at that point.**
- **As you end your meal, again bring your attention into your body, sensing its ease.**
- **Again, before getting up, feel the contact of your body on the chair, your feet touching the ground, and the sights and sounds of that moment.**

VITAMINS AND MINERALS

MICRONUTRITION

—

Our understanding of vitamins and minerals—and other micronutrients, compounds, and elements—and their role in our body has improved dramatically over the last decades. We now know that "micronutrition"—or the vitamins, minerals, and other health-giving components of our food, such as amino acids, fiber, enzymes, and lipids—is crucial to life, and that by manipulating our nutritional intake, we can not only ensure good health and address ailments but prevent illness and some of the degenerative effects of aging.

VITAMINS

—

Vitamins are a group of unrelated organic nutrients which are essential to regulate the chemical processes that go on in the body—such as releasing the energy from food, maintaining strong bones, and controlling our hormonal activity.

MINERALS

—

Minerals are inorganic chemical elements, which are necessary for many biochemical and physiological processes that go on in our bodies. Inorganic substances that are required in amounts greater than 100mg. per day are called minerals; those required in amounts less than 100mg. per day are called trace elements. Minerals are not necessarily present in foods—the quality of the soil and the geological conditions of the area in which they were grown play an important part in determining the mineral content of foods. Even a balanced diet may be lacking in essential minerals or trace elements because of the soil in which the various foodstuffs were grown.

There is some evidence that "subclinical" deficiencies—in other words, a deficiency which is not extensive enough to produce large-scale symptoms—may be the cause of certain forms of cancer, heart disease, weight and skin problems, and a host of other health conditions.

AMINO ACIDS

—

An amino acid is any compound that contains an amino group and an acidic function. There are 20 amino acids necessary for the synthesis of proteins, which are essential for life. These 20 amino acids form the building blocks of all proteins and are involved in important biological processes, such as the formation of neurotransmitters in the brain. There are 10 essential amino acids:

- Arginine (essential for children but not adults)
- Histidine
- Isoleucine
- Leucine
- Lysine
- Methionine
- Phenylalanine
- Threonine
- Tryptophan
- Valine.

The remaining 10 are called "nonessential," which means that they can usually be made by the body from other substances. In some conditions, however, nonessential amino acids are necessary, for example in cases of extreme illness or a very poor diet.

LIPIDS AND DERIVATIVES

—

Lipids are commonly called "fats," and while many fats are now known to be unhealthy, there are many that are essential to body processes and actually work to prevent the effects of "unhealthy" fats in our bodies. Many lipids, and their derivatives, including fish oils and evening primrose oil, are used to unclog arteries, work to retard the effects of aging, and to discourage heart disease and the build-up of cholesterol.

Nuts and seeds are packed with health-giving nutrients.

A HISTORY OF NUTRITION

18TH CENTURY
Although there was not yet any scientific understanding of what a "vitamin" was, in the 18th century, English sailors were given lime or lemon juice in order to prevent scurvy, a disease caused by lack of vitamin C, which occurred as a result of long periods of time away at sea without fresh fruit or vegetables.

Citrus fruits like lime are important sources of vitamin C and antioxidants.

19TH CENTURY
In the late 19th century, naturopaths drew attention to the use of food and its nutritional elements as medicine, a concept that was not new, but which had not been acknowledged as a therapy in its own right until that time. Naturopaths used nutrition and fasting to cleanse the body, and to encourage its ability to heal itself. As knowledge about food, its make-up, and the effects it has on our body became greater with the development of biochemistry, the first nutritional specialists undertook to treat specific ailments and symptoms with the components of food.

20TH CENTURY
By the middle of the 20th century, scientists had put together a profile of proteins, carbohydrates, and fats, as well as vitamins and minerals, which were essential to life and to health. More than 40 nutrients were identified, including 13 vitamins. It was discovered that minerals were needed for body functions, and a new understanding of the body and its biochemistry fed the growing interest in the subject. By the 1960s, physicians began to treat patients with special diets and supplements, prescribed according to individual symptoms, problems, and needs, but while conventional medical physicians discussed nutrition in terms of food groups, nutritionists were prescribing vitamins in megadoses. Other elements and compounds were soon identified as necessary to human life, and we are now able to purchase substances such as amino acids, lipids, and dietary enzymes.

TODAY
Today, nutrition has changed from a mainly physician-led dietary therapy, also called clinical nutrition, to a more profound theory of health based on treating the patient as a whole (holistic health), and looking for deficiencies that may be causing illness, which are specific to each individual.

Apples are one of the most popular fruit snacks. They are delicious and rich in antioxidants, vitamins, and minerals.

TAKING SUPPLEMENTS

SHOULD YOU TAKE SUPPLEMENTS?

—

Vitamins, minerals, and other elements work together within the body to ensure that all processes can be carried out. When even one element is missing, the body becomes unbalanced and unable to work at its optimum level. The best source of all micronutrients is food. Supplements are not a replacement for food, and most cannot be ingested without food. They cannot be taken in place of a good diet, but their beneficial effects will be optimized if combined with a balanced intake of nutritious foods. People suffering from chronic conditions or who smoke or drink regularly may need to take supplements to ensure optimum health.

Micronutrients work in conjunction with one another, and taking large doses of any one supplement can upset the balance within the body. A good vitamin and mineral supplement will ensure that you are getting the correct amounts of each, according to the relationships between them. Extra supplements should only be taken on the advice of a registered nutritionist or medical practitioner. Where supplements are taken to discourage the course of illness—for example vitamin C for colds or flu vit is safe to take larger doses than usual. Read the packet for further information.

Registered nutritionists have achieved great success with treating conditions such as rheumatism and arthritis, high blood pressure, fatigue, constipation, and other digestive disorders, the healing and recuperation processes following injury or surgery, skin problems, and many psychological and behavioral problems. Neuralgia, osteoporosis, PMS, postnatal illness, pregnancy problems, reduced immunities, stress, and viruses may respond to dietary treatment.

While supplements can be helpful, eating healthy food is the best source of nutrients.

WHEN TO TAKE SUPPLEMENTS

—

The best time for taking most supplements is after meals, on a full stomach, although some vitamins and minerals work best on an empty stomach. Read the label on any supplement you plan to take to find out the best time to take it.

Time-release formulas need to be taken with food, as their nutrients are slowly released over a number of hours. If there is not enough food to slow their passage through the body, they can pass the sites where they are normally absorbed before they have had a chance to release their nutrients. Take supplements evenly throughout the day for best effect.

WHEN TO SEE A PRACTITIONER

—

Most supplements can be taken safely without input from a registered nutritionist, but if you suffer from chronic health problems, or a specific ailment, it is best to seek expert advice. Amino acids and other

elements should only be taken with the advice of a professional. A nutritionist will make sure that you are taking a balanced combination of nutrients that will work together to make you healthy. Remember that everyone's needs are different, based on overall health, diet, whether or not you smoke or drink, are pregnant, and other influences. It is sensible to ensure that you receive advice that is tailored specifically to your individual needs.

Always take care to consult with a registered nutritionist or a dietician, as the term "nutritionist" is not legally protected in many states and countries. Any person can call themself a nutritionist even if they are wholly self-taught. Turn to Part Four for advice on finding a registered nutritionist.

Fruit and vegetables are excellent sources of important nutrients as well as fiber.

CHILDREN

—

Children need far lower doses than adults, and a healthy, organic diet should offer a large proportion of their nutritional needs. A good vitamin and mineral supplement will provide anything extra that is required, but if you feel your child needs further supplements, see a practitioner. If you are buying products yourself, read the label to ensure that the product is safe for children, and follow the advice carefully.

PREGNANCY

—

A growing baby puts heavy demands on your body when you are pregnant, and it is more important than ever to ensure that you have a good diet. Research has now proved that women need extra folic acid and iron during pregnancy, and a good multivitamin and mineral supplement is often suggested. Consult with your healthcare provider about which supplements are recommended during pregnancy. Do not take vitamin A supplements while pregnant (see page 72).

Supplements come in many different forms–from a gummy sweet form or liquid for children, to tablets for adults.

SUPPLEMENT FORMS

WHICH SUPPLEMENT?

—

Most supplements come in a variety of forms. They are also prepared with different quantities of the active ingredients, so read the label carefully to ensure that you are getting the correct quantity for your needs:

• **Powders** Many supplements come in powder form, which will usually provide you with extra potency, with no binders or additives. This is useful for people with allergies, or those who find it difficult to swallow a tablet. Powders are particularly useful for children—sprinkle a little powder in their breakfast juice, or stir it into some yogurt or dessert.

• **Capsules** These are convenient to take and easy to keep. Fat-soluble vitamins are normally taken in capsule form, but many contain vitamin and mineral powders which allow a higher potency. Garlic and evening primrose oil are commonly available as capsules, and the capsules can be broken apart and applied externally as necessary.

• **Tablets** Many supplements come in tablet form and these are the most practical for many people because they can be easily stored and they will keep for a long time. Check the label to see what is added to your tablets in the form of binders or fillers, which are added to preserve or bulk out the active ingredient.

• **Liquids** Liquids are appropriate for people who have difficulty swallowing tablets or capsules. Many children's formulas come in liquid form for easy administration. Liquids can be mixed with food or stirred into drinks. Liquid supplements can also be applied externally.

READING THE LABEL

—

Supplements work in different ways, and you will need to understand some of the key words that appear on the labels in order to choose which are most suitable for you.

Chelated is a term that appears on mineral supplements, and it means that the mineral is combined with amino acids to make assimilation more efficient. Most nutritionists recommend taking chelated minerals because they are two to five times more effective than other forms.

Time-release formulas are created with a process that allows them to be released into the body over an 8–10-hour period. These are particularly useful for water-soluble vitamins (see pages 207–210), any excess of which is excreted within 2 or 3 hours of taking the supplement. Time-release formulas are reputed to provide stable blood levels of the relevant supplement during the day and night.

RDA AND SUPPLEMENTS

—

Governments around the world have provided guidelines for how much of each vitamin or mineral we need in our diets. These are called RDAs (recommended daily allowance) or RDIs (recommended daily

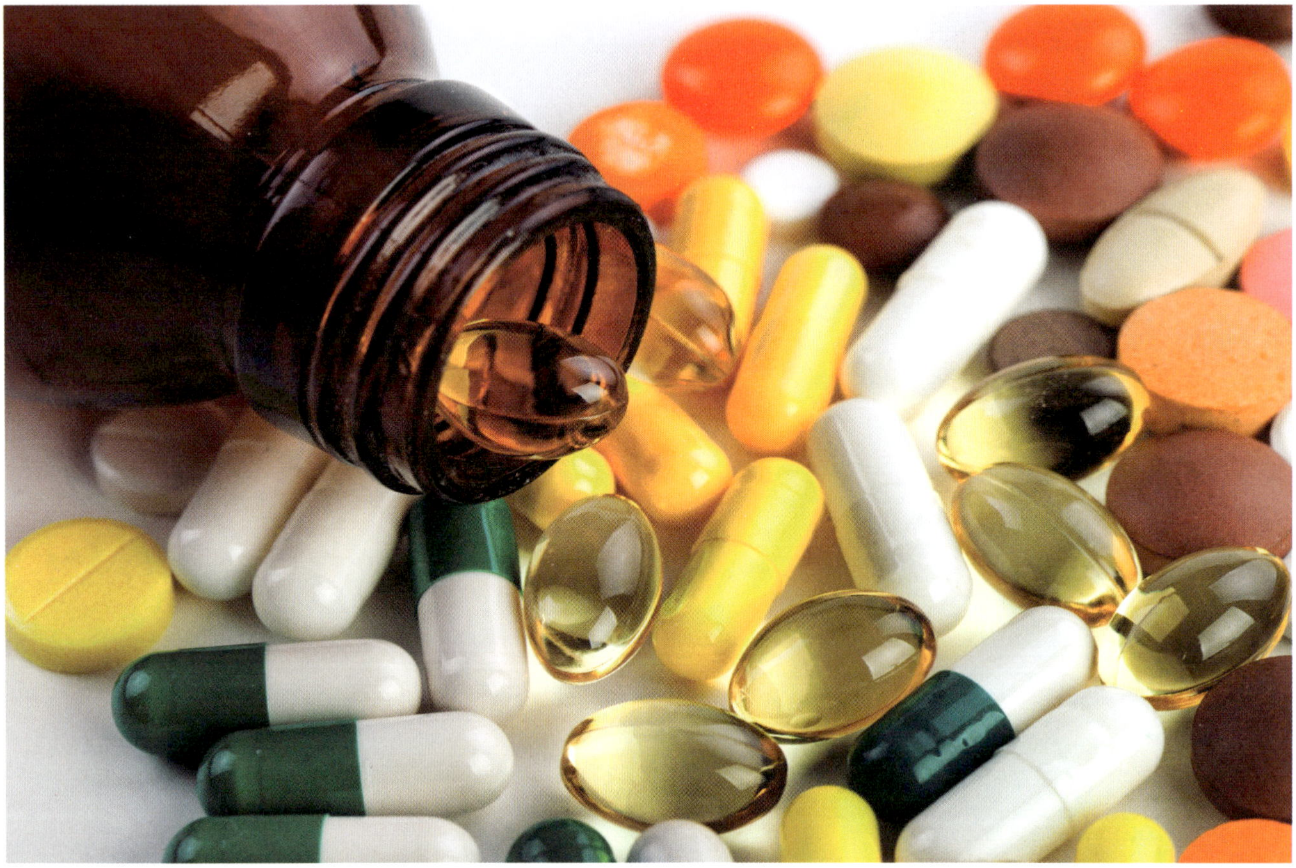

Supplements as tablets are designed to dissolve in your stomach, releasing all their nutrients.

ANTIOXIDANTS AND SUPERFOODS

Much of the cell damage that occurs in disease is caused by highly destructive chemical groups known as free radicals. These are the products of oxidation, a process that occurs naturally in our body as we breathe. Today, because of the other elements in the air, there are more free radicals than ever. In small quantities, free radicals can fight bacteria and viruses; in larger quantities they encourage the aging process and cause damage to our cells.

Many nutritionists believe that free radicals can be combated by antioxidants—the ACE vitamins (vitamin A in the form of beta carotene, vitamin C, and vitamin E), the minerals selenium and zinc, and to a lesser extent manganese and copper. Antioxidants protect other substances from oxidation. Some trials have shown that additional antioxidant vitamins—such as 2,000mg. of vitamin C and 400mg. of vitamin E daily—can reduce the incidence of heart attacks, strokes, cataracts, and other diseases, and slow down the process of aging. However, some physicians say that the jury is still out on antioxidants.

Many so-called "superfoods" are high in antioxidants, including blueberries, goji berries, pomegranate, and broccoli. Although not all physicians agree on the power of antioxidants, they do agree that these vitamin-rich, high-fiber foods are a good addition to a balanced diet. Other foods that are high in antioxidants, such as green tea and chocolate, are also high in fat or caffeine. These can be consumed as part of a healthy diet, but not to excess.

A wide range of foods are high in antioxidants, so find your favorite!

intake) and they apply to healthy individuals with a good, balanced diet. These levels are an "adequate" intake for the average person. In other words, they are not therapeutic levels and they do not take into account the varying needs of the population. People with illnesses, a stressful lifestyle, or who are on medication, or eat a highly refined diet may need much more than the RDA. RDAs are given in mg. (milligrams) or mcg. (micrograms).

The therapeutic dosage for different vitamins and minerals may be many times the RDA. For example, the RDA for vitamin C is 60mg., while the therapeutic dose is 2,000mg. The RDA for vitamin E is 10mg., while the therapeutic dose is 400mg. The RDA for zinc is 15mg. but the therapeutic dose is 30–60mg.

Liquid formulas can be added to fruit juices, making them a popular form of supplement for children.

DAIRY

In general, all dairy products are primarily good for quality protein. Eaten in moderation, they provide essential amino acids, many of which are available only from animal protein. They are also a good source of calcium. The fat content is considered a potential problem; however, balanced with foods high in antioxidants, they are an excellent component of good nutrition.

CHEESE

—

Cheeses are an important source of energy, immune-boosting protein, bone-building and tooth-strengthening calcium, and fat, vitamins, and minerals.

Eating cheese after a meal has been shown to help prevent tooth decay by forming a protective film on the tooth surface and stimulating the production of saliva, helping to guard against acid damage from other foods. The presence of conjugated linoleic acid (CLA), a muscle-building essential amino acid, has been linked with improved immune function and the prevention of cancer. Vitamin B promotes strong bones, helping to prevent osteoporosis, while vitamin K2 has been connected with maintaining a healthy heart, brain, and bones—good news for cheese lovers!

Cheese contains less lactose than milk and is therefore better tolerated by people suffering from lactose intolerance—as a rule of thumb, the older the cheese, the lower the lactose content. Many people digest goat's milk more easily than cow's milk, so chèvre (goat's milk cheese) may provide an option that's lighter on the digestion system. However, in general, cheese is high in saturated fat—if you are trying to control your weight, consider low-fat options, such as low-fat cottage cheese, or feta, which have a lower fat content than most cheeses. Most cheese is mildly inflammatory, and high levels of cholesterol and sodium mean it may not be suitable for people with hypertension (high blood pressure). As with all dairy products, cheese provides an excellent component of good nutrition as part of a balanced diet that includes foods high in antioxidants.

Cheese

RECOMMENDED FOR HELP WITH

- Healthy teeth and bones
- Immune health
- Possible cancer prevention

RECOMMENDED FOR HELP WITH

- Irritable bowel syndrome
- Healthy bones
- Immunity

KEFIR

—

An ancient drink originating in the Caucasus mountains, kefir is a fermented milk drink similar to liquid yogurt, made by adding kefir "grains" to a live culture of cow, goat, sheep, or soy milk. It contains probiotic micro-organisms, healthy bacteria that may be beneficial to the gut. Gut-friendly bacteria and yeast consume lactose during the fermentation process, so kefir can provide a suitable option for those who are lactose-intolerant. Kefir is packed with immune-boosting proteins, essential minerals, and B vitamins. Kefir products are available in larger grocery stores and health food stores. The nutrients in homemade kefir will vary depending on the type of culture used in fermentation, while nutrients in commercially available products vary by brand.

MILK

Milk provides a good source of protein, carbohydrate, and fat, except skimmed, milk, which contains virtually no fat. Milk contains essential amino acids and calcium as well as lactose. Lactose needs to be broken down by the enzyme lactase in the small intestine. Some people do not have sufficient lactase in their system and therefore find milk difficult to digest. This is known as lactose intolerance. For those who suffer from lactose intolerance (or people who avoid eating animal products), alternative lactose-free options are available, including almond milk, coconut milk, and soy milk.

MILK, WHOLE

—

Contains essential amino acids, the fundamental components of proteins and the building blocks of our tissues, important in the development of the brain and nervous system. It's also a good source of bone- and teeth-strengthening calcium. However, it is high in saturated fat, and sugars contribute a large portion of the calories.

MILK, 2 PERCENT (SEMI-SKIMMED)

—

A cup (244 g) of 2 percent milk contains 3 g less fat than whole, or full-fat milk, yet even reduced-fat milk is still fairly high in saturated fat.

MILK, SKIMMED (SKIM)

—

Low in saturated fat and cholesterol, but sugars contribute a large portion of the calories in skimmed milk.

RECOMMENDED FOR HELP WITH

- Prevention of tooth decay
- Osteoporosis
- Metabolism

RECOMMENDED FOR HELP WITH

- Heart disease
- Aging skin
- Weight loss
- Possible cancer prevention

Almond milk

ALMOND MILK

—

Made from ground almonds, high in immune-boosting antioxidants and low in cholesterol, almond milk is often used as a lactose-free substitute for cow's milk. It's also dairy-free and therefore suitable for vegans. However, it is lower in protein than cow's milk or soy milk, so you should seek alternative sources of protein if using almond milk as a substitute for these. It's easy to make at home by blending ground almonds with water, or it can be purchased in cartons from the supermarket. Its popularity has grown steadily and it is now more widely purchased than soy milk. However, it's not suitable for anyone with a nut allergy.

COCONUT MILK

—

Not to be confused with coconut water, which is simply the juice extracted from the nut, coconut milk and cream are made in a remarkably similar way to dairy products. The flesh of the coconut is mixed with water, the cream rises to the top and is skimmed off, and the resulting mixture is sieved to produce coconut milk. Rich in fiber and packed with vitamins and minerals, but lactose-free coconut products are suitable for those who are lactose intolerant. Coconut milk is a popular alternative to cow's milk for vegans in everything from baking to milkshakes, although it should be consumed in moderation because of its high fat content as well as its high calorific value.

RECOMMENDED FOR HELP WITH

- Iron-deficient anemia
- Improved digestion
- Immune system
- Good complexion

GOAT'S MILK

—

Worldwide, a larger amount of goat's milk is consumed than cow's milk. Many children in the United States have an allergy to cow's milk. This allergic reaction is caused by a protein known as alpha-s1-casein—goat's milk contains significantly less of this protein. Goat's milk also tends to be more easily digestible as it contains very little lactose. However, those who are lactose-intolerant should check with a nutritionist to determine whether goat's milk is right for them. It's also a good source of essential amino acids, the fundamental building blocks of our tissues, important to the development of the brain and nervous system.

RECOMMENDED FOR HELP WITH

- Blood pressure
- Strong bones
- Healthy teeth

SOY MILK

—

Soy milk is made by grinding soy beans and mixing with boiling water. It's high in health-boosting essential fatty acids, fiber, protein, minerals, and vitamins. A good lactose-free alternative to cow's milk, it contains no cholesterol and is higher in antioxidants. It's also a good source of bone-strengthening calcium. Soy milk has been associated with weight loss and reducing the risk of cancer. It also contains phytoestrogens, which have been linked to alleviating post-menopausal symptoms.

RECOMMENDED FOR HELP WITH

- Post-menopausal syndromes
- Weight loss
- Possible cancer prevention

Soy milk

YOGURT, PLAIN

—

Yogurt contains essential amino acids, are the building blocks of our tissues (in the form of protein), important to the development of the brain and nervous system, and the singular component of protein. It's also a good source of probiotic micro-organisms, healthy bacteria that may be beneficial to the gut. Certain probiotics have been shown to help regulate immune function and improve gastrointestinal (GI) problems such as constipation, diarrhea, and irritable bowel syndrome. Yogurt is also rich in bone-building calcium and phosphorus. However, it is high in saturated fat, so enjoy in moderation.

Plain yogurt

RECOMMENDED FOR HELP WITH

- Irritable bowel syndrome
- Strong bones and teeth
- Immunity

YOGURT, GREEK

—

Greek yogurt is traditionally made by straining the yogurt to remove the whey, resulting in a thick, creamy yogurt with less sugar, more protein, and fewer carbohydrates than regular yogurt.

It's a powerhouse of quality protein, and a good source of bone-building calcium, tissue-building essential amino acids, and probiotic micro-organisms. However, it is high in saturated fat, and it's worth noting that levels of protein, sugar, and added ingredients will vary according to the product. Check the label—the main ingredients should be active live culture and milk. Some products miss out the straining process and use added thickeners and proteins such as modified corn starch and whey concentrates instead.

Why not pair yogurt with grains and fruit for a wholesome and energy-boosting breakfast.

RECOMMENDED FOR HELP WITH

- Irritable bowel syndrome
- Strong bones and teeth
- Immunity

EGGS

As with dairy products, eggs contain an ideal mixture of essential amino acids. The high cholesterol in eggs is at least partially counteracted by the lecithin in the yolk; be careful not to overcook the yolk, though, as this will destroy the lecithin. Eggs are an excellent source of nutrition for most individuals; however, they are not suitable for those with an egg allergy or familial hypercholesterolemia. If you suffer from high cholesterol, consult your doctor about egg consumption.

CHICKEN EGGS

—

This is the most commonly eaten type of egg, and one of the best complete proteins, supplying all essential amino acids. Just two eggs supply the daily recommended amount of vitamin B12.

BOILED

—

Eggs are one of the best complete proteins, with all essential amino acids. Because no fat is used in preparing boiled eggs, they are generally lower in calories and fat than scrambled, baked, or fried eggs, which use butter in the cooking process.

POACHED

—

Like soft- and hard-boiled eggs, poached eggs are generally lower in calories and fat than scrambled, baked, or fried eggs, which use butter in the cooking process.

SCRAMBLED

—

While scrambled eggs, like other types of cooked egg, are a good source of protein, riboflavin, and selenium, they are also high in saturated fat, and very high in cholesterol.

WHOLE FRIED

—

Be sure to use olive oil or coconut oil for frying. While fried eggs, like other types of cooked eggs, are a good source of protein, riboflavin, and selenium, they're also high in saturated fat, and very high in cholesterol.

RECOMMENDED FOR HELP WITH

- Cataract prevention
- Acne
- Immunity

Chicken eggs

DUCK EGGS

—

Duck eggs are alkalizing, with anti-cancer properties. They are a good source of folate and vitamin B12, which contribute to healthy brain function. One duck egg contains over half (63 percent) of your recommended daily value of vitamin B12, which helps maintain healthy red blood cells and contributes to neurological health. Duck eggs are richer in protein than chicken eggs, but are also higher in cholesterol.

Duck eggs

FRUIT AND FRUIT JUICES

Fruits have numerous health benefits, and all except plums, rhubarb, and cranberries are alkalizing foods, which means that they maintain our PH balance. They also contain high levels of antioxidants, including vitamins A, C, and E, and a wide variety of anthocyanins, flavanoids, and polyphenols. However, many fruits provide most of their calories from sugars, so do eat them in moderation. Different types of the same fruit (such as sweet cherries and black cherries) and different preparations of the same fruit (such as fresh mango and dried mango) can have varying nutrients and health benefits. Fruits and fruit juices are a delicious—and easily portable—means of adding vitamins and minerals to your diet.

ACAI

Often called a superfood, acai berries are a purple palm fruit native to South America. Mainly available in concentrate or capsule form, acai can also be made into drinks and foods. Acai provides exceptionally high levels of antioxidants and was traditionally used to combat aging and assist in weight loss. Acai berries have a multitude of health benefits, including strengthening immunity, reducing inflammation, improving heart health, and potentially protecting against cancer. The fiber in acai maintains digestive health and bowel regularity, and has been found to help reduce the risk of diabetes, high cholesterol, and gastrointestinal disease. Some people can have allergic reactions to acai; test a small amount first.

RECOMMENDED FOR HELP WITH

- Immunity
- Heart health
- Reduces cholesterol
- Digestive health
- Blood health
- Enhanced brain function

Acai berries

ACEROLA

Acerola are dark red, cherrylike fruits that grow in hot climates. According to the United States Department of Agriculture (USDA), acerola provide more vitamin C than other food sources—reputedly up to 13 times more in acerola juice than orange juice. Acerola can be found as supplements or juices, and less commonly as the fresh fruit, syrups, or, preserves. Acerola are low in calories, fat-free, and provide dietary fiber and vitamin A.

RECOMMENDED FOR HELP WITH

- Immunity
- Heart health
- Reduces cholesterol
- Tissue regeneration
- Joint health
- Healthy skin

Acerola

APPLE

Apples are one of the most popular fruit snacks. They are delicious, and rich in antioxidants, vitamins, and minerals. The antioxidants in apples help prevent disease and strengthen the immune system, fighting bone disease and inflammation. Apples are low in calories but rich in fiber, promoting digestion. The carbohydrates and sugar in apples are good for quick energy. Apples have been recommended for acid reflux, and some people swear eating an apple dispels migraines.

RECOMMENDED FOR HELP WITH

- Immunity
- Heart health
- Reduces cholesterol
- Tissue regeneration
- Joint health
- Healthy skin

APPLE JUICE

Although it does not contain the fiber and pectin of whole apples, apple juice is an alkalizing drink. Like fresh apples, the carbohydrates in apple juice provide a boost of energy. Vitamin C is essential for immune health, and potassium maintains the good condition of organs. However, apple juice often has a high sugar content, so should be drunk in moderation.

Apple juice

APRICOT, RAW

Apricots are small orange fruits that are native to China, but are now found all over the world as fresh fruit, dried fruit, and nectar. Apricots are very low in saturated fat, sodium, and cholesterol, and a good source of dietary fiber. However, most of the calories do come from sugars. Apricots are packed with beta-carotene for heart health and are a good source of vitamins A, C, E, and K, as well as potassium. Apricots provide health benefits for the immune system, vision, skin, and bone strength. The fiber content is good for digestion. Dried apricots are also nutrition-packed and easier to transport, but if you suffer from asthma, avoid those made with sulfites.

RECOMMENDED FOR HELP WITH

- Supports immunity
- Heart and blood health
- Digestive health and bowel regularity
- Healthy skin
- Improved vision, reducing risk of macular degeneration
- Strong bones
- Tissue regeneration

Apricots

AVOCADO, RAW

—

Considered a superfood, avocados are grown in warm climates around the world. They minimize the negative effects of more inflammatory meals and contain healthy fats. They are also extremely low in sodium and cholesterol and a good source of dietary fiber, but high in calories, so should be eaten in moderation. Avocados support the body's absorption of vitamins and minerals and strengthen immunity. Avocados are rich in fatty acids that are crucial to both brain development and heart health. Vitamin K and folate maintain healthy blood cells, and avocados are also believed to promote healthy skin.

RECOMMENDED FOR HELP WITH

- Heart and blood health
- Strong bones
- Enhanced brain function
- Immunity
- Healthy skin
- Digestive health
- Developing fetus during pregnancy

Avocados

BLACKBERRIES, RAW

—

Blackberries are rich in antioxidants and very low in sodium, cholesterol, and saturated fat, and are seen as useful for weight loss. Blackberries are great for optimal health and can be eaten as a snack on their own or added to salads and porridge. Fiber maintains healthy digestion and cholesterol, and the high vitamin C is great for boosting the immune system.

Blackberries

RECOMMENDED FOR HELP WITH

- Heart health
- Reducing cholesterol
- Enhanced brain function
- Immunity
- Digestive health
- Calms diarrhea
- Developing fetus during pregnancy

BANANA, RAW

—

The USDA reports that Americans eat more than ten pounds (4.5 kg) of bananas per person per year. Bananas are often babies' first solid food. Carbohydrates provide energy, and potassium eases muscle cramps and digestion, including an upset stomach.

RECOMMENDED FOR HELP WITH

- Heart and blood health
- Brain function
- Immunity
- Healthy skin
- Easing muscle cramps
- Joint health
- Energy

Banana

BLUEBERRIES RAW

—

Considered the powerhouse of the fruits, commercial blueberries contain more antioxidants than any other commonly grown fruit—and wild blueberries are even higher in antioxidants than commercial blueberries. Blueberries contain optimal amounts of anthocyanins, hydroxycinnamic acids, hydrobenzoic acids, flavanoids, and other phenol-related polynutrients. Blueberries provide a multitude of healing benefits—from brain function, mood, and memory, to heart and skin health, strengthened immunity, bone strength, and purported cancer protection. Plus, they are great as a snack or as a healthy addition to cereals and desserts.

RECOMMENDED FOR HELP WITH

- Heart health
- Healthy blood flow
- Enhanced brain function
- Strong bones
- Eye health
- Healthy skin
- Immunity
- Digestive health
- Possible cancer protection

Blueberries

CANTALOUPE, RAW

Cantaloupe is a large melon with pale green skin and sweet, orange flesh. It is one of the most popular melons in the USA. Cantaloupe is low in cholesterol, sodium, and saturated fat. However, much of the calories come from sugar. Cantaloupe is a source of vitamins A and C and carotenoids for eye health.

RECOMMENDED FOR HELP WITH

- Heart health
- Healthy blood flow
- Enhanced brain function
- Tissue regeneration
- Strong bones
- Eye health
- Immunity

Cantaloupe melon

COCONUT, RAW

Coconut contains quality fat that is superior to most animal fat. Coconut is rich in antioxidants and high in fiber, copper, vitamin C, and manganese, strengthening bones, the immune system, and blood cells. Coconut is used in foods, drinks, and cosmetics, and can be purchased as fresh coconut, shredded, dried, coconut milk, coconut oil, and coconut water.

RECOMMENDED FOR HELP WITH

- Immunity
- Energy
- Joint health
- Heart health
- Reduced cholesterol
- Anemia
- Enhanced brain function
- Strong bones
- Digestive health

Coconut

CURRANTS

Currants are a type of berry found in North America, Europe, and Asia. They can be red, black, or white, and each has a different flavor. Currants are low in calories and fat-free. Rich in antioxidants and iron, currants have up to four times more vitamin C than oranges. Whitecurrants are slightly sweeter than red or black and are often made into preserves and desserts. Redcurrants are the tartest in flavor and in jelly form serve as a traditional condiment in the UK.

RECOMMENDED FOR HELP WITH

- Immunity
- Heart health
- Strong bones
- Joint health
- Healthy skin
- Enhanced brain function

CHERRIES

Cherries vary in color from light red to deep purple and range in flavor from sweet to tart. But all cherries are rich in antioxidants and loaded with nutrients; sour cherries trump even blueberries in this field. Cherries are ideal as a snack or flavorful addition to salads and desserts—because of their sweet flavor, they can be substituted for sugar-laden treats. Cherries are high in water and low in calories, which keeps you fuller for longer, and the fiber helps with digestion and weight loss. Cherries contain melatonin, which helps regulate sleep cycles, and the vitamin and mineral content promotes healthy bones and strong immunity. Dried cherries provide slightly less nutrients than raw.

RECOMMENDED FOR HELP WITH

- Heart health
- Healthy blood flow
- Enhanced brain function
- Tissue regeneration
- Strong bones
- Eye health
- Immunity

CRANBERRIES

Cranberries have a long history, including their use by Native Americans as traditional remedies and food. When choosing cranberries, the US Centers for Disease Control and Prevention recommend cranberries that are darker in color, shiny, plump, and able to bounce, in order to garner the most benefit. Cranberries are well known as a remedy for urinary tract infections, but they are also great at maintaining gastrointestinal health, maintaining heart health, and preventing kidney stones. Cranberries are high in antioxidants and vitamin C to boost the immune system and fight colds. Because of fresh cranberries' limited season, dried cranberries are a good option, but have more sugar and less vitamin C than fresh.

RECOMMENDED FOR HELP WITH

- Immunity
- Heart health
- Healthy blood flow
- Healthy skin
- Enhanced brain function
- Digestive health
- Urinary tract infections
- Kidney stones

Whole cranberries

DATES

Dates are the fruit of the date palm tree, which grows in warm climates around the world. The dates most commonly found in the USA are Medjool or Deglet Noor, both of which are packed with nutrients. Dates are an excellent source of dietary fiber, keeping digestion regular and leaving you feeling fuller for longer. The potassium level of dates is high—great for building muscle and maintaining organ function. Magnesium boosts energy and helps regulate blood pressure. However, dates are high in calories and energy density, so eat these—and all dried fruit—in moderation.

Dates

RECOMMENDED FOR HELP WITH

- Digestive health
- Easing constipation
- Reduced cholesterol
- Heart health
- Strong bones and muscles
- Energy
- Joint health
- Healthy skin
- Mood stabilizer

ELDERBERRIES

—

Elderberries grow in both hemispheres, though more common in the Northern. The berries are dark purple or red and are made into drinks, preserves, syrups, and teas. Elderberries have a long history as a traditional remedy. Today, they are used to boost immunity, and research is being carried out on their potential as a flu treatment. They may also help weight loss and cholesterol. Always cook elderberries before eating.

Elderberries

RECOMMENDED FOR HELP WITH

- Heart health
- Reducing cholesterol
- Strong bones
- Eye health
- Healthy skin
- Immunity, which may include flu
- Mood stabilizer
- Weight loss
- Gout

FIGS

—

Figs are delicious, sweet-tart fruit that are grown in warm climates. Figs are rich in antioxidants and can be eaten both fresh and dried. Figs provide a healthy amount of dietary fiber and carbohydrates, making them great for digestive health and bowel regularity, and good in moderation for weight management. Fresh figs can be eaten whole as a snack or added to salads and other dishes. Because of fresh figs' seasonality, dried figs are a good year-round alternative and provide nearly the same amount of vitamins and minerals as fresh.

RECOMMENDED FOR HELP WITH

- Digestive health
- Easing constipation
- Reducing cardiovascular disease
- Strong bones
- Healthy skin
- Enhanced brain function

GRAPEFRUIT

—

The botanical name of grapefruit translates to "paradise citrus," and it's no wonder when you consider the vitamin-filled beauty of this fruit. Grapefruit come in pink, red, or white, each with varying degrees of sweet or tart flavor. All types are low in calories and high in fiber, as well as providing a wealth of fatty acids, vitamins C and A, and calcium. Grapefruit is known as an immunity booster, cholesterol-reducer, metabolism-increaser, and potentially a cancer-preventer as well. Some medications, including statins, may not react well with grapefruit; for any concerns, discuss with your doctor.

Grapefruit

GRAPEFRUIT PINK AND RED, RAW

—

Pink grapefruit juice is high in antioxidants and, in particular, lycopene, which has anti-tumor properties.

GRAPEFRUIT WHITE, RAW

—

Referred to as both "white" and "yellow," this grapefruit has a tarter taste and marginally more vitamin C than pink/red.

GRAPEFRUIT JUICE, PINK

—

Pink grapefruit juice is high in antioxidants and, in particular, lycopene, which has anti-tumor properties.

RECOMMENDED FOR HELP WITH

- Reducing cardiovascular disease
- Joint health
- Immunity
- Enhanced brain function, including memory
- Weight loss
- Easing constipation

GRAPES

Grapes are grown around the world, from the USA to China, and Chile to South Africa. They come in a wide variety of colors and flavors and can be eaten raw, turned into juice and wine, and added to salads. Grapes are low in calories and a great replacement for a sugary treat; they help you maintain a healthy weight by filling up on fewer calories. All grapes contain antioxidants—in particular, resveratrol, which is higher in dark-skinned grapes than in white, and fights inflammation and heart disease. Grapes also provide vitamins A, C, and K, and provide good dietary fiber, helping and help with bowel regularity.

GRAPES, GREEN

—

While lower in resveratrol than darker-skinned grapes, these grapes (called both white and green) are still loaded with antioxidants and vitamins and are often a more popular choice for children.

Grapes

GRAPES, RED

—

Red grapes, also known as black, are a richer source of the antioxidant resveratrol than green grapes.

GRAPE JUICE

—

Grape juice is rich in antioxidants and good for the heart.

RECOMMENDED FOR HELP WITH

- Digestive health
- Weight loss
- Easing constipation and maintaining bowel regularity
- Immunity
- Heart and blood health
- Joint health
- Enhanced brain function
- Strong bones
- Healthy skin

GUAVA

—

Guava is a tropical fruit that remains rare in mainstream grocery stores, but its growing popularity means it can now be found in many specialist health food stores. Guava originated in Central and South America and is now grown in a range of warmer regions. Guava comes in different types, including pineapple and strawberry, with the common guava also called the green apple guava. It can be eaten raw, cooked, or as nectars and preserves. This seed-abundant fruit is an excellent source of vitamins A and C, as well as carbohydrates and fiber. This makes guava good for the digestive system and it assists in appetite control, as well as boosting bone strength and immunity. Some pediatric specialists advise that guava is a rich nutrient source for nursing mothers.

Pineapple guava, also known as feijoa or guavasteen, is rich in antioxidants and folate. It is oval with green skin and cream flesh. Strawberry guava provides an excellent source of vitamin C and potassium. The skin and flesh are a reddish-purple.

RECOMMENDED FOR HELP WITH

- Digestive health
- Reducing cholesterol
- Weight loss
- Easing constipation and calming diarrhea
- Immunity
- Developing fetus during pregnancy and nutrient source for nursing
- Enhanced brain function
- Strong muscles
- Healthy skin and eyes

Guava

Honeydew melon

HONEYDEW, RAW

—

Honeydew is a type of muskmelon. It is sweet and juicy and often eaten raw as a snack or dessert. The nutrients promote immunity and skin health. Some people can have a melon allergy. If your lips feel numb, consult a doctor.

RECOMMENDED FOR HELP WITH

- Immunity
- Healthy skin
- Reducing risk of cardiovascular disease
- Strong bones and muscles
- Enhanced brain function
- Digestive health

KIWI FRUIT

—

The kiwi fruit (often simply "kiwi") is a delicate, small fruit with brownish-green, fuzzy skin and bright-green flesh. Kiwi fruit are often peeled and eaten raw or added to fruit salads or desserts. On their own, kiwi fruit are an alkalizing food that provide a huge dose of vitamin C, as well as being a good source of carbohydrates, vitamins A and E, potassium, and lutein. As a result, this fruit strengthens immunity, improves eye health, prevents cardiovascular disease, and keeps the organs in good condition.

RECOMMENDED FOR HELP WITH

- Immunity
- Heart health
- Strong bones and muscles
- Eye health
- Healthy skin
- Enhanced brain function
- Reducing cholesterol
- Improving metabolism
- Developing fetus during pregnancy
- Possible cancer protection

Kiwi fruit

LEMON

—

Lemons are not commonly eaten raw, but with the nutritional punch they provide whole, you may think again! However, even by adding its juice or pulp to drinks and dishes, your body is still absorbing this fruit's mighty offerings. Lemons and their juice are an excellent source of vitamin C. The skin provides a huge dose of vitamin C, so for added immune strength, try adding zest the next time you're cooking with lemons. Lemon and honey is a great simple recipe for sore throats.

Lemon

RECOMMENDED FOR HELP WITH

- Immunity
- Colds and illnesses
- Strong bones
- Digestive health
- Easing constipation
- Reducing risk of cardiovascular disease
- Blood health
- Enhanced brain function

LEMONGRASS

—

Nicknamed "fevergrass," lemongrass is a type of grass native to Asia. Lemongrass was traditionally used to quell fevers and fight infection. The anti-inflammatory properties help to reduce nausea, relieve dyspepsia, and aid digestion.

RECOMMENDED FOR HELP WITH

- Digestive health
- Reducing nausea
- Heart health
- Bones and muscles
- Immunity
- Energy
- Enhanced brain function
- Developing fetus during pregnancy

Lemongrass

LIME

—

This small citrus fruit is rich in antioxidants and an excellent source of vitamin C, and one lime contains 22 percent of the average RDV for adults—great for boosting immunity and fighting illness. Citrus fruits are recommended as a remedy for chemotherapy patients and others experiencing dramatic changes in taste.

RECOMMENDED FOR HELP WITH

- Chemotherapy patients
- Immunity
- Bones and muscles
- Heart health
- Reduces cholesterol
- Brain function
- Developing fetus during pregnancy
- Digestive health

Mandarin

LYCHEE

—

Native to Asia, the lychee (or litchi) was once considered an aphrodisiac. Distinctive in appearance, this alkalizing food has pink, bumpy skin, juicy, white flesh, and a floral aroma. It can be found in specialist Asian stores and health food stores. It is loaded with vitamin C and provides a huge boost to immune function. The polyphenols have been found to combat obesity and prevent liver disease.

RECOMMENDED FOR HELP WITH

- Immunity
- Protection against liver disease
- Digestive health
- Combating obesity
- Energy
- Heart health
- Strong bones and muscles
- Joint health

Whole lychee

MANDARIN (SATSUMA)

—

The mandarin, or satsuma, looks like a small orange. It is commonly understood to be the same as the tangerine, although some retailers distinguish the two by skin color. Mandarins provide 80 percent of your vitamin C RDV, boosting immunity, and the fiber is important for weight loss and cholesterol reduction. Studies suggest the juice can help protect against liver cancer.

RECOMMENDED FOR HELP WITH

- Digestive health
- Reducing cholesterol
- Immunity
- Heart health
- Bones and muscles
- Healthy skin and eyes
- Enhanced brain function

MANGO, RAW

—

Mangoes are large fruits with a stone, covered in reddish-green skin, with juicy yellow flesh. They are a rich source of antioxidants, providing high levels of vitamins A, C, and E for immune strength, healthy skin and eyes, and cardiovascular health, and they are known to reduce symptoms of gastritis.

RECOMMENDED FOR HELP WITH

- Immunity
- Eye health
- Healthy skin
- Blood health
- Strong bones and muscles
- Energy
- Enhanced brain function
- Digestive health, reducing gastritis
- Possible cancer protection

MANGO, DRIED

—

Dried mango is an energy-boosting, vitamin-A-packed snack, but it does contain more sugar than the fresh fruit. Dried mango is recommended for help with immunity, energy, digestion, and healthy eyes and skin.

MANGO, NECTAR CANNED

—

While higher in calories and sugars than fresh mango, mango nectar is still a great source of vitamins A and C. Look for nectar without added sugar.

Mango

Nectarine

NECTARINE

—

Nectarines belong to the same species as peaches. The dietary fiber and low calories assist with weight loss, and because of their sweet taste, nectarines are an ideal replacement for sugary treats. Nectarines are an alkalizing food with vitamins A and C, and potassium. Like peaches and plums, they can cause an allergic reaction in those suffering from birch-pollen allergies.

RECOMMENDED FOR HELP WITH

- Immunity
- Digestive health
- Weight loss
- Skin and eye health
- Heart health
- Bones and muscles
- Energy
- Enhanced brain function

OLIVES

—

Both green and black olives are a good source of vitamins and nutrients. The difference in color is down to preparation methods, with black olives being left longer on the vine. Green olives are picked before they are ripe, and both are soaked in lye and brine. However, they are high in antioxidants and omega fatty acids and provide fiber and vitamins A and E, protecting against cardiovascular disease, high cholesterol, and arthritis. Green olives contain more sodium, and black olives are slightly higher in calories. Because of the sodium content, olives should be eaten in moderation.

RECOMMENDED FOR HELP WITH

- Heart health
- Digestive health
- Reducing cholesterol
- Skin and eye health
- Reducing inflammation and arthritis
- Strong bones and tissue
- Immunity
- Energy
- Enhanced brain function
- Possible cancer protection

Olives

PAPAYA

—

The papaya is a tropical tree-growing fruit originating from Central America. Outside of the Americas, it is occasionally called "pawpaw," "papaw," or "red papaya." Papayas are sweet and juicy and tend to have pinkish-red flesh. They can be cut up and eaten straight, or added to salads and desserts. Papayas are rich in antioxidants and provide a huge amount of vitamin C, as well as vitamin A and potassium, contributing to strong immunity and healthy skin, bones, and body functions. The digestive enzymes contribute to digestive health, including reducing the symptoms of gastritis. The antioxidant lycopene reduces the risk of cardiovascular disease and, with vitamin A, macular degeneration.

RECOMMENDED FOR HELP WITH

- Immunity
- Reducing symptoms of gastritis
- Reducing cardiovascular disease
- Eye health
- Healthy skin
- Strong bones and tissue
- Improved stamina
- Enhanced brain function
- Developing fetus during pregnancy
- Possible cancer protection

PASSION FRIUT

—

Passion fruit, or purple granadilla, is a tropical fruit that is native to South America. The fruit is small and round, with purple skin and sweet-tasting, yellow, seed-filled flesh. It can be eaten on its own or turned into juices, smoothies, sauces, and desserts. Passion fruit is an alkalizing food that provides fiber and vitamins C and A. Both passion fruit and its flower contain a sedative compound called harman, used as a traditional remedy for insomnia and anxiety.

RECOMMENDED FOR HELP WITH

- Immunity
- Insomnia and anxiety
- Heart health
- Strong bones and joint health
- Eye and skin health
- Energy
- Digestive health

Passion fruit

ORANGE

—

Originating in Asia, oranges are an incredibly popular citrus fruit, believed to be the most cultivated fruit in the world. Oranges are rich in antioxidants, best known as an excellent source of vitamin C. Due to their carbohydrates, they are a good source of energy and help maintain metabolism—a great snack for weight control. Fiber protects against cardiovascular disease and aids digestion. Vitamins A and C, and thiamin promote healthy skin and cell regeneration. Like other citrus fruit, oranges are acidic, which can cause damage to your tooth enamel and, in rare cases, trigger an allergic reaction. Consult your dentist or doctor if symptoms develop.

RECOMMENDED FOR HELP WITH

- Immunity and fighting colds and illnesses
- Eye and skin health
- Reducing inflammation
- Reducing cholesterol
- Reducing risk of cardiovascular disease
- Strong bones and muscles
- Energy
- Enhanced brain function, including memory and mood
- Developing fetus during pregnancy

ORANGE JUICE

—

Orange juice is reputedly the favorite fruit juice in North America and Europe. It is rich in antioxidants, full of vitamins and minerals, and comes in a wide array of brands and styles. A whole orange packs more nutritional punch than juice, and fresh-squeezed orange juice more than from concentrate—but neither juice type provides much fiber. Vitamins C and A boost immunity and skin health. Large amounts of juice can cause weight gain and damage oral health.

RECOMMENDED FOR HELP WITH

- Immunity and fighting colds and illnesses
- Energy
- Digestive health
- Weight loss
- Heart health
- Strong bones and muscles
- Skin and eye health
- Tissue regeneration
- Enhanced brain function
- Developing fetus during pregnancy

Orange juice

PEACH

—

Peaches are soft, fuzzy fruit that originated from China. They are related to nectarines and plums. Peaches are delicious when eaten fresh, but with their limited season they can also be enjoyed in canned form throughout the year. Peaches can be eaten raw, or prepared as preserves, juices, sauces, and desserts. Peaches are antioxidant-rich and a good source of vitamins A and C, boosting immunity and skin health, as well as potassium and calcium for strong bones and organs. Fiber and carbohydrates promote digestive health. Peaches can provide a good alternative to sugary treats but should be eaten in moderation due to their own sugar content. Dried peaches are higher in sugar than raw.

PEACH CANNED

—

Canned peaches tend to be skinless, which limits their fiber. The preserving process also increases the sugar content. However, canned peaches still provide vitamins A and C. If eating commercially canned peaches, look for "no sugar added" on the label.

PEACH NECTAR

—

Peach nectar is an alkalizing juice that is good for digestive troubles, including easing constipation. It provides vitamins and nutrients, but be aware of the sugar content and drink in moderation.

Peach

RECOMMENDED FOR HELP WITH

- Immunity
- Digestive health
- Strong bones and tissue
- Heart health
- Eye and skin health
- Energy
- Brain function
- Possible cancer protection

PEAR

—

There are believed to be more than 3,000 types of pears, including Asian, Anjou, Bartlett (the most popular in the USA), Bosc, Comice, Conference (considered the most popular in the UK), and European (or common). Pears are an alkalizing food that can be eaten raw, baked, or poached, and added to salads and desserts. Pears are rich in carbohydrates, fiber, and potassium, making them a great energy snack that is also good for digestive health and good body function, including easing constipation.

RECOMMENDED FOR HELP WITH

- Immunity
- Digestive health
- Easing constipation
- Energy boost
- Heart and blood health
- Strong bones and muscles

Pear

PEAR DRIED

—

Higher in sugar and calories than fresh pear, this should be eaten in moderation. However, it remains an alkalizing food that provides fiber and carbohydrates.

PINEAPPLE

—

Pineapple is a large tropical fruit with tufted leaves that grows from a plant of the bromeliad family in many warm regions worldwide. It is named for its pinecone resemblance. Pineapples are an alkalizing food and are low in fat, cholesterol free, and provide manganese and vitamin C, exceptional for skin, digestive health, and immunity. They may also reduce the risk of heart disease, stroke, and gout.

The enzyme bromelain may treat arthritis, sinusitis, and digestive troubles. The acid can cause a tingling sensation in your mouth. If it is more severe, consult a doctor about possible allergies.

RECOMMENDED FOR HELP WITH

- Immunity
- Healthy skin
- Heart health
- Reducing inflammation from arthritis and gout
- Easing sinusitis
- Energy
- Enhanced brain function

Pineapple

PLUM

—

Plums are small, juicy fruit with purple skin and yellow flesh, closely related to peaches and nectarines. Plums are low in calories and a good source of fiber, which makes them great for weight management. Plus, their sweet flavor makes them a suitable alternative to sugary snacks. Plums are rich in antioxidants and a good source of vitamins C and A, important for immunity, cellular repair, and bone and eye health. Like peaches and nectarines, plums can cause an allergic reaction in those suffering from birch-pollen allergies.

RECOMMENDED FOR HELP WITH

- Digestive health
- Easing constipation
- Blood and heart health
- Strong bones and tissue
- Healthy eyes and skin
- Immunity
- Energy
- Enhanced brain function
- Joint health

PRUNE (DRIED PLUM)

—

Prunes are rich in antioxidants and a good source of fiber, and their digestive benefit of curing constipation is their best-known trait. However, prunes also provide iron and copper, good for healthy blood.

RECOMMENDED FOR HELP WITH

- Digestive health
- Easing constipation
- Blood and heart health
- Strong bones and tissue
- Healthy eyes and skin
- Immunity
- Energy
- Enhanced brain function
- Joint health

POMEGRANATE

—

Some religious scholars believe that pomegranates were the original forbidden fruit in the Garden of Eden. These gorgeous purple-red fruit, and their seeds, pack a considerable amount of nutrients. This superfood boasts an impressive level of antioxidants, plus vitamins C and K, and potassium, for immunity, cellular repair, and blood health, as well as maintaining prostate health. The seeds alone contain fiber, but it is a personal preference whether to eat them alongside the fruit itself.

RECOMMENDED FOR HELP WITH

- Immunity
- Heart and blood health
- Improves prostate health in men
- Strong bones and muscles
- Digestive health
- Enhanced brain function
- Joint health

Pomegranate

RASPBERRIES

—

Raspberries come in a beautiful array of colors, including pale gold, red, purple, blue, and black. Red and black are the most common. Raspberries are rich in vitamin C and manganese and packed with antioxidants. These berries are also a good source of fiber, omega fatty acids, and vitamin K. In all, raspberries are good for the heart and blood, as well as important for the immune system and bone strength, and a purifier for the skin.

Raspberries

RECOMMENDED FOR HELP WITH

- Immunity
- Digestive health
- Weight loss and improved metabolism
- Blood and heart health
- Strong bones and muscles
- Healthy skin
- Energy
- Enhanced brain function and memory
- Developing fetus during pregnancy
- Possible cancer protection
- Joint health

RHUBARB, RAW

—

Rhubarb provides fiber, antioxidants, and vitamin K, great for digestive, heart, and blood health. Rhubarb also provides calcium for bone strength, and lutein, protecting against cataracts and macular degeneration. Due to its laxative qualities, use it in moderation. Significant overuse of rhubarb can also potentially cause kidney stones and uterine contractions.

Rhubarb

RECOMMENDED FOR HELP WITH

- Skin health and tissue regeneration
- Reducing inflammation associated with arthritis
- Immunity
- Heart and blood health
- Bones and muscles
- Eye health
- Digestive health
- Possible cancer protection

ROSEHIPS

—

Rosehips have many times more vitamin C than oranges, although the amount is dependent on freshness. Rosehips aid the immune system and protect against arthritis. They may disrupt blood sugar regulation in diabetics.

RECOMMENDED FOR HELP WITH

- Skin health and tissue regeneration
- Reducing inflammation associated with arthritis
- Immunity
- Heart and blood health
- Bones and muscles
- Eye health
- Digestive health
- Possible cancer protection

TANGERINE

—

Tangerine is often used as another name for the mandarin orange, although some retailers differentiate between the two based on skin color (with darker-skinned mandarins sold as tangerines in the USA), and is sometimes considered the generic term for the mandarin. Regardless of nomenclature, tangerines are high in vitamin C, boosting the immune system and combating illness, and dietary fiber, assisting with weight loss and reducing cholesterol. This fruit is believed to help protect against liver cancer. In the UK, tangerines are traditional Christmas stocking fillers, and in China, a symbol of happiness and prosperity.

Tangerine

Rosehips

STRAWBERRIES

—

Strawberries are an alkalizing food that is loaded with folate, important for brain function, especially for the developing fetus during pregnancy. Additionally, strawberries are a great source of immune-boosting vitamin C, organ-maintaining potassium, and digestion-calming fiber. Due to potential allergic reactions, some doctors recommend not feeding strawberries to babies.

RECOMMENDED FOR HELP WITH

- Immunity
- Digestive health
- Heart and blood health
- Healthy skin
- Enhanced brain function
- Developing fetus during pregnancy

Strawberries

WATERMELON

—

In North America, nothing signifies summer like juicy wedges of watermelon—and this green-skinned, pink-fleshed melon is growing in popularity elsewhere, too. Because of its high water content, watermelon is a healthy, very low-calorie fruit that can be eaten raw (cut into wedges), served in salads, or even grilled. Watermelon provides vitamins A and C, and potassium, as well as moderate amounts of fiber and carbohydrates. The color comes from the compound lycopene, which reduces the risk of heart disease and cancers. Most seeds are spat out, but they can be roasted for a healthful treat, providing protein and magnesium.

RECOMMENDED FOR HELP WITH

- Heart and blood health
- Reducing cardiovascular disease
- Strong bones and muscles
- Eye health

Watermelon

GRAINS

Over the course of the past 10,000 years, grains—bread, cereals, rice, pasta, noodles—have increasingly been consumed, and even recommended, as the staff of life. Unfortunately, since the 20th century, genetic modifications have increased the gluten content of wheat, and with new technology has come even greater changes. In general, wheat, rye, barley, and spelt contain naturally occurring gluten, and there is good evidence that some oats have been contaminated with gluten. Gluten-free grains include corn (maize), rice, amaranth, millet, buckwheat, quinoa, sorghum, and teff; however, over the past few decades the vast majority of corn has also been significantly genetically modified.

BRAN FLAKES

—

Packed full of fiber. Many breakfast cereals contain bran flakes, which are high in fiber and therefore beneficial for those prone to constipation. However, they also contain gluten and should be avoided by celiacs. Bran flakes are low in fats and sugars and high in immune-boosting vitamin A and metabolism-boosting iron, but these amounts can vary so it's worth checking individual products.

RECOMMENDED FOR HELP WITH

- Cholesterol
- Diabetes
- Immune health

Bran flakes

Granola

RECOMMENDED FOR HELP WITH

- High blood pressure
- Anemia
- Osteoporosis

GRANOLA

—

A high-protein breakfast cereal with a low glycemic load. Granola is a general term covering cereals which feature oats as their main ingredient. Look for varieties which are high in fiber to aid digestion, and low in added sugar and fat. Better still, make your own. Low in cholesterol and sodium, granola is also a good source of vitamin E (alpha tocopherol), known for its antioxidant properties. Nutrients vary between products.

MUSESLI

—

High in protein with a low glycemic load. Like most cereals, muesli is low in saturated fat and cholesterol, and is a good source of the free-radical-zapping antioxidant vitamin E (alpha tocopherol). B vitamins and iron promote the production of "good" cholesterol, which can help protect against heart disease, and contribute to maintaining good overall health. Muesli is also an excellent source of manganese, providing about 93 percent of your recommended daily intake. This trace mineral is very important for maintaining the normal functioning of the brain and proper activity of the nervous system, as well as bone health. The only downside is that muesli often has quite a high sugar content.

RECOMMENDED FOR HELP WITH

- Allergies
- Diabetes (type 2)
- Metabolism

Muesli

OATS

Some oats are gluten free, and all are high in protein. A steaming bowl of porridge for breakfast is packed with minerals, including calcium, potassium, and magnesium. Along with the B-complex vitamins, these are vital for maintaining a healthy nervous system, building strong bones and teeth, and supplying lots of silicon for healthy arterial walls. No wonder oats have been the staple food of some of the hardiest peoples, such as the Scottish Highlanders.

Dried oats

OAT CEREAL, REGULAR

—

In common with most cereals, oats are low in saturated fat and sodium and contain no cholesterol. They are a good source of dietary fiber, bone-building phosphorus, and antioxidants selenium and manganese. Oat cereal products can be obtained in many different forms, often with added vitamins (fortified).

Rolled oats

OATS, ROLLED

—

Rolled oats, sometimes called old-fashioned or regular oats, are made when whole oat groats are steamed and then rolled into flakes. The healthy oils are stabilized, they stay fresh longer, and they cook more quickly. The Scots traditionally stone-grind their oats, creating broken bits of varying sizes, resulting in the familiar porridge oats.

Whole oats

WHOLE OAT CEREAL, GROATS

—

A groat is the basic grain kernel with the inedible outer husk removed. They are low in saturated fat and very low in cholesterol and sodium, but lack the manganese and selenium content of rolled oats and cereals.

RICE, BLACK

—

Black rice contains a high level of antioxidants, which help to combat free radical damage to cells, which if left unchecked can lead to disease. Anthocyanins, the antioxidants also found in blueberries, are responsible for the dark purplish color of black rice. Anthocyanins have been linked to a decreased risk of heart disease and cancer. Black rice is also rich in metabolism-boosting iron and zinc.

RECOMMENDED FOR HELP WITH

- Immunity
- Heart disease
- Possible cancer protection

Black rice

RICE, BROWN, LONG-GRAINED, COOKED

—

A better source of protein than white rice. It is gluten free, making it suitable for those on gluten-free diets. Brown rice takes longer to cook than white rice, but the nutritional benefits are worth the wait. The outer bran and germ layers are where the health-boosting vitamins, minerals, and fiber are stored. As a rule of thumb, the longer the grain, the less sticky and starchy the rice. Long-grain rice is ideal for light, fluffy, pilaf-style dishes.

RECOMMENDED FOR HELP WITH

- Lowering cholesterol
- Digestion
- Heart disease

Red rice

HERBS, SPICES, AND SEASONINGS

In general, all spices, seasonings, and herbs have much greater concentrations of antioxidants than fruits and vegetables. Carbohydrates, fats, and meats tend to be relatively low in antioxidants, and many of these create inflammation.

One of the most interesting reports on the benefits of antioxidants was published in *The Journal of Nutrition* in 2011. The study, from the University of Pennsylvania, demonstrated that two tablespoons of high-oxidant spices lowered oxidative stress and triglyceride levels by 30 percent after high-fat and high-carbohydrate diets. An article by Monica H. Carlsen, et al, in *Nutrition Journal* (2010, 9:3) listed the total antioxidant content of more than 3,100 foods, beverages, spices, herbs, and supplements. The highest mean antioxidant values of the dried and ground herbs and spices ranged from 44 to 277 mmol/100 g, with the highest in clove, "followed by peppermint, allspice, cinnamon, oregano, thyme, sage, rosemary, saffron, and estragon (tarragon)."

The best way to measure antioxidant capacity is Oxygen Radical Absorbance Capacity (ORAC). The recommended daily intake is 5,000 ORAC, while 10,000 is more ideal! According to Modern Survival Blog's Top 100 High ORAC Value Antioxidant Foods, the highest ORAC content foods are: ground cloves, sumac bran, ground cinnamon, raw sorghum bran, oregano, turmeric, freeze-dried acai berry, and cumin seed.

The bottom line is that virtually all herbs and spices are excellent additives and help mitigate the inflammatory aspects of the more inflammatory foods. All of the following are strongly recommended for overall health. Use liberally, except for the Himalayan salt, of which half a teaspoon daily is optimal. In general, a teaspoon or less of most of these will add 5,000 to 10,000 ORAC units to your diet.

ALLSPICE

—

Popular in Mexican and Central American cuisine, allspice is warming, soothing, and fragrant. Like black peppercorns, it's thought to aid the motility (or contractions) of the gastrointestinal tract, and promote digestion by boosting the secretions of enzymes in the stomach and intestines. Rich in minerals, a tablespoon of allspice provides 2 percent of your recommended daily values of iron and potassium, contributing to the healthy function of the blood and heart. It's also high in vitamin C, a powerful natural antioxidant that helps the body combat infection.

Allspice

Cinnamon

CINNAMON

—

A powerhouse of the spices, with higher antioxidant properties than almost any other food. The brown bark of the cinnamon tree native to Sri Lanka is popular for its warm, woody flavor and sweet, fragrant aroma. For centuries, it's been prized as a spice, a trading commodity, and for its medicinal properties. There are two types of cinnamon. Cassia cinnamon comes mainly from China, Vietnam, and Indonesia, while Ceylon cinnamon, which is slightly sweeter, is produced in Sri Lanka, India, Madagascar, Brazil, and the Caribbean. Cinnamon is available as dried quills or ground powder.

BASIL

—

Popular for its fragrant aroma and sweet, punchy flavor, just a handful of basil leaves will transform a bland snack into a delicious treat. Loaded with antioxidants which help prevent cell damage from free radicals, basil offers more than just a flavor boost. Considered one of the healthiest of the herbs, just two tablespoons of chopped fresh basil are packed with over a quarter of your recommended daily value of vitamin K, essential for blood clotting. For a basil-packed flavor hit, try making your own pesto.

Whole cloves

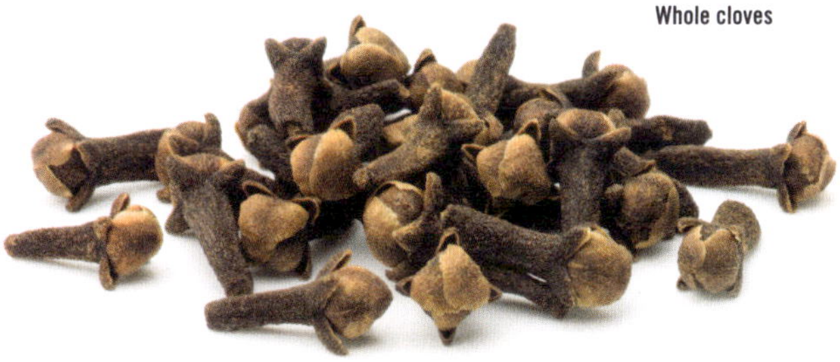

Basil

CLOVES

—

Native to the rainforests of Indonesia, cloves are the unopened flower buds of the evergreen clove tree. The manganese content in cloves is higher than in almost any other food. Just a couple of teaspoons of cloves provides in excess of your daily recommended value of this trace element, a potent antioxidant that helps protect cells against free radical damage and contributes to healthy skin. For millennia, cloves have been prized for their warm, sweet flavor and medicinal properties.

CUMIN

Packed with energy-boosting iron, cumin is an ordinary-looking little seed with extraordinary health benefits. One teaspoon contains almost a quarter (22 percent) of your recommended daily value of iron. An integral component of hemoglobin, which transports oxygen from the lungs to the cells around the body, iron is particularly important for menstruating women, who lose iron each month during menses. Growing children and adolescents have an increased need for iron, as do women who are pregnant or lactating. As well as packing a healthy punch, cumin is popular for its nutty, peppery taste, and adds a distinctive flavor to Mexican, Middle Eastern, and Indian cuisine.

RECOMMENDED FOR HELP WITH

- Metabolism
- Digestion
- Immune health
- Possible cancer protection for stomach and liver

Cumin seeds

FENNEL

Loaded with antioxidants and fiber, fennel has long been used in folk remedies to aid digestion and combat a variety of ailments, from congestion to conjunctivitis. A storehouse of many vital vitamins and minerals, it was used by the ancient Chinese to stimulate appetite, soothe sore throats, and increase the flow of breast milk in lactating mothers. Native to southern Europe, fennel is sought after for its distinctive anise flavor, and is a favorite in many Mediterranean dishes.

Fennel

RECOMMENDED FOR HELP WITH

- Digestion
- Possible prevention of colon cancer
- Rheumatoid arthritis

OREGANO

Oregano takes its name from the Greek *oros* and *ganos*, meaning "mountain joy." It has long been prized in Europe and is a staple of Italian cuisine. So much more than a tasty pizza topping, oregano is packed with fiber to aid digestion, and vitamins A, C, E, and K to boost the immune system, provide antioxidant power to protect against cell damage from free radicals, and prevent unwanted blood clotting.

RECOMMENDED FOR HELP WITH

- Digestion
- Immunity
- Lowering cholesterol

Oregano

Dill

DILL

Dill takes its name from a Saxon word meaning "to lull," which is apt given its soothing effect on the digestive tract. Rich in antioxidants, both the feathery leaves and the seeds have been used in healing remedies since ancient Greek and Roman times. Just one tablespoon of dill seeds contains 10 percent of your recommended daily value of calcium, an integral ingredient in maintaining healthy bones.

RECOMMENDED FOR HELP WITH

- Digestion
- Possible cancer protection
- Rheumatoid arthritis

PARSLEY

—

An excellent source of vitamins A, C, and K. Just one cup (60 g) of fresh raw parsley contains in excess of your recommended daily value of vitamins A and C, and a huge 1,230 percent of your recommended daily value of vitamin K. Vitamin C is one of the most critical vitamins supporting immune health, while vitamin A also boosts immune health as well as vision. Vitamin K prevents unwanted clotting of the blood and promotes bone health. Add to that twice the amount of iron as in spinach, and it's easy to see why parsley is so much more than just a garnish.

RECOMMENDED FOR HELP WITH

- Macular degeneration
- Alzheimer's disease
- Immunity

Parsley

PEPPERMINT

—

Popular for its cool, fresh flavor, peppermint has long been prized for its distinctive taste and medicinal properties. The essential oil menthol is what gives peppermint its distinctive aroma, taste, and cooling sensation. Menthol is also thought to be responsible for the calming effect of peppermint on the digestive system and bowels, alleviating the symptoms of irritable bowel syndrome. It is also beneficial for respiratory function and heart health.

Peppermint

RECOMMENDED FOR HELP WITH

- Irritable bowel syndrome
- Blood pressure
- Asthma

ROSEMARY

—

The piney flavor of rosemary is a favorite accompaniment to lamb, pork, chicken, and salmon dishes. Not only is rosemary a flavorsome addition to many recipes, it is associated with numerous health benefits and has long been used in folk remedies for boosting circulation, improving blood flow to the heart and brain to enhance concentration and memory, stimulating the immune system, and aiding digestion. What's more, it's hardy and easy to grow, making it a perfect potherb for your kitchen garden.

Rosemary

RECOMMENDED FOR HELP WITH

- Asthma
- Digestion
- Immune health

SAFFRON

—

Saffron has long been highly prized for its distinctive, vibrant yellow color and unique flavor. The spice is made from the dried stigmas of the crocus flower. It takes around 4,500 crocus flowers to produce 1oz (28g) of saffron spice. This labor-intensive process, which is carried out by hand, means saffron comes with the highest price tag of any of the common spices. However, its many health benefits—as an antioxidant, immune booster, and blood sugar regulator—coupled with its distinctive flavor and hue means it remains a popular commodity.

Saffron

RECOMMENDED FOR HELP WITH

- Immune health
- Skin
- Maintaining blood sugar levels

Sage

SAGE

—

For centuries, sage has been revered for its culinary and medicinal uses, and it was considered sacred by the Romans. Like its sister herb, rosemary, sage contains a potent blend of essential oils, flavonoids, and phenolic acids, including rosmarinic acid, with powerful antioxidant and anti-inflammatory properties. It's also packed with vitamin K, with just one tablespoon containing 43 percent of your recommended daily value, helping to prevent unwanted clotting of the blood and maintain healthy bones. Sage has been used as a folk remedy for millennia to treat ailments from excessive perspiration to sore throats.

RECOMMENDED FOR HELP WITH

- Rheumatoid arthritis
- Bronchial asthma
- Atherosclerosis
- Alzheimer's disease

RECOMMENDED FOR HELP WITH

- Immunity
- Digestive health
- Blood pressure

Soy sauce

SOYA SAUCE

—

Very low in saturated fat and cholesterol. A good substitute for salt. Research suggests that soy sauce may not carry the same cardiovascular health risks linked to other high-sodium foods, including high blood pressure. However, those on a salt-restricted diet or at risk of excessive salt intake should still consult with a healthcare provider before including more soy sauce in a meal plan than would otherwise be allowed based on sodium content. Look for products that do not contain artificial colors or flavors. Wheat-free varieties are also available—"tamari" soy sauces are made using less or no wheat.

Sorghum

SORGHUM BRAN

—

Native to Africa, sorghum is said to be the fifth most important cereal crop grown in the world. It is very low in saturated fat, cholesterol, and sodium, and is gluten free, making it a good alternative to wheat bran for celiacs or those on a gluten-free diet. Sorghum bran also packs a healthy antioxidant punch, helping to protect cells against free radical damage. A good source of fiber, a 3½ ounce (100g) serving of sorghum bran contains a quarter of your recommended daily value of fiber. Sorghum bran is also rich in iron and niacin, fueling healthy metabolism and immune function.

RECOMMENDED FOR HELP WITH

- Digestion
- Metabolism
- Immune health

TARRAGON

—

Tarragon is rich in immune-boosting antioxidants, and minerals such as calcium, iron, and manganese, contributing to healthy bones, blood, and skin. Also known as dragon wort, in folk traditions tarragon's cooling properties make it a popular remedy for menopausal hot flushes, as well as for a variety of ailments from stimulating the appetite to hiccups. Different varieties include French, Russian, and Spanish tarragon, French being the most popular and widely used as a flavorsome addition to a range of dishes, from roast chicken to omelets.

French tarragon

RECOMMENDED FOR HELP WITH

- Carpal tunnel syndrome
- Pre-menstrual syndrome
- Atherosclerosis

RECOMMENDED FOR HELP WITH

- Immune health
- Bronchitis
- Digestion

Thyme

THYME

—

This delicate-looking herb packs a healthy antioxidant punch—it's loaded with immune-boosting vitamin C, anti-microbial thymol, and free-radical-zapping manganese. Thyme has long been used in natural remedies for chest and respiratory complaints, including coughs, bronchitis, and chest congestion, and as an antiseptic mouthwash. The ancient Greeks prized thyme for its aromatic qualities, burning it as incense in sacred temples. It is one of the herbs in the French bouquet garni, used to season soups, stocks, and stews. Enjoy its distinctive flavor in a bean, beef, or lamb stew on a cold winter's day for an immune system boost.

RECOMMENDED FOR HELP WITH

- Inflammatory bowel syndrome
- Rheumatoid arthritis
- Coronary artery disease
- Atherosclerosis

Turmeric

TURMERIC

—

Turmeric is made from the bright orange root of the *Curcuma longa* plant, native to the sub-Himalayan mountain region. A powerhouse of the spices, it has long been used in Indian and Chinese medicine for its anti-inflammatory, pain-killing, and antioxidant properties. Just one tablespoon of turmeric contains over a quarter of your recommended daily value of manganese, a potent antioxidant that helps protect cells against free radical damage and contributes to healthy skin. Use it to add a unique, warm, peppery kick to curry dishes—even small amounts can have a beneficial health impact.

LEGUMES (PULSES)

In general, legumes—including peas, beans, and lentils—are high in fiber and protein; however they are "incomplete" proteins, lacking some essential amino acids. They need to be eaten alongside milk, meat, or egg protein to be complete. Legumes are also high in carbohydrates, which is where most of their calorific content comes from.

GARBANZO BEANS (CHICKPEAS)

—

Like other beans, garbanzo beans are rich in soluble and insoluble fiber. Soluble fiber helps with the removal of cholesterol, and insoluble fiber prevents constipation. Garbanzo beans are low in saturated fat and sodium, and a very good source of anemia-busting folate and free-radical-zapping antioxidant manganese. These beans produce less intestinal gas than many legumes.

Garbanzo beans

RECOMMENDED FOR HELP WITH

- Constipation
- Blood circulation
- Cholesterol reduction

ALFALFA SEEDS, SPROUTED

—

Low in saturated fat, sodium, and cholesterol, sprouted alfalfa seeds are the shoots of the plant harvested before they are fully grown. They're packed with concentrated amounts of essential vitamins and minerals, including vitamin K, essential for blood clotting, immune-boosting vitamin C, and bone-strengthening calcium. Wash thoroughly before eating and add to salads for a tasty nutritional boost.

Sprouted alfalfa seeds

RECOMMENDED FOR HELP WITH

- Lowering cholesterol
- Healthy blood
- Immunity

HARICOT BEANS

—

Also known as Navy beans, as they were a staple of the United States army in the early 20th century. They are low in saturated fat, cholesterol, and sodium. Haricot beans are packed with fiber and anemia-busting folate. They are also a good source of energy-boosting thiamin (B1). All animals require vitamin B1, which is made in bacteria, fungi, and plants, but a big portion of the nutritional B1 content of foods is often lost due to modern food processing.

RECOMMENDED FOR HELP WITH

- Diabetes
- Constipation
- Good general health

Haricot beans

KIDNEY BEANS

—

Low in saturated fat, cholesterol, and sodium, kidney beans are packed with protein and digestion-boosting soluble and insoluble fiber. One cup of boiled kidney beans contains more than half (58 percent) of your recommended daily value of anemia-busting folate, which contributes to healthy heart and brain function. In common with most legumes, cooking red kidney beans by boiling will considerably reduce the sodium content, which is high in the raw product.

Kidney beans

RECOMMENDED FOR HELP WITH

- Heart health
- Digestion
- Brain function

Peanuts

RECOMMENDED FOR HELP WITH

- Lowering cholesterol
- Bone formation

PEANUTS

—

Low in cholesterol, but high in sodium and calories, peanuts are one of the anti-inflammatory and alkalizing legumes. They're a good source of free-radical-zapping manganese and niacin (vitamin B3). Nutritional properties vary according to variety: for example, Virginia peanuts are much more anti-inflammatory than Valencia peanuts. It's worth noting that although they are called "nuts," peanuts are actually legumes and therefore not harmful to nut-allergy sufferers. However, some people do have a specific allergy to peanuts.

Snow peas

RECOMMENDED FOR HELP WITH

- Cardiovascular health
- Maintaining healthy blood sugar levels
- Immunity

SNAP BEANS (FRENCH BEANS)

—

Also known as green beans or string beans. Low in sodium and very low in saturated fats and cholesterol, snap beans are packed with dietary fiber, vision-boosting vitamin A, immune-boosting vitamin C, and vitamin K, essential for blood clotting. They are also a good source of the antioxidants folate and manganese, which help to protect cells from free radical damage.

RECOMMENDED FOR HELP WITH

- Age-related macular degeneration
- Blood clotting
- Storing energy

Snap beans

SNOW PEAS, SUGAR SNAP PEAS (MANGETOUT)

—

Snow peas are flatter than round garden peas, while sugar snap peas are a cross between the garden pea and the snow pea. Both snow peas and sugar snap peas have edible pods and are sweeter than garden peas. Eat them raw in salads for a healthy crunch or enjoy them sautéed in a range of dishes. They're loaded with antioxidants, including vitamins C and E, and zinc, as well as anti-inflammatory nutrients associated with a lowered risk of conditions such as type 2 diabetes.

MEATS

All meats have optimal essential amino acids, including taurine, which is vital for many biological functions in humans. Meats are also one of the best sources of vitamin B12. No plant food contains either taurine or vitamin B12. Including a couple of servings of red meat in your weekly meal plan as part of a healthy diet can provide your body with many vital nutrients.

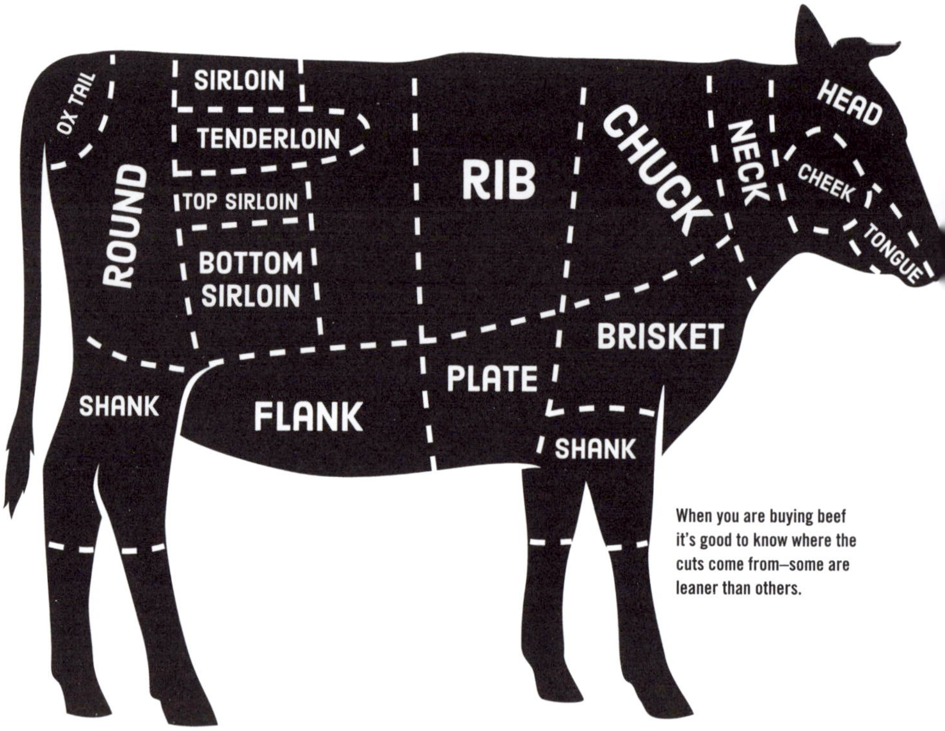

When you are buying beef it's good to know where the cuts come from—some are leaner than others.

BEEF

—

Depending on the cut and the preparation method, beef tends to be low in sodium and is a good source of many vital nutrients. However, it is relatively high in saturated fat, which can lead to a build-up of cholesterol in the arteries and a higher risk of heart disease, so should be included in your diet in moderation. As a rule of thumb, the leaner the beef, the lower the levels of saturated fat. Choose lower-fat cuts such as top round, bottom round, eye round, flank, and strip for healthier options. Higher-fat cuts such as tenderloin, porterhouse steak, or ribeye contain higher levels of total fat, saturated fat, and calories, which can be difficult for the body to process. Cooking methods impact the level of fat as well as cut. Grilling, baking, poaching, or steaming are healthier options, while frying or roasting increase the fat content.

BEEF, RAW, GRASS-FED

—

Research has shown that grass-fed beef contains more than double the carotenoid content of conventionally fed beef. Carotenoids are a family of yellow, orange, and red compounds, essential for a healthy immune system. Grass-fed beef contains significantly lower levels of cholesterol than conventionally fed beef. Labeling on beef products can be confusing or misleading—even products that state "pasture-fed" or "grass-fed" do not guarantee that cows have spent a significant amount of time in an outdoor pasture setting. Look for labels that state "100 percent grass-fed beef."

Grass-fed beef is a healthier option for red meat, with lower cholesterol and more carotenoids.

KIDNEY, BEEF

—

Beef kidneys are protein-rich, with a three-ounce (85g) serving containing nearly half of your recommended daily value of protein. They're a good source of iron and B vitamins. However, they are also high in cholesterol and trans fat.

LIVER, BEEF

—

Rich in vitamin B12, which helps maintain healthy red blood cells and aids neurological health. Vitamin B12 deficiency leads to pernicious anemia, and damage to the spinal cord and brain. However, liver is high in cholesterol and trans fat. Pan-frying compared to braising increases the glycemic load. Calves' liver tends to be more tender and milder in flavor than meat from older animals.

RECOMMENDED FOR HELP WITH

- Iron-deficient anemia
- Immune health
- Muscle maintenance

ROUND STEAK

—

Round steak comes from the rear leg of the cow. It's a lean cut, making it a healthier option than cuts such as porterhouse steak. However, it is high in cholesterol. The lack of fat and marbling means it can dry out when cooking, so slow, moist heat methods of cooking such as braising help retain the moisture.

TONGUE, BEEF

—

Rich in anemia-busting iron and immune-boosting zinc. However, tongue is high in saturated fat and trans fat. Like other organ meats, such as liver, it is high in cholesterol and should be eaten in moderation.

The flavor of lamb is beautifully enhanced when cooked with either delicate or punchy herbs and spices.

LAMB

—

Lamb is low in sodium, and a good source of protein, energy-boosting niacin, immune-boosting zinc, and vitamin B12, essential for red blood cell production and nerve function. Most meat products lack dietary fiber, and should be eaten with vegetables to provide this essential nutrient. It is worth noting that most meat is high in saturated fat and cholesterol, though the presence of vitamin B complexes help to control "bad" cholesterol. Lamb is a source of purines, which your body converts into puric acid, which can increase the risk of kidney stones and gout—people susceptible to these conditions should avoid foods high in purines, including lamb.

LAMB LOIN, COOKED

—

Along with shank and leg, loin is one of the leaner, healthier cuts of lamb, and is comparable to beef or pork in terms of calories and fat. Lamb is an excellent source of essential amino acids. It is, however, high in saturated fat and cholesterol.

LAMB CHOPS

—

Grilling is one of the healthiest, most delicious ways to prepare lamb chops. Broiling is another healthy cooking method that maintains the healthy benefits of grilling. They are, however, high in saturated fat and cholesterol.

LEG, LAMB

—

Along with shank and loin, leg is one of the leaner, healthier cuts of lamb, and is comparable to beef or pork in terms of calories and fat. High in saturated fat and cholesterol.

As with beef, certain cuts of lamb, such as leg, are leaner and lower in calories and fat.

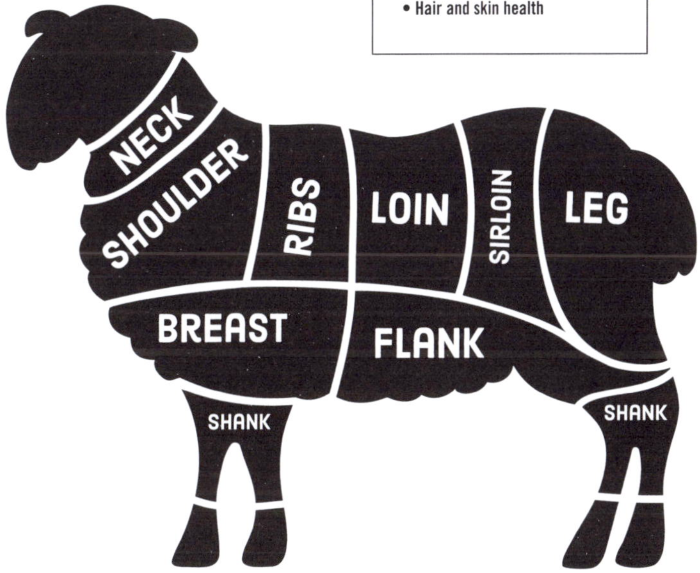

LIVER, LAMB

—

Lamb liver is particularly rich in vitamin A, which helps promote healthy skin and hair, and iron, essential to delivering oxygen around the body. However, it is also very high in cholesterol, high levels of which can lead to heart problems.

RECOMMENDED FOR HELP WITH

- Immune health
- Bone building
- Hair and skin health

MIXED MEATS

While not considered health foods, even mixed meats, such as sausages, can provide the body with essential nutrients that contribute to body maintenance and muscle building. These include choline for cell membrane construction and relieving pain and depression. The iron available assists in healthy red blood cells, and protein is vital for building and maintaining muscle.

PORK

—

Like most meats, pork is a good source of protein, iron, energy-boosting niacin and thiamin, bone-building calcium, and selenium, which has been linked to combating cancer. However, pork is also high in saturated fat, cholesterol, and, depending on the cut and preparation method, can be high in sodium. Most meat products lack dietary fiber, and should be eaten with vegetables to provide this essential nutrient. Including a couple of servings of pork in your weekly meal plan as part of a healthy diet can provide your body with many vital nutrients.

BACON, CANADIAN (BACK BACON)

—

Two slices of Canadian-style bacon provide just over a quarter (26 percent) of your recommended daily value of energy-boosting thiamin. However, this food is also high in cholesterol and sodium. Two slices contain 30 percent of your recommended daily value of sodium, so should be avoided by those on a sodium-restricted diet.

BACON, CURED

—

Bacon contains protein, niacin, and selenium. However, it is high in sodium, so should be avoided by those on a sodium-restricted diet. Low-sodium bacon is a good alternative for those on a sodium-restricted diet. Nutrient quantities for low-sodium bacon are the same as below, except that the sodium content is 82 mg.

PORK CHOPS, CENTER LOINS

—

The loin runs along the back of the pig from the legs to the shoulder and includes the upper portion of the pig's body. Blade chops come from near the shoulder, sirloin chops from near the rump, with center between the two. Center is the leanest choice. All provide an energy-enhancing vitamin B boost.

GROUND PORK (MINCE)

—

Three ounces (85g) of ground pork contain over 40 percent of your recommended daily value of thiamin, which helps to maintain the healthy function of your heart, muscles, and central nervous system. All animals require vitamin B1, which is made in bacteria, fungi, and plants, but a big portion of the nutritional B1 content of foods is often lost due to modern food processing.

HAM RUMP

—

Ham rump is a very good source of copper, which helps to boost the body's antioxidant defenses, protecting against free radical damage to cells. It also plays an important role in energy production and contributes to bone and blood vessel health. However, rump is high in cholesterol and very high in sodium (30 percent recommended daily value in three ounces /85g, so should be eaten in moderation.

HAM, WHOLE LEG

—

Whole leg of ham is lower in sodium than cured cuts of ham. Three ounces (85g) of roasted whole leg of ham contains just 2 percent of your recommended daily value of sodium. It's also a very good source of protein—3oz (85g) contains half your recommended daily value. However, it is high in cholesterol.

LIVER CHEESE, PORK

—

Liver cheese is an outstanding source of vision-boosting vitamin A and vitamin B12, which maintains healthy red blood cells and contributes to neurological health. Around 3oz (85g) contains 133 percent and a huge 155 percent of vitamin A and vitamin B12 respectively. However, it is high in saturated fat, cholesterol, and sodium, so should be eaten in moderation.

PORK TENDERLOIN

—

Low in sodium and rich in energy-enhancing B vitamins, pork tenderloin is a lean cut, providing a lower-fat alternative to other cuts, such as chops or bacon. It is also a good source of metabolism-regulating selenium and bone-tissue-strengthening phosphorus.

RECOMMENDED FOR HELP WITH

- **Nerve function**
- **Energy**
- **Immunity**

Pork is high in saturated fat and cholesterol, but choosing the right cut means you can enjoy this protein-packed meat.

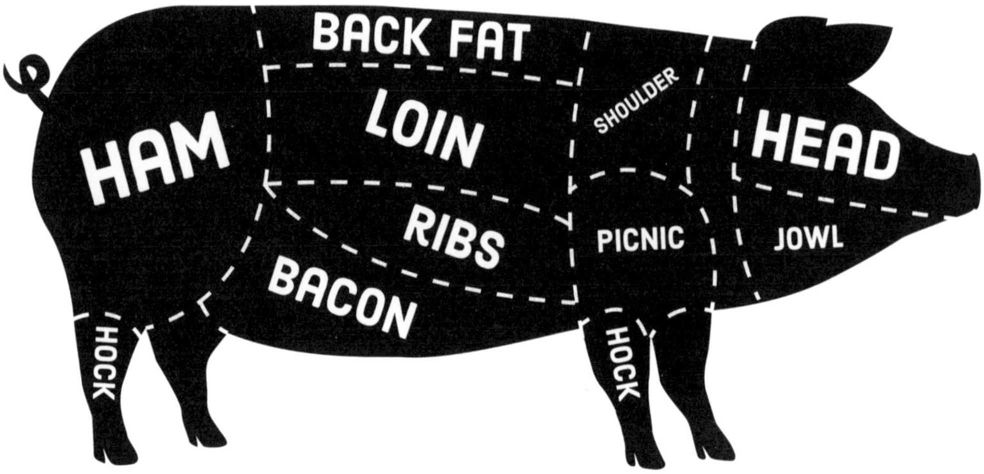

VEAL

—

Veal is the meat from young cattle, usually less than twenty weeks old. Like pork, veal tends to be lower in fat than beef. It is also richer in energy-boosting thiamin and niacin. Like other red meats, veal is a good source of protein and can contribute to meeting your daily protein requirement, whether in stir-fries, grilled, stewed, or using ground meat to make burgers or meatloaves. The nutritional value of meats varies according to the type and the cut, while cooking methods impact the level of fat: broiling, baking, poaching, or steaming are healthier options, while frying or roasting increase the fat content.

VEAL LOIN

—

Veal loin is a good source of B vitamins, which are necessary for energy systems and metabolism. However, it is high in saturated fat and cholesterol.

VEAL RUMP

—

Veal rump is a good source of selenium; studies have shown a link between consumption of the trace mineral selenium and a reduction in the risk of cancer.

RECOMMENDED FOR HELP WITH

- Heart health
- Energy levels
- Immunity
- Iron-deficient anemia

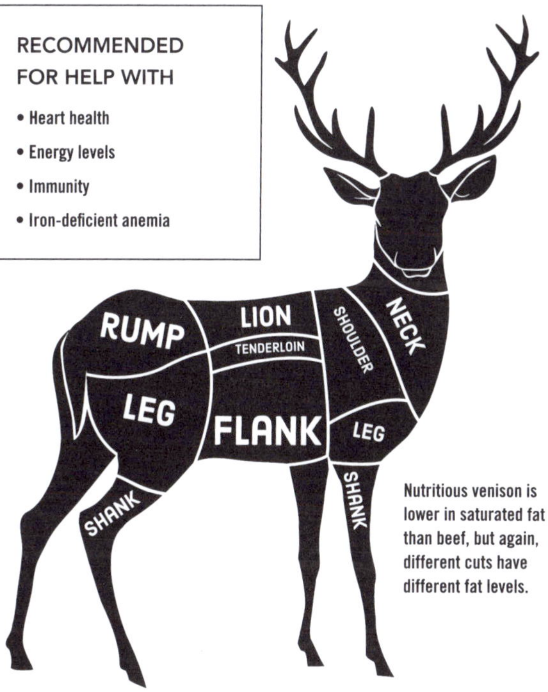

Nutritious venison is lower in saturated fat than beef, but again, different cuts have different fat levels.

Delicately flavored and lower in fat, veal is delicious with light flavorings and fat-free cooking.

VENISON (DEER)

—

Wild deer (venison) is high in protein and stacked with vitamins and iron. From a nutrient perspective it is similar in some ways to beef, but different in others. Venison is lower in saturated fat than beef. For example, a 4oz (110g) serving of beef flank steak has more than 0.3oz of total fat, nearly 0.1oz of which is saturated. An equivalent serving of venison contains only 0.1oz of total fat, 0.05oz of which is saturated. Both meats provide many other important nutrients, notably iron and complex B vitamins, which are necessary for maintaining healthy energy systems and metabolism. Including a couple of servings of red meat in your weekly meal plan as part of a healthy diet can provide your body with many vital nutrients.

RECOMMENDED FOR HELP WITH

- Muscle maintenance
- Energy
- Immune health

LIVER, VEAL

—

Veal liver is very high in vision-boosting vitamin A, which also helps promote healthy skin and hair; and iron, essential to delivering oxygen around the body. However, it is also high in cholesterol.

VEAL SHOULDER

—

Veal shoulder is a good source of energy-boosting B vitamins, including niacin, and immune-boosting zinc. However, it is high in cholesterol. recommended for help with:

GROUND DEER (MINCE)

—

Ground deer can be made into patties or meatloaf. It is a good source of energy-boosting B vitamins, but is high in saturated fat and cholesterol.

DEER LOIN

—

Deer loin is a healthy, lean choice of cut. It is rich in energy and immune-boosting B vitamins. However, it is high in cholesterol.

MUSHROOMS

Mushrooms are widely known for their high levels of nutrition and their many health benefits. Low in calories, saturated fat, cholesterol, and sodium, they also contain many vital nutrients, and are being hailed as one of the "superfoods."

RECOMMENDED FOR HELP WITH

- Immune health
- Digestion
- Metabolism protection

Portobello mushrooms

MOREL MUSHROOM

A great source of vitamin D, essential for helping your body absorb calcium, thus supporting bone health. The morel has an intense, woodsy flavor. Dried morels are also flavorful and less expensive than the fresh variety, ideal for cooking. Morel mushrooms are low in calories and a good source of fiber and iron, supporting healthy digestion and oxygenation of the blood.

PORTOBELLO MUSHROOM

Portobello mushrooms are fat-free, low in calories, and a rich source of antioxidant-boosting copper and selenium, as well as metabolism-enhancing B vitamins. They are instantly recognizable by their large tan brown caps, dark undersides, and thick white stems. Their dense, meaty texture makes them a versatile ingredient in the kitchen, and an ideal meat substitute in many dishes, from hamburgers to Bolognese.

Flavorful morel mushrooms add an intense and nutritious hit to dishes.

RECOMMENDED FOR HELP WITH

- Digestion
- Immune health
- Bone strength

SHIITAKE MUSHROOM

—

Great for maintaining a healthy immune system, and also thought to lower cholesterol. These meaty and flavorful mushrooms contain a substance called eritadenine, which encourages body tissues to absorb cholesterol and lower the amount circulating in the blood. Shiitakes are also thought to have anti-viral and anti-cancer effects. Widely available fresh or dried, the dried variety have a particularly intense smoky flavor. Sauté for roughly 7 minutes to get the best flavor, while keeping maximum nutritional value.

SHIITAKE MUSHROOM, RAW

—

Raw shiitake mushrooms are a good source of antioxidant-boosting copper and selenium, as well as metabolism-enhancing B vitamins. Wash raw mushrooms to remove earth—you may want to chop off the bottom of the hard stem, then slice thinly and scatter over salads to add a flavorful nutritional boost.

SHIITAKE MUSHROOM, DRIED

—

A three-cup (100 g) serving of dried shiitake mushrooms provides more than double your recommended daily values of copper and the B vitamin pantothenic acid. Dried shiitake mushrooms also contain even higher levels of niacin, riboflavin, vitamin B6, manganese, selenium, zinc, and dietary fiber than raw. Soak dried shiitake mushrooms in water before using. Chop and use to add depth of flavor to soups, stews, and stir-fries.

RECOMMENDED FOR HELP WITH

- Immune health
- Lowering cholesterol
- Possible cancer protection

Button mushrooms

RECOMMENDED FOR HELP WITH

- Immune health
- Digestion
- Metabolism

BUTTON MUSHROOM, WHITE

—

Low in saturated fat and sodium and very low in cholesterol. A good source of the immune-boosting B-complex vitamins riboflavin, niacin, pantothenic acid, and folate, as well as antioxidant-boosting copper and selenium. White button mushrooms are the most common and least expensive mushrooms. Their mild taste means they can be used in a wide range of dishes, from salads to sauces, yet their flavor intensifies when cooked, making them ideal for sautéing and grilling.

NUTS AND SEEDS

Nuts and seeds are among the nutritional "superfoods"—packed full of health-giving nutrients, such as proteins, healthy fats, and fiber. Though please beware and avoid if you have a nut allergy.

ALMONDS

—

Eating almonds five times a week may lower the risk of coronary artery disease by 50 percent. All nuts are good, but almonds and Brazil nuts are the only two that produce an alkaline reaction in the body. Since most people's bodies are far too acidic, almonds are a welcome addition to any diet. They also have more magnesium than other nuts and are an excellent source of monounsaturated fat. And, of course, its excellent taste means that the almond is an all-time favorite. Additionally, almond butter is terrific, either alone or with many other foods.

Almonds

ALMOND BUTTER

—

Almond butter is an alkalizing food that's low in cholesterol: add a spoonful of almond butter to your breakfast shake for a flavorsome protein boost. Almond butter provides folate, iron, magnesium, potassium, and zinc.

ALMOND OIL

—

Almond oil is a great substitute for more unhealthy fats and oils. While it lacks the B vitamins of whole almonds or almond butter, just one ounce of almond oil contains over half your recommended daily value of antioxidant vitamin E, helping to protect cells from free radical damage.

Almond butter

BRAZIL NUTS, DRIED

—

Native to the Amazon rainforest, Brazil nuts are one of only two nuts (almond is the second) that produce an alkaline reaction in the body. Since most people's bodies are too acidic, Brazil nuts are a welcome addition to any diet. They are also an excellent source of selenium: just one ounce contains a huge 767 percent of your recommended daily value, making them the highest natural source of this mineral.

Brazil nuts

RECOMMENDED FOR HELP WITH

- Lowering cholesterol
- Reducing the risk of heart disease
- Type 2 diabetes

RECOMMENDED FOR HELP WITH

- Diabetes
- Coronary artery disease
- Possible cancer protection
- Carpal tunnel syndrome

CASHEW NUTS

—

Native to the Amazon, these sweet, crunchy nuts are packed with free-radical-zapping antioxidants, energy, vitamins, and minerals—as well as energy-boosting copper and bone-strengthening magnesium. They are low in cholesterol and sodium. Cashews are one of the best legumes, with excellent fat ratios and protein, though with incomplete amino acids. Delicious as a snack, raw, or roasted, and as an addition to salads and stir-fry dishes.

Cashews

CASHEW BUTTER

—

Cashew butter is low in cholesterol, with good-quality fats. One tablespoon four times a week can help to lower the risk of cardiovascular disease and coronary heart disease. It provides copper, folate, protein, and zinc.

Cashew butter

RECOMMENDED FOR HELP WITH

- Lowering cholesterol
- Reducing the risk of heart disease
- Diabetes

CHESTNUTS, ROASTED

—

Unlike most nuts, chestnuts are rich in complex carbohydrates. They are chiefly composed of starch and have a similar nutritional composition to staple starch foods such as sweet potato. Chestnuts stand out from other edible nuts for being rich in vitamin C, nature's own powerful antioxidant, which helps prevent cell damage from free radicals. One ounce of roasted chestnuts contains 12 percent of your recommended daily value of immune-boosting vitamin C. Chestnuts are also a good source of energy-boosting copper.

RECOMMENDED FOR HELP WITH

- Lowering cholesterol
- Reducing the risk of heart disease
- Immunity

Chestnuts

FLAXSEEDS

—

A powerhouse of the seed kingdom, flaxseeds are a great source of fiber, omega-3s, and antioxidants. They make a nutritious addition to everything from muffins, cookies, and breads, to pizza crusts and casseroles. And the good news is that studies suggest that the cooking process doesn't impact the effectiveness of the omega-3 fatty acids, which help to lower LDL or "bad cholesterol" and increase HDL or "good cholesterol" levels in the blood. Flaxseeds are also ranked as the number one source of lignans—phytonutrients that provide both antioxidant and fiber-like benefits to the body. They contain a whopping seven times the amount of lignans as sesame seeds, the closest runner-up in the lignan-rich food stakes.

FLAXSEED OIL

—

One of the best sources of essential fatty acids, which help to lower LDL or "bad cholesterol" and increase HDL or "good cholesterol" levels in the blood. One ounce provides 5 milligrams of vitamin E.

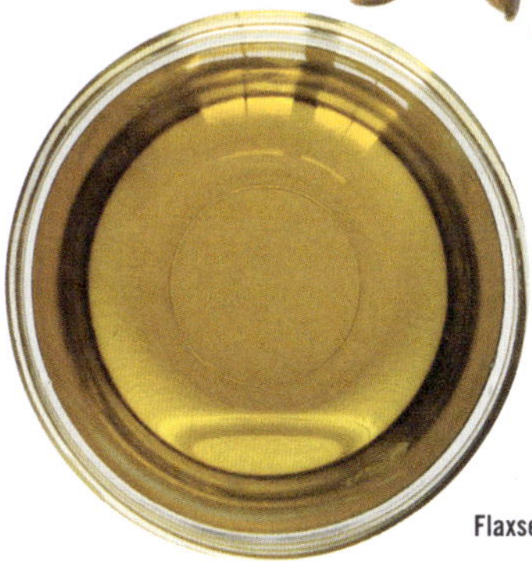

Flaxseed oil

RECOMMENDED FOR HELP WITH

- Reducing the risk of heart disease and diabetes
- Lowering cholesterol
- Colon health
- Immunity

GINKGO NUTS (GINGKO)

—

Traditionally used in Chinese medicine in a range of contexts, from easing asthma to improved memory and concentration. Ginkgo nuts decrease the ability of the blood to clot, and should be discontinued a week before elective surgery. Despite the health benefits of ginkgo nuts, it's recommended to limit consumption to no more than ten a day as ginkgotoxin can cause poisoning by interfering with vitamin B6, causing symptoms from stomachache to vomiting, and can even prove fatal.

RECOMMENDED FOR HELP WITH

- Boosting memory
- Immunity

Ginkgo nuts

CHIA SEEDS

—

A super-quality protein and source of fiber, chia seeds are also packed with omega-3s. There may be no other food as rich in overall nutrients and health benefits as chia—the "strength" food of the Aztecs. If I had only one food to eat, I would choose chia! No other food has the overall balance of quality protein, fat, and fiber, and these small black or white seeds pack more energy and value than any other known food. Plus, no other plant protein comes close in terms of the quality of the protein/amino mix. Just four tablespoons of chia seeds contains as much quality protein as a glass of milk.

RECOMMENDED FOR HELP WITH

- Irritable bowel syndrome
- Diabetes
- Hypertension
- Weight loss protection

Chia seeds

HAZELNUTS

—

These sweet, nutritious nuts are a good source of healthy fats, which help to lower cholesterol, and of free-radical-zapping vitamin E, which also contributes to healthy skin. Hazelnuts are packed with the antioxidant manganese and energy-boosting copper. One ounce of hazelnuts contains nearly a quarter (24 percent) of your recommended daily value of copper, which plays an important role in keeping your energy levels well stoked.

Hazelnuts

RECOMMENDED FOR HELP WITH

- Reducing the risk of heart disease and diabetes
- Weight loss
- Lowering cholesterol

PECAN NUTS

—

These rich, buttery nuts are the most antioxidant-rich tree nut, protecting cells against damage from free radicals. They're also packed with energy, and rich in omega-6 fatty acids, which can help lower the risk of heart disease. They're popular in sweet desserts, such as pecan pie, but can also be enjoyed as a healthy snack raw or roasted (with or without salt), or as a healthy addition to a range of dishes.

RECOMMENDED FOR HELP WITH

- Reducing the risk of heart disease and diabetes
- Lowering cholesterol

Pecan nuts

PINE NUTS, DRIED

—

The sweet, crunchy, edible seeds of the pine tree are a good source of protein and dietary fiber. Low in cholesterol and sodium, they're packed with cardiovascular-system-boosting vitamins E and K, and the antioxidant manganese to help protect cells from free radical damage. Just 1oz (25g) of pine nuts contains in excess (123 percent) of your recommended daily value of manganese.

RECOMMENDED FOR HELP WITH

- Reducing the risk of heart disease and diabetes
- Weight loss
- Maintaining healthy levels of cholesterol

Whole pine nuts

PISTACHIO NUTS

—

One of the healthiest, low-calorie nuts. Pistachios are a good source of "heart-friendly" monounsaturated fats, which help to lower cholesterol. They're packed with antioxidant minerals, such as free-radical-busting manganese and copper, to help protect cells from free radical damage, and crammed with vitamins too—just 1oz (25g) of pistachios contains almost a quarter (24 percent) of your recommended daily value of nervous-system-boosting vitamin B6.

RECOMMENDED FOR HELP WITH

- Reducing the risk of heart disease and diabetes
- Lowering cholesterol

Pistachio nuts

MACADAMIA NUTS

—

Native to the rainforests of Australia, macadamia nuts are packed with energy and contain high levels of monounsaturated fats, which may help to lower cholesterol. They're also rich in antioxidants, which protect cells from free radical damage. Just 1oz (25g) of macadamia nuts contains over half (58 percent) of your recommended daily value of free-radical-zapping manganese.

RECOMMENDED FOR HELP WITH

- Reducing the risk of heart disease and diabetes

Macademia nuts

PUMPKIN SEEDS

—

A great source of magnesium and zinc. Eating the entire seed, including the shell, will maximize your intake of zinc. They can also be enjoyed roasted, though it's worth noting that roasted seeds have a significantly higher glycemic load (10) compared to dried seeds (0). It's recommended to roast pumpkin seeds for no more than 15–20 minutes, as after this time unwanted changes occur in the fat structure, altering their nutrient content.

Pumpkin seeds

RECOMMENDED FOR HELP WITH

- Reducing the risk of heart disease and diabetes
- Prostate health
- Immunity

SUNFLOWER SEEDS

—

A rich source of vitamin E and the B-complex group of vitamins. A handful of these mildly nutty seeds provides a tasty, nutritious, health-boosting snack. Not only do they stave off hunger, sunflower seeds are packed with vitamin E and magnesium, which help keep your heart and bones healthy. Upping your intake of vitamin E can significantly reduce the risk of developing atherosclerosis and boost heart health. B-complex vitamins also provide a boost to the metabolism, ensuring energy levels are well stocked.

RECOMMENDED FOR HELP WITH

- Reducing the risk of heart disease and diabetes
- Possible cancer protection

Sunflower seeds

WALNUTS

—

Walnuts contain valuable and rare nutrients not found in many other food sources, including the tannin tellimagrandin and the flavonol morin. These antioxidant and anti-inflammatory phytonutrients have been linked with a decreased risk of breast cancer and prostate cancer related to walnut consumption. It's thought that walnut skin—the whitish outermost part of the nut—contains many of the key nutrients, so eating the skin is encouraged to gain the full nutritional benefit of these marvelous nuts.

BLACK WALNUTS, DRIED

—

Black walnuts contain more protein than English walnuts, and are a great source of essential fatty acids, which help to lower cholesterol.

ENGLISH WALNUTS

—

A great source of omega-3 fatty acids, they contain slightly higher levels of energy-boosting thiamin, and can help with weight loss.

English walnuts

RECOMMENDED FOR HELP WITH

- Reducing the risk of heart disease
- Type 2 diabetes
- Lowering cholesterol
- Boosting memory

SESAME SEEDS

—

An excellent source of copper and other minerals, sesame seeds are packed with a rich mix of nutrients to maintain healthy bones and muscles, and contribute to good overall health. Sesamin and sesamoli are a type of lignan—phytonutrients with antioxidant and anti-inflammatory properties that have been shown to help lower cholesterol. Sesame seeds add a delicate nutty crunch and a nutritional boost to a range of foods, from breads to desserts, and salads to cereals. Sesame seed butter paste is a healthy, nut-free alternative to peanut butter, containing large amounts of omega fatty acids, as well as calcium, copper, and iron.

RECOMMENDED FOR HELP WITH

- Reducing the risk of heart disease and diabetes
- Prostate health
- Liver health

Sesame seeds

POULTRY

"Poultry" includes chicken, turkey, duck, goose, pheasant, and quail. In general, poultry meat is low in fat and high in protein. The white meat found in most poultry is lower in fat than the dark meat, so consider this when choosing your cut. Additionally, baking and broiling are healthier means of cooking poultry than frying. All poultry is even healthier if it is grass-fed and/or pasture-fed, rather than restricted to only being fed grains. Grass-fed poultry meat is also considered tastier and more tender.

CHICKEN

Chicken is one of the best sources of complete protein, featuring all essential amino acids. Protein is a building block of bones, muscles, and the components of the body's make-up. The human body requires a large amount of protein, so chicken is a good part of any meat-eater's well-balanced diet. Amino acids are required for cell development and muscle development, and chicken also has a healthy ratio of fats. White meat is considered healthier than dark meat, while breast meat is particularly low in fat; gizzards and giblets are especially high in protein, and liver contains high levels of iron and vitamin B12. Breast meat has a lower fat content than other pieces of chicken. Chicken giblets are particularly high in protein. Chicken livers contain high levels of iron and vitamin B12.

Choosing the right cut is important; white meat (and breast meat in particular) is lower in fat than dark meat. However, dark meat contains higher vitamins.

RECOMMENDED FOR HELP WITH

- Muscle maintenance
- Increased energy
- Oxygenation of the blood
- Possible cancer prevention
- Iron-deficient anemia

Chickens that have been allowed to roam and forage are happier birds and provide the tastiest meat.

DUCK

Duck is an excellent source of protein, with all essential amino acids and a good ratio of fats. While less common in the USA, duck is a prevalent and delicious food choice in Asia and Europe. There are three main varieties of duck for cooking. In the USA, mild Pekin or Long Island duck is the most common, while the stronger Muscovy is popular in France. Duck has the reputation of being fatty, but in small portions duck is nutritious and protein-packed. The dark color of the meat of this bird comes from high levels of oxygen-storing protein, creating the richer, meatier flavor. Duck has a thick layer of fat under the skin; either remove the skin or score it before cooking to allow the fat to escape.

RECOMMENDED FOR HELP WITH

- Muscle maintenance
- Increased energy
- Iron-deficient anemia
- Possible cancer prevention
- Oxygenation of the blood

PHEASANT

Pheasant is a good-quality protein, with all essential amino acids and a good ratio of fats. Pheasant is more common in the UK and Europe than in the USA. As with duck and goose, pheasant has a higher fat content than chicken and turkey, but about half the amount of fat as beef. Pheasant provides a high level of protein, as well as significant amounts of niacin, potassium, selenium, and vitamin B12, and is one of the best dietary sources of vitamin B6. Pheasant is often roasted, and can either be purchased fresh or frozen from specialty food stores; the fat is reduced by removing the skin.

RECOMMENDED FOR HELP WITH

- Muscle maintenance
- Strong bones and teeth
- Improved circulation
- Immune health
- Stroke prevention
- Possible cancer prevention

TURKEY

Turkey is a lean white meat that can be purchased in many forms. In the USA, turkey is most commonly served roasted whole for Thanksgiving, but turkey can be used in many dishes and is available in a variety of cuts. Turkey is a quality protein, with all essential amino acids. Turkey also has a good ratio of fats, and is a great source of tryptophan, which, as a precursor to serotonin, can help with mood and relaxation. Turkey is a versatile and inexpensive meat and has more protein and less fat and cholesterol than other meats. Turkey livers are a particularly good source of vitamin B12.

RECOMMENDED FOR HELP WITH

- Muscle maintenance
- Strong bones and teeth
- Improved circulation and blood oxygenation
- Enhanced immune health
- Possible cancer prevention

GOOSE

Goose is an excellent-quality protein, with all essential amino acids and a good ratio of fats. Goose has a higher total fat content than chicken or turkey, but lower than beef and slightly lower than duck. Like duck, goose meat is rare in the USA but a Christmas dinner staple in the UK. Goose provides similar nutrients to duck and can also be a flavorsome and nutritious meal when carefully prepared and served in modest amounts. Goose meat is red, due to the high levels of the oxygen-storing protein. Employ the same methods of preparation as duck to reduce the amount of fat when cooking.

RECOMMENDED FOR HELP WITH

- Muscle maintenance
- Enhanced immune health
- Strong bones and teeth
- Possible cancer prevention

Cooking the whole bird allows all the flavors of the fat and bones to permeate the meat.

QUAIL

Quail is an excellent-quality protein, with all essential amino acids and a good ratio of fats. Quail is another less-common game bird, but one that can be found in dishes served in European restaurants. Why not consider preparing quail at home as part of a delicious, well-balanced meal? A small quail is usually served per person; where quails are larger in size, consider serving the breast meat. Search online or try specialist food stores to find quail.

RECOMMENDED FOR HELP WITH

- Muscle maintenance
- Increased energy
- Oxygenation of the blood
- Possible cancer prevention
- Iron-deficient anemia

SEAFOOD AND FISH

Seafood is among the most health-enhancing of all foods. The quality of the protein, with all essential amino acids, is crucial for building antibodies to strengthen the immune system, and building muscle for strength and endurance. The high quantity and quality of omega-3 fatty acids found in seafood enhance heart and brain health as well as memory. Seafood contains minimal carbohydrate, and helps maintain low blood sugar and normal body fat. Many freshwater fish also have significant levels of omega-3s. The American Heart Association recommends eating two servings of fish per week to promote heart health. Seafood and fish can have high levels of mercury and other toxins, which can be of concern to pregnant women in particular. Each country has its own recommendations regarding the consumption of fish and seafood during pregnancy; these should be referred to. Additionally, allergy to shellfish (including lobster and scallops) is relatively common; if you suffer from any symptoms, get treatment immediately.

ABALONE (MIXED SPECIES), RAW

—

Abalone is the name for a group of sea mollusks or snails. They are also called "ormer" in the UK. Abalone contain essential amino acids and are very low in saturated fat. They are a good source of protein, selenium, and vitamin K, as well as providing high levels of vitamin E and iron. However, abalone are also high in sodium and cholesterol, so eat in moderation. Abalone have a special place in many Asian cultures due to their far-reaching health benefits.

RECOMMENDED FOR HELP WITH

- Reducing cardiovascular disease
- Oxygenation of the blood
- Possible cancer prevention
- Enhanced brain function and memory
- Immunity

ANCHOVY

—

Anchovies are small, oily ocean fish. They are very nutritious, if eaten in moderation. They contain essential amino acids and are high in selenium, calcium, iron, and potassium, great for healthy eyes, bones, and muscle. Canned or raw, anchovies are high in cholesterol—canned, they are also high in sodium. Anchovies are a great source of omega-3s. If you suffer from gout, watch your consumption. Low in mercury, they can be eaten during pregnancy.

BASS

—

Bass is low in calories and an excellent source of protein. Whether freshwater bass or sea bass, this white fish is high in cholesterol, so maintain portion control and eat in moderation. Freshwater bass in particular is high in manganese and vitamin B12, promoting a strong heart and blood cells and healthy skin. Sea bass is high in selenium and phosphorus, assisting in cellular repair and a reduction in inflammation. It is recommended that bass be avoided or limited during pregnancy due to possible exposure to mercury.

RECOMMENDED FOR HELP WITH

- Heart health
- Reducing cardiovascular disease and diabetes
- Strong bones
- Joint health
- Immunity
- Enhanced brain function

BREAM (SEA)

—

Sea bream, also known as porgy, include numerous sea and freshwater species around the world. Sea bream recommendations for pregnant women vary considerably from country to country, and the toxins in this white fish are considered too high for safety by many during this time. However, for non-pregnant people, sea bream is delicious and low in calories. It is also high in omega-3s and seen to lower blood pressure and promote good eye health.

RECOMMENDED FOR HELP WITH

- Reducing risk of cardiovascular disease
- Heart health
- Immunity
- Energy boost
- Eye health
- Anemia

Oily fish are high in omega-3 fatty acids, which are good for heart and brain health.

RECOMMENDED FOR HELP WITH

- Metabolism
- Stamina
- Eye health
- Heart and blood health
- Possible cancer protection

CARP

—

Carp are large, oily freshwater fish. They contain essential fatty acids and are low in sodium but high in cholesterol. Carp are a good source of phosphorus, vitamin B12, selenium, and zinc. Good for promoting heart health, carp consumption also supports the immune system and assists in cellular repair. Due to higher levels of mercury, the American Pregnancy Association recommends limiting carp during pregnancy.

RECOMMENDED FOR HELP WITH

- Strong bones
- Reducing risk of cardiovascular disease
- Heart health
- Immunity
- Enhanced brain function
- Reducing joint inflammation

CATFISH

—

Catfish is a popular dish in the American South, but a less well-known food source elsewhere. If catfish is prepared correctly and carefully, it can be a delicious and nutritious meal. However, catfish poisoning does result from lack of careful preparation, so ensure you purchase from reputable sources and cook it thoroughly. Catfish contains essential amino acids and is a great source of vitamin B12, phosphorus, and selenium. It is also high in omega-6, which is especially high in farmed catfish. But due to its high cholesterol, it should be eaten in moderation. Due to the low purine content, catfish is considered safe in moderation for those suffering from gout, and because of low mercury, it is deemed safe to eat during pregnancy by the American Pregnancy Association. The same amount of wild catfish provides similar levels of nutrients, but with 89 calories and lower omega fatty acids.

Catfish needs to be prepared carefully to prevent food poisoning.

RECOMMENDED FOR HELP WITH

- Enhanced brain function
- Heart health
- Reduced cardiovascular disease
- Immunity
- Reduced joint inflammation
- Strong bones
- Anemia

CAVIAR

—

Caviar is a delicacy in many parts of the world. It is simply fish eggs (notably from the beluga sturgeon), but these little bundles are actually nutritional sources for unborn fish, providing a rich source of nutrients for humans, too. Caviar is very high in cholesterol and sodium, so consume it only as a rare treat—which is just as well, due to the cost. Caviar is extremely high in omega-3 and vitamin B12 (93 percent of your daily value), as well as vitamins D and A, and selenium. Avoid eating uncooked fish eggs during pregnancy.

RECOMMENDED FOR HELP WITH

- Immunity
- Heart health
- Reduced cardiovascular disease
- Anemia
- Enhanced brain function
- Strong bones
- Healthy skin

CLAMS

—

Clams are a type of bivalve mollusk that live in the water. They are eaten all over the world, from Italian shellfish pastas to American clam chowder and Indian curries. Clams contain the highest natural source of the amino acid taurine, believed to lower blood pressure and help fat digestion. They are very low in saturated fat but they are high in cholesterol. Clams are protein-rich and have astoundingly high levels of vitamin B12, plus very high levels of iron and selenium. Clams are low in mercury and can be eaten in moderation during pregnancy.

RECOMMENDED FOR HELP WITH

recommended for help with:

- Lowering blood pressure
- Anemia
- Enhanced brain function
- Immunity
- Healthy skin
- Possible cancer prevention

COD

—

Atlantic cod, also called whitefish or scrod, is a distinctively different type of fish from Pacific cod, with varying nutritional contents. Both Atlantic and Pacific cod have incredibly high levels of protein per calorie. There are concerns about the overfishing of cod, so it is best to monitor this. Atlantic cod is one of the least mercuric fish, and safer to eat during pregnancy. Atlantic cod contains essential fatty acids and is high in selenium, vitamin B12, and vitamin B6, and low in mercury. However, it is high in cholesterol. Pacific cod contains essential fatty acids and is very low in saturated fat. It is a good source of selenium, vitamin B6, and phosphorus, but is high in cholesterol.

RECOMMENDED FOR HELP WITH

- Strong bones
- Immunity
- Lowering blood pressure
- Anemia
- Blood health
- Reducing risk of cardiovascular disease
- Possible cancer prevention

CRAB

—

Crab is a low-calorie food that is very low in saturated fat and high in protein. Crabs are very high in sodium and cholesterol. As a result, ensure you do not add extra salt or butter when preparing crab and limit your intake of this meat. However, crab meat is very high in vitamin B12 (almost twice the recommended daily value) and also has high levels of copper, selenium, and zinc. Crab meat is low in mercury and can be eaten in moderation during pregnancy.

RECOMMENDED FOR HELP WITH

- Reducing cardiovascular disease
- Immunity
- Strong bones
- Energy
- Enhanced brain function
- Developing fetus during pregnancy
- Healthy skin
- Blood health
- Possible cancer protection

CRAPPIE (WILD)

—

Crappie is a freshwater sunfish that is also referred to as croppie, white perch, calico bass, and papermouth, and comes in both white and black varieties. It is a common game fish in USA and Canada and is often caught for sport. Crappie contains essential amino acids and is low in saturated fat, sodium, and cholesterol. It is also very high in vitamins E and A, as well as manganese and iron.

RECOMMENDED FOR HELP WITH

- Blood health
- Vision and eye health
- Reduces risk of cardiovascular disease
- Boosts stamina
- Healthy skin

EEL

—

While eel may not sound delectable to everyone, it is a delicacy in many cuisines, including jellied eel in the UK and the healthier grilled eel in Korea. Eel is low in sodium and high in omega-3, omega-6, zinc, phosphorus, and vitamins A and B12. However, it is also high in calories and cholesterol, so this meat should be eaten sparingly. With these nutrients, eel can reduce the risk of type-2 diabetes, arthritis, and cardiovascular disease. In Korea, it is believed to improve stamina, but research has so far proved inconclusive.

RECOMMENDED FOR HELP WITH

- Anemia
- Reduces risk of cardiovascular disease
- Strong bones
- Protection against diabetes
- Brain function
- Healthy skin
- Immunity

FLOUNDER

—

Flounder is a flat ocean fish that is low in calories and protein compared to the density of the meat, meaning you feel fuller quicker. It is low in saturated fat and contains all essential amino acids. Flounder is very high in omega-3 and selenium, as well as vitamin B12, aiding to blood and heart health and a stronger immune system. Due to the low purine content, flounder is considered safe in moderation for those suffering from gout, and because of low mercury is generally considered safe to eat while pregnant.

RECOMMENDED FOR HELP WITH

- Weight loss
- Reduces risk of cardiovascular disease
- Strong bones
- Heart health
- Joint health
- Possible cancer protection

GROUPER

—

Grouper can grow very large—but as long as you choose small fillets, the health benefits are sizable. Grouper contains essential amino acids and is low in sodium, calories, and saturated fat, and very high in selenium, protein, and iron. Because of the low calorie content, grouper is excellent for those watching their weight. Both the high protein and selenium are important for repairing new body tissue, and the iron for maintaining healthy red blood cells. Due to high levels of mercury, the American Pregnancy Association recommends limiting consumption during pregnancy.

RECOMMENDED FOR HELP WITH

- Weight loss
- Blood health
- Anemia
- Reduces risk of cardiovascular disease
- Strong bones
- Heart health
- Joint health
- Possible cancer protection

HADDOCK

—

Haddock is a popular choice for those less keen on strong fishy flavors. Haddock is a mild white fish that is versatile in the kitchen. Containing essential amino acids, haddock is very low in saturated fat and an excellent source of protein. It is very high in cholesterol, and smoked haddock in particular is high in sodium and should be eaten in moderation. The high vitamins and minerals in haddock help in the prevention of a number of chronic diseases, such as cancer, heart disease, and diabetes. In moderation, haddock is considered safe to eat while pregnant by the American Pregnancy Association, but smoked haddock should be avoided due to possible listeria contamination.

RECOMMENDED FOR HELP WITH

- Strong bones
- Blood health
- Reduces risk of cardiovascular disease
- Heart health
- Energy
- Joint health
- Possible cancer protection

HALIBUT (ATLANTIC AND PACIFIC)

—

According to the USDA, halibut is one of the highest-protein fish available, making it a great choice for muscle maintenance and energy. Halibut also contains essential amino acids and is low in saturated fat and sodium. It is high in omega-3, selenium, and niacin, promoting heart health and boosting the immune system. In moderation, halibut is considered safe to eat while pregnant by the American Pregnancy Association.

RECOMMENDED FOR HELP WITH

- Strong bones
- Heart health
- Reduces risk of cardiovascular disease
- Immunity
- Energy
- Joint health
- Possible cancer protection

LOBSTER

—

Lobster is a good source of vitamins and minerals. However, due to its high sodium and cholesterol content, it should be eaten in moderation. Lobster contains essential amino acids and is low in fat. The calcium and phosphorus build strong bones, vitamin B12 works towards brain function and nerve communication, and copper increases energy and assists in cell regeneration and skin health. Lobster has traditionally been considered an aphrodisiac. Because of higher mercury, lobster should be limited during pregnancy. Allergy to lobster and other shellfish is relatively common; if you suffer from any symptoms, get treatment immediately.

Although containing many nutrients, lobster's high cholesterol and sodium content mean it should be enjoyed as a treat.

RECOMMENDED FOR HELP WITH

- Strong bones
- Anemia
- Blood health
- Energy
- Immunity
- Healthy skin
- Possible cancer protection

MACKEREL

—

Mackerel is an oily fish, and the name applies to several types. Mackerel provides high levels of omega-3—crucial for heart health—and jack mackerel is considered highest of all. Mackerel is a good source of potassium, which, together with the high omega-3, works to control blood pressure, if eaten in moderation. The vitamin B12 strengthens red blood cells. The USDA and American Pregnancy Association recommend avoiding king mackerel during pregnancy due to high mercury levels, but other types of mackerel can be eaten on occasion.

RECOMMENDED FOR HELP WITH

- Heart health
- Reduces risk of cardiovascular disease
- Blood health
- Lowers blood pressure
- Enhanced brain function
- Strong bones
- Immunity
- Possible cancer protection

HERRING

—

Herring contains extremely high omega-3s and is high in protein, but also high in cholesterol. The fatty acids and protein promote healthy brain function and bone strength, and the potassium assists in nerve communication. Herring is rich in iron and vitamin B12, which keep red blood cells healthy. Herring is considered safe to eat during pregnancy due to its low mercury levels, but the American Pregnancy Association recommends avoiding kippers (smoked herring) during pregnancy due to possible listeria contamination. If you suffer from gout, watch your consumption of this food. Grilling or poaching are the healthiest cooking options; kippers and pickled herring are high in sodium—eat these in moderation.

Herring is a nutritious fish, but also high in cholesterol, so eat in moderation.

RECOMMENDED FOR HELP WITH

- Anemia
- Cardiovascular disease
- Strong bones
- Brain function
- Healthy skin
- Immunity

MONKFISH

—

Monkfish is a type of anglerfish that, while not considered a thing of beauty, is a delicious and healthy fish. However, the sustainability of monkfish fishing has been brought into question in some parts of the world, so bear this in mind when purchasing. Monkfish is a low-calorie, high-protein fish that contains essential amino acids and is low in sodium, as well as being high in selenium and phosphorus, great for energy and brain function. It is advised that monkfish consumption be limited during pregnancy due to mercury levels.

RECOMMENDED FOR HELP WITH

- Strong bones
- Blood health
- Anemia
- Immunity
- Energy
- Mood
- Possible cancer protection

MULLET

—

The striped mullet is found in various guises in the cuisines of the world, and the fish can be both farmed and wild. Mullet contains essential amino acids and is low in sodium, high in selenium, and provides a good source of iron and omega fatty acids. However, it is also high in cholesterol. Protein is important for strong bones, healthy blood, and tissue repair, and iron maintains healthy red blood cells and is particularly important for growing children, and women who are menstruating, pregnant, or lactating. Mullet is low in mercury and can be eaten in moderation during pregnancy.

RECOMMENDED FOR HELP WITH

- Strong bones
- Blood health
- Immunity
- Energy
- Possible cancer protection

OCTOPUS

—

Octopus is an ocean mollusk related to squid and cuttlefish. It is believed there are over 300 species of octopus, but only a limited number of these are caught for human consumption. Octopus is a low-calorie seafood that contains essential amino acids and is low in saturated fat and high in protein, but also high in cholesterol and sodium. Both Atlantic and Pacific octopus provide high levels of copper, iron, zinc, and vitamin B12. Copper boosts energy and helps form connective tissue; it also metabolizes iron, itself important for healthy red blood cells. Together, copper and zinc strengthen the immune system.

RECOMMENDED FOR HELP WITH

- Strong bones
- Blood health
- Immunity
- Energy
- Healthy skin
- Heart health
- Possible cancer protection

OYSTER

—

Oysters are bivalve marine mollusks. They are low in fat and contain essential amino acids. They are also a good source of copper, iron, and zinc—which is especially high in canned oysters. Alongside copper, zinc boosts a healthy immune system, and iron promotes healthy red blood cells. However, oysters are very high in cholesterol and relatively low in protein. Oysters are low in mercury and can be eaten in moderation during pregnancy.

RECOMMENDED FOR HELP WITH

- Strong bones
- Blood health
- Immunity
- Energy
- Eye health
- Heart health
- Possible cancer protection

PERCH (OCEAN)

—

Perch is low in saturated fat and rich in protein. It contains essential amino acids, selenium, phosphorus, vitamin B12, and calcium, but is high in cholesterol. Selenium promotes good metabolism and may reduce the risk of cancer, while phosphorus and calcium maintain healthy bones. Due to mercury levels, the American Pregnancy Association recommends limiting perch consumption during pregnancy. The risk of mercury and other toxins in ocean perch can be reduced by careful preparation, especially by removing skin and fat and cooking to a high temperature.

RECOMMENDED FOR HELP WITH

- Strong bones
- Metabolism
- Blood health
- Healthy skin
- Immunity
- Energy
- Heart health
- Possible cancer protection

PIKE

—

Pike is a freshwater fish with low sodium and high protein and vitamin B12. It is also very low in saturated fat and a good source of phosphorus, which makes pike a positive option for weight-loss programs. Pike comes in many types: Northern pike is common in the Northern Hemisphere; walleye pike (or simply "walleye" or "pikeperch") is native to North America and the official state fish of Minnesota. It is recommended that pike be avoided during pregnancy.

RECOMMENDED FOR HELP WITH

- Weight loss
- Strong bones
- Blood health
- Heart health
- Healthy skin
- Immunity

POLLOCK (ATLANTIC)

—

Pollock is a good source of protein and contains essential amino acids. This white fish is low in saturated fat and is a source of vitamin B12, selenium, and phosphorus. However, it is quite high in cholesterol. Vitamin B12 is essential for a healthy nervous system, and phosphorus and selenium boost the immune system and strengthen bone and tissue. Due to low mercury, pollock is considered safe to eat in moderation while pregnant by the American Pregnancy Association.

RECOMMENDED FOR HELP WITH

- Strong bones
- Blood health
- Enhanced brain function
- Energy
- Heart health
- Possible cancer protection

RED SNAPPER

—

Red snapper is most prevalent along the southeastern Atlantic coast. Much of what is labeled as "red snapper" is actually snapper of a different type. Red snapper is low in calories, rich in protein, and contains all essential amino acids, as well as high levels of selenium and vitamin B12. It is also low in saturated fat and sodium. Due to higher levels of mercury, the American Pregnancy Association recommends limiting snapper during pregnancy. This fish may be in danger of overfishing so you should bear this in mind when buying.

RECOMMENDED FOR HELP WITH

- Heart health
- Strong bones
- Blood health
- Immunity
- Possible cancer protection

ROE (MIXED SPECIES)

—

Roe is the ripe ovaries or unfertilized eggs of fish, and cod and salmon are some of the more common types of roe. It is a delicacy in some countries, such as Norway, but less common in others, such as the USA. It comes as either "hard" or "soft" roe. The remarkably high omega-3 content makes this a very healthy food, despite the high cholesterol levels—although it should still be eaten in moderation. Roe is extremely high in vitamin B12, as well as being high in selenium, riboflavin, and phosphorus. Avoid eating uncooked fish eggs during pregnancy.

RECOMMENDED FOR HELP WITH

- Reducing cardiovascular disease
- Blood health
- Enhanced brain function and memory
- Immunity
- Energy
- Possible cancer protection

ROUGHY (ORANGE)

—

Orange roughy, or deep-sea perch, is a widespread ocean fish with an incredible lifespan of over 100 years. They are vulnerable to overfishing, so it is important to monitor your region's advice on this fish prior to purchase. Orange roughy contains essential amino acids, is very low in saturated fat, and is high in omega-6, protein, and selenium—but very high in cholesterol. The American Pregnancy Association recommends avoiding orange roughy during pregnancy due to high mercury levels, and it is recommended that this fish be eaten in moderation by all others.

RECOMMENDED FOR HELP WITH

- Reducing cardiovascular disease
- Heart health
- Strong bones
- Immunity
- Possible cancer protection
- Enhanced brain function and memory
- Immunity

SALMON

—

Salmon is believed to be among the top five most-consumed fish in the USA, and fresh salmon sales are on the rise in the UK Salmon meat comes in many varieties, from salmon steaks to raw sushi, and lox/smoked to canned. Salmon is primarily found in the Atlantic and Pacific Oceans, with contention over the best farming and fishing practices. Salmon is full of essential vitamins and minerals: incredibly rich in omega-3 and omega-6, with essential amino acids, low sodium, and high selenium, vitamins B12 and B6, and folate. Salmon is lower in saturated fat than beef. Due to the low purine content, salmon is considered safe in moderation for those suffering from gout. The American Pregnancy Association recommends avoiding smoked fish during pregnancy due to possible listeria contamination, but fresh or canned salmon can be eaten in moderation.

RECOMMENDED FOR HELP WITH

- Reducing cardiovascular disease
- Blood health
- Enhanced brain function and memory
- Strong bones
- Immunity
- Possible cancer protection

Salmon is still the most frequently bought fish, for its flavor and health benefits.

SARDINES

—

Sardines are small, oily saltwater fish known to promote heart health, with high omega-6 and omega-3. It is recommended that you look for BPA-free canned sardines (or opt for fresh), as BPA is shown to increase cancer growth and diabetes. Sardines are also very high in cholesterol. They are a rich source of protein, vitamins, and minerals, and one of the few natural food sources of vitamin D. Sardines strengthen the cardiovascular and digestive systems and reduce the risk of disease. Sardines are low in mercury and can be eaten in moderation during pregnancy.

RECOMMENDED FOR HELP WITH

- Regulating blood pressure
- Blood health
- Enhanced brain function and memory
- Strong bones
- Immunity

SHRIMP (PRAWN)

—

Shrimp are a widespread marine crustacean. The term "shrimp" is often used generally for a number of similarly shaped crustaceans and sometimes synonymously with "prawn." In North America, "shrimp" is the prevalent term, where they are the most popular seafood; however, in the UK, "prawn" is most often used, especially for larger shrimp. According to the American Heart Association, moderate consumption of shellfish (including shrimp) contributes to a heart-healthy diet. Shrimp contain essential amino acids, including tryptophan, which helps stabilize mood and sleep, as well as selenium, which boosts immunity. However, they are high in cholesterol. If you suffer from gout, watch your consumption. Shrimp are low in mercury and can be eaten in moderation during pregnancy. Allergy to shrimp and other shellfish is relatively common; if you show symptoms, get treatment immediately.

RECOMMENDED FOR HELP WITH

- Heart health
- Strong bones
- Mood
- Blood health
- Energy
- Immunity
- Possible cancer protection

SOLE (FLATFISH)

—

Sole is a flatfish, related to flounder, that dwells on the sea bed. There are a number of types, from common or Dover sole to American sole. Like flounder, sole is a low-energy, dense fish, creating fullness on fewer calories. Sole is a good source of protein and low in saturated fat, but high in cholesterol. Due to the low purine content, sole is considered safe in moderation for gout sufferers, and due to low mercury is considered safe to eat in moderation during pregnancy. Common sole is at risk of unsustainable sourcing.

RECOMMENDED FOR HELP WITH

- Weight loss
- Heart health
- Strong bones
- Blood health
- Anemia
- Immunity
- Joint health
- Possible cancer protection

RECOMMENDED FOR HELP WITH

- Weight loss
- Heart health
- Enhanced brain function
- Blood health
- Immunity
- Joint health

Scallops are a delicious treat for those on a weight-loss diet.

SCALLOPS

—

Scallops are marine bivalve mollusks found in oceans all over the world. Scallops are a lean source of protein that is low in calories and saturated fat, making them good for weight management. They are, however, high in cholesterol. They are high in vitamin B12 and super-rich in fatty acids—in particular, omega-6, which is integral to brain and immune system function, which, with omega-3, reduces the risk of heart disease and high blood pressure. If you suffer from gout, watch your consumption of this food. Scallops are low in mercury and can be eaten in moderation during pregnancy.

STURGEON

—

Sturgeon is best known for its eggs, which produce caviar. However, sturgeon meat itself contains essential amino acids and is low in sodium, though high in cholesterol. It is a great source of vitamin A, pivotal to tissue regeneration, preventing acne, and reducing the risk of heart attack or stroke. Vitamin B12 maintains healthy red blood cells, and niacin is important for energy production.

RECOMMENDED FOR HELP WITH

- Heart and blood health
- Strong bones and tissue
- Anemia
- Immunity
- Healthy skin
- Joint health
- Developing fetus during pregnancy

SWORDFISH

—

Swordfish is an excellent source of protein and omega-3, and one of the few natural food sources of vitamin D. Protein and fatty acids help build and protect bone and tissue, as well as protecting the body against stroke and heart disease. Vitamin D contributes to healthy bones. Selenium may help protect against cancer and, alongside vitamin D, boosts immune system function. Swordfish is high in cholesterol and mercury. The USDA and American Pregnancy Association recommend avoiding swordfish during pregnancy, and swordfish should be limited in the diets of others, too.

RECOMMENDED FOR HELP WITH

- Heart health
- Enhanced brain function
- Strong bones
- Blood health
- Anemia
- Energy
- Healthy skin
- Immunity
- Joint health
- Possible cancer protection

TILAPIA

—

Tilapia are believed to have originated in Africa but have since found their way to other warm climates and fish farms in colder climates, and are now one of the most commonly consumed fish in the USA. Tilapia are low in sodium and amino acids, but high in cholesterol. Their high levels of protein are important for muscle maintenance and energy. Selenium improves immunity. Due to low mercury, tilapia are considered safe to eat in moderation while pregnant by the American Pregnancy Association. Serve tilapia grilled, baked, or steamed.

RECOMMENDED FOR HELP WITH

- Strong bones
- Blood health
- Anemia
- Immunity
- Energy
- Mood
- Possible cancer protection

TROUT

—

Trout refers to a large family of oily freshwater fish, although some do travel to the ocean. In the USA, there are a number of species, including lake trout and rainbow trout. Trout are rich in omega-3 and omega-6, as well as amino acids and protein, and low in sodium but high in cholesterol. Amino acids and protein work together to build and repair bones and tissue and maintain organ function. Omega fatty acids work together to decrease the risk of heart disease and high blood pressure, as well as helping with brain function. Vitamin B12 helps maintain healthy blood cells. Freshwater trout are low in mercury and can be eaten in moderation during pregnancy.

RECOMMENDED FOR HELP WITH

- Heart health
- Strong bones
- Tissue regeneration
- Enhanced brain function
- Blood health
- Energy
- Immunity
- Joint health
- Possible cancer protection

TUNA

—

Tuna is a saltwater fish with widespread habitat and a number of species, including bluefin, yellowfin (ahi), bigeye, and albacore. Bluefin tuna is especially high in omega-3 and protein and low in sodium. It is also a good source of vitamins B12 and A. Yellowfin tuna is low in saturated fat and sodium, but high in cholesterol. It is a good source of selenium, niacin, and vitamin B6. Both are protein-rich. Due to the low purine content, light canned tuna is considered safe in moderation for those suffering from gout. The American Pregnancy Association recommends avoiding ahi and bigeye tuna during pregnancy due to high mercury levels.

RECOMMENDED FOR HELP WITH

- Strong bones
- Blood health
- Anemia
- Immunity
- Energy
- Mood
- Possible cancer protection

WHITEFISH

—

Whitefish is a large family of fish that are mainly of the freshwater variety. Outside of the USA, whitefish is not a common term found on menus or in stores; rather, the individual fish name is used. Whitefish are low in sodium, and whitefish meat is exceedingly high in omega-3, while the eggs are high in vitamin B12. However, whitefish are very high in cholesterol. These fish are low in mercury and can be eaten in moderation during pregnancy.

RECOMMENDED FOR HELP WITH

- Heart health
- Strong bones
- Blood health
- Enhanced brain function
- Energy
- Immunity
- Joint health
- Developing fetus during pregnancy

WHITING

—

Whiting refers to a number of different species, including English, Japanese, and Pacific whiting, and can sometimes refer specifically to hake or pollock. Whiting contains essential amino acids and high protein, strengthening bones and protecting the heart. It is low in saturated fat but very high in cholesterol. Whiting is a good source of vitamin B12, selenium, phosphorus, and potassium. These nutrients maintain bone strength, blood health, and organ function, and strengthen the immune system. Whiting are low in mercury and can be eaten in moderation during pregnancy. Pacific whiting in particular is reported to be sustainably sourced.

RECOMMENDED FOR HELP WITH

- Heart health
- Enhanced brain function
- Strong bones
- Blood health
- Anemia
- Energy
- Healthy skin
- Immunity
- Joint health
- Possible cancer protection

VEGETABLES, NON-STARCHY

Non-starchy vegetables contain lower amounts of carbohydrates and calories than starchy vegetables, and are packed with vitamins, antioxidants, and fiber.

ARUGULA (ROCKET), RAW

—

Arugula is also known as rocket. This zesty salad leaf is an excellent source of nitric oxide, which improves heart health. It's loaded with health-boosting nutrients, from antioxidant vitamin A to immune-boosting zinc. A favourite in Italian cuisine, the younger, paler leaves have a more delicate flavour suited to salads and pesto, while the older, darker leaves pack a peppery punch, ideal for adding pizzazz to your pizza.

RECOMMENDED FOR HELP WITH

- Possible cancer prevention
- Liver health
- Gastrointestinal ulcers

Arugula

Asparagus

RECOMMENDED FOR HELP WITH

- Possible cancer prevention
- Regulating blood sugar levels and blood pressure

ASPARAGUS

—

Succulent asparagus spears have been considered a delicacy for many centuries. They're loaded with antioxidants, which help protect cells from free radicals, molecules which damage cells. Rich in phytonutrients known as saponins that have been shown to have anti-inflammatory and anti-cancer properties, asparagus packs a healthy, nutritious punch. Delicious in salads or on its own.

BEET (BEETROOT) GREENS

—

The leafy tops of the beetroot plant contain nitrates to help the body produce nitric oxide, which improves heart health. Beet greens are packed with even more health-boosting nutrients than the beetroot. They are very low in cholesterol, yet loaded with free-radical-zapping antioxidants, making them one of the healthiest greens. Just 1oz (25g) of beet greens contains in excess of your recommended daily value of vitamin K—raw greens provide about 140 percent, while cooked greens provide a huge 871 percent. Vitamin K helps blood to clot properly and promotes bone strength.

RECOMMENDED FOR HELP WITH

- Weight loss
- Cardiovascular health
- Vision

Beet

Artichoke

ARTICHOKE

—

Artichokes contain more immune-boosting vitamin C than oranges. They're packed with vitamins and minerals, including vitamin K, essential for blood clotting, free-radical-zapping manganese, and cholesterol-regulating folate. They're also a very good source of fiber: just 1oz (25g) contains 10 percent of your recommended daily value, helping to maintain a healthy digestive system.

RECOMMENDED FOR HELP WITH

- Immunity
- Digestion

Bell peppers

RECOMMENDED
FOR HELP WITH

- Immunity
- Age-related macular degeneration

BELL PEPPERS

—

Also known as sweet peppers or capsicums. Bell peppers are native to South America, but have spread to the rest of the world. They come in a variety of colours, red and green being the most common. Their crunchy, sweet, brightly coloured skin makes them a favourite ingredient in a range of dishes from salads to sautées. Bell peppers are a great source of antioxidants, compounds that help decrease free radical molecules, which damage cells. Higher-heat cooking can damage some of the delicate phytonutrients in bell peppers, so use lower-heat methods for a short period of time to keep the nutrients intact. Just 1oz (25g) of boiled red bell pepper contains 16 percent of your recommended daily value of vision-boosting vitamin A and 80 percent of immune-boosting vitamin C, compared with 3 percent and 35 percent in the equivalent amount of boiled green bell pepper.

BROCCOLI

—

Broccoli is loaded with antioxidants to help protect cells against free radical damage, and sulforaphanes, molecules that may help to combat cancer. Nutrients in broccoli help the body to eliminate unwanted contaminants, resulting in a strong, positive detoxification impact. It's also rich in the flavanoid kaempferol, which lessens the impact of allergy-related substances on your body, providing broccoli with unique anti-inflammatory benefits. Its green or purple florets make a nutritious addition to a range of dishes from salads to stir-fries.

Broccoli

RECOMMENDED
FOR HELP WITH

- Possible cancer prevention, especially prostate and colon
- Detoxing
- Immunity

Brussels sprouts

RECOMMENDED
FOR HELP WITH

- Possible cancer prevention
- Immunity
- Detoxing

BRUSSELS SPROUTS

—

A great source of digestion-boosting fiber, immune-boosting vitamin C, and various phytochemical compounds, including glucosinolates which have been linked with protecting against cancer. Just one ounce 1oz (25g) of boiled Brussels sprouts contains nearly a third (29 percent) of your recommend daily value of vitamin C and almost half (49 percent) of vitamin K, which helps proper blood clotting and maintaining healthy bones.

BURDOCK ROOT

—

Burdock root is the tuber of the greater burdock plant. It is high in free-radical-zapping antioxidants, soothing mucilage, and carbohydrate- and fat-regulating insulin. Burdock root has long been used in traditional medicines to help purify the blood due to its diuretic properties. Its soothing, demulcent properties mean it has also traditionally been used to treat throat and chest problems.

Burdock root

RECOMMENDED
FOR HELP WITH

- Regulating blood sugar
- Mild laxative
- Cardiovascular health

Cabbage

CABBAGE

—

This leafy vegetable is packed with antioxidants and is high in fiber—1oz (25g) contains 3 percent of your recommended daily value of dietary fiber. It's also packed with immune-boosting vitamin C and vitamin K, essential for blood clotting and bone nourishment. Steaming or sautéing cabbage can also provide special cholesterol-lowering benefits. The fiber-related components in cabbage do a better job of binding together with bile acids in your digestive tract when they've been steamed, making it easier for bile acids to be excreted. The result is a lowering of your cholesterol levels.

Savoy cabbage is a particularly good source of sinigrin, a glucosinolate which has been linked with unique cancer preventive properties, especially with respect to bladder cancer, colon cancer, and prostate cancer.

RECOMMENDED FOR HELP WITH

- Digestion
- Possible cancer prevention, especially bladder, prostate, and colon
- Weight loss
- Lowering cholesterol

CELERY

—

Celery is one of the most alkaline foods you can eat. Since most people's bodies are far too acidic, celery is a welcome addition to any diet. Popular for its flavourful leaves and shoots, and crunchy roots, celery is rich in immune-boosting, anti-cancerous antioxidants, which help protect cells against free radical damage; its leaves are a good source of vision-boosting vitamin A. Enjoy celery roots in salads for a healthy, nutritious crunch, or boiled in soups and stews.

Celery

RECOMMENDED FOR HELP WITH

- Lowering cholesterol
- Reducing anxiety levels
- Immunity

CHICORY (CURLY ENDIVE)

—

Chicory is a woody plant native to Europe, North Africa, and Asia, which is now cultivated widely in the USA. Its long tap root is most commonly used as a caffeine-free coffee substitute, while its leaves are popular in salads. Chicory was prized by the ancient Egyptians for its healing benefits for the liver and gallbladder. It is loaded with free-radical-zapping antioxidants.

Chicory roots are a good source of inulin, which aids digestion and helps to regulate cholesterol. Chicory roots can also be roast, ground, and used as a caffeine-free coffee substitute. Chicory greens are loaded with vitamin K, essential for blood clotting and bone nourishment—just 1oz (25g) is packed with 108 percent of your recommended daily value.

Chicory

RECOMMENDED FOR HELP WITH

- Digestion
- Lowering cholesterol
- Liver detoxification

Celeriac

RECOMMENDED FOR HELP WITH

- Possible cancer protection, especially colon
- Immunity

CELERIAC

—

Also known as root celery, celeriac is loaded with antioxidants, which help prevent cell damage from free radicals. Research has shown that falcarinol, a poly-acetylene antioxidant found in celeriac, may help to protect against colon cancer. It's also a good source of vitamin K, essential for blood clotting and bone nourishment. Enjoy celeriac in a range of dishes, from mash to soups and stews, for a healthy nutritional boost.

COLLARDS (COLLARD GREENS)

—

Collards are a great source of phytonutrients—natural compounds that may help prevent disease and help to keep your body working properly. They're packed with vitamin K—just one 1oz (25g) of raw collards contains a huge 179 percent of your recommended value of this bone-nourishing vitamin. Steamed collards may have the greatest cholesterol-lowering ability of all commonly eaten cruciferous vegetables, outshining steamed kale, broccoli, and mustard greens. The glucosinolates glucoraphanin, sinigrin, gluconasturtian, and glucotropaeolin provide unique cancer protection, too, making collards a highly nutritious addition to any diet.

RECOMMENDED FOR HELP WITH

- Possible cancer prevention
- Strong bones
- Immunity

Cucumber

RECOMMENDED FOR HELP WITH

- Digestion
- Strong bones
- Vision

CUCUMBER

—

Cool, refreshing cucumbers are low in calories and packed with nutritious vitamins and minerals. Because their rough outer skin can be difficult to chew and digest, cucumbers are often peeled. However, what many people don't know is that most of the beneficial nutritional value of cucumbers, including bone-nourishing vitamin K, comes from the peel. Leave the peel on to reap all of the nutritional benefits this vegetable has to offer.

DANDELION GREENS

—

Dandelions have long been revered for their healing properties. They are rich in free-radical-zapping antioxidants and other nutritious minerals and vitamins, including vitamin K, essential for blood clotting and bone nourishment. Just 1oz (25g) of raw dandelion greens contains a huge 272 percent of your recommended daily value of vitamin K. Dandelions are also a good source of vision-boosting vitamin A. Choose young, tender greens to add a tasty nutritional boost to salads.

RECOMMENDED FOR HELP WITH

- Digestion
- Bone strength
- Vision
- Alzheimer's disease

Dandelion greens

CRESS, GARDEN

—

Garden cress is packed with vitamins, essential minerals, and free-radical-zapping antioxidants. Just one 1oz (25g) contains a huge 190 percent of your recommended daily value of bone-nourishing vitamin K. Cress is also loaded with vision-boosting vitamin A and immune-boosting vitamin C, as well as bone-building calcium, potassium, and phosphorus. The nutritional value of cress is often overlooked—it's so much more than just a garnish. Add cress to salads and sandwiches for a tasty, nutritious boost.

Garden cress

RECOMMENDED FOR HELP WITH

- Iron-deficient anemia
- Diarrhea
- Immunity

EGGPLANT (AUBERGINE)

—

Also known as aubergine and brinjal, eggplant is rich in free-radical-scavenging antioxidants, including nasunin, which has also been shown to contribute to healthy brain cells. Phytonutrients in eggplant help to lower cholesterol and have been linked with the prevention of cancer and rheumatoid arthritis. Many of the nutrients are contained in the glossy purple skin; be sure to include this to reap eggplant's full nutritional value in dishes from ratatouille to stews.

RECOMMENDED FOR HELP WITH

- Weight loss
- Cardiovascular health
- Vision

Eggplant

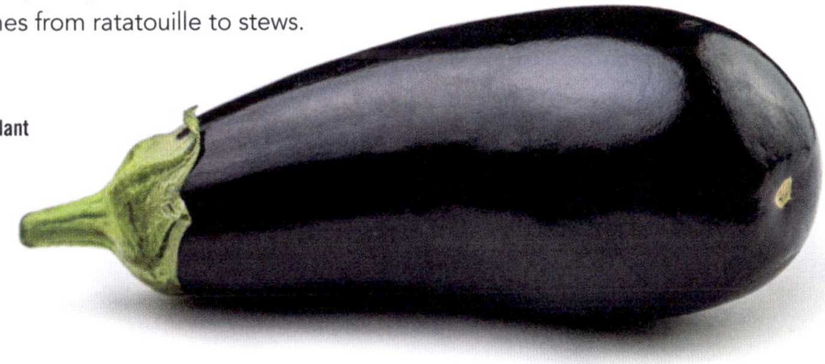

ENDIVE

—

This leafy green salad veg is rich in antioxidants, which protect cells in the body from free radical damage. It's bursting with bone-nourishing vitamin K, immune-boosting vitamin C, vision-boosting vitamin A, and energy-stoking B vitamins, as well as digestion-aiding dietary fiber. Include endives in salads for a tangy nutritional boost.

Endive

RECOMMENDED FOR HELP WITH

- Lowering cholesterol
- Vision
- Immunity

FENNEL BULB

—

Succulent fennel bulb is loaded with free-radical-zapping antioxidants and dietary fibre. Its anise-like flavour makes it a favourite in Mediterranean dishes. Anethole, the essential oil that gives fennel its distinctive flavour, has been shown to have anti-fungal and anti-bacterial properties, while heart-friendly potassium contributes to a healthy cardiovascular system, helping to regulate heart rate and blood pressure. Fennel is a flavourful, healthy addition to many dishes, from roast chicken to seared salmon.

RECOMMENDED FOR HELP WITH

- Lowering blood pressure
- Digestion

Fennel bulb

Garlic

RECOMMENDED FOR HELP WITH

- Possible cancer prevention
- Lowering cholesterol
- Immunity

GARLIC

—

Garlic has long been celebrated as a king of healing plants in cultures around the world, used in traditional remedies for a wide range of ailments, from heart problems to premature aging. It also has a reputation as a natural antibiotic. Add garlic to soups, stews, fish, and meat dishes for a tasty, healthy boost, or chop it raw into salads. Not only does it pack a flavourful punch, it's loaded with health-boosting nutrients. Allowing garlic to sit after you've chopped or crushed it, before heating or adding to other ingredients, increases the health benefits.

LEEKS

—

Leeks are rich in antioxidants, protecting cells against damage from free radicals. They're also a good source of immune-boosting vitamin C, vision-boosting vitamin A, and vitamin K, essential for blood clotting and bone nourishment. For a healthy cooking option, slice thinly and briefly sauté. As with garlic and onions, allowing leeks to sit after chopping, before heating or adding to other ingredients, enhances their nutritional benefits.

RECOMMENDED FOR HELP WITH

- Lowering cholesterol
- Reducing anxiety levels
- Immunity

Leeks

Kale

RECOMMENDED FOR HELP WITH

- Possible cancer prevention, especially prostate and colon
- Detoxing
- Macular degeneration

KALE

—

Green leafy kale is rich in antioxidants and high in calcium. It's also a good source of immune-boosting vitamin C, vision-boosting vitamin A, and vitamin K, essential for blood clotting and bone nourishment. Flavanoids in kale have been shown to have strong antioxidant and anti-cancer properties.

Lettuce

RECOMMENDED FOR HELP WITH

- Digestion
- Vision
- Immunity

LETTUCE

—

A very low-calorie food. Lettuce is loaded with vision-boosting vitamin A and vitamin K, essential for blood clotting and bone nourishment, as well as dietary fiber, iron, and energy-enhancing B vitamins. A good rule of thumb is that the nutritional value becomes greater the darker green the leaves, with iceberg at the lower end and green leaf lettuce at the higher end of the spectrum. However, all varieties are low in calories and provide fiber, vitamins, and minerals, making lettuce a healthy addition to any diet.

ONION

—

Loaded with antioxidants, which help prevent cell damage from free radicals. Many of the nutrients in onion are concentrated in the outer layers of the flesh. To reap maximum health benefits from the outer layers, avoid over-peeling onions. Onion is a wonderfully versatile ingredient, adding a healthy boost to a huge range of dishes, from salads and soups, to sauces and curries. As with garlic and leeks, allowing onions to sit after chopping, before heating or adding to other ingredients, enhances their nutritional benefits.

Red onions are distinct from other onions because of their dark purplish color. They have a milder flavor than white onions, making them a popular choice raw in burgers or salads. Sharper and more pungent than red onions, white onions add a crisp bite to burgers and salad dishes, or provide a pungent, robust base for a wide range of savory dishes.

Okra

White onion

RECOMMENDED FOR HELP WITH

- Lowering cholesterol
- Reducing anxiety levels
- Immunity

RECOMMENDED FOR HELP WITH

- Possible cancer protection
- Diabetes
- Heart health

OKRA

—

Also known as "lady's fingers," okra is high in fiber, which is beneficial for digestion, as well as being a good source of vision-boosting vitamin A, immune-boosting vitamin C, brain-boosting folate, and vitamin K, essential for blood clotting and bone nourishment. Okra is popular pickled, fried, or grilled and in dishes such as gumbo. It is sometimes known as "gumbo pod."

PEPPER, JALAPENO

—

Native to Mexico, these hot, fiery green peppers contain the natural plant compound capsaicin, which has anti-inflammatory properties. These little peppers pack a nutritious punch—one jalapeno contains in excess of your recommended daily value of immune-boosting vitamin C, as well as providing bone-nourishing vitamin K, vision-boosting vitamin A, and health-boosting minerals. Add jalapenos to salsa, mashed avocado, or eggs for a spicy, nutritious kick.

RECOMMENDED FOR HELP WITH

- Lowering cholesterol
- Immunity

Jalapeno pepper

Radicchio

RECOMMENDED FOR HELP WITH

- Lowering cholesterol
- Vision
- Immunity

RADICCHIO (RED CHICORY)

—

This Mediterranean, cabbage-like vegetable is rich in antioxidants. It's also loaded with the flavanoids zeaxanthin and lutein, which help to protect your eyes from harmful ultraviolet rays, as well as bone-nourishing vitamin K and energy-enhancing B vitamins. Its wine-red, bitter-flavored leaves have long been a popular ingredient in Italian salads.

SCALLION (SHALLOT)

—

These small, slender bulbs have a milder, more delicate flavor than onions. On a weight per weight basis, shallots are richer in minerals, vitamins, and antioxidants than other types of onion, making them a welcome addition to any diet. Shallots are rich in antioxidants, which help cells combat free radicals, and a good source of vision-boosting vitamin A. As with onions, allowing shallots to sit after chopping enhances their nutritional benefits.

Scallions

RECOMMENDED FOR HELP WITH

- Lowering cholesterol
- Vision
- Immunity

TOMATO

—

RECOMMENDED FOR HELP WITH

- Lowering cholesterol
- Vision
- Immunity

Tomatoes are a nutritional powerhouse. Tomatoes and tomato products, including tomato sauce and tomato juice, are rich in vitamins and antioxidants, including lycopene. Research has shown that diets rich in lycopene may help decrease the risk of heart disease, age-related macular degeneration, stroke, high cholesterol, and certain types of cancer. Cooked tomatoes and tomato products in the form of tomato paste or sauce contain significantly more lycopene than raw tomatoes. However, whether eaten raw or cooked, freshly picked or canned, tomatoes provide a healthy addition to most diets, though high acidic levels may aggravate reflux or heartburn in those prone to these conditions. Include a mixture of cooked and raw tomatoes in your weekly meal plan to reap the most health benefits from tomatoes.

Raw red tomatoes are rich in dietary fiber, vision-boosting vitamin A, immune-boosting vitamin C, and bone-nourishing vitamin K. Lycopene is the antioxidant that gives tomatoes their rich red colour. However, tomatoes do not necessarily have to be deep red to be an outstanding source of lycopene. Research suggests that lycopene from orange tomatoes may actually be better absorbed by the body.

Like other tomato products, canned tomato juice contains the antioxidant lycopene. The lycopene content in all-natural, or homemade, tomato juice is similar to that found in fresh raw tomatoes. Look for products with no added salts, sugars, or chemicals.

Cooking tomatoes increases the lutein content, which helps prevent prostate cancer. Cooking also increases the content of the antioxidant lycopene. Eating cooked tomatoes with a healthy source of fat or oil enhances the absorption of lycopene, so try tomato sauce made with olive oil to maximize lycopene uptake.

Due to their moisture content, tomatoes deteriorate rapidly after being picked. Sun-drying removes the water to preserve the tomato, while retaining the flavour and many of the nutrients. Sun-dried tomatoes are low in fat, and high in fiber and immune-boosting vitamin C.

SPINACH

—

One of the most alkaline foods you can eat. Since most people's bodies are far too acidic, spinach is a welcome addition to any diet. Spinach is a storehouse of vitamins and minerals—1oz (25g) of raw spinach contains 169 percent of your recommended daily value of vitamin K, essential for blood clotting and bone nourishment, over half (53 percent) of your recommended daily value of vision-boosting vitamin A, and 4 percent of iron.

Spinach

RECOMMENDED FOR HELP WITH

- Lowering cholesterol
- Vision
- Immunity

WAKAME SEAWEED

—

Wakame seaweed has a delicate briny flavour and is popular in Japanese cuisine in dishes such as miso soup. It is traditionally cultivated in Japan on ropes tied to offshore rafts. Wakame seaweed is one of the few foods containing iodine, which improves thyroid function, and has been linked to the prevention of breast cancer. It can be eaten raw or cooked. Enjoy in salads or soups for a healthy "umami" flavour boost. However, it is high in sodium, so should be consumed in moderation.

Wakame seaweed

RECOMMENDED FOR HELP WITH

- Lowering cholesterol
- Vision
- Immunity

Watercress

RECOMMENDED FOR HELP WITH

- Lowering cholesterol
- Vision
- Immunity

WATERCRESS

—

This aquatic leafy green plant is found near springs and slow-moving streams. It's a close cousin to arugula and cabbage, yet it is often overlooked as a nutritional food source. Watercress is packed with vitamins and contains more vitamin C than oranges—1oz (25g) of raw watercress provides 20 percent of your recommended daily value of this immune-boosting vitamin, as well as 18 percent of vision-boosting vitamin A, and a huge 87 percent of bone-nourishing vitamin K. It's also rich in iron. Add raw to salads or steam as a side vegetable for a subtle, peppery health boost.

Swiss chard

SWISS CHARD

—

Also known as silverbeet or spinach chard, this leafy green vegetable is a storehouse of nutrients. It's rich in antioxidants and loaded with immune-boosting vitamin C, bone-nourishing vitamin K, and vision-boosting vitamin A, as well as health-boosting flavanoids.

RECOMMENDED FOR HELP WITH

- Lowering cholesterol
- Vision
- Immunity

RECOMMENDED FOR HELP WITH

- Lowering cholesterol
- Vision
- Immunity

Zucchini

ZUCCHINI (COURGETTE)

—

Also known as courgette, zucchini is one of the most popular summer squashes in the Americas. Zucchinis are low in calories, and high in vision-boosting vitamin A and heart-friendly potassium. The skin is particularly rich in nutrients, so leave it on to reap the full nutritional benefits of zucchini.

VEGETABLES, STARCHY

Starchy vegetables are higher in calories than non-starchy vegetables, but their health benefits are enormous as they are rich in vitamins, minerals, and fiber. They are also high-quality carbohydrates, so those with diabetes need to be wary of their intake.

Cauliflower

BEET (BEETROOT)

—

Beets are commonly found sliced in Greek salads, boiled down in Russian borscht, and can be delicious roasted or served in a salad. The most commonly found beets are reddish-purple, but beets also come in white, orange, and yellow. Beets are a good source of many nutrients, including vitamin C, iron, magnesium, potassium, folate, manganese, and dietary fiber. The nitrates in beets help the body to produce nitric oxide, which improves heart health. The traditional red beets are a gorgeous color, but do be careful when preparing, as they easily stain surfaces and skin. Avoid eating beets if you suffer from kidney stones.

CARROT

—

With the nickname of rabbit food, carrots are anything but basic animal feed. Raw carrots are a delicious, crunchy snack, but carrots also make flavourful soups, nutritious sides, and are a delightful and colourful addition to stir-fries, casseroles, and stews. Carrots can now be found in white, purple, or red due to inventive breeding programs. Carrots are one of the richest sources of beta-carotene, which the body converts into vitamin A. Carrots also have no fat and no cholesterol, which makes them a great choice for anyone watching their weight.

CAULIFLOWER

—

Most vegetables that are highly rated for their nutritional value are deep greens or bright reds—but in spite of its pale color, cauliflower is just as jam-packed with nutrients as its vivid cousins. It is very low in saturated fat and cholesterol, and a good source of both protein and dietary fiber. Delicious raw on its own or in dips, excellent in stir-fries and casseroles, cauliflower is a real powerhouse for its immune system and anti-cancer benefits.

RECOMMENDED FOR HELP WITH

- Weight loss
- Good intestinal health
- Immunity
- Possible cancer protection
- Reducing risk of cardiovascular disease

A broad range of fruit and vegetables provides the best intake of vitamins and minerals for a strong body, mind, and immune system.

RECOMMENDED FOR HELP WITH

- Constipation and diarrhea
- Lowering cholesterol levels
- Improves heart health
- Increasing brain function
- Immune health
- Healthy bones
- Healthy skin
- Good for pregnant women
- Iron-deficient anemia

RECOMMENDED FOR HELP WITH

- Weight loss
- Good intestinal health
- Stroke and heart attack prevention
- Lowering cholesterol
- Heart health
- Immunity
- Promotes eye health

Ginger root

GINGER ROOT

—

Long used for its medicinal properties, fresh ginger root has a very high level of antioxidants. It can be used fresh or dried and is popular in Asian cooking, as well as in some desserts and teas, and has a fresh and distinctive flavour. Ginger has traditional uses as a nausea suppressant, and has been recommended to stave off feelings of nausea from chemotherapy, morning sickness, and travel sickness. If you experience heartburn or gallstones, consult your doctor before incorporating too much ginger into your diet.

RECOMMENDED FOR HELP WITH

- Nausea and upset stomach
- Nausea due to chemotherapy, travel sickness, pregnancy, and menstruation
- Improves immune health
- Improved circulation
- Reduces inflammation and osteoarthritic pain

CORN (MAIZE)

—

Corn is considered a nutritional powerhouse: it is a healthy, alkalizing food that is rich in antioxidants, low in saturated fat, cholesterol, and sodium, and is a good source of dietary fiber. Corn can be eaten as corn on the cob, boiled from frozen, or as baby corn in stir-fries or as a side dish. Corn also comes in a variety of colors, although yellow corn is the most common. This is often referred to as "sweetcorn" in the UK, but just simply "corn" in the USA. Corn is good for your heart, eyes, and digestion. If you suffer from kidney trouble, discuss potassium intake with your doctor.

RECOMMENDED FOR HELP WITH

- Immunity
- Good intestinal health, alleviating constipation and diarrhea
- Heart health and circulation
- Eye health, protecting against macular degeneration and cataracts
- Reducing risk of cardiovascular disease

Corn

PARSNIP

—

Parsnips are related to carrots, celeriac, and fennel. Parsnips are not a widely used root vegetable in the USA, but they are popular as a roasted side dish in Europe, and can also be made into a delicious spiced or curried soup. Parsnips are rich in antioxidants and a very good source of potassium, dietary fiber, vitamin C, folate, and manganese. They are also very low in saturated fat, cholesterol, and sodium.

RECOMMENDED FOR HELP WITH

- Digestive health
- Maintaining blood pressure and cholesterol
- Enhanced brain function
- Strong bones and teeth

Parsnip

Pumpkin

PUMPKIN

—

Not just a fun Halloween tradition, pumpkin is also a delicious and nutritious food. Beautiful in colour and versatile to cook with, pumpkin is equally delicious in curries and casseroles as it is in desserts (but, of course, the sugars in most pies will outweigh the nutritional benefits, so keep this in moderation). While fresh whole pumpkin is best, canned pumpkin does still maintain a good amount of vitamins and minerals for a healthy diet. Pumpkin is a low-calorie, appetite-satisfying, alkalizing food that is rich in antioxidants.

RECOMMENDED FOR HELP WITH

- Digestive health
- Maintaining blood pressure and cholesterol
- Reducing risk of stroke and heart attack
- Eye health
- Enhanced brain function
- Strong bones and teeth
- Weight loss

RADISH

—

A healthy, alkalizing food, radishes are often overlooked as a foodstuff and relegated to the place of a pretty garnish on the side of a plate. But think again. Radishes can be a tasty snack or crunchy salad addition, as well as great in soups or casseroles, and are packed with vitamin C, potassium, and fiber. As a low-calorie food, they are excellent for anyone watching their weight. White icicle radishes provide slightly more vitamin C.

RECOMMENDED FOR HELP WITH

- Enhanced brain function
- Blood pressure and cholesterol
- Strong bones and teeth
- Possible cancer prevention
- Weight loss

Radish

RUTABAGA (SWEDE)

—

A rutabaga (also called the swede or Swedish turnip) is a cruciferous root vegetable that is closely related to the turnip. Both the purple-yellow vegetable itself and the green leaves can be eaten. Rutabaga is most commonly either roasted or mashed. It is high in antioxidants and a good source of both fiber and vitamin C.

Rutabaga

RECOMMENDED FOR HELP WITH

- Immune health
- Digestive health
- Strong bones and teeth
- Healthy skin
- Possible cancer protection, especially prostate and colon

Sweet potato

SWEET POTATO

—

One of the healthiest of all vegetables, and certainly the healthiest of all starchy vegetables, sweet potatoes are delicious and versatile. Why not try them in place of a baked potato, mashed, or in casseroles for a healthy and filling meal? As mashed potatoes, they require very little butter and milk, making them a healthy alternative. Sweet potatoes are loaded with antioxidants and a good source of dietary fiber (especially if you leave the skin on), potassium, and a huge array of vitamins, as well as being low in sodium, saturated fat, and cholesterol.

RECOMMENDED FOR HELP WITH

- Weight loss
- Immune health
- Digestive health and regularity
- Strong bones
- Healthy skin
- Eye health
- Increased energy
- Lowering cholesterol
- Reducing risk of stroke and heart attack
- Possible cancer prevention

TURNIP

—

Turnips are an incredibly nutritious root vegetable that are high in antioxidants. They are also a good source of dietary fiber, vitamins A, C, and K, as well as a range of other minerals. They are low in saturated fat, sodium, and cholesterol. Turnips are underused in everyday cooking, but they are delicious roasted on their own or alongside carrots and paired with meats and in casseroles. Turnips have a central role in Scottish tradition, being served in the Burns Night dish of haggis, neeps (turnips), and tatties (potatoes). Turnip greens provide fiber, folate, and very high vitamin K.

Turnip

RECOMMENDED FOR HELP WITH

- Immune health
- Digestive health and regularity
- Strong bones
- Healthy skin
- Eye health
- Lowering cholesterol
- Reducing risk of stroke and heart attack
- Possible cancer prevention, especially prostate and colon
- Weight loss

RECOMMENDED FOR HELP WITH

- Lung health
- Pregnancy and health of fetus
- Immune health
- Digestive health
- Healthy skin
- Eye health
- Lowering cholesterol
- Reduce risk of stroke and heart attack

WINTER SQUASH

—

Winter squash comes in several varieties, including acorn, butternut, spaghetti, and more. Winter squash is a healthy, alkalizing food that is versatile and delectable—bake it whole, add it to a casserole, or make a warming winter soup. Winter squash is full of vitamin A, which improves lung health, and a good source of folate, a beneficial vitamin during pregnancy.

Winter squash

EXERCISE

CHAPTER THREE

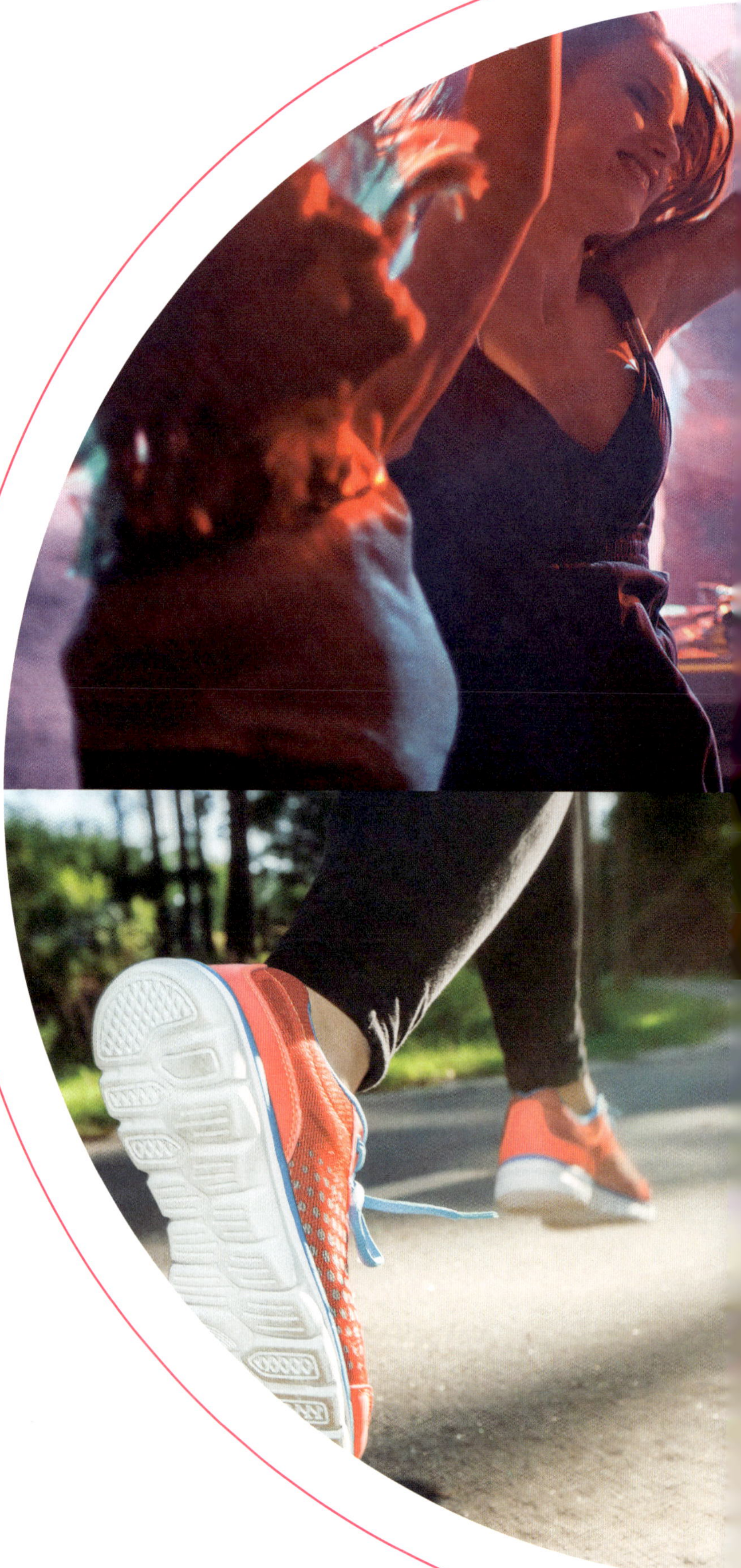

EXERCISE FOR YOU

WALKING

—

Walking is one of the most convenient, accessible—and also free—forms of exercise. You don't have to buy lots of expensive equipment (the only thing you'll need is a good pair of shoes) and you can walk (almost) anywhere, be it in a city or in the countryside.

Walking is a gentle form of exercise, so it's ideal if you haven't been physically active recently. You can walk as fast or as slow as you like and build up your pace over time as you get fitter.

Walking outdoors gives you the chance to breathe in fresh air and enjoy the environment. A simple stroll and a change of scene can help reinvigorate you, boost your mood, and clear your head.

If you're not keen on going out on your own, or you would like to make this an opportunity to connect with other walkers and try new routes, look out for local walking groups you could join. Many areas operate health walks, while some neighborhoods have groups that meet regularly. You could try starting your own; for example, post a message on social media and ask if there's anyone near you who'd like to get together for a walk. If you're wary of meeting strangers, choose somewhere public for your first outing, like a park.

JOGGING

—

Like walking, jogging is another convenient and free form of exercise. Once you have a decent pair of running shoes, you can get started straightaway.

Again, as with walking, you can pick your pace and enjoy being outdoors and getting some headspace. Local parks are a great place to jog and, if you go frequently or at the same time of day, you may find you begin to spot other regulars, with the added bonus of making it a sociable time as well.

If you don't want to jog on your own, see if any friends or family would like to join you. There are also lots of local running clubs where new members are always welcome, or you could try out a Park Run to meet other like-minded people.

Exercising brings both physical and mental health benefits–particularly if you make it a social event.

DANCE CLASSES

—

One of the best things about dance classes is that they often don't feel like exercise. You can get so absorbed in the rhythm of the music and enjoying yourself that the time will fly.

There are a host of different styles of dance classes available, from ballroom, ballet, tap, and salsa to street dance, swing, Bollywood, jive, and jazz.

If you're unsure what type of dance class would be best for you, see if you can go along to a few classes and have a taster session. That way you can try out the different methods and see which suits your fitness level, interests, and ability the best. Look out for details of local dance classes running at community centers or gyms or ask on social media for recommendations. In most cases, you don't need to worry about needing a dance partner—there'll always be someone at the class that you can pair up with if required.

GYM

—

If you prefer to exercise inside, going to the gym is the ideal choice. You can use exercise equipment such as rowing machines, treadmills, or exercise bikes, or take advantage of one of the many classes that gyms offer.

Buying a gym membership can help with motivation and encourage you to go regularly. The wide variety of classes gyms offer also gives you the chance to try out different forms of exercise and helps increase the chance of you finding something that you enjoy, making fitness fun.

When you're looking for a gym to join, find out if they do taster days or weeks and take advantage of everything that's on offer. Look out for special offers on gym membership that could save you money.

Exercise doesn't have to be aerobic every time—a good stretch is really beneficial, too.

If you're going to the gym for the first time, do take advice on the most appropriate exercises that you should do. If there's a free fitness assessment available with a trainer, it's well worth having it.

Nobody cares if you can't dance well. Just get up and dance.

Martha Graham

AEROBIC WORKOUTS

Aerobic, or cardio, exercise is so called because it gets your heart pumping and increases the flow of blood to your muscles and lungs. Aerobic exercise is known to improve fitness, burn calories, help with weight loss, and boost your overall physical and mental health.

Medical practitioners recommend that adults should do at least 150 minutes (2 hours and 30 minutes) a week of moderate-intensity aerobic physical activity or 75 minutes (1 hour and 15 minutes) of vigorous-intensity aerobic activity each week. Vigorous-intensity activity means an activity that makes you breathe hard and fast—you're unlikely to be able to talk much without needing to pause for breath while you're doing it.

It's possible to meet your weekly target from just one single session of aerobic activity, but a lot of people find it more practical to break it into several smaller sessions spread out over a couple of days, or even do a little each day. Smaller chunks of exercise may fit in with your schedule and work commitments more easily and be more achievable than one long workout.

One of the benefits of aerobic exercise is that there are a lot of options to choose from, so hopefully you should be able to find something that meets your needs and that you enjoy. You can mix it up, too, trying out different exercises when you fancy a change.

Types of aerobic exercise include running, swimming, hiking, aerobics, dancing, kickboxing, brisk walking, rollerblading, water aerobics, tennis, working out on cardio machines, and spinning.

To get you started, here are some simple aerobic workout ideas that you can perform at home, indoors, or outdoors, to meet your fitness and exercise goals.

WARM UP

—

Before you start doing an aerobic workout, you'll need to warm up. This will help reduce the risk of injuries and prepare your body by releasing the tension in different parts of your body. Ideally, aim to warm up for at least five minutes before you start exercising, or longer if you feel your body is stiff and needs it.

Start your warm-up by marching in place, then march backward and forward, swinging your arms as you go.

• Do 10 shoulder rolls—continue marching in place with your arms loose by your sides and roll your shoulders forwards 10 times, then backwards 10 times.

• Do 10 head rolls—stand and rotate your head gently in a clockwise direction, then repeat in a counterclockwise direction.

• Do 10 upper body twists—stand with your feet shoulder-width apart, bend your arms in front of you, and have your hands clasped loosely in fists. Turn your body and hips to the right, hold for a few seconds, and return to the center. Repeat on the other side.

• Do 10 knee lifts—stand and, keeping your back straight, bring one knee up and touch it with the opposite hand, then repeat with the other knee and other hand.

• Do 10 knee bends—stand with your feet shoulder-width apart and your arms stretched out in front of you, parallel with your shoulders. Bend your knees slightly, lower yourself down a little, then stand back up and repeat.

• Do 10 simple squats—stand with your feet shoulder-width apart, with your knees facing forward, and let your arms hang down by your sides. Gently lower yourself down

A few minutes spent warming up before a workout will prepare your body properly for exercise.

If you're new to exercising, it's a good idea to get some professional advice first on what's right for your body.

by bending your knees and pushing your bottom back, your chest over your knees. For extra balance, you can extend your arms forward as you bend.

MAIN WORKOUT

—

Once you've warmed up your body sufficiently, you can start your aerobic workout. The following exercises can be performed in the order listed or mixed up for a bit of variety. Each exercise is beneficial to different parts of your body, while also giving you a good, thorough aerobic workout. Aim to repeat each exercise 10 times before moving on to the next one, then try to do a few more each time as you build your fitness level. Even a short 10-minute aerobic workout will be beneficial.

Jump, squat, and turn

Stand with your feet slightly wider than hip-width apart. Jump on the spot, and on the second jump, turn to face the opposite way. Jump again and drop down into a squat by bending both your knees. If you feel comfortable, reach down and touch the floor with one hand. To vary things, try skipping the turn and just do the jump and squat.

Squat thrust

Stand with your feet hip-width apart and put your hands by your sides. Bend down, place both hands flat on the floor, and hop your feet so they land behind you in a high plank position with your legs straight, hips level, and your wrists in line with your shoulders. To complete the squat thrust, hop forward and stand up straight. If it's too much for you to hop back both feet together, try doing them one at a time.

Squats are not just beneficial for your leg muscles; they provide a full-body workout.

You can continue your aerobic workout with these heart pumping exercises.

Jumping jacks
Starting in a standing position, bend your knees slightly and jump, while extending your legs to each side and putting your arms straight up into the air. Jump again and move back to your original position. As you get fitter, try jumping a bit higher each time, with less time between jumps.

Toe taps
Put a small object that won't roll around (for example, a small cushion or a book) on the floor in front of your feet to act as a target. The aim is to tap the target with your toes while jumping from one foot to the other. Start with one foot resting lightly on the target, then quickly jump and swap so that your other foot is on the target. Repeat the move, alternating your feet and lightly tapping your toes on the target. The more you practice this, the quicker you'll get.

Fast feet punches
Stand with your feet slightly wider than hip width, with your knees slightly bent. Close your fists, then bend your arms to bring your fists up to chin height. Take quick, fast steps with your feet, and at the same time, move your arms out forward in a punching motion. If you find it tricky to do both movements at once, start by practicing either the punches or the quick footsteps, then build them in together.

Skipping gives you a full body aerobic workout.

TIP: SKIPPING

If you have a skipping rope, skipping is perfect to add to your aerobic workout. Do 10 to 20 single skips with the rope, seeing how fast you can go. The fitter and more practiced you get, the faster you should be able to skip.

Squat jumps
Start these jumps from a squatting position, with your thighs parallel with the floor, your back straight, and your arms bent so that your fists are at chin height. Jump to turn 90 degrees, extending your arms down by your sides as you do so. You should land in a squat position. As you get better at this exercise, try to turn 180 degrees as you jump.

Hop and touch
Stand up and raise your right leg in front of you, keeping it as straight as possible. Hop on your left foot, then swing your opposite arm in front of your body and touch your right knee. Repeat with the other leg and try to keep hopping and moving as you go. As you get more flexible, aim to reach further down your leg, until eventually you are able to touch your ankle.

Mountain climber
Start in a high plank position, with your palms flat on the floor and your hands shoulder-width apart. Your shoulders should be parallel with your hands and your legs extended. Move your right knee so that it comes up to your chest, while keeping your left leg and back straight. Move your leg back to the original position and repeat with your left leg.

Aerobic exercise is even better when it's done in the open air!

Cool down

Once you've finished your exercises, don't forget to cool down. In the same way that it's important to warm up before you exercise, it's also important to cool down properly; it will slow your heart rate and help you relax after your exercise session. Spend at least 5 minutes—longer if you feel you need it—cooling down.

Here are some gentle stretches you can try.

Upper body stretch

In a standing position, link your fingers together and turn your palms upward. Keeping your back straight, lift your hands up and backward as far as you comfortably can. Hold for a few seconds, then repeat.

Calf stretch

In a standing position, move your right leg forward, resting the foot on the floor, bend at the knee slightly, and lean forwards a little. Keep your left leg straight and gently lower your left heel to the floor. Repeat the stretch with the other leg.

Hamstring stretch

Lie on your back and raise your left leg, keeping your right leg bent with the foot on the floor. Hold your left leg with both hands, below the knee, and gently pull your left leg towards you. Hold for a few seconds then repeat with the other leg.

Thigh stretch

Lie on the floor on your left-hand side, with your arm bent and supporting your head. Slowly bend your right leg upward and reach out to hold the top of your right foot. Aim to gently pull the heel towards your bottom to stretch your thigh. Keep your knees together and touching as you do this. Hold for a few seconds, then repeat with the other leg.

Child's pose

Sit on the floor on your heels with your knees open wide. Bend forward at your hips and gently lower yourself down, using your hands to walk your body along the floor until your forehead is resting on the ground. Extend your arms and place your palms on the ground. Hold for 30 seconds.

Always spend time cooling down after a workout, to prevent injury.

PILATES

The main principle of Pilates is that exercise is essentially a mind–body technique. Therefore, when you exercise you mentally focus on the muscle groups that you are using. Pilates recognizes that it is only through the synchronizing of thought and action that an exercise is truly effective. In order to create a healthy and fit body you need to integrate the mental, physical, and spiritual spheres.

MIND OVER MATTER

—

It has long been established that the mind has a enormous influence on the health of the body. Research shows that the mind has an infinite capacity to induce positive physiological effects, which have both an internal and external effect. You may have noticed that when you're in a good mood you automatically seem to look and feel better. Scientists ascribe this phenomenon to the activity of the billions of nerve cells in our brain, which transmit chemical messages to the rest of the body. Our thoughts and emotions play a vital role in influencing this intercellular communication. Think for a moment how you feel when you are stressed. Not very pleasant. This is because your body produces an excess of "stress" chemicals (e.g., adrenaline and cortisol), which causes your whole system to speed up. Your heart beats faster, your blood pressure goes up, your breathing becomes rapid and shallow. At times, this type of response is necessary. It is what motivates you when you are faced with a crisis. In large doses this type of reaction can, however, be extremely harmful and can lead to all sorts of unpleasant symptoms such as dizziness, shaking, profuse sweating, insomnia, and migraines. It is easy to see what effect negative, stress-inducing emotions can have. Positive feelings of calm and contentment have a much more beneficial effect, as they induce the body to produce health-enhancing, feel-good chemicals (e.g., endorphins and serotonin), which are vital for well-being. They promote a sense of serenity—you breathe more easily and deeply, your heart rate is slower, and your blood pressure lowers. The more relaxed you feel, the less tension you hold in the muscles throughout your body. This has a beneficial effect on your general bearing and posture. Tight, tense muscles make your body shrink and constrict. This stops the energy from flowing freely throughout the body and, in time, this will be reflected in a weak, misshapen musculature.

Pilates is an excellent mind-body technique that's beneficial for all ages.

MINDFUL EXERCISE

—

If thoughts are so powerful, it makes sense to try and harness your thinking to bring about positive changes in your body. This is, in fact, the very essence of Pilates. By learning to execute each exercise correctly you are also allowing your mind to exert a greater influence over your body. With Pilates you only do a limited number of repetitions. You do them slowly, so that you can concentrate more clearly on directing your energy towards what it is you are trying to achieve. If you view your body in a negative way you will need to reverse your direction of thought. Positive thoughts bring about positive changes.

To ensure that an exercise can be of real benefit and bring about the changes that you desire, for example a strong, straight back, it is necessary to complement each physical action with a mental focus. By practising creative visualization regularly, you will gradually develop the intellectual and emotional ability to internalize the physical changes that you wish to make.

Once you've done this, the external changes will start to appear. As you become aware of your body and its needs, you can consciously start to make changes through exercise. Pilates is based on lengthening and stretching the body to its full potential. This eventually creates a longer, leaner shape, increased flexibility, and a suppleness that promotes a greater ease of movement. These exercises concentrate on strengthening weak muscles and stretching those which are too tight and constricted.

What you really want is a body in which strength and flexibility complement each other. It is possible to totally restructure the way you are. It is not, however, just a matter of getting your body to make the right moves. An integral part of Pilates is the way you perceive the exercise. This is why attitude and creative imagery are so important. Each time you work through a series of movements it is essential that you can envision what it is that you wish to achieve. Painting a picture in your mind helps your body to respond in the right way. This not only makes the whole process more stimulating but the effects of each exercise

If you can't find a class nearby or prefer to work out at home, you can find Pilates exercises online.

are much more powerful. Initially it may take a while to fully understand the mechanisms. I always tell a new client to expect to do only about 30 percent of what they will eventually be capable of doing. It takes about 10 sessions to really comprehend the technique. Pilates is the only form of exercise that gets progressively more difficult, but the results are worth it. In time you will look taller, slimmer, and more toned.

CREATIVE VISUALIZATION

—

Whatever we create in our lives begins as a basic image in our minds. Many of these images are unconscious. Through creative visualization it is possible to alter these thoughts and pictures. With Pilates, the idea is to create an image in your mind that will help you to focus on the area of the body that you are working. This requires a very deep level of concentration, which does become easier with practice. On a superficial level, many of the exercises appear quite simple. How you physically position your arms and legs, however, is only part of the process. Pilates, unlike many other disciplines, is actually much more complex as with each movement you must be constantly aware of what your entire body is doing. You don't concentrate only on the stomach, or the inner thigh, and exclude the rest of your body. Even when you are doing a series of movements specifically designed to work a certain group of muscles, such as your abdominals or your quads, you must always remember to be equally focused on the rest of your body. Where are your feet? Are you holding your head in exactly the right way? Is your body properly aligned?

Initially, this can seem quite difficult and using visualization techniques can be enormously helpful. Understanding how your body should be feeling means it becomes easier to assume the correct position. Eventually, these images will arise naturally through association, without too much effort. Visualization is one of the best methods to bridge the gap between mind and body. By creating mental pictures that correspond to what you are trying to do physically you will, in time, develop a level of body awareness which is unique to Pilates.

BASIC TECHNIQUES

—

Anyone can learn to visualize. It helps though if you can begin by feeling relaxed. A still mind is more conducive to conjuring up images.

- Spend a few minutes gathering your thoughts. Try to forget about external influences such as work, what you should be doing, and any worries you might have. Remember, this is your time.
- Do some gentle stretches and focus on your breathing. Slow, deep breathing has an instantly calming effect because it helps to promote soothing alpha brainwaves. Once you are feeling sufficiently relaxed you can start your exercises.
- As you exercise, focus on each part of your body. How does it feel? With each exercise try to perceive a specific picture. If you are trying to envision yourself on a sandy beach, focus clearly on how this feels. Do your feet feel relaxed, warm and comfortable? Are your arms hanging loosely by your sides, like a puppet? Where is your head? Think of images that will help you to get into exactly the right position.
- Invite each image to emerge with as much intensity as possible, so that you can almost feel it. Once you have created a familiar picture, eventually all you will have to do is to focus on it and your body will automatically respond.The concept of Pilates is to bring about permanent changes. You can hasten this process by using visualization techniques when you are not exercising. These will automatically help you to walk, stand, and sit in the correct way.

With practice, vizualization and concentration improves so you get the full benefits of Pilates for your mind as well as your body.

PILATES POSTURE AND BREATHING

PERFECT POSTURE: HOW TO LOOK INSTANTLY TALLER AND SLIMMER

—

Not sure if you're standing correctly? Then practice this position for a few minutes daily. After a while it will feel so natural that you no longer have to think about it.

Stand with your feet hip-width apart. Imagine that you're standing on sand. Your feet are relaxed. Think of your weight being over the middle of each foot, with your toes gently lengthening into the sand. Close your eyes and make a mental note of the following:

• Don't sink back into your heels or lean forward. Keep your weight evenly distributed over your feet.

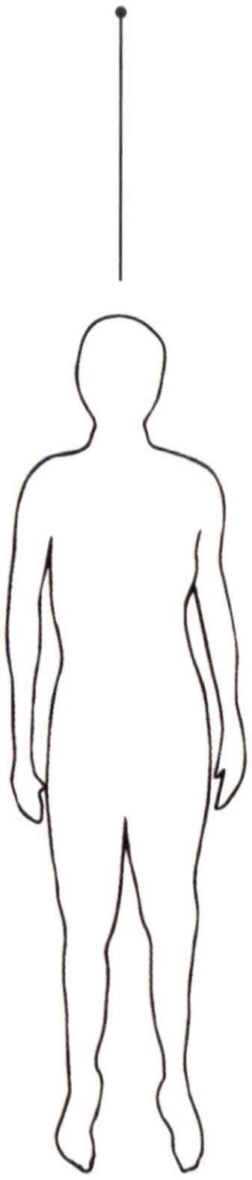

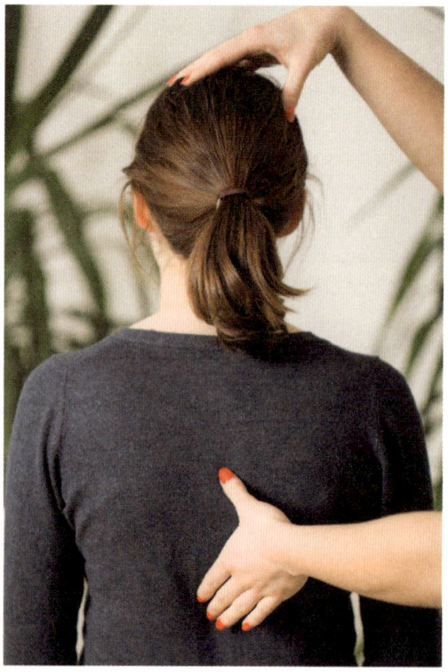

Pilates can even be beneficial to posture and balance.

• Let your arms fall naturally in front of your body.
• Let your hands hang from the shoulders, totally loose and relaxed.
• Don't lock your knees. They should feel relaxed and not rigid.
• Keep your inside thighs and bottom relaxed.
• Imagine that your head is like one of those nodding dogs in the back of car. It's not going backwards and forwards but resting directly upon your shoulders and rocking gently until it settles into a comfortable, neutral position.
• Think of the bones directly behind your ears. Try to imagine them "reaching" towards the ceiling.
• Pull your stomach in, without tipping the pelvis forward. Think of a piece of string from your pubic bone to your navel. It is shortening as you pull up and in. Feel your tailbone drop—as if it is weighted to the floor. This will seem much easier after you've done more of the stretches to release the pelvic girdle.
• Keep the front of your thighs relaxed. Now your whole body is perfectly aligned—you should feel as if you are floating an inch off the ground.

BREATHING

—

Correct breathing is a very important facet of Pilates. By remembering to breathe properly, you'll find it becomes much easier to exercise. The problem is that most people don't breathe deeply enough. Breathing slowly and deeply is very energizing. It ensures there is sufficient oxygen circulating throughout the body.It may sound obvious, but when you exercise do not hold your breath. It's better to breathe incorrectly than not at all. Practice the following exercise before you start any of the stomach work.

Correct breathing helps you get the most out of Pilates, and helps with relaxation.

BASIC BREATHING EXERCISE

—

Lie on your back in a relaxed position, resting your head on a folded towel, with your knees bent.

- Place one hand on your stomach and, very gently, breathe in through your nose. Feel your lungs filling with oxygen and slowly expand and relax your stomach. Breathe out.
- With one finger on your pubic bone and one on your navel, try and shorten that gap as you breathe out, and flatten your stomach to your spine without tilting your pelvis.
- Breathe in again and feel that gap slightly expand.
- Breathe out. Imagine there is a piece of string or an elastic band that links your pubic bone to your navel. Very gently feel it pulling up and in. This will get all three sets of stomach muscles working, including your oblique muscles, which will tighten your waist. Make sure you breathe slowly and deeply. One of the main rules of Pilates is to breathe out on the point of effort. If in doubt, particularly on the stretches—breathe naturally. When you breathe in your stomach gently expands. However, it shouldn't swell in an exaggerated way. Try and think of your ribcage expanding gently to the sides so that you're not just breathing into your throat and upper chest.

PILATES BETTER BALANCE

If you're worried about slipping, tripping or not being able to catch objects thrown towards you, your sense of balance is most probably poor. What seems to occur, as you get older or as a result of any injury, is that you lose your awareness of balance and your reflexes are no longer as sharp. This can cause great feelings of insecurity. Perhaps you begin to worry more about safety. We all know that the simplest of falls might have serious consequences. This is reflected in the body, which becomes stiff and constricted as a result. The easiest way to change this is to practice the following exercises every day. In time, you will start to feel lighter and more confident in the way you move. For each of these exercises all the same rules as the "perfect posture" exercise apply (see the checklist in the previous spread).

STANDING ON ONE LEG

—

Traditional Chinese medicine uses terminology that sounds strange to most Westerners. Instead of talking about rheumatic diseases or neurological diseases, it classifies diseases as being caused by *w* which regulates the overall body temperature and the upper, and lower parts *[jiaos]* of the body. There are also six extra meridians, one of which runs up the front center line of the body (the *ren mai* or conception vessel), and one of which runs up the spine (the *du mai* or governor vessel).

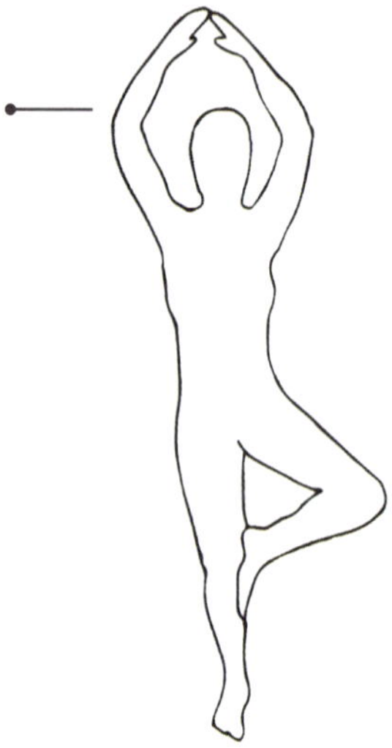

STANDING ON ONE LEG WITH A TOWEL

—

Do exactly the same as above, standing on a flat towel. This gives you a slightly more unstable surface and makes the exercise more difficult. Even if you don't regularly exercise, try to do these every day—especially if you are over 45.

WALKING BACKWARDS

—

Start in the "perfect posture" position and, with feet approximately an inch apart, start to walk backwards. Slowly drag your foot back, so that it never entirely leaves the floor. The easiest way to master this is to imagine that you are trying to remove some chewing gum from under your feet.

Look in the mirror—but do not look down at your feet.

This exercise is even more effective if you imagine you are walking on sand.

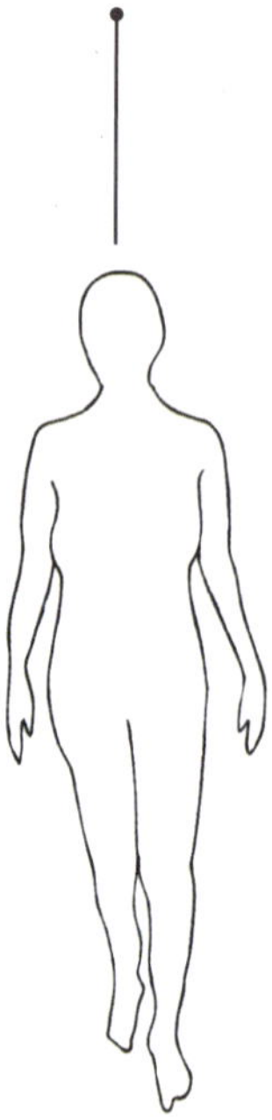

Improving your sense of balance will help your posture and prevent risk of falls and injury.

YOGA

THE CONSULTATION

—

The word yoga means union of body, mind, and spirit with the universal spirit. The yogis of ancient India realized that for perfect health and inner peace, both body and mind must work together in perfect harmony. Yoga's combination of intricate physical postures, deep breathing exercises, balances, relaxation, and meditation are the perfect discipline to relieve stress, calm the mind, and tone the entire body, both inside and out. In our quest to earn more, do more, and have more, modern humans subject ourselves to increased physical and mental stress. The pace of life is now so fast that few of us have time to enjoy the present moment and just be.

Continued stress on both body and mind increases our vulnerability to disease. Unfortunately, although medicine has made many amazing breakthroughs in the West over the last hundred years, the focus continues to be on treating diseases and not their causes. This is where yoga can help us all so much. Stress or tension literally strangles our bodies, inhibiting blood flow to our tissues.

Yoga's beautiful physical movements, combined with deep breathing exercises, will carefully rid the body of tension and stimulate oxygen-rich blood to our cells, so providing them with the nutrients that they require. As well as toning all our muscles, the physical exercises will also strengthen our bones and keep our spine and joints flexible. The lymphatic system, which fights infection and carries away toxins, is inhibited during times of stress, but as yoga carefully smoothes away the tension, it can resume its natural functions. Yoga's calming balances necessitate tremendous concentration and so they take the mind off its day-to-day activities, giving it a rest. The most difficult thing to discipline, however, is the human mind. Here again yoga offers us many techniques, from breathing exercises to relaxation and meditation, which may be used to calm a turbulent mind. Gradually and with continued practice the combined discipline of the exercises together with the breathing and meditation will help us to achieve the peace and calm we desire. And just as stress inhibits our energy flow, a calm and peaceful mind will lead to abundant energy and that genuine "good to be alive" feeling.

Yoga is both a relaxing and enjoyable exercise, which relieves stress and tones the body.

Eventually, we stop looking elsewhere for our pleasures and concentrate on "looking within," disciplining our mind to search inside ourselves for our joy and happiness. We then start to enjoy the present moment, and listen to our gut instincts, finally achieving self-realization and finding the true health and happiness that is within us all.

ORIGINS OF YOGA

—

It is unclear when yoga actually originated, but seals were discovered depicting a yoga posture during the excavation of some ruins in prehistoric India in an area that now lies in Pakistan. These ruins revealed a very advanced civilization dating to around 5000 B.C.The earliest texts mentioning yoga were the Vedas, and these seem to have spanned about 2,000 years, from 3000–1200 B.C. These texts were followed by the Upanishads, written between 800 and 400 B.C. The word Upanishad literally describes a sitting where the master or guru instructs his pupils. This is how yoga has been passed on from generation to generation, over the years. The spirit of the Upanishads can be compared with that of the New Testament "The Kingdom of God is within you." "Meditation is a truth higher than thought. The earth seems to rest in silent meditation: and the waters and the mountains and the sky and the heavens seem all to be in meditation."

"When a man achieves greatness on this earth, he has his reward according to his meditation."

Chandoya Upanishad *7.6*

The Bhagavad Gita, dating from about 500 B.C, tells of the struggle of the human soul, helping it to find God in all things and all things in God. It tells of a great battle for the rule of a Kingdom or the Kingdom of the soul, a battle between the forces of light and darkness. It shows that this is a battle that affects us all.The Patanjalis Yoga Sutras, written between 200 B.C and 200 A.D., are a crucial yoga text. Patanjali wrote of a practical eight-part approach to yoga, frequently referred to as the Eight Limbs of Yoga.

Yoga classes can be an enjoyable way to get a full workout of body and mind while also being sociable.

Yoga involves a series of physical movements that rid the body of tension.

"Restraint, observance, posture, breath-control, sense withdrawal, concentration, meditative-absorption and enstasy are the eight members of yoga. Non-harming, truthfulness, non-stealing, chastity and greedlessness are the restraints."

Patanjalis Yoga Sutras *II, 29–30*

These eight limbs were not regarded as a ladder to be climbed one rung at a time, but more the necessary ingredients in the recipe for life. The ancient yogis realized that life can be a difficult and complicated journey but its careful teachings and disciplines guide us along our path. They had a deep understanding of human nature and of the mind–body connection, and they devised this system to help us obtain happiness and peace of mind, as well as a perfectly toned healthy body.

THE EIGHT LIMBS OF YOGA

1. Yamas

These are guidelines necessary for our moral conduct and are the basic principles of right living and restraint; they include no violence, stealing, or envy and they command us to be truthful with both others and ourselves. Yoga teaches us that happiness is not in external objects but within ourselves and that the spirit of God is within each one of us.

2. Niyamas

These are the personal disciplines of daily life. They are cleanliness of mind and body, purity, contentment, study, work, and devotion to God or the universal spirit. Yoga teaches us that the body is the temple of the spirit and keeping the body in perfect condition is our duty.

3. Asanas

These are the yoga exercises or postures. It is said that there are 840,000 of them! These movements work the entire body, freeing it from tension, toning and firming and strengthening every muscle, internal organ, and gland. The balancing postures teach us the power of concentration and focus. Deep relaxation calms the mind and rids the body of chronic tension, and meditation trains the mind to achieve stillness and peace.

4. Pranayama

This is yoga's breath control. There are many breathing exercises in yoga to stimulate life-giving oxygen to every cell, to energize the body and calm and soothe the mind. The word pranayama means "controlling the energy flow." Yoga teaches us how to use our breathing to control our life.

5. Pratyahara

This is the withdrawal of the senses from the external world to the self within to give one peace and calm. This is achieved by practicing the asanas and pranayama. Most of our daily activities necessitate our concentration and involvement with external objects and thoughts, but by concentrating on our body as we do the movements, and by concentrating on our breathing, the mind and body become peaceful and calm.

6. Dharana

This is the power of constant concentration and focusing of the mind. The mind is like the rays of the sun. When spread over a wide surface, the rays will be warming, but concentrate the rays and they become powerful enough to burn. Yoga balances start us on this path. They discipline the mind to concentrate on just one spot while performing the balances. This skill develops so that eventually one is able to concentrate and focus on a subject of interest even in the midst of turmoil.

7. Dhyama

This is meditation. Meditation is a powerful tool for freeing our minds from the pressures of life, helping us feel peaceful and calm. When this is accomplished, new ideas appear and the way ahead looks clearer.

8. Samadhi

This is the result of our total efforts and is the experience of enlightenment and bliss, living in the present moment, and the realization that we can manifest whatever we wish. The mind becomes full of joy and peace. It is the state of union with the universal spirit or God.

YOGA TODAY

—

The collective knowledge of these ancient texts began to appear in the West at the end of the 19th century and since then interest in yoga has grown and today it is at an all time high. Students of all ages are pouring into classes to learn yoga, and for many diverse reasons. Some come simply to improve their body shape, some to cure an aching back, some to relieve stress. Whatever the reason, yoga can help you live healthily in this chaotic, exciting, and wonderful modern world.

While Hatha yoga remains the most widely practiced form of yoga in the West, other forms include:

- Raja Yoga—the yoga of the mind;
- Karma Yoga—the yoga of action;
- Bhakti Yoga—the yoga of devotion;
- Jhana Yoga—the yoga of the intellect.

Because of the many approaches to teaching yoga, finding a class to suit you can be very confusing. I often receive phone calls from people inquiring as to what sort of yoga I teach. I suppose that since I have been teaching for over 30 years, by now I have put my individual stamp on the ancient art. Throughout this time, I have tried to make yoga understandable, enjoyable, and available to everyone. It is my firm belief that everyone can benefit tremendously from yoga practice.

But how can you find a class that will be to your liking? I am afraid that this will be a bit like trying to find everything else—from a plumber to a dentist. Often you have to try several until the perfect one appears. There are some excellent yoga teachers around, so quite simply search for a class until you find one that works for you. As a first move, you can't do better than to look in your local newspaper to find classes running near where you live.

GUIDELINES FOR PRACTICING

—

You need very little equipment for your yoga practice so it is easy to fit in with any lifestyle. Once you have learned your basic movements you can do them at home or on vacation. Your yoga will go with you wherever you go. Having said this, there are a few basic guidelines that you should take note of before you start.

You need a warm airy room if you are practicing inside, but in warmer climates it is wonderful to do your yoga in the fresh air in the warmth of the early morning or evening. Never practice in the heat of direct sun.

- You need a mat or blanket to sit on. My preference is for a blanket or thick warm mat for indoor practice. However, if you are practising yoga outside, perhaps on a beach, you need a waterproof mat to keep you clean and dry.
- Wear loose clothing, ideally a leotard and leggings for women, or leggings and a close fitting T-shirt. Jogging bottoms or shorts and a T-shirt are best for men. If you are outdoors in a warm climate, your swimsuit is just fine.
- Bare feet are essential for yoga practice. Always wait at least 2 hours after a main meal before you practice yoga.
- The golden rule of yoga is never ever to strain. Don't worry if you are stiff and uncoordinated to start with. This is quite normal. Just persevere, work at your own pace, and you will be delighted at how quickly your body responds to the movements and how much more flexible you are after only a few weeks of practice. You will start to feel better almost immediately and will soon be delighted with your new svelte shape.
- Although yoga is for everyone, if you have any health concerns it is always wise to check with your doctor before you begin. Never substitute yoga for your doctor's treatment. Yoga is good for your health and some movements are particularly beneficial for certain conditions. However, they must never replace medical attention.
- If you are pregnant and have not done any yoga before, then please wait until after your check-up at about 15 weeks. If everything is OK and your doctor is happy, then you may start to practice yoga very gently, omitting the movements marked unsuitable for pregnancy.
- Following the baby's birth, wait until after your 6-week check-up before you recommence your yoga practice. If your doctor is happy for you to restart, then inform your teacher of the nature of your delivery. Go gently and soon you will find your shape and energy coming back fast.
- Breathing—in yoga, we breathe deeply with every movement to help to stimulate oxygen to every cell, and energize our entire systems. Breathing is done through the nose. As a general rule, gently allow your abdominals to push out as you inhale deeply through the nose at the start of a posture and exhale slowly and quietly through the nose as you go into the movement. While in the positions, breathe calmly and peacefully through the nose.

Try different styles of yoga and various classes until you find the one you most enjoy.

MORNING YOGA ESSENTIAL

Have you ever watched an animal wake up after a rest? It stretches its body from top to toe. This gets rid of tension and makes sure it is in perfect condition to start the day. The Morning Yoga Essential is an ideal sequence to start your day. It will greatly improve your shape and flexibility, give you bundles of energy, and can be a tremendous help to people with an aching back.

THE ENERGIZING BREATH

—

This is a wonderful breathing exercise. It is a great tonic when done first thing in the morning, but it will give you that "good to be alive" feeling anytime anywhere.

1 *Stand straight with your feet together.*

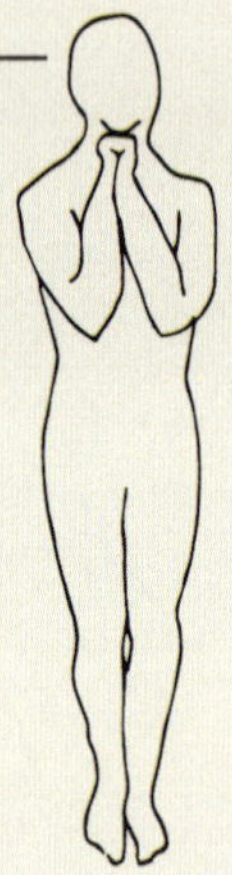

Place your fingertips interleaved under your chin with your elbows together.

Inhale slowly through your nose for a count of five. As you do this bring your elbows up as high as possible. Feel the breath at the back of your throat.

NOTE

This movement sounds simple, but standing straight and moving your head back can be quite difficult at first. Please don't worry. Many people have a lot of tension in their necks, but as you progress in yoga you will find it becomes easier. Also, some people feel dizzy or light-headed at first. If so, start by doing the movement only twice and take your head just a tiny way back, gradually building up to five times as you progress.

2 *Gently let your head drop back and exhale slowly and thoroughly through your mouth. At the end of the exhalation, slowly bring your elbows together as your head slowly returns to its normal position.*

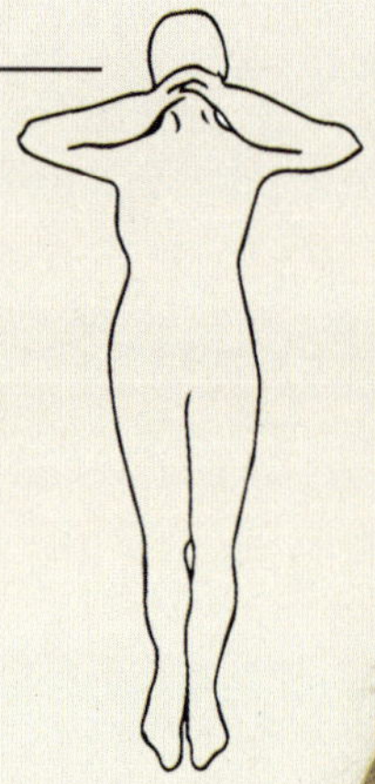

Repeat this cycle five times to begin with, increasing to ten times as you become used to the movement.

BENEFITS

This stretch is brilliant for slimming and toning the midriff and waistline, and releasing tension in the lower back.

SIDEWAYS STRETCH

Stand straight with your legs at least 3 feet apart, your toes facing forwards. Inhale deeply and lift your right hand in the air. As you exhale, gently bend over to the left side, sliding your left hand down your left leg. Don't strain. Go just as far as you can with ease.

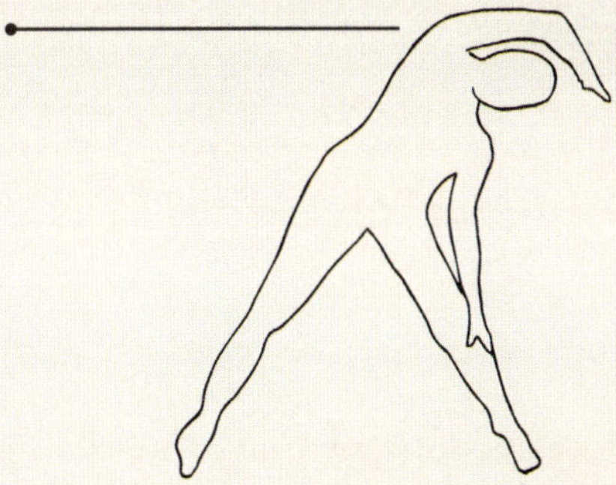

Breathing normally, hold the position for a count of five, increasing to ten as you progress. Inhale and slowly return to an upright position. Exhale, slowly lower your arm and relax. Repeat the movement to the other side, and then repeat the entire movement.

BENEFITS

Because of our sedentary lifestyle, most people use less than one third of their lung capacity. This wonderful movement helps to increase lung capacity, so increasing the oxygen supply to all our cells. This will give you energy and help to relieve stress.

HEAD TO KNEE POSTURE

—

1 Stand straight with your legs together. Inhale and lift your arms up above your head. Place the palms of your hands together and stretch your body upward. This is great for helping to realign your spine and releasing tension from your entire body.

As you lower your arms, exhale slowly through your nose. Repeat the movement. Now place your right foot about 3 feet in front of your left foot.

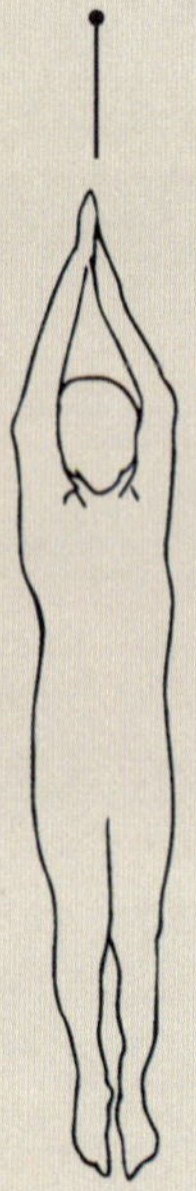

2 Inhale and lift your arms up above your head with your palms together. As you exhale with your head up, back flat, and legs straight, start to move forward aiming your chin just past your knee.

Don't worry if you are nowhere near this position to start with. Just relax in your maximum position and stay there for a count of five, breathing normally. Take note of your maximum stretch on this side.

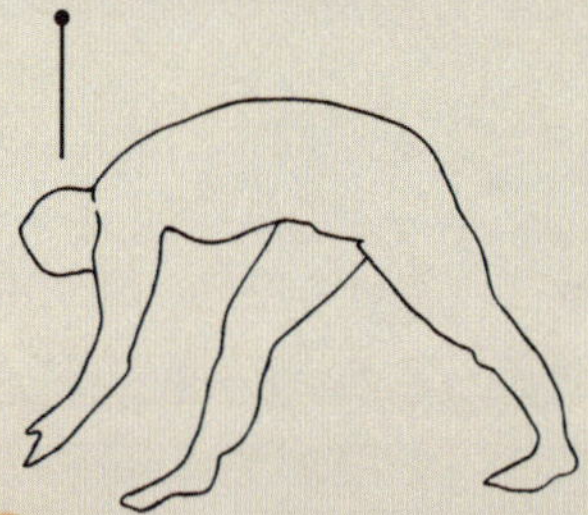

3 Inhale and, lifting your head, slowly return to your upright position. Exhale, lower your arms, and relax. Repeat the movement to the other side placing your left foot 3 feet in front of the right. Take note of how far you can manage this side.

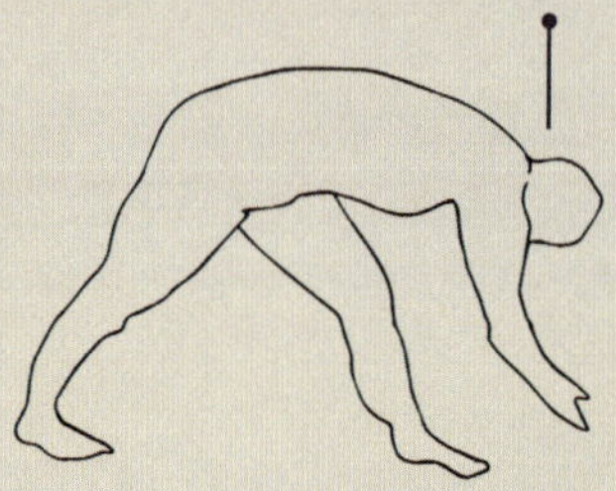

BENEFITS

This movement helps to correct imbalances in the lower back. It firms the backs of the thighs and calves and the bottom, and slims the midriff and waistline.

FORWARD AND BACKWARD BEND

1 *Stand straight with your feet about a foot apart, your toes facing forward. Inhale deeply and slowly lift your arms in the air, stretching them upward. Exhale slowly through the nose as you move calmly and gently forward, keeping your back flat and your legs straight.*

Relax in your maximum position and stay there, breathing normally. Don't worry if your maximum position isn't very far in the beginning. It will improve quicker than you can imagine. Do not strain yourself.

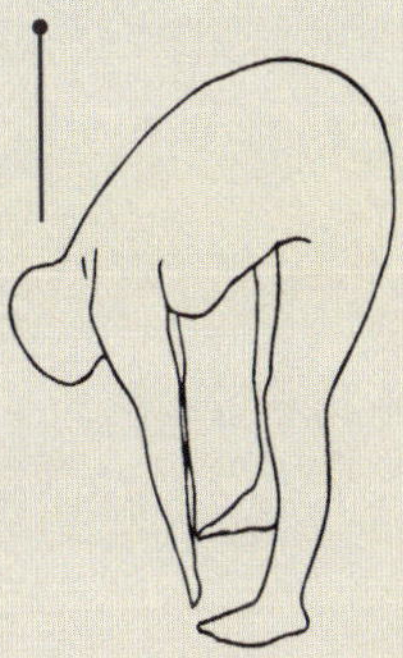

2 *Breathing normally, stay in the maximum position for a count of five, increasing to ten as you progress. Eventually your chin will be on your shin. Again, this might seem impossible at first, but with practice you'll get there, I promise!*

3 *Slowly lift your head and, as you inhale, continue to come up slowly into an upright position with your hands stretched up above your head. Keeping your eyes on your thumbs, start to relax gently backward, exhaling in your maximum position.*

Again, don't worry if only an inch is possible to begin with. Breathing normally, hold your backward stretch for a count of five. Then inhale and slowly return to an upright position. Exhale, lower your arms, and relax. Repeat this movement once.

BENEFITS

An excellent stretch, this gently releases tension from the whole body and ensures wonderful flexibility of the spine. It tones the legs, especially the backs of the thighs, and firms the abdomen, midriff, waistline, and throat. It is great for the skin and hair because it increases circulation to these areas.

RISHI'S POSTURE

—

1 Stand straight with your feet 3 feet apart. Inhale and stretch your arms up in the air.

As you exhale, move forward slowly and, with your legs straight and back flat, grasp your left leg with your right hand. Eventually you will be able to slide your right hand under your left foot, but in the early stages just grasp the leg where it feels comfortable, keeping both legs straight.

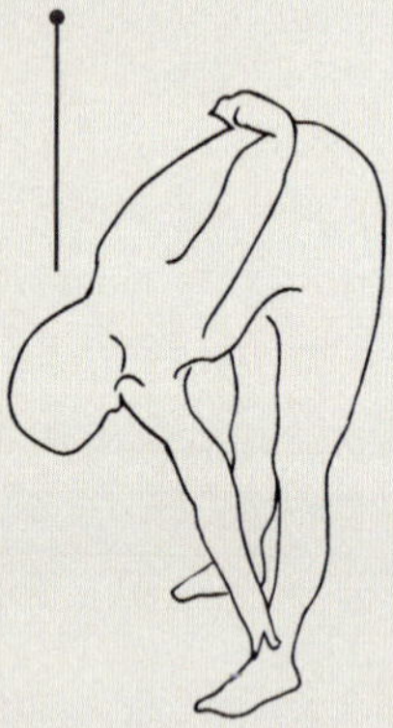

2 Slowly lift your left arm in the air and carefully turn your body so you are looking at your left hand. Breathing normally, hold for a count of five. Then slowly lower your arm and relax forward, clasping your legs and gently pulling your upper body toward the legs. Breathe normally.

Inhale and then, as you exhale, grasp your right leg with your left hand and slowly lift your right arm in the air. Again, turn your body carefully to enable you to look up at your right hand. Breathing normally, hold for a count of five.

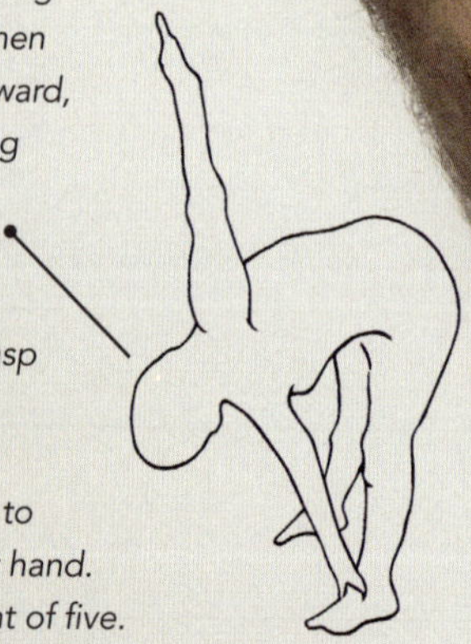

3 Relax forward, clasping both legs and drawing the body inward. Inhale and lift your head, then slowly return to an upright position, stretching your arms above your head.

Now place your hands at your waistline with your thumbs in front and fingers behind, and with full lungs gently bend backward, exhaling as you reach your maximum backward bend.

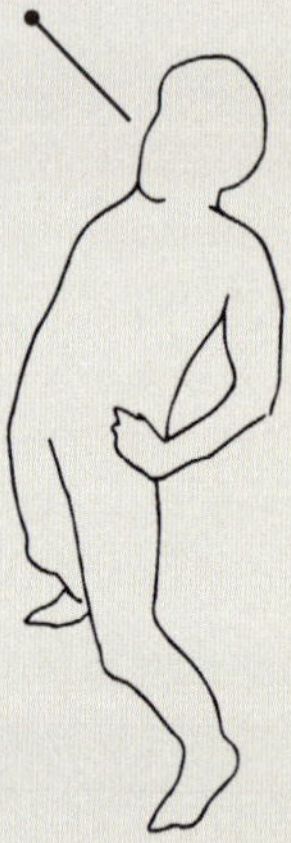

Breathing normally, hold your maximum backward bend for a count of five. Then inhale as you return to an upright position. Exhale, relax, and repeat the entire movement.

BENEFITS

This is excellent for rebalancing the lower back and is great for people who suffer from tension in this region. I recommend it for tennis players and golfers, who can frequently suffer from aches and pain in the lower back. The movement also firms the midriff, waistline, bottom, and thighs and keeps the spine in an excellent condition, giving it great flexibility. A real gem of a movement.

THE AWKWARD POSTURE

1 *Stand straight with your feet about 1 foot apart and your toes facing forward, not outward.*

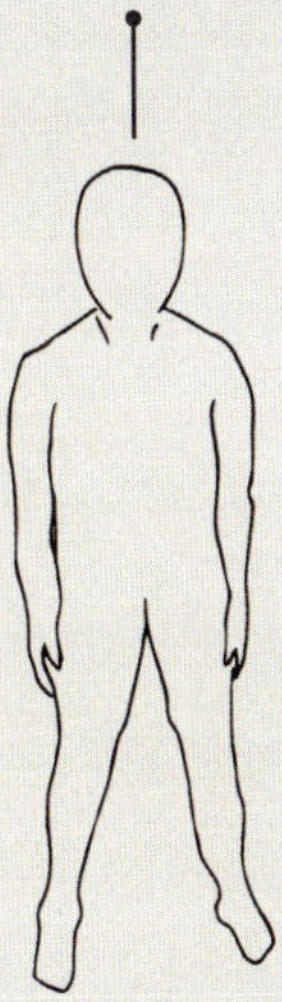

2 *Take a deep breath in and, as you exhale keeping your back straight, gently lower your bottom to your heels. Don't worry if only halfway is possible in the beginning stages. Just do your best without straining.*

3 *Hold your maximum movement for a count of five. Then inhale and gradually return to an upright position, keeping your back straight (do not bend forward). Exhale, relax, and repeat this movement twice.*

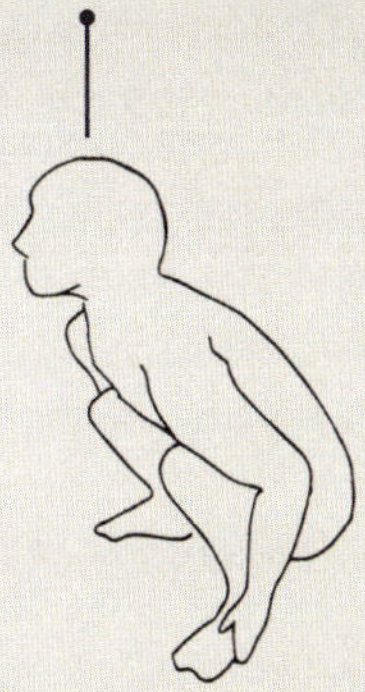

BENEFITS

This does wonders for your thighs—it really tones and firms them. It also greatly improves the flexibility of the knees and strengthens the arches of the feet, and the toes and ankles. In my opinion, this simple 10-minute sequence is worth its weight in gold. It will give you energy, improve your shape, and is excellent for helping with and preventing back problems.

YOGA TONING OF THIGHS AND BOTTOM

Yoga balances firm, tone, and strengthen virtually every muscle in the legs and bottom and are excellent for keeping our joints and lower back flexible. They help to strengthen the bones in the legs since the entire weight of the body is transferred to just one leg during these movements.The balances also teach us the power of focus and concentration as we learn to concentrate on a spot to enable us to do the movements. This takes our mind off our daily activities and gives it a rest, making us concentrate on the present moment. Although difficult to begin with, most beginners are delighted that they are able to do these movements with ease in a relatively short time.

POSE OF A TREE

1 *Standing straight, inhale and lift your right foot on to your left thigh. This sounds easy but can be quite difficult to start with. Don't worry or strain yourself. Even if you start by placing your foot on your ankle, calf, or knee in the beginning stages, you will assist your joints back to their natural flexibility. Yoga and perseverance will get you there!*

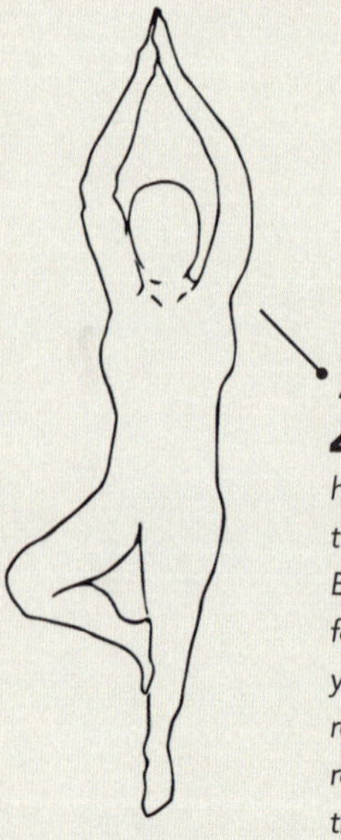

2 *Inhale and lift your arms in the air. Placing the palms of your hands together, stare at a spot on the floor or wall to help your balance. Breathing normally, hold this position for a count of five, increasing to ten as you progress. Exhale, lower your arms, replace your foot on the floor, and relax. Repeat to the other side, and then repeat the entire sequence.*

BENEFITS

This movement is excellent for toning and firming your inner and outer thighs and strengthening your legs. It also aids the flexibility in your ankles, knees, and hips. The balances take your thoughts off your day-to-day activities, so giving your mind a rest.

STANDING STICK BALANCE

Standing straight with your feet together, inhale and lift your arms in the air, placing the palms of your hands together, crossing the thumbs. Inhale and place your right foot 1 foot in front of the left. Exhale and, leaning forward, lift the left leg so that the entire body resembles a capital T. Stare at a spot to aid your balance. Breathing normally, stretch the body fingers forward and the left leg back and hold for a count of five, increasing to ten as you progress. Inhale and return to an upright position. Exhale and relax.

Repeat on the other side, then repeat the entire sequence.

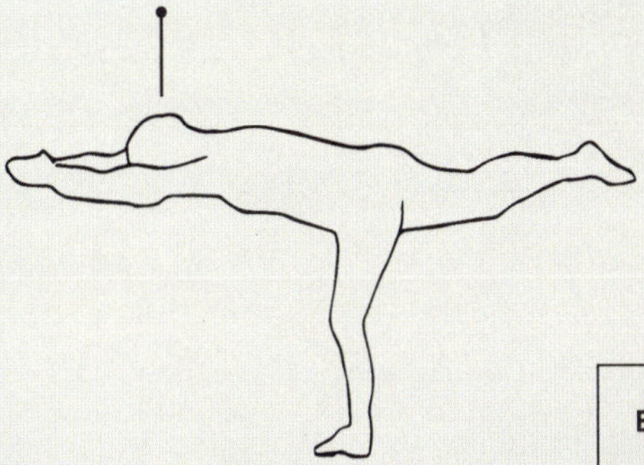

BENEFITS

This movement is excellent for toning and firming your inner and outer thighs and strengthening your legs. It also aids the flexibility in your ankles, knees, and hips. The balances take your thoughts off your day-to-day activities, so giving your mind a rest.

HALF MOON BALANCE

1 *Standing straight with both feet together, inhale and stretch your right arm out to the right side, and gently place your hand on the floor. If necessary, bend your knees to enable you to do this.*

2 *Staring at a spot on the floor, exhale as you lift your left leg in the air. When you have your balance in this position, carefully lift your left arm in a straight line with your right one, and then gently pull your shoulder and head back to gaze at your left hand. Breathing normally, hold for a count of five, then gradually lower your leg. Inhale and return to an upright position.*

3 *Exhale, relax and repeat the movement to the other side, then repeat the entire sequence once, increasing the hold to a count of ten as you progress.*

BENEFITS

This movement tones and slims the hips and thighs, increasing the flexibility in the hips and lower back. It is incredibly good for your balance and coordination.

BIG TOE BALANCE

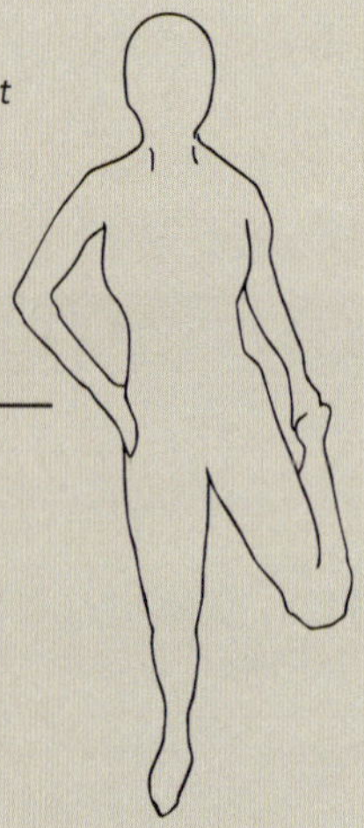

1 *Standing straight with both feet together, place your right hand on your right hip. Inhale and take hold of your left big toe in your left hand. Don't worry if this is too difficult at first. Just place both your hands under your left knee.*

2 *Staring at your spot as you exhale, try to straighten your left leg, making sure you keep your right leg perfectly straight. This is difficult at first, but do persevere. It is well worth it. Eventually the leg will straighten.Hold your maximum stretch for a count of five at first, increasing to ten as you progress. Gently lower your leg to standing position, relax, and repeat to the other side. Repeat the entire sequence.*

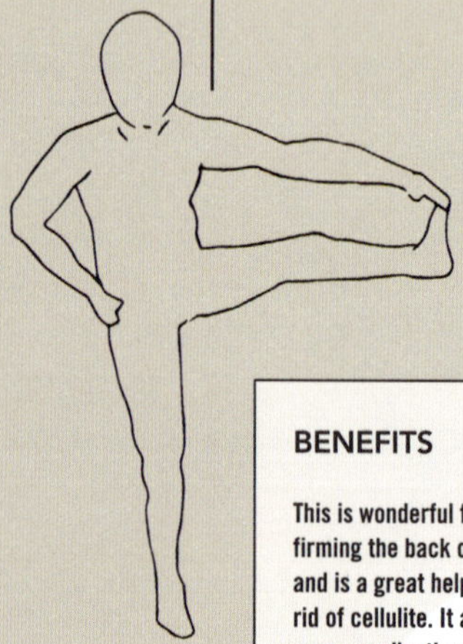

BENEFITS

This is wonderful for toning and firming the back of your thighs and is a great help in getting rid of cellulite. It also helps your coordination and balance, and releases tension in the hips and lower back.

HEAD TO KNEE BALANCE

1 *With your feet together, lift your arms in the air and place the palms of your hands together, crossing the thumbs. Inhaling, place your right foot about 2 feet in front of your left foot. As you exhale, carefully stretch forward aiming your hands to the floor either side of your right foot. In the beginning stages, you may have to bend your right knee to enable you to do this.*

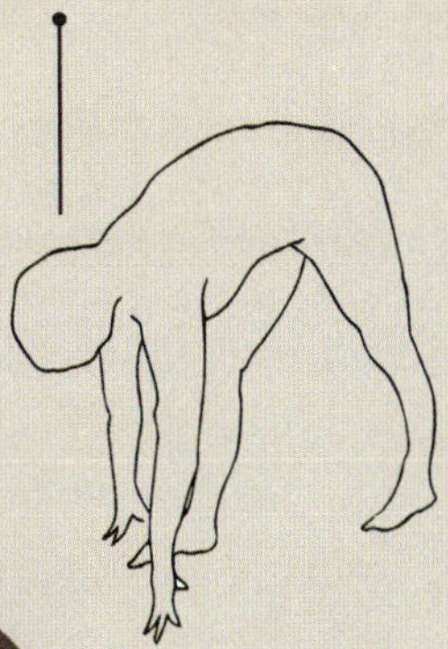

2 *Gently lift your left leg in the air, aiming to point the toe toward the ceiling, drawing your chin towards your shin. Relax in the position, breathing normally, and hold for a count of five. Slowly lower the left leg. Now, with your hands flat on the floor by your right foot, aim to carefully straighten your legs. Don't strain—just persevere! Inhale as you lift your head, then your arms, and return to an upright position. Stretch your entire body, then exhale and relax. Repeat to the other side and notice if you find one side is easier than the other. This is often the case. Happily, in time yoga will help to correct this imbalance for you. Repeat the entire movement. Finally, after the last position in your maximum forward bend, place your feet together and gently aim your chin to just below your knees. Inhale and return to a standing position, stretch your arms above your head. Exhale and relax.*

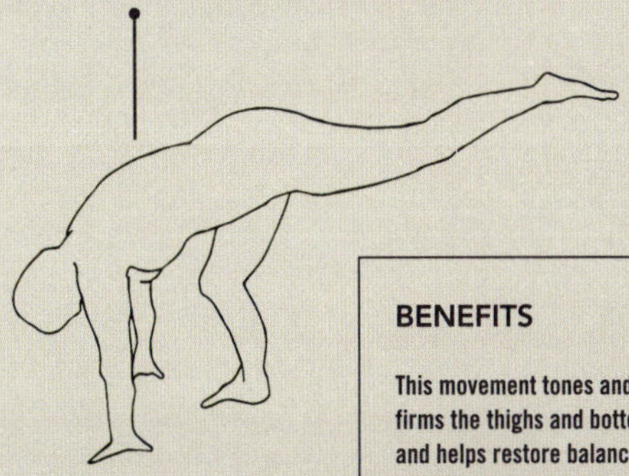

BENEFITS

This movement tones and firms the thighs and bottom, and helps restore balance and relieve tension in the lower back. It stimulates blood flow to the head and neck area, and helps boost the condition of the skin and hair.

EAGLE BALANCE

1 *Standing up straight with your feet together, stretch both arms straight out in front of you.*

Inhale as you cross your right upper arm over your left upper arm, bend the elbows and place both hands in prayer position with the thumbs together in line with your nose. Don't worry if your hands do not fit in the beginning. They soon will as flexibility is improved.

BENEFITS

This can be a nightmare to start with. It is difficult to balance. Your joints just do not seem to fit together. Your arms won't entwine. Don't worry, we have all started like this—just persevere. Yoga is like an oil can, carefully increasing the flexibility of all your joints in one go. The Eagle Balance tones your upper thighs, helps your concentration and balance, relieves tension in your lower back, and helps stimulate extra blood flow to the lower abdominal organs. None of us realize how quickly our joints can stiffen and this wonderful movement will really help.

2 *Exhale as you repeat this movement with your legs, crossing the right thigh over the left and, bending the left leg, entwine the right foot around the left calf, eventually aiming to have your toes around your calf. Now interleave your fingers and place your chin on your upper hand, your elbow on your upper knee, and hold this amazing balance for a count of five, breathing normally while staring at a spot on the floor. Inhale as you come out of the position. Stand straight, exhale, and relax and repeat on the other side. Repeat the entire movement.*

DANCER'S POSTURE

—

This is one of yoga's most beautiful movements.

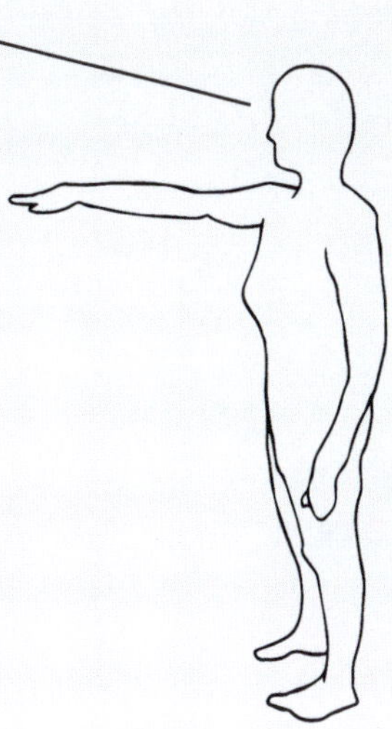

1 With your feet together and with perfect posture, lift your right hand in the air, concentrate on a spot in front of you, and inhale.

2 As you exhale, grab your left foot in your left hand behind your back, and gently lift the leg as high as possible. Breathing normally, hold for a count of five.

Gently lower your leg and relax. Repeat to the other side and gradually increase the hold to a count of ten as you progress. Repeat the entire movement.

BENEFITS

A beautiful movement—as well as helping your concentration and balance, it relieves tension in your lower back, lifts and firms your bottom, and tones your thighs while strengthening the supporting leg.

YOGA TONING OF ABDOMINALS AND WAIST

Do not attempt any of the movements in these exercises during pregnancy. The abdominals drop as we get older and these exercises are invaluable for keeping the abdomen firm, toned, uplifted, and youthful. The contraction massages your internal organs (your small intestine, colon, pancreas, gall bladder, and heart). The movement can help tremendously in stimulating peristalsis and relieving constipation and gives relief to those who suffer from irritable bowel syndrome and abdominal bloating.

YOGA ABDOMINAL LIFT AND CONTRACTION

—

This movement is like a wonderful gift. It only takes 30 seconds a day and is brilliant for those stomach muscles! It must be done on an empty stomach—the ideal time to do it is before breakfast. Don't worry if you do not appear to be getting much movement in the beginning stages—just persevere. The resulting slimmer, firmer, and flatter tummy is well worth it!

BENEFITS

We do not always appreciate how much our body is affected by our mind. We all have experienced a "gut reaction," the feeling of a knot in the lower abdomen. This wonderful movement is excellent for helping to release this feeling of tightness.

Stand straight with your legs about 1 foot apart, placing your hands on your upper thighs. Inhale deeply, then exhale fully. Keeping the air out of your lungs, pull your abdominals in and up. Hold for a count of ten, then release the abdominals, inhale, and relax. Repeat the movement twice.

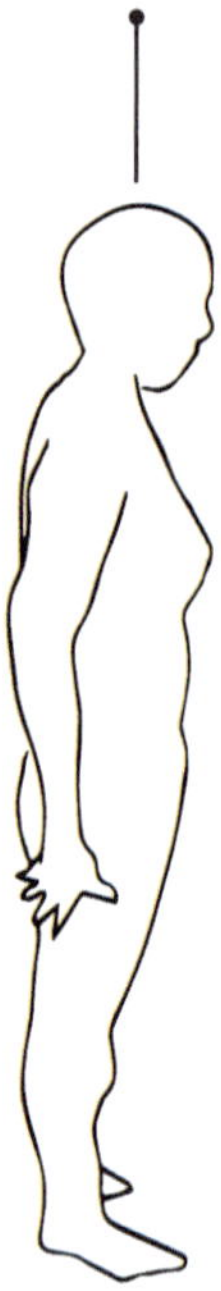

You can then try an abdominal contraction. Inhale, then exhale and lean slightly forwards. Keeping all the air out of your lungs, snap your abdomen in and out ten times, increasing gradually to twenty as you progress. Relax, inhale, and repeat the movement twice.

TUMMY AND THIGH TONER

—

This deceptively simple movement is like dynamite!

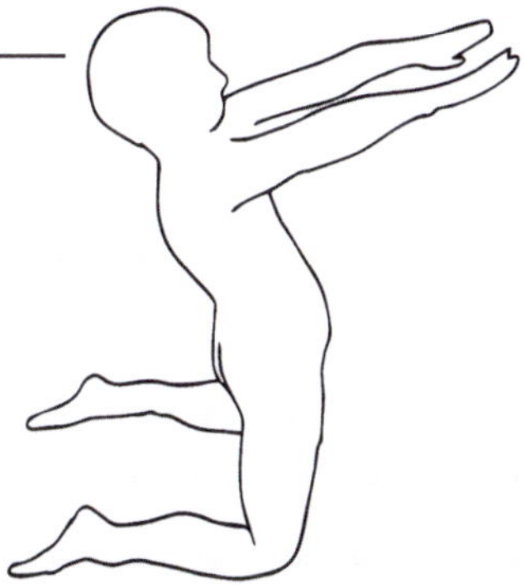

Kneel with your knees about a foot apart. Lift your bottom from your heels and, keeping your back straight, place your arms parallel to the floor making sure that your thighs are straight and perpendicular to the floor. Inhale and, as you exhale, lean back a small way, increasing the stretch as you progress. Don't let your bottom sag. Breathing normally, hold the position for a count of five, then inhale, and return to an upright position. Repeat the movement twice.

BENEFITS

This powerful movement really tones and firms your tummy. It gives your thighs that beautiful firm, toned, slim yoga shape.

POSE OF A BOAT

This is a fantastic firmer for both tummies and thighs. It also greatly strengthens the lower back. Sit on a thick mat or blanket for this exercise.

1 Sit straight with both legs straight out in front of you. Stretch out your arms parallel to the floor. Inhale and, as you exhale gently, lift your legs from the floor and balance on your bottom. Hold the position for a count of one to begin with, gradually increasing to ten as you progress, then gently lower your legs to the floor and relax.

Repeat the movement twice. This can be hard work but move carefully and build it up gently. Remember, never strain in the posture. Following the movement, lie on your back, draw your knees to your chest, and gently rock your back from side to side to relieve any tension in your lower back.

BENEFITS

This is a really powerful hamstring stretch. It does wonders for the shape of the back of your thighs and is a great help in getting rid of cellulite.

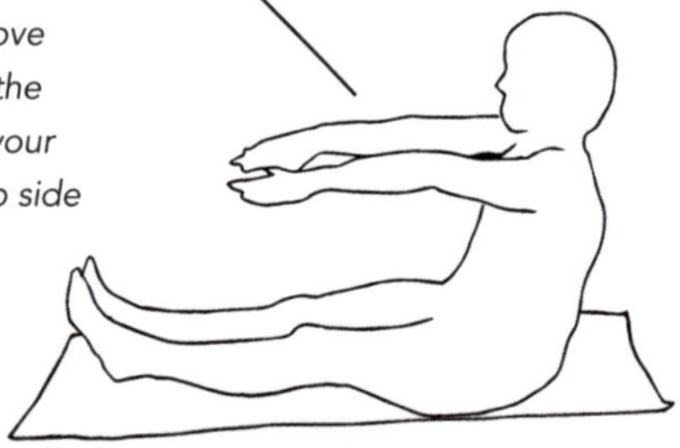

2 Sitting on your mat with both legs stretched out in front of you, place your hands interlocked behind your head. Take a deep breath and, as you exhale gently, lift your legs from the floor. Hold for a count of one to start with, increasing to ten as you progress. This is very powerful —do not strain!

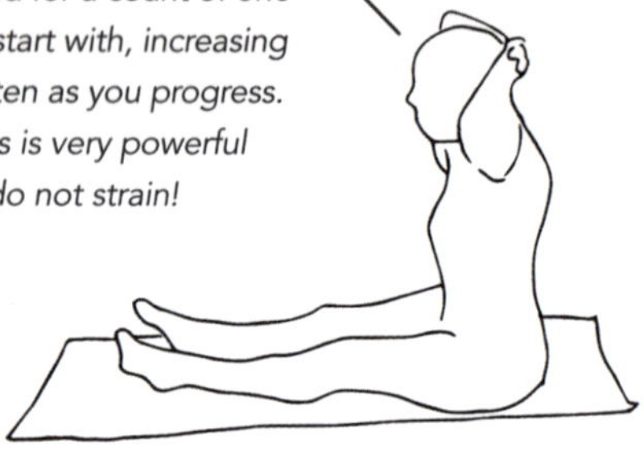

3 Gently lower our legs to the floor and then relax. Repeat the movement twice. Following the movement, lie down and gently draw your knees to your chest and rock from side to side.

BENEFITS

Again, this is a powerful toner for your abdomen, thighs, and lower back.

SLOW MOTION FIRMING

—

This beautiful sequence not only gives you a lovely firm, strong, and flat tummy, but also is delightfully relaxing and is great to do after a long hard day before going to sleep at night. The movement is performed in one slow continuous motion.

1 Sit up with your back straight and with both legs straight out in front of you and together. Place both arms parallel to your legs. Inhale and lift your arms in the air.

2 Exhale as you slowly move forwards, keeping your back and legs straight—do not strain, just allow your body to flow easily and gently into your maximum position. You should eventually aim to clasp your feet and draw your chin to your knees.

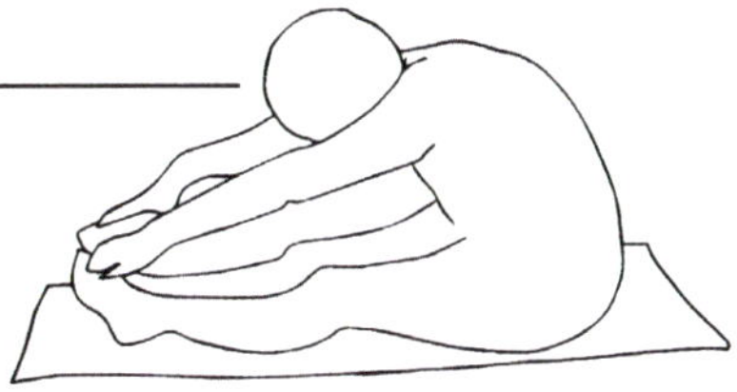

3 Inhale as you slowly return to an upright position, then exhale as you gently lie flat. Place your arms flat on the floor behind your head. Inhale and gently bend your knees, lift your legs up, and straighten them so that they are at right angles to your body.

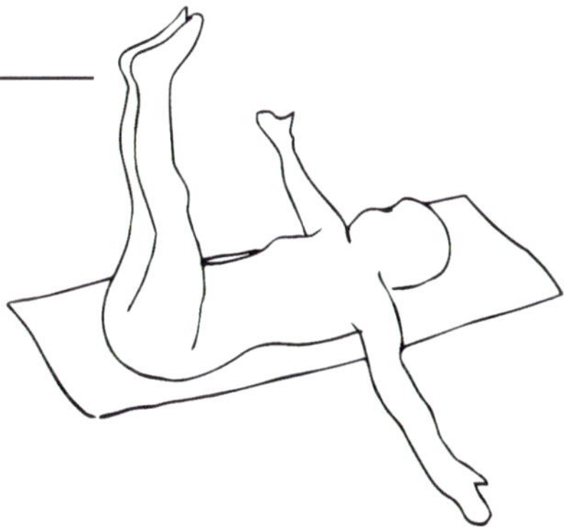

4 Exhale as you slowly lower your legs to the floor. In the beginning stages, make this part of the movement relatively fast, then slow it down as your abdominals firm and strengthen. For people with weak backs, you may feel a small pull in your lower back to start with. If this occurs, immediately bend your knees and then continue to lower your legs with your knees bent. As you progress you will find that you will be able to go further before having to bend your knees. Inhale as you slowly come up into a sitting position, stretching your arms up in the air. If you find this difficult in the beginning stages, then use your elbows to help you push off. Exhale as you relax and stretch forward into a back stretch.

Repeat this sequence twice, increasing to four times as your back and abdominals become stronger. Then lie down, draw your knees into your chest, and gently relax your back into the floor, gently rocking from side to side. Then lie flat, slow your breathing down, and relax.

BENEFITS

This beautiful sequence will deliver the results you want—a beautiful, firm tummy and nice strong back—and it will really relax you. If your back is stiff and tense, you may toss and turn and find sleep difficult. This movement is perfect for unwinding this tension and helping you to deep restful sleep.

YOGA TONING OF ARMS, BUST, AND NECK

On the physical level, these exercises are amazing in how they tone your upper arms, neck, jaw, and throat, while releasing the tension in the back of your neck and shoulders. They also stimulate blood flow to the head and neck area, so benefiting your skin, hair, and brain cells. The tensions of the mind are frequently stored in the back of the neck (the proverbial pain in the neck) and lumbar spine. These powerful exercises carefully relax both these areas.

THE CHEST EXPANSION

—

These movements are not only dramatic in the way that they tone and firm the arms and the muscles that support the bust, but they are also excellent for correcting posture, relieving tension in the neck and shoulders, and realigning the spine.

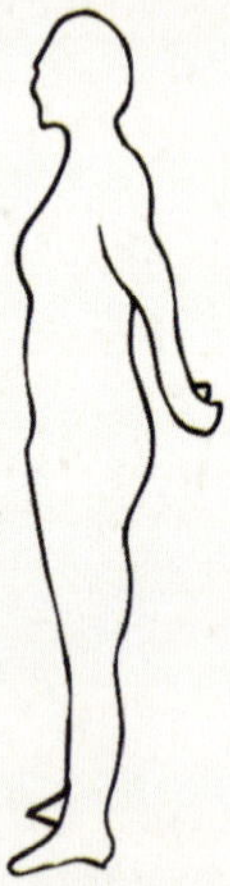

1 Stand with your feet together and your back straight. Interlock your hands behind your back, gently pulling your shoulders back and straightening your arms.

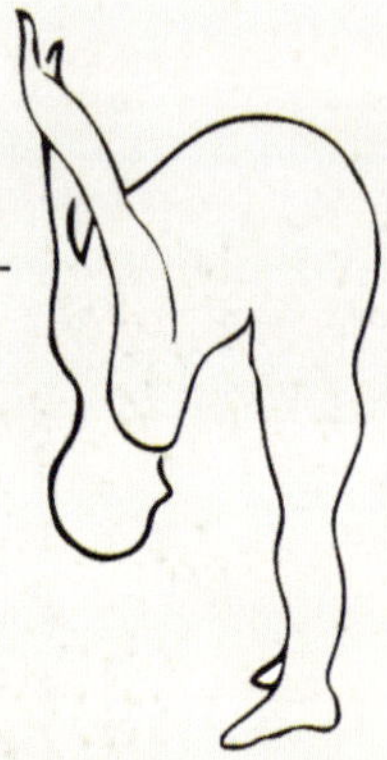

2 Inhale and lift your arms up as high as possible behind your back, then exhale as you slowly bend forward into your maximum forward bend, keeping your back and legs straight. Breathing normally, relax and hold your maximum position for a count of five. Your aim is to be able to place your chin on the top of the shin, just under the knee. It will happen eventually, but remember not to strain!

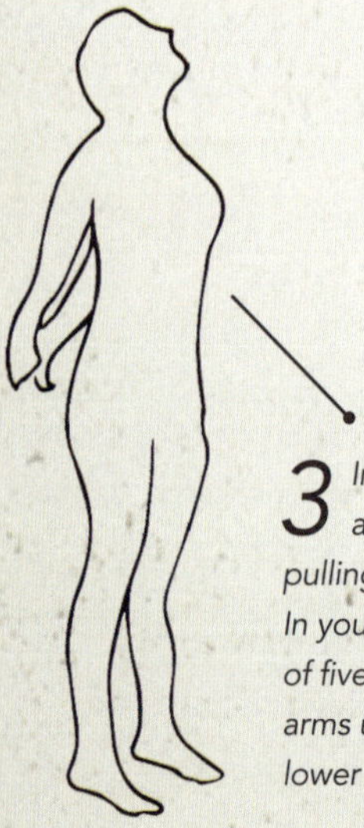

3 Inhale and lift your head, then slowly return to an upright position and gently bend backward, pulling your arms back down and under your bottom. In your maximum position, exhale, and hold for a count of five. Inhale and return to an upright position, hold your arms up behind your back for an extra count of two, then lower them and relax. Repeat the movement twice.

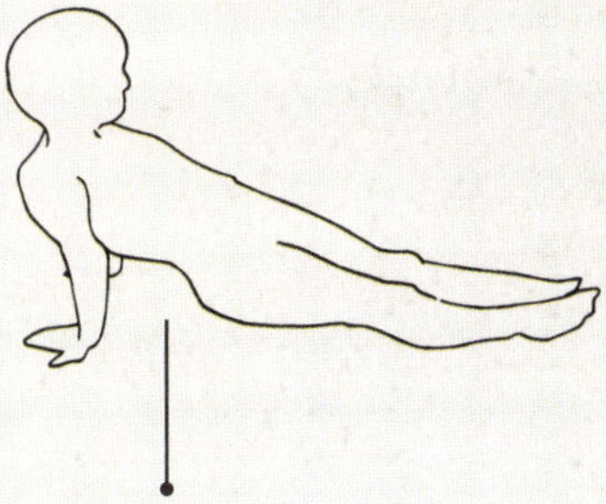

BENEFITS

This is so good for the strength of your hands, arms, wrists, and fingers. It gives great shape to your upper arms and shoulders. It helps to correct drooping shoulders and releases tension in the lower back.

POSE OF A PLANET

—

This movement, as well as strengthening your arms and shoulders, releases tension in the lower back.

Sit straight with your hands comfortably on the floor behind you, about 1 foot behind your bottom with your fingertips facing backward. Your legs should be straight out in front of you. Inhale and, as you exhale, keeping your body in a straight line, place your weight on your arms, and gently lift your body from the floor. Ensure that your legs are straight and your toes are on the floor. Hold for a count of one at first, increasing to ten as you become stronger. Slowly lower your bottom to the floor and relax. Repeat this movement once.

SIDEWAYS BODY RAISE

—

This is another excellent arm shaper and strengthener. We have a built-in response to put a hand out to break a fall should we slip. If our wrists and arms are weak, this can easily result in a break. Yoga hand balances such as this perfectly address the problem. If you have had a wrist or arm problem, follow the directions below but do not lift your bottom—just put a little weight on your hands to strengthen them gradually. Follow these instructions only when your arms are sufficiently strong.

Place both hands on the floor to the right-hand side of your body. Keep your knees bent and make sure that your hands and feet are on a non-slip surface. Inhale and, as you exhale, lift your body from the floor, ensuring that your weight is supported on both hands and both feet.

Adjust your body so that your right shoulder is directly above your right wrist and that your arm is straight. Lift your bottom and make sure the left foot is on top of the right one and that the body is in a straight line.

When, and only when, you feel strong enough, lift your left arm from the floor and stretch it in a straight line, with the inside of the arm alongside your left ear. Concentrate on a spot on the floor and hold your balance for a count of five, then relax. Gently lower your bottom to the floor and repeat on the other side. Repeat the whole movement once.

BENEFITS

An excellent arm toner and firmer that gives excellent shape to your upper arms and shoulders. This movement greatly strengthens the wrists, hands, elbows, and shoulders. An extra benefit is in the way it stretches the hands. For those who spend many hours at the computer, the wrists can become very stiff and painful and this movement can help tremendously.

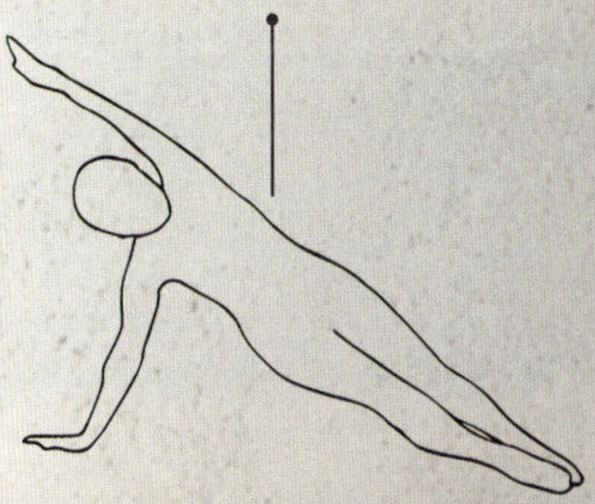

THE MOUNTAIN POSE

We tend to "shoulder our problems" and this beautiful movement helps lift away the pressures of the day. Although yoga cannot remove the problem, it can help remove the tension resulting from the problem.

1 Kneel down on your mat with your bottom on your heels. Some people find this very difficult to begin with. You can help yourself by placing a thick cushion on top of your calves under your bottom. If this still doesn't feel comfortable, then sit in a cross-legged position. Interlock your hands in front of you so that you are looking into the palms, then gently turn them inside out so that you are now looking at the back of your hands. Inhale and stretch your arms up above your head. Exhale and straighten your arms—imagine you are pushing the ceiling a little higher. Breathing normally, hold this stretch for a count of five in the maximum position. Inhale, undo your hands, exhale, and slowly lower them. Repeat the movement.

BENEFITS

The Mountain Pose helps to lift the pressures of life from your shoulders, it tones and firms your upper arms and enhances the flexibility of your wrists and fingers. It is excellent for strengthening the spine and, in the advanced stage, ensures flexibility of the hips, knees, and ankles.

2 Once your knees have acquired sufficient flexibility to do the Mountain Pose with ease, then (and only then) try this slightly stronger stretch.

With your knees a hip-width apart, place your hands on the floor and, keeping your weight on your hands, aim to lower your bottom between your heels.

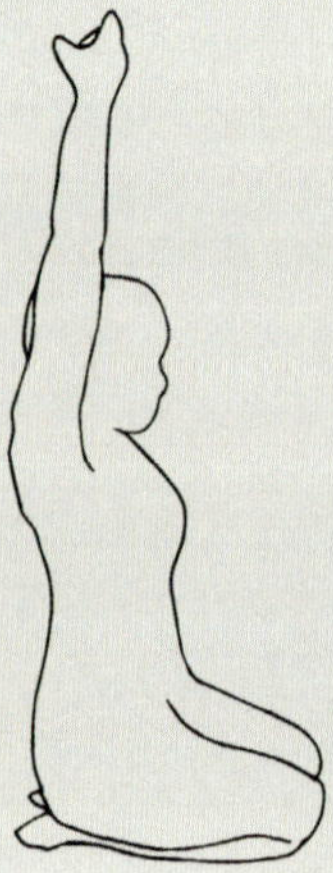

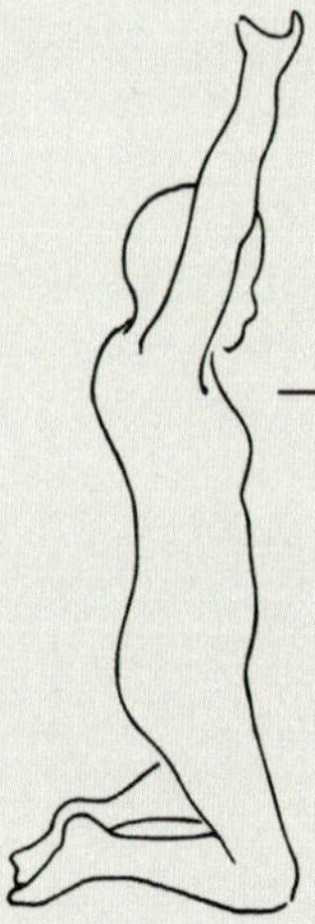

3 Once you can sit comfortably in this position without strain, repeat the Mountain Pose for this advanced stretch—inhale, interlock your hands, turn them inside out, exhale, push them upward aiming to straighten the arms. Breathing normally, hold for a count of five, then exhale, and relax. Repeat twice.

POSE OF A COW

This position helps to correct neck tension and realign the neck and shoulders. These can frequently be imbalanced due to such things as carrying heavy shoulder bags, constant use of one arm at the expense of the other, and playing lop-sided sports.

This position can be astounding, with one side seeming easy and the other almost impossible. It is good to discover our imbalances. Rest assured that daily practice of this movement will gradually help correct the problem for you. Repeat the entire sequence just once.

BENEFITS

Pose of a Cow helps to correct imbalances in your shoulders. It tones and firms your upper arms and firms the muscles that support the bust. In the advanced position, it is excellent for toning the thighs and ensuring the flexibility of your hips, knees, and ankles.

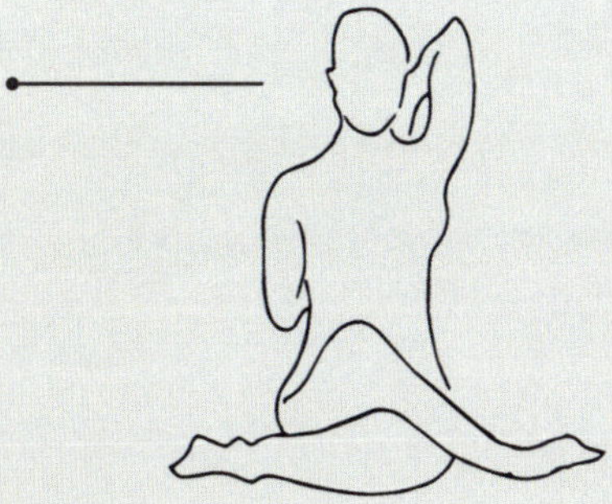

1 Sit in a kneeling position with your bottom on your heels. If this is not possible, adopt a cross-legged pose. Inhale, lift your right hand in the air, and drop it over your right shoulder. Exhale and lift your left arm up behind your back, aiming to join your hands in a clasped position. Don't worry if you cannot join them at first, just practice and soon you will be able to. In the meantime, remember your maximum position is fine. Inhale and, as you gently exhale, bend forward and aim your forehead to the floor. Breathing normally, hold this position for a count of five, then inhale and return to an upright position. Unclasp your hands, relax, and then repeat on the other side, noticing if there is a difference between the two sides.

2 Once you find the Pose of a Cow easy in all respects, you can try the advanced stage for a stronger stretch. Before you attempt this you must be able to sit on your heels with ease. In an all fours position, ensuring that your weight is on your hands, place your right leg over your left and then gently lower yourself down to sit between your heels. Go carefully. It may take a while to accomplish this position and remember that the only way to get there is daily practice without strain. If it is too difficult, just remain in a kneeling position. Lift your right arm in the air and drop it down behind your right shoulder. Take the left arm up behind your back and clasp your hands together.

3 Inhale and, as you exhale gently, bend forward and place your forehead on your upper knee. Breathing normally, stay in this position for a count of five, then inhale and return to an upright position. Exhale and relax and perform the movement on the other side. Repeat the movement once on each side.

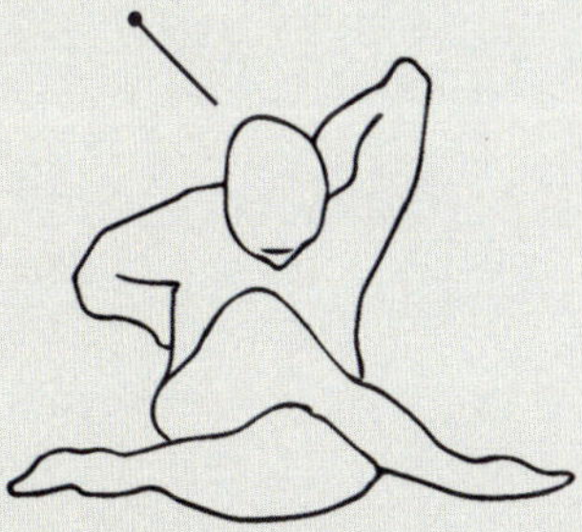

MASSAGE

CHAPTER FOUR

ORIGINS OF MASSAGE

Massage is probably one of the most popular forms of health activity today. It is used in relaxation groups and workshops, in leisure centers, and as a form of natural therapy for injury and the wear and tear of daily life. Whether performed by a trained professional or a gifted amateur, it offers the experience of touch, movement, and energy, qualities that are associated with the well-being of the whole person, and the act of giving massage has deep significance for both the giver and the receiver.

By treating symptoms, or suppressing them, we are doing nothing to treat the root cause of a problem. Eczema sufferers apply ointments and creams to the surface of the skin; they may take anti-inflammatories or antihistamines to ease the itching, but the cause of the eczema is still there, and the body's reaction has been masked by drugs. They have not been cured; their illness has merely been controlled.

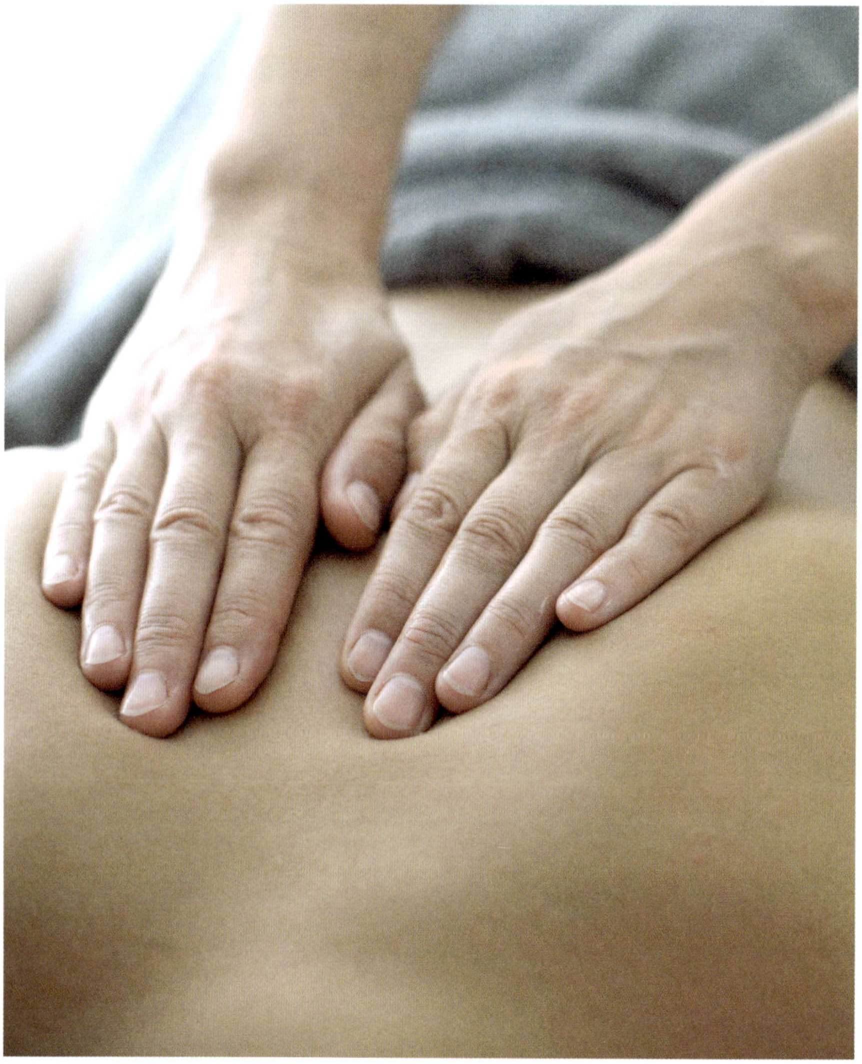

The physical and psychological benefits of massage have been recognized since ancient times.

ORIGINS OF MASSAGE

—

The physical and psychological benefits of massage have been recognized and valued since ancient times. Working within their limited concepts of body function, early physicians were able to use massage very effectively in the treatment of fatigue, illness, and injury. In the 5th century B.C. Hippocrates described *anatripsis*—literally, "rubbing up"—as having a more favorable effect than rubbing down on the limbs, although the understanding of the blood's circulation was at that time incomplete. Esthetically, the ancient Greeks associated physical culture with the unfolding of mental and spiritual faculties, and set up massage schools in their beautifully built centers of health known as gymnasiums. In the Far East, performing musicians and actors have always learned massage practices as aids to their artistic development; exponents of *kathakali*, an early dance form originating in South India, are treated with deep massage from the feet of their teachers. In some societies, massage has even been used socially as an act of hospitality; in Hawaii, for example, passive movements called *lomi-lomi* are traditionally bestowed on honored guests.

In Europe, massage remained an important element of healthcare throughout the duration of the Roman Empire and is widely referred to in the literature of the era. The development of massage in the West seems to have been interrupted by the disintegration of the Roman civilization, although an unbroken tradition continued in the East. It is not until the 16th century, at a time when relatively sophisticated surgical techniques were being developed in France, that we hear of massage reemerging in Europe in connection with healing.

In the late 19th century, the demand for therapeutic massage led to the formation of societies of therapists. These societies had the objects of promoting the science of massage, organizing training, and "safeguarding the interests of the public and the profession." The desirable characteristics of a practitioner were held to be "good health, intelligence, and a high moral tone." At the time they succeeded in their aims, but later developments were to undo much of their work.

ECLIPSE AND REVIVAL

—

In the 20th century, the great strides made by conventional medicine have tended to eclipse traditional therapies, even though —or perhaps because—they have been practiced for centuries. Dazzled by the achievements of science and technology, most people in the developed world all but ignored the therapeutic value of human touch until a few decades ago. Yet massage and its sister therapies are enjoying a renaissance. This can be partly explained by a return to "natural" values in reaction to the highly stressful conditions of modern life, but there is also a growing resistance to the dehumanizing aspects of modern healthcare.

Today many people yearn for an approach to healthcare that is based, not on drugs and technology, but on the healing value of physical contact. There is nothing mystical or romantic about this idea. The human body is a physical object that responds to physical influences, and a grasp of human anatomy is central to any understanding of the role of massage. This book is partly a celebration of our wonderful anatomy: an appeal to the imagination, because anatomy is imagination. You can learn little about the body unless you can imagine, for example, your heart's powerful beating, the delicacy and strength of your muscles, and the balance of the bony arrangements that support you. An appreciation of the body's engineering is as vital to good massage as any psychological insight.

Some massage therapists will use oils to nourish the skin and leave it hydrated.

Massage is now firmly established as an effective therapy, yet despite growing awareness of its value, the idea of massage often meets with some resistance. Massage has been abused socially, leading to doubts about its morality, and there is still much confusion about its role in healing. Should it be seen as an alternative to conventional medicine, or a complementary therapy? How safe is it? Does it have any real physiological effects, or is it primarily psychological in value? These questions, and no doubt many more, will be examined in the pages that follow.

Massage is a popular and effective treatment for relaxation.

MASSAGE STYLES

There are many interpretations of massage, and each emphasizes the benefits of a particular technique or style. There are two main categories: Oriental and Western. Oriental styles tend to be stimulating, and use direct, focused pressures. Western styles are more concerned with soothing and calming the patient. The rationale for massage is quite different in each culture. Although formal anatomy is accepted in the East, practitioners there use unconventional theories to explain the interactions between the body and its "owner." So, whereas a Western therapist may speak of the liver as an organ of the body, the Eastern therapist refers to the energy that organizes the liver, and will use massage to adjust that sense of energy, rather than treat the organ in isolation.

MASSAGE FOR ILLNESS

Traditional healthcare systems throughout the world recognize that massage can play an important role in treating illness. In India, for example, it is not uncommon to see children massaging the legs of their hospitalized parents. For many years, massage has been ignored by orthodox Western medicine, but, increasingly, medical practitioners have come to recognize the potential of massage therapy, especially in connection with those diseases of civilization, in which personal stress is acknowledged to be an important factor. In many such cases, orthodox treatments have achieved limited success, while holistic therapies involving massage have been of significant help.

We recognize illness as having two distinct aspects: "acute," which is an active or regenerative stage, and "chronic," in which degenerative processes feature. The stimulating and supportive influence of massage has much to offer in both cases, helping to alleviate acute conditions and reduce the emotional and psychological disturbance associated with chronic conditions. There are circumstances in which full body massage may be inappropriate, but such circumstances rarely rule out massage entirely. Evidence from hospices where people are terminally ill suggests that, even then, a modified form of massage is entirely beneficial.

Massage is valuable during illness because of its recognition that being ill involves being disordered neurologically. The term "being ill" is another way of expressing that the body is under the dominance of the sympathetic nerves: the part of the autonomic nervous system which governs the system's response to irregularity. Sympathetic nerve activity is also associated with fear and distress, and this is why even the simplest manifestation of disease tends to be associated with emotional upset.

A gentle hand massage can be very soothing for elderly patients.

MASSAGE TYPES

WESTERN MASSAGE
Swedish Massage (Europe)
Esalen (California)
Aromatherapy (Anglo-French)
Holistic Massage

INNOVATIVE
Bowen Technique (Bowen)
Polarity (Randolph Stone)
Rolfing (Ida Rolf)
Reflexology (Bailey)

PHYSIOTHERAPY
Vacuum Suction (Effleurage)
Gyrator (Kneading)
Ultrasound (Petrissage)
Vibrator (Percussion)

EASTERN
Ayurveda (India)
Tuina (China)
Lomi-Lomi (Hawaii)
Shiatsu (Japan)

Extreme cases such as these are sometimes described as psychosomatic conditions, in which the fear generated and the condition provoking it fuel each other in a relentless, self-perpetuating cycle.

Massage can interrupt this cycle and relieve the distress of illness by modifying sympathetic nerve activity and encouraging the activity of the parasympathetic nerves, which have a relaxing effect. This increases the patient's tolerance of pain, which is a good indicator of recovery, enabling the patient to make a swifter return to full health.

MASSAGE FOR INJURY

—

The influence of massage on the circulation is very helpful in alleviating pain after accidents and injuries. In the case of serious injury, the pain can be greater during the recovery stage than immediately after the accident, and is often associated with the return of functioning. Vigorously massaging the opposite limb to the injured one, or the lower limbs in cases of upper body injury, alleviates pressure without compromising the healing processes.

Targeted massage therapy can help to alleviate pain from injuries and promote healing.

An injury harms the tissue, interrupting normal functioning. It is accompanied by pain, swelling, and inflammation. Pain draws conscious awareness to the site of the injury so that irritating movement is discouraged. The increased circulation to the injured tissue is responsible for the swelling, which also helps immobilize the damaged area. Inflammation involves a rise in local temperature that helps destroy debris within the injury. Appropriate massage treatment helps modify these responses so that injuries are easier to bear and quicker to heal.

The blood that is attracted to an injury is thicker than usual because of the increase in white cell activity. The lymphatic system is also mobilized to supply a watery disinfectant that protects the body from any external contamination. It is unwise to reduce the resulting swelling artificially since it contains healing ingredients. Raising the injured part higher than the heart usually makes the congested state much more tolerable; meanwhile the gentle strokes of massage, above and below the injury, are helpful in maintaining an effective drainage.

The inflammatory response is necessary to help dispose of disintegrating body tissue. It is an uncomfortable experience, however, and the most obvious, effective way to minimize this discomfort is through the use of cooling hydrotherapy. The heat from the inflammation is transferred to a cool compress and the effect on the nerves and the blood vessels is very soothing.

BENEFITS OF MASSAGE

The benefits of massage are extensive. Massage can be used to help preserve health and treat illness. It can work in conjunction with orthodox and complementary therapies and is in itself an enjoyable and healthy activity. As the popularity of massage increases, more opportunities are being identified for its use—from easing the discomforts of childbirth to providing emotional and physical support to a wide range of individuals.

In India, massage is considered to be indispensable, and beneficial literally from the cradle to the grave. In Japan, people are regularly roused by the shiatsu practitioner who calls from house to house asking "Shiatsu today?"; the whole family may then each enjoy 10 minutes of refreshing treatment. Throughout the world, massage is employed in preparation for surgery and the manipulative adjustments of chiropractic, and it is also used for postoperative therapy. In the United States it is an important element of stress management programs, and it has been found that the act of giving simple massage reduces stress even in the givers.

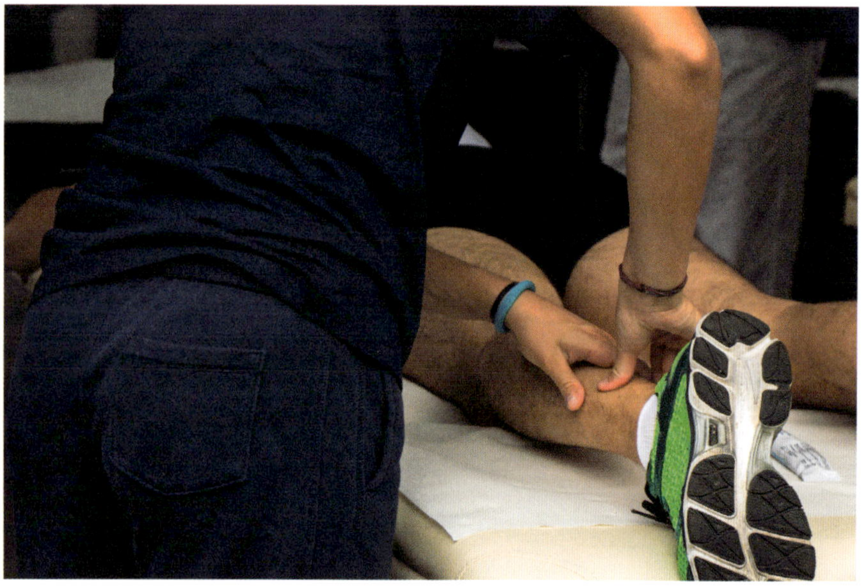

Massage has become an important part of the self-care routines of many sportspeople.

PHYSIOLOGICAL BENEFITS

—

The benefits of massage as injury therapy have always been appreciated in sports, but in recent years its use has developed and expanded. Massage is now an intrinsic part of an enlightened attitude that embraces the care as well as the repair of athletes. Its importance as a means of combating the stresses of competitive sports has made it a major component of training and fitness regimes.

The value of massage as therapy for a variety of subclinical conditions has been demonstrated by its application to long-distance air travel. Although in some respects less arduous than in the past, modern air journeys are nevertheless capable of producing symptoms such as dehydration, indigestion, stiffness, and disorientation. Massage can help with all these, and one airline company offers in-flight therapy, in which passengers receive facial, foot, or hand massage. They are also advised on simple de-stressing movements. Another airline has developed a seat with inbuilt massage technology that intermittently stimulates passive posture throughout the flight. Passengers have reported that these treatments definitely reduce the impact of jet lag, especially when combined with rest and further massage soon after landing.

PSYCHOLOGICAL BENEFITS

—

It is one of the many joys of massage that its therapeutic benefits are not exclusive to professional treatment. Even at a spontaneous level, massage provides an opportunity for us to offer help to both family and friends.

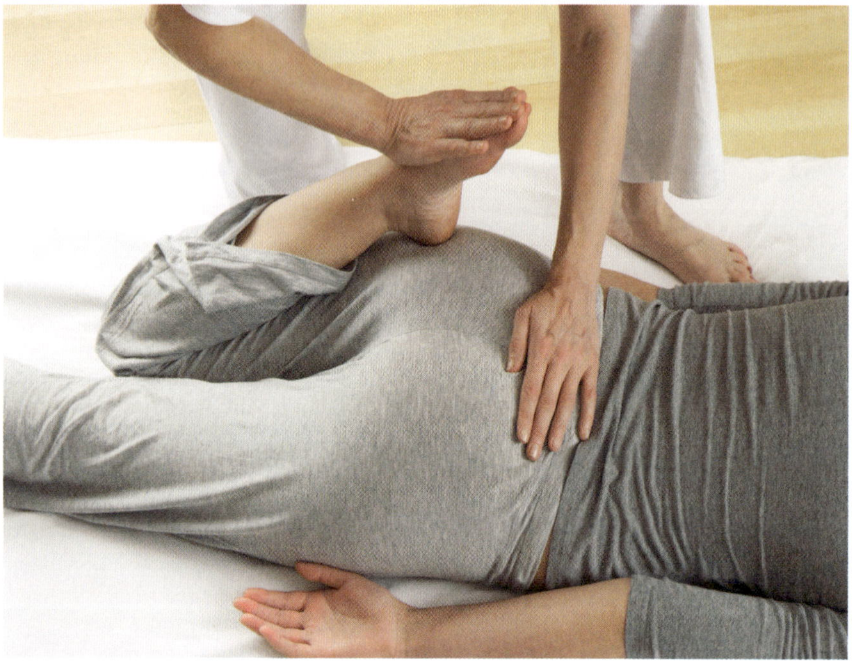

Shiatsu massage treatments are an indispensible part of life in eastern countries and are now popular in the West.

It seems almost instinctive to squeeze the shoulders of a tired or anxious friend and smooth the brow of a startled child. Most people know how it feels to be under strain, and this may be our guide when giving untutored massage. For those who find it natural to extend a helping hand, it is not difficult to convert a tentative approach into a lasting, beneficial exchange for both receiver and giver. A little experience, coupled with a little knowledge about how massage works, can transform the instinctive touch into a precious gift.

A simple massage is just as beneficial for mind as body, effectively reducing stress.

Massage has been found to be a useful extension of communication between partners or colleagues when verbal and familiar patterns of relating become exhausted. Massage can create emotional space, reducing the intensity of conflict, and provide cooling-off time without repressing the real issues. The powerful nonverbal communication of massage enables friends to address the physical burden of each other's problems without necessarily involving direct or unwanted confrontation.

ULTIMATE BENEFIT

—

Enjoying and appreciating the benefits of massage requires a physical receptivity and a willingness to be benefited by our bodies. Throughout history, certain religious codes of conduct have demanded restraint and control at all times and these precepts have become ingrained in our culture. Consequently, some people find their access to the pleasure of massage blocked by their own physical inhibitions. Fortunately, nature has arranged that the benefits of massage, once they have been experienced, become inviting, magnetic, and irresistible.

MASSAGE TECHNIQUES

Massage is given in a flowing sequence, in which one stroke blends seamlessly with another. This classic formula for massage shows the strokes needed to give an effective treatment. The vital transition between the pressure strokes is provided by effleurage, which both introduces and concludes the massage.

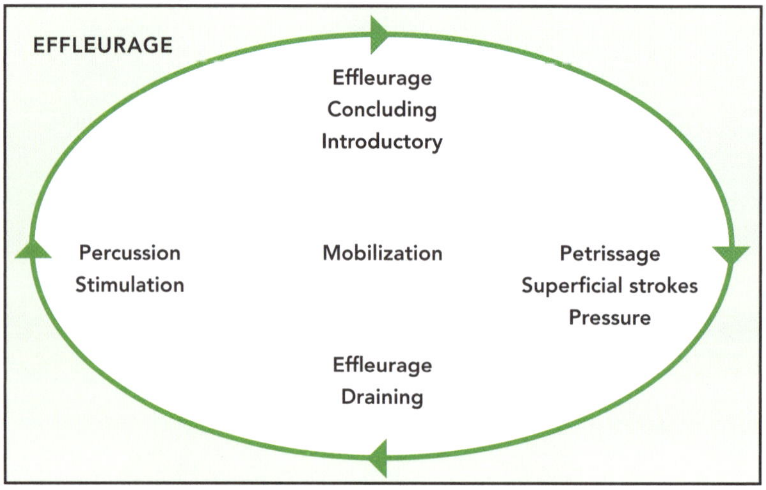

EFFLEURAGE

—

For effleurage, lay your hands across the patient's body with fingers together and thumbs slightly stretched. Stroke smoothly, initially without pressure, following the contours of the body. Smooth the skin in the direction of the heart after petrissage strokes.

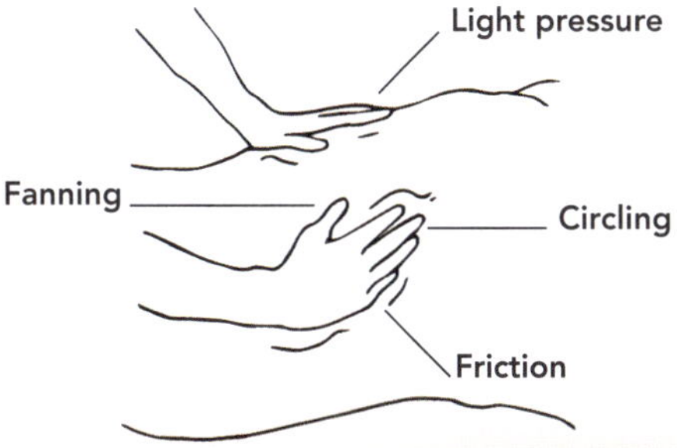

PETRISSAGE AND KNEADING

—

For kneading, use the whole hand, with fingers together and thumbs outstretched, to squeeze the rounder contours of the body. Petrissage is a lighter squeezing action, using only the thumbs and fingertips to work on slimmer or flatter muscles.

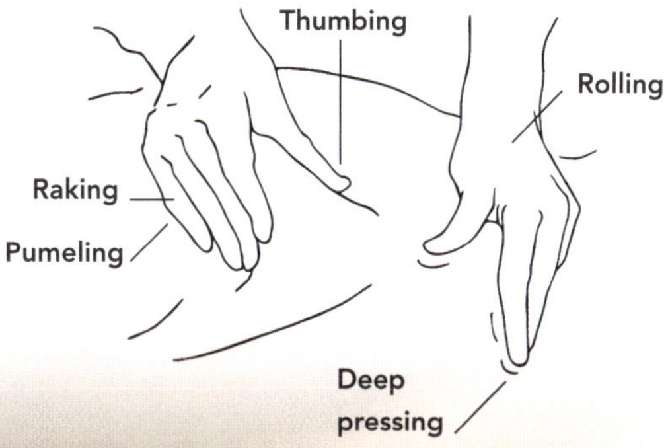

PERCUSSION

—

Apply percussion by lightly striking the body using different parts of your hands, keeping your wrists loose. Begin slowly, increase to moderate speed, then build to a crescendo before stopping abruptly.

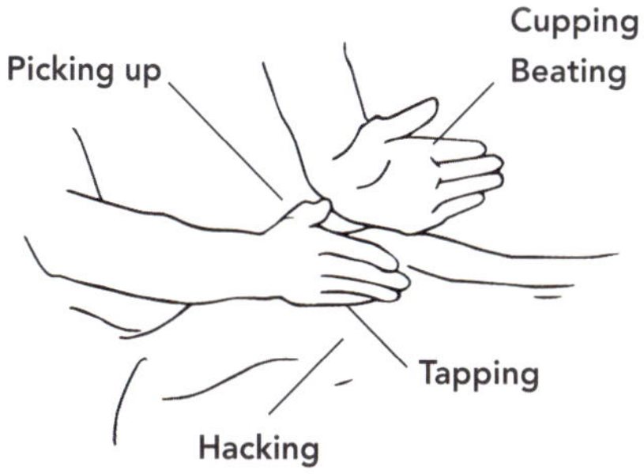

MASSAGE AS SELF-TREATMENT

Self-massage on an injury can ease pain or get to work on alleviating symptoms quickly.

While massage is generally most beneficial when given by another person, it can also be used as a safe and effective self-treatment. Practitioners often teach self-applied movements to use at home to extend the effects of a professional massage. There may also be occasions when treatment is required urgently, and such emergencies nearly always occur when helpful friends or therapists are unavailable. When the immediate need is to contain a problem or deal with acute pain, self-treatments can be extremely valuable. Aside from any physical benefit, the feeling that you are able to respond physically to a problem can be very reassuring as you await the attention of an expert therapist.

Self-massage has a variety of applications. Chronic conditions and problems associated with wear and tear often respond well to self-treatment. It is very comforting to have techniques readily available that are helpful in managing pain, refreshing, and emotionally sustaining. Respiratory distress and exhaustion are two instances where self-massage is known to be beneficial. Self-massage can also provide stress relief in the workplace. In parts of China, for example, it is a recognized part of the daily routine of many workers. Occupationally, the most obvious practitioners of self-massage are massage therapists, who enjoy its benefits through the rhythmic strokes and movements they apply to their patients.

A SOFTER OPTION

—

While self-treatment is primarily a maintenance therapy, it has a role in the prevention of problems. By including self-massage as part of a fitness program, it is possible to avoid the build-up of conditions that may precede an emergency. Learning self-massage can also be an important step toward accepting treatment from someone else. If given massage feels too pressurizing or threatening for those who are reclaiming their bodies from self-harm or another type of trauma, tentative self-massage can encourage recognition of positive sensory experiences.

This is particularly true of reservations about abdominal massage. It is understandable that we should feel physically protective of the abdomen since, considering its importance, it is a relatively unprotected area of the body. It is quite possible that, because of the ideal position of our hands relative to the abdomen and the sensitivity of its muscles, self-massage of the abdomen may initially be more effective than given massage. The realization of its benefits may then allow a deeper, therapeutic treatment to be received from an experienced massager later.

Our modern working habits mean that neck strain is common, but can be alleviated with a gentle massage.

By locating the area that is inflamed or aggravated, it is possible to target and treat muscular pain.

SELF-MASSAGE IN PRACTICE

Given reasonable privacy, self-treatment can be applied wherever and whenever possible. There are some simple movements that can be done anywhere, such as squeezing the fists while walking or wriggling toes within shoes; both of these are useful for relieving tiredness. It is also possible to apply self-help therapy at unreasonable or antisocial times, such as in the middle of the night. Self-applied neck massage, for example, can help deal with broken sleep.

Self-treatment is rarely contraindicated, even when given massage may be inadvisable. This is because you have total control over the level of pressure—an important feature of appropriate massage. There is also less chance that the treatment may irritate underlying conditions, because the feedback is immediate and the movements can be finely adjusted. Self-massage can even assist in reclaiming self-control after the incapacitation of illness or injury.

Self-massage is easy to perform anywhere, and does not need any special equipment.

NECK SELF-MASSAGE

The neck is a vulnerable structure. The heels of shoes cause the head to tilt backward and shorten the neck; most of us hear better from one ear and twist the neck around to the clearer side; violent movements may tear at the neck's delicate nerves and blood vessels. This in turn may lead to referred pain in the head and arms. Compensatory tensions build up around the bones, often heard as crackling during neck exercises. This self-massage encourages a relaxed centeredness of the neck. It is also worth trying for sinus congestion, with the addition of a hot cloth over the cheeks and a cold cloth around the feet.

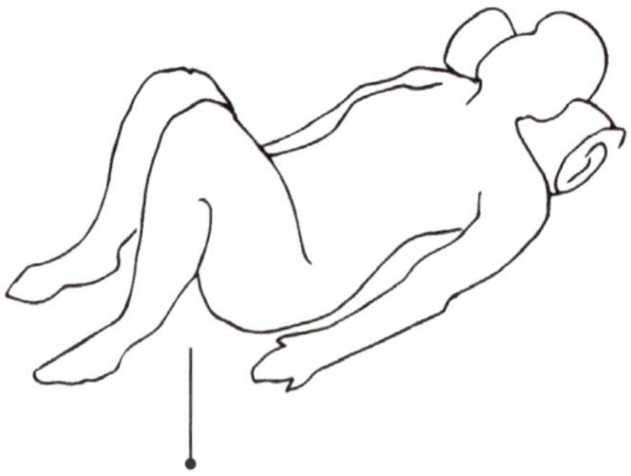

1 Roll a small towel to a diameter of roughly 3 inches (7.5 cm). Lie down and place the towel directly beneath your neck, taking up the normal neck curvature. Relax your jaw.

2 Draw your feet up closer to your hips. Without deliberately moving, your head will have rocked slightly backward.

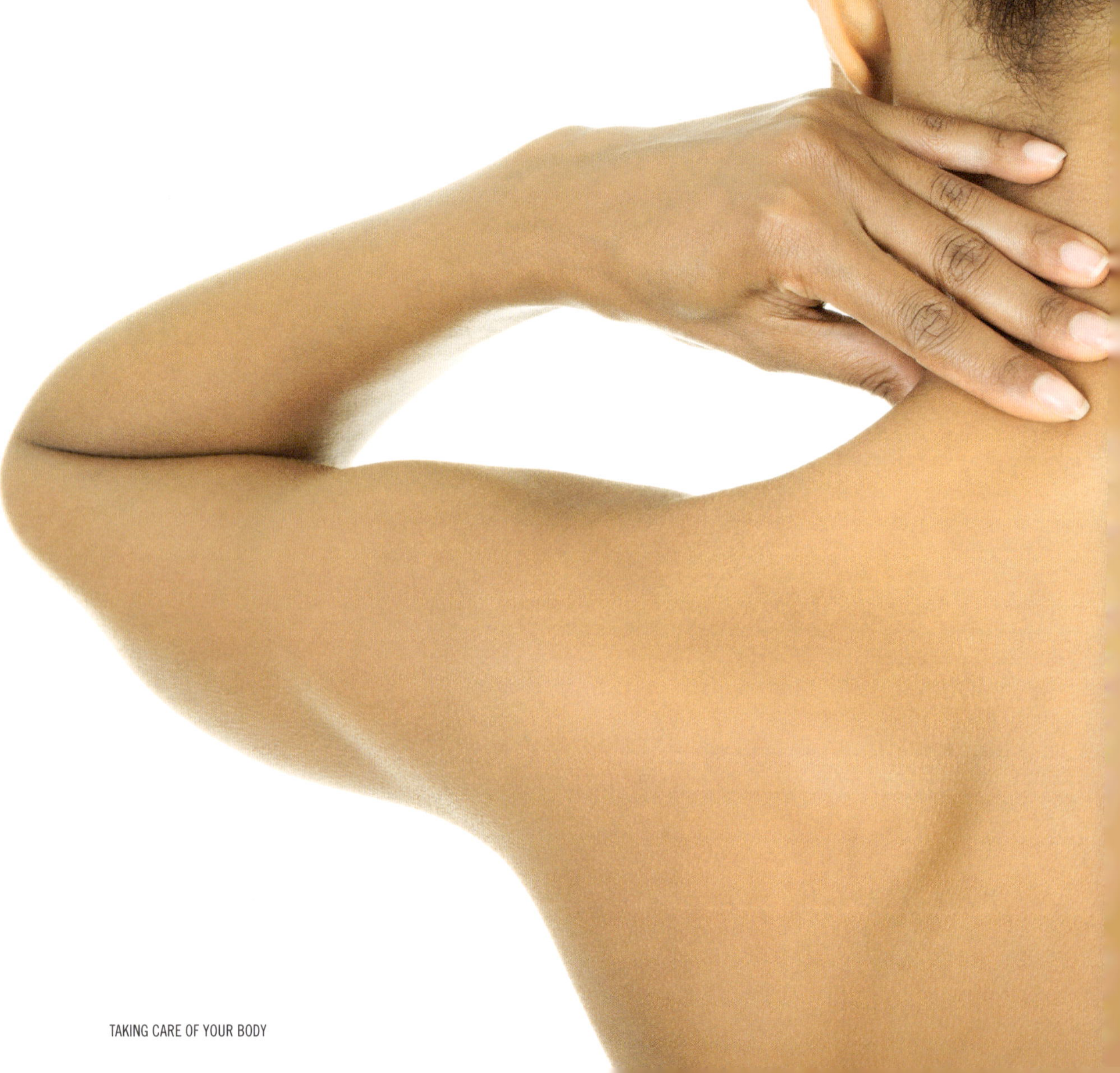

3 Keeping your head in contact with the floor, roll the head to the left and right against the towel a few times, then come to rest on the right side. Breathe deeply for a few seconds.

4 Roll again two or three times and rest on the left side, breathing as before. If one side of the neck feels tighter, roll the head back toward the stiffness for a few seconds, then slowly roll as far as possible in the opposite direction.

5 Return to center, reach up, and hold the ends of the towel. After a deep inward breath, exhale while at the same time rolling your supported head comfortably forward, chin toward your chest. Repeat once more.

6 Lower your head slowly and replace your arms by your sides. Relax completely with your mouth slightly open. To recover without strain, roll your whole body over and push yourself upright from the side.

ABDOMINAL SELF-MASSAGE

MASSAGE FOR ABDOMINAL PAIN

—

The usual cause of abdominal pain is indigestion. Excessive consumption of any food tends to overwhelm the system, and when someone is exhausted or nervously upset, food that has been eaten is hardly processed at all. The pain associated with the symptoms is connected to the slow but steady cramping of the muscles of digestion, which normally squeeze food gently through the system. Since this process is itself a massage system for food, self-massage is a very appropriate treatment.

1 Lie down with a pillow under your knees. Take a few deep breaths. Investigate your abdomen with gently probing fingers. If you feel a tightening over a painful area, begin a smooth, continuous, reinforced effleurage, clockwise, massaging with lighter pressure over the uncomfortable part.

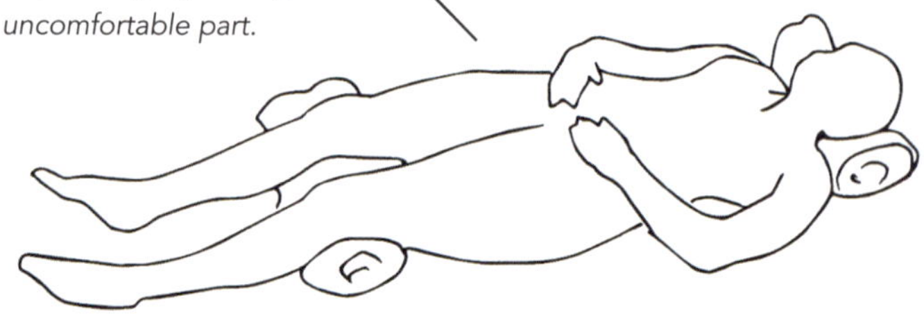

2 If this helps, use the knuckles or fingertips to give little bounces over the painful part, pressing enough to stretch the skin. You may detect some movement within the abdomen. Alternate this pressure with effleurage.

3 Where there has been focused tension in the abdomen, the remaining area will have gone slack. Do a quicker, upward effleurage with one or both hands to encourage toning.

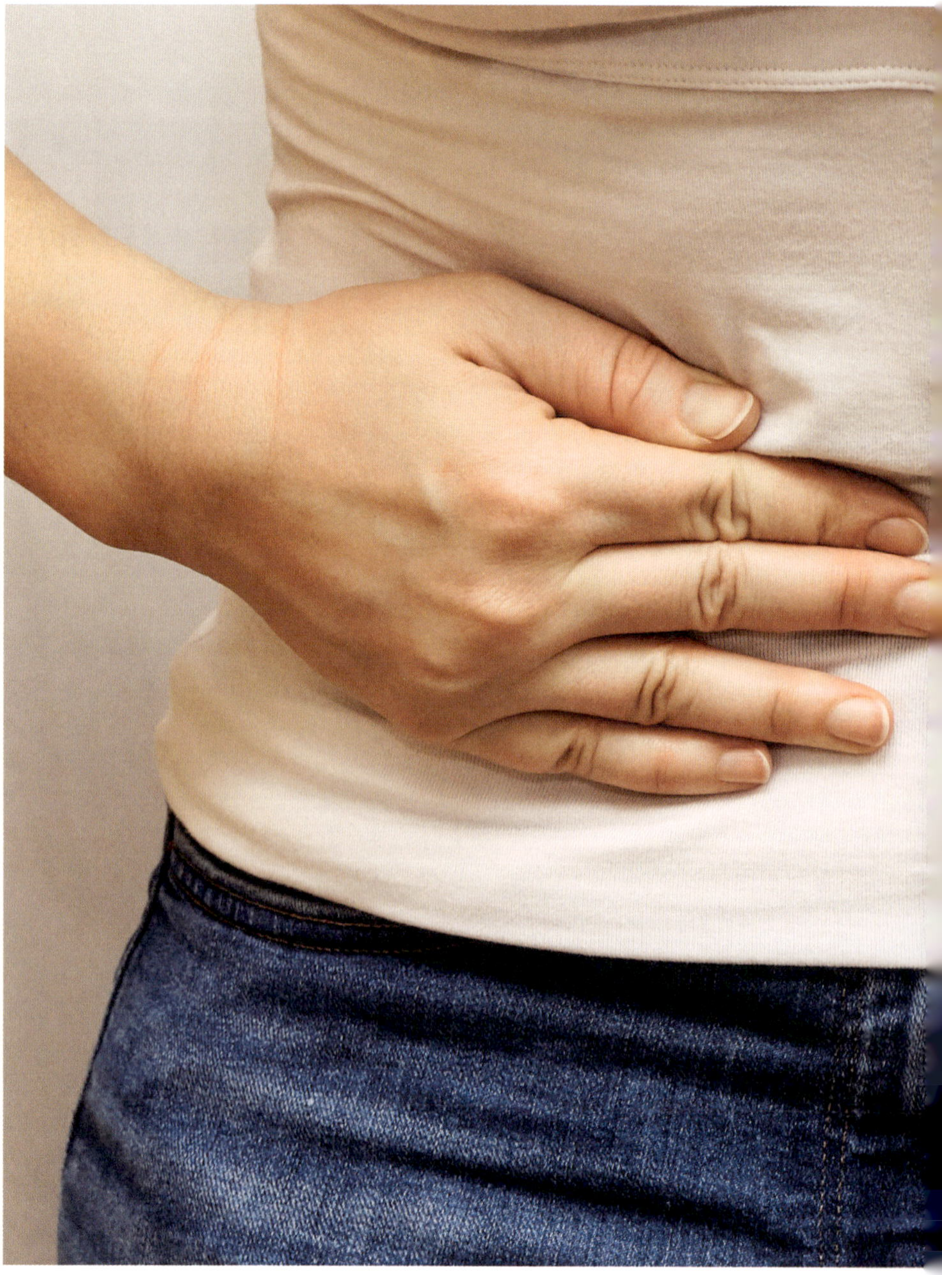

MASSAGE FOR CONSTIPATION

The internal body massage responsible for moving food through the digestive tract is called peristalsis. The action of peristalsis is continuous to the very end of the digestive process in the large intestine or colon, but action of the sympathetic nervous system can disrupt the activity of the colon and cause constipation. Self-massage can help relieve the problem by converting the sympathetic nervous activity to parasympathetic activity. The position adopted for this massage is well known outside English-speaking countries.

1 Practice squatting by holding on to a stable chair or door handle and lowering your hips between your feet. Try to keep your feet flat.

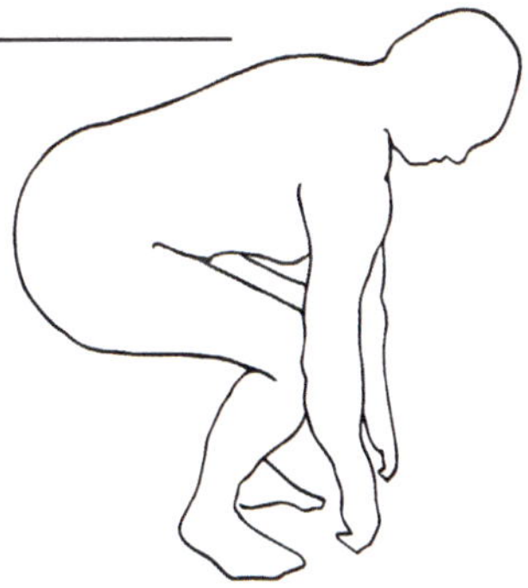

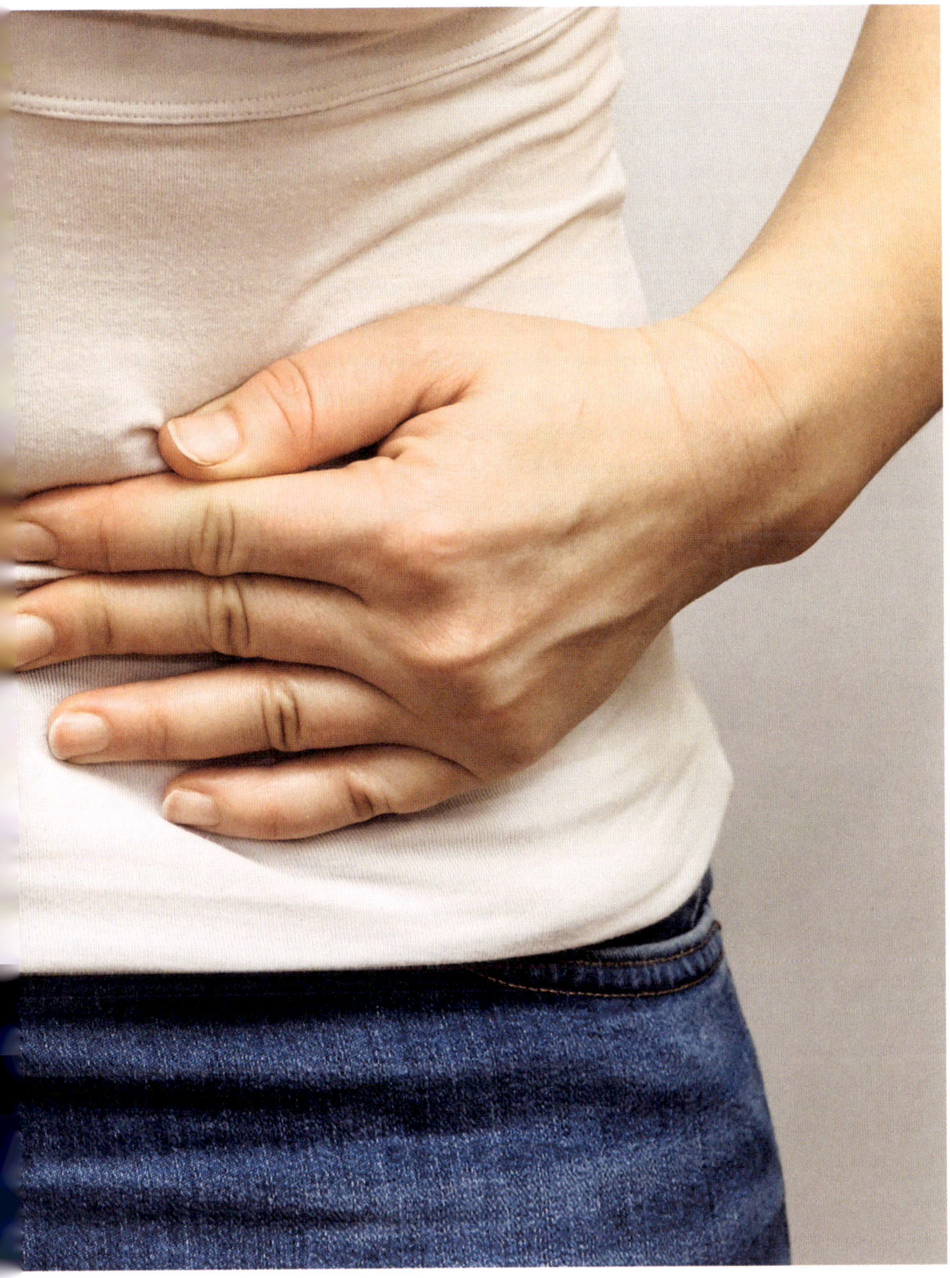

2 When you have made your hips supple, squat on the toilet seat in the same way. If you can't manage this without fear of falling, sit down and raise your feet on a box so that your knees are higher than your hips.

3 Retract and slowly release your abdomen a few times. Make a fist and press gently but deeply around the edge of the abdomen, especially on the left side. Relax and breathe deeply and avoid bearing down.

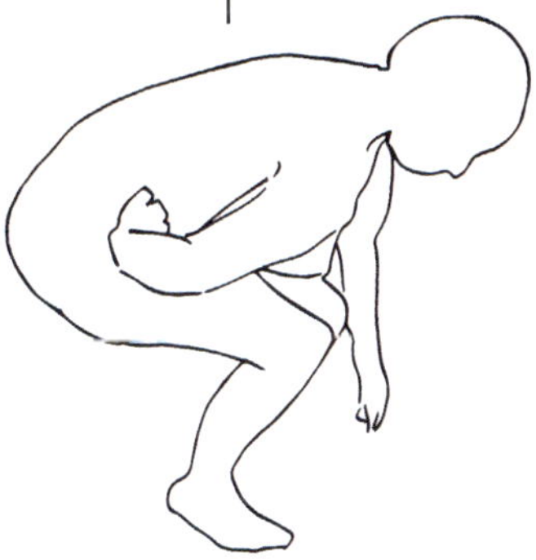

MENSTRUAL PAIN SELF-MASSAGE

The discomfort experienced during menstruation and after childbirth can be relieved by simply inverting the pelvis. This reduces pressure within the blood vessels and gives a welcome traction to the lower back. This self-treatment can be used to relieve discomfort as necessary, but may bring a long-term improvement if it is practiced throughout the cycle. Immediately after birth, begin the treatment by raising the legs at the lower end of the bed by 3 inches (7.5 cm) and gradually progress to the full sequence.

1 *Lie flat on your back and place your feet over the back of a chair. Keep your knees slightly flexed and relax your arms by your sides.*

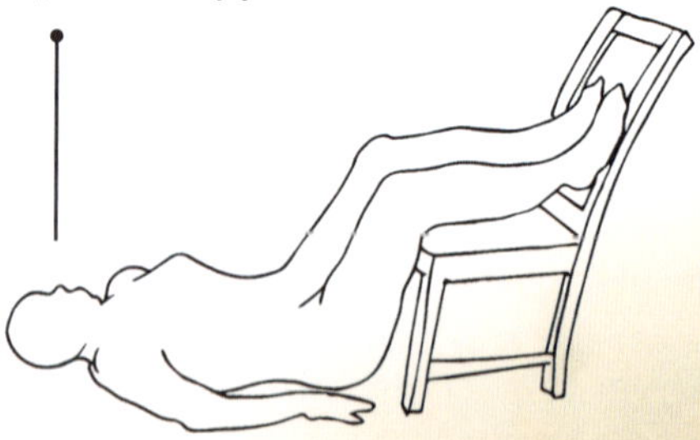

2 *Raise your pelvis and your lower back slowly by pressing down on your hands and heels. Rest and repeat, raising your pelvis as high as possible.*

3 *While your pelvis is raised, tense your legs to hold the position and gently scoop the abdomen from pelvis to rib cage, with alternate hands. Lower slowly and do a simple effleurage of your abdomen and the tops of your thighs.*

4 Place both arms over your head and breathe deeply. Draw your knees to your chest, keeping your back flat. Briefly drop your toes to the floor, then swing your legs into the air, rolling your pelvis and lower back up as high as possible.

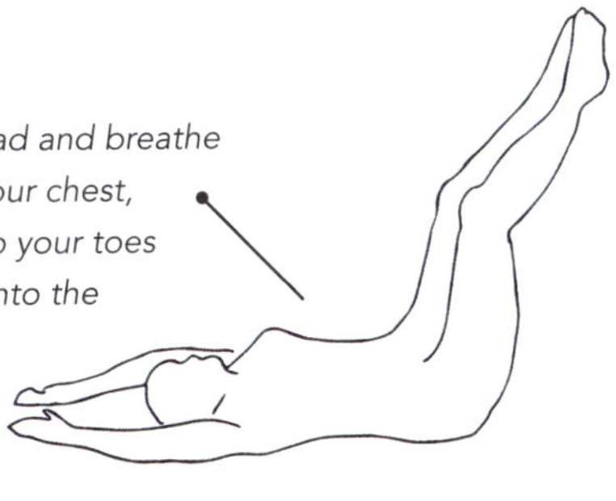

5 Initially, your legs will tend to point beyond your head, but with practice you will achieve a more upright position. The point of this section of the treatment is to encourage a gentle struggle to remain in the air, so don't overstrain. Remain in the air for as long as you feel comfortable.

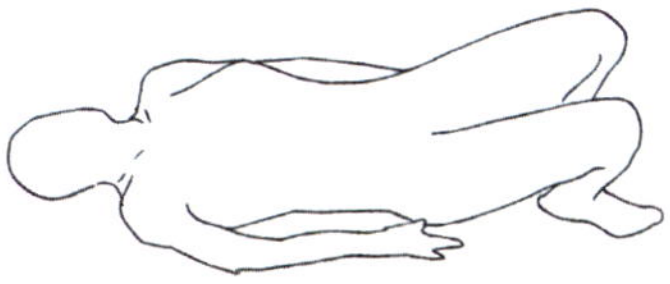

6 Recover by rolling down carefully on to your spine and pelvis. Place your feet close to your hips and rest for a while, breathing deeply.

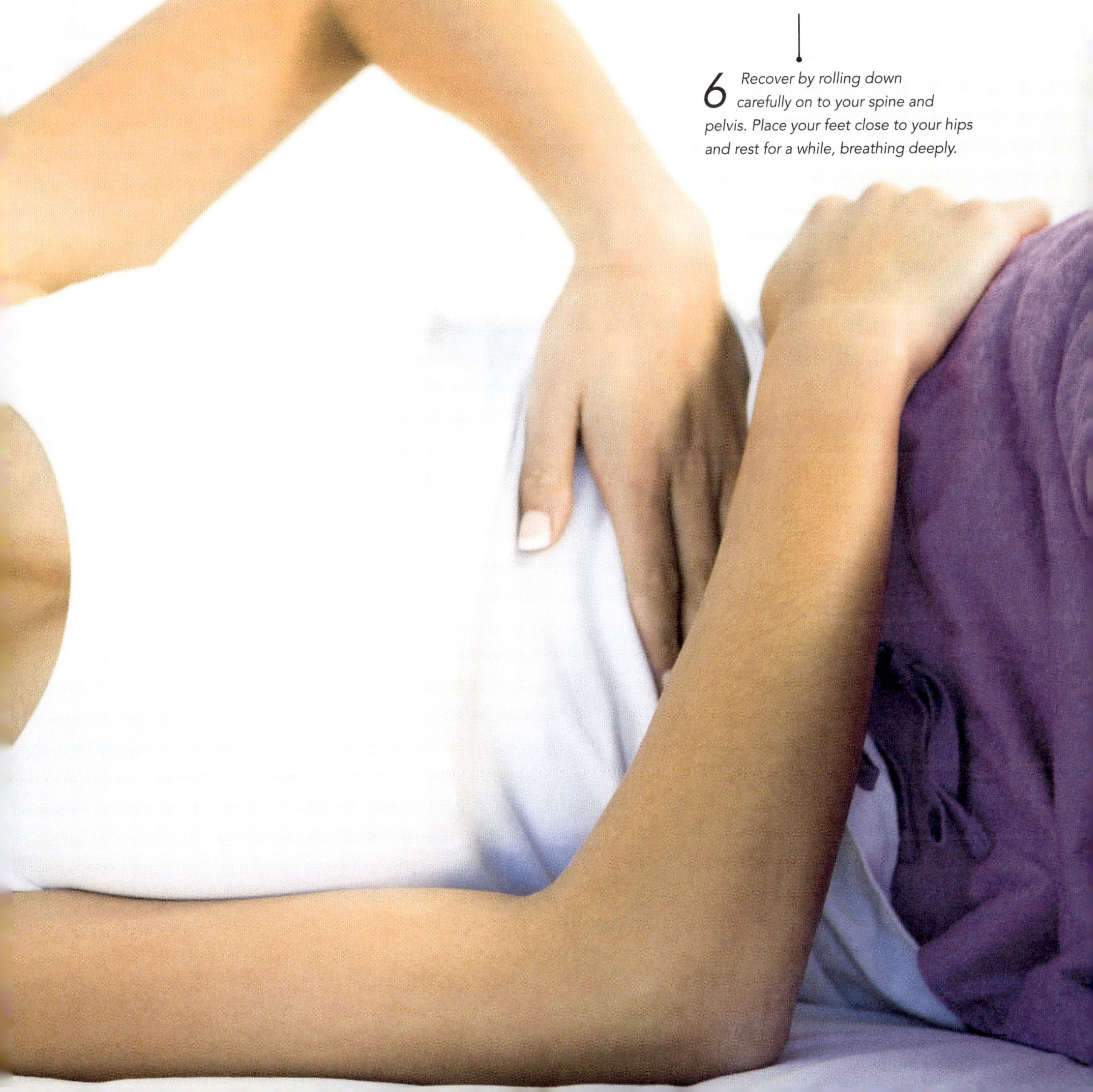

EYES AND FEET SELF-MASSAGE

MASSAGE FOR TIRED EYES

—

Although it may not seem possible to overuse the eyes, the monotonous gazing and fixed focusing associated with modern living can become strenuous. The strain affects the eyes' external muscles, causing them to sting and ache. Eyesight is also known to be affected by stressful events. This self-massage, known as palming, has both physical and mental benefits. It deeply relaxes the eyes and eases tension in the neck muscles, which is important for the circulation to the eyes. If you are becoming concerned about your eyes, do these movements twice a day and try doing a neck massage.

1 *Wearing loose-necked clothing, sit close to a table. Shrug your shoulders, rolling them forward and backward six times.*

2 *Rub your hands together vigorously for a few seconds to generate some friction and make the palms feel warm.*

3 *Place both your palms (not your fingers) over your closed eyes so that no light can leak through the gaps.*

4 *Rest your elbows on the table and take a few deep breaths. You will begin to feel your neck muscles relaxing.*

5 *Let your arms slide apart a little and slowly sink your head into your hands, taking more weight on your elbows. Spend a few moments visualizing a vivid, colorful scene from nature, with changing perspectives.*

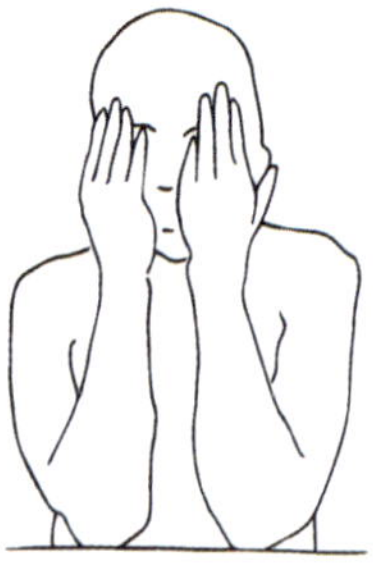

6 *After approximately one minute, let the imagery fade and breathe deeply six times. Lightly make contact with the eyeballs by extending your thumb and fingers and flattening your palms over your eye sockets.*

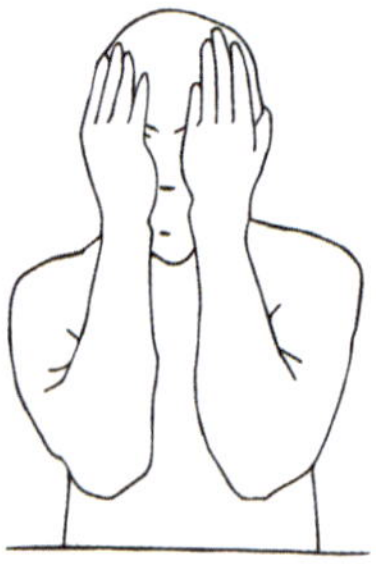

7 *Lower your hands to your cheeks and make smooth effleurages from between the eyebrows to the temples, six times.*

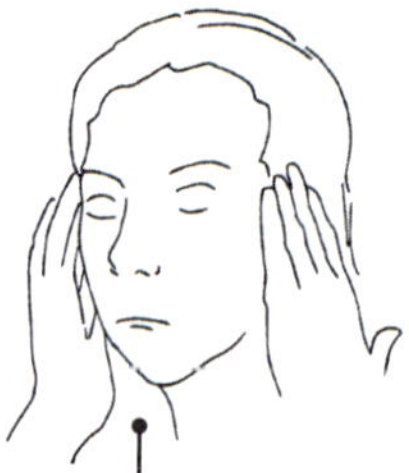

8 *Relax your arms. Widen your eyes for a moment and breathe deeply to conclude the self-massage treatment.*

Regular self-massage to the face, and especially the eye and temple area, can soothe tired eyes, as well as easing tension in the head and neck.

MASSAGE FOR FEET

—

From an early age our feet are confined by shoes in a way that would be unacceptable to any other part of the body. This may result in irreversible compensations such as fallen arches and toe deviations; freely moving feet are known to provide significant help in preventing heart disease and assisting postoperative circulation. This self-massage can be helpful with headaches, as well as foot discomfort. The water massages are useful when you are suffering from low energy or just getting back on your feet after an illness.

1 *Fill a basin with ankle-deep cool water. Take off your shoes and socks and paddle for two minutes, lifting the feet clear of the water.*

2 *Mop your feet dry. Place a ball under one instep and roll the foot backward and forward for one minute. Repeat with the other foot.*

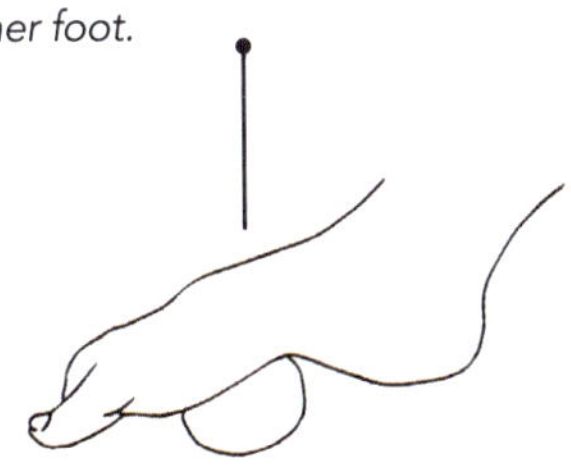

3 *Walk your feet slowly forward, one foot length at a time, using creeping movements of your toes. Then creep backward.*

4 *Press your left toes onto the floor while drawing your right toes firmly upward, keeping the foot flat. Hold for three seconds, then repeat on the other side.*

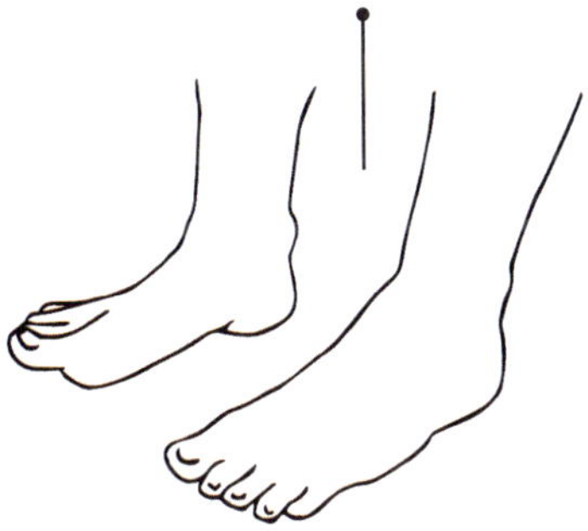

5 *While keeping the toes on the ground, bounce the heel of each foot up and down 20 times.*

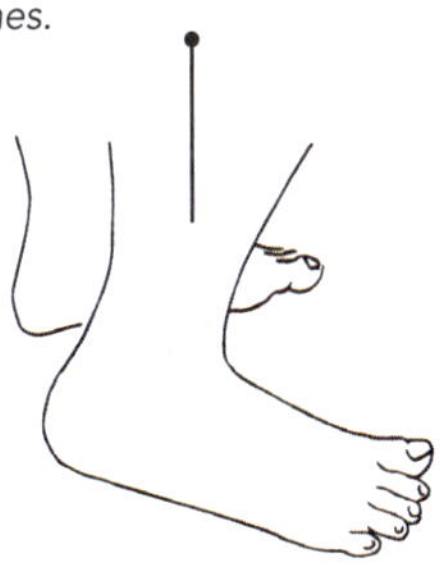

6 *Keeping the heels on the ground, bounce the rest of the foot up and down 20 times. Paddle again for one minute, wrap the feet in a towel without drying, and rest with your legs elevated.*

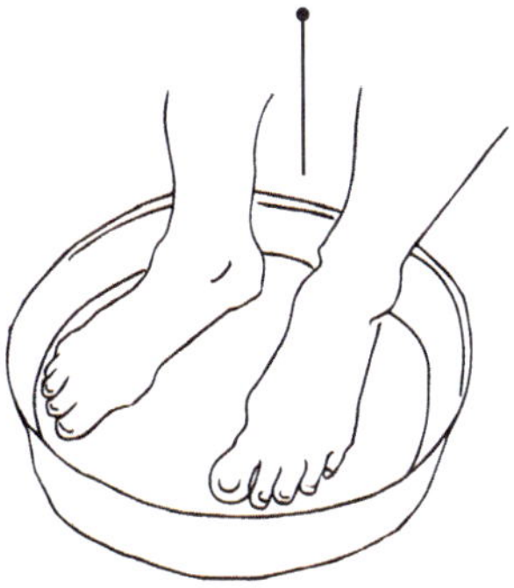

TAKING CARE OF YOUR MIND

EMOTIONAL WELLNESS

PART TWO

HEALING THE MIND

CHAPTER FIVE

EXPLORING POSSIBILITIES

The first step to physical and emotional well-being is a clear, unstressed, and positive mindset. When it comes to healing the mind, there is a wealth of possibilities to explore, from meditation and mindfulness, to art and music, talking and ecotherapy. Some therapies can easily be practiced on your own, while others are best carried out in classes or on a one-to-one basis with a professional therapist, but they all share the common goal of helping to harness the healing power of your mind. Many of the therapies can be successfully combined, offering an even better boost to your mental and physical well-being. If troubling or negative thoughts and feelings are overwhelming or affecting your ability to live your daily life, consult with your healthcare provider about next steps.

Explore different therapies to find out what suits you—alone or in a group.

PRAYER AND BREATHING

Sitting quietly to say a prayer can ease the mind. You may choose to pray for yourself or for others, or to focus on being thankful for all the good things in your life. You do not need to be religious to give thanks, and it is a technique that you can try at any time, on your own or in a group.

Controlled breathing techniques can help you relax and manage stress. Diaphragmatic breathing helps you learn how to breathe slowly and deeply from your abdomen and is particularly useful for dealing with panic attacks. Even if you think you breathe properly already, trying a specialist class can be an eye-opener into your normal breathing habits.

To get a taster of the technique, lie flat on your back, with your knees bent and your head on a pillow. Place a hand on your upper chest and the other just below your ribcage. Slowly breathe in through your nose so your stomach moves out against your lower hand. Now tighten your stomach muscles as you exhale through pursed lips. Throughout your inhalation and exhalation, the hand on your chest should remain as still as possible.

You don't have to be religious to give thanks; a prayer can ease the mind.

MEDITATION AND MINDFULNESS

Practicing meditation involves learning to clear your mind, so it becomes silent and you reach a sense of peace. Meditation helps the mind become free of random thoughts and feelings. Even a few minutes of meditation a day can be beneficial for relieving stress. Meditation is accessible to anyone and you can try it out at any time, anywhere, or join an organized group. If you find it hard to clear the chatter in your head, try focusing on the flame of a burning candle.

In contrast to meditation, where the emphasis is usually on clearing your mind, mindfulness focuses on giving full attention to the present moment. The idea is to focus on and be aware of "now," while acknowledging and accepting the feelings and thoughts in your body and mind. Doing so allows you to reconnect with sights, sounds, tastes, and smells, as well as how you feel, without judging yourself. It encourages calm and awareness, so you can learn to manage negative thoughts and the effect they have on you. Research has found that mindfulness can help manage mild depression, anxiety, and other mental health problems.

Art therapies are great for all ages, and you don't need to be a skilled artist to benefit.

BIOFEEDBACK

—

Biofeedback is a form of noninvasive therapy that helps to promote relaxation. A series of electrodes are attached to your skin and send signals to a monitor via a biofeedback device. Beeps, flashes, and images appear on the monitor, giving details on your heart rate, breathing, blood pressure, muscle activity, and temperature.

As your heart rate and other bodily functions change when you are under stress, you can see them as they happen and then get feedback to learn to control them better yourself. Other mind–body healing methods can be combined with biofeedback to help improve relaxation, such as mindfulness and deep breathing.

There are a range of talking therapies that can help you to cope with stressors in your life.

TALKING THERAPIES AND PSYCHOTHERAPY

—

There is a lot to be gained from talking to someone else and getting a different perspective on life and problems. A range of different talking therapies can be used to help you understand your behavior and feelings, and learn how to cope better with overwhelming emotions, difficult life events, and traumatic experiences.

Psychotherapy is one form of talking therapy that can be used to help you identify problems, habits, and worries, and devise ways to find solutions. As well as talking, psychotherapy sometimes combines the use of art, music, or drama, too, all with the help of a professional therapist.

ART AND MUSIC THERAPIES

—

Art, music, dance, and drama therapies are often recommended or provided by psychotherapists and counselors. It can sometimes be hard to express your feelings, especially if you are confused about them yourself, so these therapies allow you to go beyond words to express how you feel and what you are going through.

One of the benefits of these therapies is that you do not need any prior experience or artistic skills. The key aim is to be guided to create something, such as a play, dance routine, piece of music, or painting, to express yourself in a way you feel comfortable with. Arts therapies can be physically relaxing and open up another outlet for mind–body healing.

ECOTHERAPY

—

Ecotherapy is a relatively new term in treatment programs, but the idea behind it is by no means new. Ecotherapy means using outdoor activities involving nature to help heal your mind and boost your mental and physical well-being. Ecotherapy can include activities like gardening, taking exercise outside, getting involved with a conservation project, helping with animals on a farm or refuge, or cycling through woodland. Research into ecotherapy shows that it can help with mild to moderate depression, and reduce anger and low self-esteem. It also offers the chance to connect with nature, other people, and improve your mood.

Ecotherapy offers the chance to connect with nature and improve your mood.

Here are some ideas and possibilities to try, from journaling and music to setting up your own sacred space.

JOURNALING

—

Putting pen to paper and journaling your thoughts, emotions, and memories can be a great way to harness your creativity and help improve your emotional well-being. Journaling gives you the opportunity to focus on your feelings in a different way and it can be an easier approach to expressing thoughts than talking about them in person. Studies have shown that journaling can help reduce stress, relieve anxiety, and ease depression.

The act of writing in a journal can unlock your more creative side and help you become more intuitive and confident in expressing yourself. It offers a therapeutic way to help you examine, understand, and identify particular habits and patterns of behavior that you may not be consciously aware of, to devise ways in which you could solve problems and issues, and examine how you approach situations.

Journaling can also give you the opportunity to work on setting and achieving personal goals. Writing down your aims and making plans on paper gives you a structure to work toward and can make goal-setting clearer and more achievable. The good thing about journaling is that there's no right or wrong way to go about it. If you're not sure how to start, and you feel anxious when faced with a blank page, try one of these strategies:

• Start small—you don't have to write much; try just writing a sentence per day, or journaling for five minutes.
• Be specific—if you're not sure what to write, choose a focus. For example, you could try gratitude journaling, where you write what you're grateful for each day, or focus on using your journal first thing in the morning to write your aims for the day.
• Write regularly—get into the habit of writing in your journal often, however long or short a time you spend on it.
• Kick-start your journaling—look out for journals that are designed with writing prompts; they can help you get started in a more structured way and take the stress out of knowing where and how to begin.
• Try a bullet journal—if you're overwhelmed by racing thoughts and ideas, try this type of journal instead. Bullet journaling focuses on being mindful of your plans and aims and can help you track habits in a coherent, at-a-glance manner.

MUSIC

—

The link between music and emotional well-being is well documented. Research has shown that listening to music can release dopamine, the feel-good chemical, into your brain, and levels increase even more when people listen to music they enjoy. If you feel in need of a mind detox, play your favorite music at home or in the car. Listening on headphones is a practical option when you're out and about, commuting to work, or when you're taking a lunch break. Uplifting music can have a positive effect and help you feel energized and uplifted, while listening to calming music before going to bed can be relaxing. Choose the music most suited to your mood and needs.

Making music is also beneficial, from playing instruments to singing. In fact, there's evidence that singing in a choir can be a great source of stress relief. There are lots of choirs and community groups that let you sing for pleasure, rather than performance, so why not find one near you?

Journaling is a great way to understand your life in a private way.

SACRED SPACE

—

Create your own sacred space at home, so you can retreat to an oasis of calm when you need to. You don't necessarily need a complete room to dedicate to this, it can just be a section of it—a cozy corner or a small nook. You could use your sacred space to meditate, practice mindfulness, or simply have it as somewhere that you can sit and take a few moments to quietly relax and unwind when you need to.

Ideally, your sacred space should be free of distractions, clutter, and technology. Aim to have things in your sacred space that make you feel good—houseplants you love, scents and aromas you enjoy, or inspirational quotes and artwork. If you're religious, you could include a religious icon or figurine of a deity, or you might like to have a few special crystals.

Native Americans use dry white sage to purify and clear a space of negative energy, and you could try the same as you prepare your space. You'll need a special stick of white sage—this is not the same as the commonly grown garden herb sage—which can be purchased from health or holistic stores. Light the stick of sage, extinguish the flame and let it gently smoke and waft around your space.

Consider creating a sacred space at home as an oasis of calm. This can be a cozy corner or a whole room. For some people, this includes personal altar of things that bring you joy.

Creativity is a popular form of self-care for your mind and there is a vast array of different ways in which you can be creative. While some methods do require a few existing skills or knowledge, there are others that are accessible for anyone to have a go at.

COLORING

—

There used to be a time when coloring in was viewed as purely a childhood activity, but it's become much more mainstream and acceptable for adults to color, too. In fact, the world of coloring books for adults has become big business.

Sitting down with your pens and pencils and indulging in a spot of coloring in can be highly therapeutic. It's a chance to unleash your creativity, explore colors, try your hand at art, and just enjoy yourself.

It's not just hearsay—one research study has found that coloring can indeed be a therapeutic form of emotional self-care. This is because it is a mindful activity and can soothe a stressed mind, helping ease anxieties and worries.

There are lots of adult coloring books available these days, as well as digital downloads that you buy online and print off yourself. If you need inspiration, take a look on YouTube, where colorists frequently share videos and record color-a-longs.

ZENTANGLE

—

Another popular way of exploring your creativity and soothing your mind is to try Zentangle.

Zentangle is a form of art, often produced in black pen on white paper, that involves drawing structured patterns or tangles. There's a whole series of different patterns to learn and they're commonly drawn on small square pieces of paper, called tiles, as well as drawn together to form larger designs.

The Zentangle patterns are all easy to learn and are made up of simple combinations of hand-drawn lines, curves, and dots. You don't need to be good at drawing or have expensive equipment to have a go, so it's something creative that's very accessible.

Focusing on drawing in this way can be rather like a mindfulness exercise. As you concentrate on what you're drawing, anxieties and worries are pushed to the back of your mind. Many people find it relaxing and it's also really rewarding to see what you have created.

MIXED-MEDIA ART JOURNAL

—

Exploring mixed-media art ideas is another option for unleashing your creativity in a fun and unstructured way. A mixed-media art journal provides you with a place to explore your creativity and, like written journaling, it can be a great way of unloading and expressing yourself.

One of the benefits of a mixed-media art journal is that there are no rules or set methods to use—it's down to you what you'd like to create. Popular methods include painting (watercolors or acrylic), drawing, using pastels, creating textured prints and surfaces, making patterns, or collaging with materials such as paper, magazines, or ephemera.

If you're not sure where to start, browse the Internet for ideas or look up mixed-media art videos online. There are tutorials you can follow, or you can just play with art materials and see what you create.

HOBBIES

—

Hobbies are a great form of self-care, as they're all about doing things you love and enjoy. It's good to incorporate plenty of time for yourself into your life and the things you take pleasure in, and it will give you the opportunity to help your emotional wellness at the same time.

When you indulge in hobbies you typically immerse yourself in focusing on the activity in hand, be it reading, sewing, crochet, or fossil hunting. It's natural to find yourself losing track of time, being absorbed in the rhythm of the craft and temporarily switching off from the stress and worry of everyday life.

If you had an old hobby that you used to enjoy in the past, such as horse riding or cycling, but haven't done it for ages, have a go at it again. Some skills are never lost and it may simply be a case of rekindling your love for the activity.

Or set yourself the challenge of discovering a new hobby. There's nothing to be lost from trying out new activities and you may find something that really resonates with you. Look out for local activity classes or taster sessions, where you can go along and try several different options. Of course, don't spend loads of money on equipment or supplies before you're sure it's definitely for you.

Alternatively, look online for activity videos and see if you can find something that appeals to you. A new skill might be just what you need to boost your self-care!

Coloring in can be a wonderfully therapeutic and mindful activity.

Starting a new hobby can be something you can share with all the family.

STARTING TO MEDITATE

We all long to be happy and free from the struggles and conflicts that scar our lives. We search for ways to find a heart of wisdom and a mind of calm. We yearn to be a conscious participant in creating a world for ourselves and others that is imbued with peace and understanding. Throughout our lives we do all that we can to bring an end to feelings of alienation, estrangement, and suffering, and to forge relationships of intimacy and warmth. Meditation is intended to transform us, to show us the way to free ourselves from the grip of fear, division, and confusion. The practice of meditation illuminates our life, inwardly and outwardly, showing us the path to freedom and wakefulness.

Meditation is a path that teaches us to be awake in each moment of our lives.

A HEALING PATH

Meditation is not a means of fleeing from life, nor is it a quick-fix solution to all of the difficulties and challenges we may meet. But it is a path that teaches us to be increasingly present, honest, and awake in each moment of our lives. It is a direct means of healing the estrangement and division that too often separate us from others and ourselves.

Depth of wisdom, compassion, and peace are not sought in transcendent experience, nor projected into the future, but are nurtured within this heart, mind, body, and life in the present.

For thousands of years people have retreated to the solitude and stillness of deserts, mountain tops, and monasteries seeking an inner renewal, depth, and authenticity. But the great teachers of the past and present who truly inspire our own journeys do so not solely because of some dramatic spiritual breakthrough experienced in solitude, but through their commitment and capacity to embody their wisdom and depth of compassion in every area of their lives.

Initially, when we face the struggles, challenges, and conflicts that are part of living, we react with the belief that they are obstacles to be overcome or subdued. When we meet the swirls of confusion that can cloud our own minds or the emotional storms that shatter our hearts, we are prone to believe that they are wrong or a personal imperfection. But through our own experience in meeting the difficult and challenging, we come to understand that resistance, blame, judgment, or suppression do little to bring about healing and the end of sorrow. A path of meditation, directed towards the release of our hearts and minds, encourages us to turn our attention directly towards the places of challenge and difficulty we are most prone to flee from or abandon. This is where the seeds of peace and understanding plant their roots.

Meditation encourages us to step out of the pathways of blame, judgment, and rejection, and ask ourselves where healing begins in this moment. The end of sorrow, we begin to understand, does not rely upon eradicating everything unpleasant or challenging in our lives—that is an impossible task. The end of sorrow and struggle is born of our capacity to make peace with all things and to hold the events of our life in a heart of loving kindness and understanding.

Meditation is a path of awakening, an inner journey of direct experience. It has a direction and clear sense of aspiration—serenity, balance, open-heartedness, compassion, and deep inner wisdom all lie at the heart of meditative teachings and paths. Equally, meditation is a path of embodiment, teaching us to approach all of the events, people, circumstances, and moments in our lives with profound integrity, loving kindness, and equanimity. Meditation is not a journey of self-improvement—it is dedicated to the relief of anguish and struggle wherever they appear. Meditation is greater and more vast than just a technique or formula for living—it is the cultivation of a heart of wisdom and mind of calm.

MOMENTS OF PEACE

—

Genuine meditation is no stranger to any of us. Long before we undertake a formal meditation practice we have all encountered glimpses of profound peace, compassion, and serenity, moments of deep inner stillness, times of genuine connectedness with nature, other people, and ourselves. There have been times when the busyness of our minds has calmed and we have found ourselves listening, seeing, and responding with a natural sensitivity and patient intimacy. We have all met moments when our hearts have opened and we have found ourselves able to receive the sorrow and distress of someone we care for, or even a person we don't know, without fear and with a natural compassion. We have all experienced times when we have felt truly at ease within our own bodies, minds, and lives.

Too often these moments of depth and stillness feel like random occurrences. We are inspired and touched by them and yet they feel so fleeting and are too often inaccessible to us. Meditation practice teaches a way of being present and awake at all times, to ourselves and to the world, a way of resting in inner stillness, receptivity, and understanding.

Meditation is a path of cultivation and a discipline born of dedication to peace and depth. Patient intimacy lies at its heart. It is also a path of the present. None of us can alter or recover a past that has already gone by; the future is yet to come and we cannot guarantee how it will unfold. The moment that we are in is the only moment that can be lived fully and in which we can find transformation. Meditation encourages us to turn directly towards our lives and this moment. They are the grist for awakening. It is not a quest to find a perfect moment, but a way of cultivating balance, sensitivity, and clarity within all the joys and sorrows of our lives. We come to understand that the source of genuine happiness, joy, and peace lies within our own hearts and minds, and not within the changing events of our life. Meditation is not a denial of past or future, but an understanding that we are writing the history of all the future moments in our lives through the way in which we attend to and experience the moment we are in.

Patience and dedication are key to deepening meditation.

Too often we live in a fog of confusion and busyness, governed by impulse, habit, and reactivity. We find ourselves frantically trying to do more and more each day, torn between the multiplicity of demands that compete for our attention. Our lives can be filled with lost moments—interactions, conversations, sounds, sights, and feelings that we have neglected to attend to. Leaning into the future or floundering in thoughts of the past, we lose the richness and simplicity available to us in the present. Meditation practice is a direct way of reclaiming those lost moments—the life we can miss through neglect, inattention, and busyness.

Our meditation practice begins right where we are, in the life we are living, with our willingness to take the first steps of being attentive and present. There are a vast variety of spiritual paths, lineages, and traditions available to us. They vary in their styles, yet they share an emphasis on integrity, commitment, serenity, and wisdom. All meditative paths serve to nourish our hearts and minds, inviting us to explore the possibility of great depth, authenticity, and compassion in our lives. We nurture, through meditation practice, a climate of heart, an inner culture that is receptive to deep understanding and transformation. We learn to shed the layers of confusion and agitation that too easily cloud our capacity to live with great sensitivity.

THE ART OF MEDITATION

—

Meditation is an art, and like any other art it asks for both dedication and discipline. At the heart of every meditative path is a dedication to peace, compassion, authenticity, and freedom. Genuine discipline is not a tyrannical code governing our actions and life, but is born of our dedication to all that is truly liberating and healing. The styles, practices, and techniques of meditation are the container or discipline in which we bring to fulfillment the peace and freedom we deeply treasure.

There are two dimensions to meditation: one is the form and the other is the spirit. They are interwoven and indivisible. Meditation is much more than becoming proficient in a particular technique. The techniques of practice are ways to articulate and cultivate the spirit of awakening. It is equally true to say that the paths and the goals of meditation cannot be separated. If we aspire to peace, understanding, sensitivity, and compassion, then we are also asked to practice meditation in their spirit. If our meditation practice is to lead to an open heart, clear mind, and greater loving kindness in every area of our lives, then it asks us to cultivate those qualities in every step on our path. Patience and dedication are key elements in the deepening of meditation.

CREATING A MEDITATIVE SETTING

Initially as you begin to practice developing attention it is worthwhile to create an environment around you that is supportive. A corner of your bedroom or any space in your home that is simple and quiet will serve. Find a chair or cushion that you can return to and as far as possible create in that space a meditative environment. Dedicate a period of time each day to spend in formal meditation. There is no prescribed right amount of time; however long you are able to give to your meditation practice is worthwhile. Don't expect that every time you sit down to meditate you are going to have amazing breakthroughs, peak experiences, or moments of great rapture.

What you meet in your meditation is the mind and heart you bring to it. Sometimes you will be sitting with a mind of chaos, filled with the plans or memories of your day. What is valuable is making the effort to be aware of that mind, however it is. The moments of stillness you commit to each day are always worthy moments. They are times of cultivating calm attention, awareness, and sensitivity that will begin to impact upon every area of your life. When you sit down to meditate, ensure that you turn off your telephone, radio, and television. Allow yourself to unhook for a time and care for the quality of your own heart and mind. Increasingly we feel compelled to be perpetually available and engaged. Times of meditation are times to be engaged with stillness, appointments we make with ourselves. It is often helpful to dedicate a period of time at the beginning and the end of the day to be wholeheartedly committed to cultivating our meditation practice. The effects of these times of stillness and focus will increasingly begin to pervade all of our day.

We will come to see that calm attention, peace, sensitivity, and open-heartedness are not random experiences or accidents we occasionally encounter in life. They live within our own hearts and minds, born of awareness and wise attention.There is no right posture to meditate in—you can use a chair, bench, or cushion—but find a posture that is upright and alert. In your meditation posture you are embodying the qualities of heart and mind you are seeking to develop.

Within that uprightness, also find a deep sense of ease and relaxation. Battling with bodily discomfort in meditation is not conducive to finding the well-being and sensitivity we are seeking to nurture. If your body is particularly exhausted or distressed, it is even fine to lie down to meditate, although in this posture you may need to make a resolved commitment to be awake and present. The posture to seek is one that allows you to be at home and at ease within your body.

Approach your meditation times as moments of dedication. Commit yourself to being as fully present as it is possible for you to be. As you begin to practice, clarify your sense of intention. Take a few moments to reflect upon why you are engaging in this meditation, what this time is dedicated to.

The meditation is in the service of peace, calm, and sensitivity. Dedicate yourself to being attentive, clear, and focused.

Let go of all preoccupations with the past and future. This is not a time for planning and rehearsing the future, nor for recycling thoughts about the past. Beginning your meditation with a clear sense of intention is an encouragement to establish yourself in the present. Meditation is a time of caring for your well-being and cultivating serenity and depth.

Meditation can introduce us to moments of great joy and opening. It will also make us increasingly aware of the places where we react most habitually and close down most persistently. Through sustained and dedicated practice we learn to embrace the difficult and the delightful, the joyful and the sorrowful with the same welcome, interest, and inner balance. In essence, meditation teaches us to be awake and present in the midst of all things. This is the home of genuine understanding and depth.

Create a space for meditation where you can relax and feel comfortable.

CULTIVATING ATTENTION

Attention is the key that opens the door to inner peace and awareness. Learning to bring a loving and mindful attention to all the moments of our lives, we find ease everywhere. Without attention we live only on the surface of life. The song of a bird, the beauty of a sunset, the cries of someone who needs us are lost to us. It is only when we are attentive that we are able to explore our inner landscape and learn the lessons we are asked if we are to live with authenticity and freedom. To be touched by anything in the world, to love and to live fully, we need to be present and awake. If we are to live with compassion, balance, and generosity, we need to cultivate the art of attentiveness.

Wise attention is a means of simplifying our inner landscape. Observing our own minds, we see that they seem to be filled with a cascade of thoughts, obsessions, memories, and preoccupations. We can feel overwhelmed by the fragmented thoughts and images that saturate our consciousness, a casualty of the busyness of our own minds.

Attention teaches us to calm this busyness and agitation. Learning to be attentive, one moment at a time, is learning to rest in a deep sense of inner ease. The art of clear, focused attentiveness is finding calmness in the midst of agitation, serenity in the midst of chaos, simplicity in the midst of complexity. We do not need to flee the world to discover this profound inner calm; we do need to learn how to release ourselves from fragmentation and distractedness.

Interest is the primary building block of wise attention. Wherever there is interest in our lives, energy and attention naturally follow. Wise attention is founded upon our interest in being free of confusion and fragmentation. It grows in the heartfelt interest we bring to understanding what it means to live a life of peace, calmness, and understanding.

Attention is the common thread that runs through every meditative discipline and art. It enables us to cut through the habits of entanglement and speculative thought and the reactions that trigger agitation. Through calm and gentle attention we learn to cultivate the clarity and sensitivity that allow understanding and stillness to deepen. Wise attention is a gesture of kindness to ourselves, freeing us from the chaos and abrasiveness of a mind that is too easily scattered and divided. Attention is cultivated through learning to focus upon one object, one moment at a time. Learning to attend wholeheartedly to that object, we illuminate it, forming a bond of connection. It becomes our anchor in the present moment. Whenever our attention drifts away, we learn to come back, renewing our connection with that anchor.

Cultivating attention requires great patience, for we are sometimes swimming against the habits of a lifetime of being distracted and entangled. Yet attention is not born of willpower or control, but a calm commitment to being present and awake. In the practice of developing attention we need to bring a deep sense of ease and relaxation, yet also to balance that ease with a committed perseverance and dedication. It is important that meditation does not become yet another task to add to a list of things we must do. It should be approached as a time of deep ease, a time of reconnecting with our capacity to rest with calmness and wakefulness in all the moments of our lives. The attention we develop in meditation practice will begin to make an impact on our lives. As our inner busyness begins to calm, we will be more aware of the nature of our minds and bodies. We will find that we are less prone to being governed by impulse and reactivity. Our capacity to be more present with all things will be enhanced and we will discover a refuge of serenity and balance within our own hearts and minds.

Attention is the art of cultivating happiness and well-being. We do not need to postpone that ease to a time in our lives when there are fewer demands upon our attention. We can discover it now—in the midst of a life of activity, a mind that has thoughts and a world that is ceaselessly bombarding us with a multiplicity of impressions and demands.

Attention awakens us—to ourselves and to everything that comes into our world. There are a variety of ways of learning to develop attention and calm in our lives. Spending some time on a daily basis in formal meditation cultivating a focused and single-pointed attention will make a significant impact upon the quality of our lives. Learning to bring that wise attention to all the contacts and interactions we engage in daily will deepen and enhance our capacity to live with spaciousness and calm. Attention in itself is not difficult; it is remembering to be attentive that is challenging. But in discovering that wise attention is the source of deep inner happiness and well-being, our dedication to its cultivation will grow.

GUIDED MEDITATION

THE CONCENTRATED MIND

• Find a posture for your body that is as balanced and relaxed as possible. Gently close your eyes. Take a few moments just to be aware of your body, bringing your attention to all the places where your body makes contact with the ground, cushion, or chair. Just be aware of the sensations at those points of contact—warmth, pressure…Bring your attention to your breath just at the point where it enters and leaves your body. Focus your attention calmly yet fully on the area of your upper lip and nostrils.

• As your breath enters your body, just be aware of the sensations that arise—the coolness of your breath, tingling, whatever sensations appear in the area of your upper lip and nostrils. Sustain your attention in that area, with whatever sensations are present, until you sense the touch of the out-breath at your upper lip and nostrils as your breath leaves your body. Be aware of the warmth of your out-breath as it leaves your body.

• Let your attention rest clearly and gently in the area of your upper lip and nostrils. You might find that your breath becomes almost imperceptible. If this occurs, let whatever sensations are present at your upper lip and nostrils be the focus of your attention. Don't try to make your breathing fuller or deeper, just let the sensations of the breath entering and leaving be the point where your attention rests.

• You may be aware of thoughts arising, but notice that few of them linger or have the power to draw your attention away from your selected focus.

• Bodily sensations may also arise, but as your concentration deepens you may notice a perceptible change in your sense of your body. A very deep sense of bodily ease and relaxation may appear as your concentration becomes more established. You may notice that the boundaries of your body begin to blur and the sense of solidity in your body softens. This is fine. Just continue to keep your attention focused on the area of your upper lip and nostrils. If there are moments when your attention is drawn to a thought or bodily sensation, just notice this and gently return to focus once more on the area of your upper lip and nostrils.

• As you focus on this area, notice how the sensations change, at times becoming very subtle. Sense the ease and simplicity that come with deepening attention. Let yourself rest within that ease. As your concentration deepens further, notice the deeper calmness and spaciousness that begin to pervade your body and mind. Rest with ease within that calmness, allowing it to deepen from moment to moment. When you are ready, open your eyes and come out of the posture.

Mindfulness isn't difficult;
we just need to remember to do it.

Sharon Salzberg

MINDFULNESS OF BREATHING

When you sit down to meditate there are times when you find yourself sitting with a mind that is overfull with thought, distraction, and busyness. Your first reaction to this may be to feel that this is the wrong time for you to meditate. In reality, the times of agitation in our lives are the times that most urgently invite us to cultivate calm and simplicity. Finding it difficult to be with ourselves and to explore our inner landscape is a cue that signals the immediate need to find a sanctuary of inner calm.

It is helpful to cease thinking of agitation or turmoil as an insurmountable obstacle to mediation and to developing serenity. The obstacle lies not in the agitation and chaos, but more often in our resistance to these states.

Accepting that our minds and hearts are chaotic, confused, and overfull is the first step in developing calm. Dismissal and judgment only add a further layer of tension to the turmoil already present. Acceptance is the beginning of the transformation we seek. The next step is to approach that chaos with a calm and gentle attentiveness.

It is just one moment at a time we are asked to care for and make peace with. Discovering our capacity to nurture even a little serenity and attention in the midst of chaos will deeply enhance our confidence in ourselves and rescue us from foundering in agitation.

Finding attention and serenity in the midst of chaos is an important part of self-care.

GUIDED MEDITATION

RISING AND FALLING

- Take a few moments to relax into an upright and alert posture.
- Let your eyes close gently and your whole body soften and relax.
- For a few moments take some slightly fuller breaths, paying particular attention to your outgoing breath and releasing it fully.
- Let your breathing relax and find its own natural rhythm.
- Bring your attention to rest in your abdomen, noticing how your abdomen responds to each inhalation and each exhalation.
- Sense the rising and falling of your abdomen with each breath.
- With each movement of your abdomen make a quiet mental note to mark what is happening.
- Note "rising" with the in-breath and "falling" with the out-breath.
- Ensure that the mental noting is directly linked to what is actually occurring in your abdomen.
- Let your attention rest within the noting and the movement in your body simultaneously—rising, falling, rising, falling.
- Sometimes you may find it helpful to place your hands gently over your abdomen as you are practicing. This will enable you to feel more fully connected with the movement of rising and falling as it happens moment to moment.
- At times your attention will move away, into past, future, images, sensations. As far as possible just notice those departures and note where your attention has gone with simplicity and calmness.
- Return your attention to your abdomen, once more noticing the rising and falling in your abdomen with each breath.
- Sense your breathing calming and focusing your attention. Sense yourself letting go of busyness and agitation, moment to moment.
- When you are ready, open your eyes and come out of the posture.

GUIDED MEDITATION

MINDFULNESS OF BREATHING

- Find a posture that is as relaxed and comfortable as possible.
- Gently close your eyes. From the top of your head to the tips of your toes, gently and systematically move your attention down through the whole of your body. As you do so, consciously relax any part of your body that is registering tension or agitation. Soften any knots of tightness that you become aware of. Pay particular attention to your face, shoulders, and hands, allowing them to soften and relax.
- Let your hands rest on your legs or rest together lightly. Focus your attention for a few moments on the palms of your hands, being aware of whatever sensations are present. Let your body relax into a sense of ease, consciously being still in your posture. Gently bring your attention to rest within your breathing. Be aware of the whole movement of your breath from its beginning to its ending. Be aware of the expanding and relaxing of your chest and abdomen with each breath.
- Now make your breath slightly deeper and fuller, sensing the movement of the in-breath as it moves into your abdomen. Don't exaggerate the movement of your breath too much, just deepen it slightly.
- Bring your attention to the movement of your out-breath. Follow your outgoing breath to its very end, sensing when it has fully left your body.
- With each breath you take, give particular attention to the out-breath, to the release of your breath and your body relaxing. Sense yourself breathing out tension and agitation.
- When your mind is agitated, thoughts will clamor for your attention. Each time your attention is drawn into the thoughts or images that appear, just notice them, not pushing them away but also not becoming lost within them. Give them the barest of attention, acknowledging them but knowing that this is the time for cultivating stillness and calmness.
- Gently bring your attention back to be fully aware of the next out-breath. Breathe out the agitation. You may notice that the pressing thought patterns have an impact on your body, making it feel restless. If this happens, just consciously recommit yourself to being still and relaxed within your body.
- Continue focusing upon your breathing, keeping it just slightly fuller and deeper than it would normally be.
- Let yourself be fully present within each out-breath, staying with it until the beginning of the next in-breath. Notice the slight pause between the ending of one out-breath and the beginning of the next in-breath.
- Let yourself rest calmly within that pause.
- Sense the beginning of the next breath and your body's response. When you are ready, open your eyes and come out of the posture.

Stress is a problem when it becomes overwhelming and exhausting.

STRESS

Stress describes the feelings you have when the demands made on you, or that you feel are being made, are more than you are able to fully cope with. Stress can affect all ages and is a normal reaction to pressure. It can be caused by external stressors, such as pressure from work, life experiences, family, or finances; or internal stressors, such as thoughts and feelings of inadequacy, uncertainty, or low self-esteem.

Sometimes the effect of stress can be positive; for example, if it acts as encouragement or motivation to get on with the task in hand. This is because stress is a physical response, causing your body to move into the fight or flight mode. As it does so, the body releases a mix of hormones and chemicals, such as adrenaline, cortisol, and norepinephrine, that prepare your body for action. That is what causes physical symptoms such as a pounding heart, a rush of energy, and fast breathing, which can prove to be exhilarating and motivational for some.

However, stress is healthy and positive only when it is short-lived. Stress becomes a problem when you experience too much of it, causing it to become overwhelming and resulting in both physical and mental exhaustion. Too much cortisol can also affect your immune system, making it less efficient.

Stress can cause emotional and behavioral changes. You may be plagued by feelings of anxiety, fear, anger, depression, and frustration, and lack concentration, sleep, and the ability to make decisions. In turn, a build-up of all these feelings can produce physical symptoms, such as heart palpitations, headaches, and aches and pains.

Stress can be a highly unpleasant experience, and an important part of tackling stress is to accept you have a problem. As well as identifying the root causes and making lifestyle changes, exploring ways to release your stress, relax your mind, and rebalance your body are some of the key ways of combating it.

COMBATTING STRESS THROUGH NUTRITION

—

Eating a good, balanced diet will make your body stronger and able to cope more efficiently with stress. B vitamins are often depleted by stress, so ensure that you are getting enough in your diet, or take a good supplement. There is some evidence that bee and flower pollen can boost immunity and energize the body. However, do not eat them if you are allergic to honey or stings.

An amino acid called L-tyrosine appears to energize, and studies show that people taking this supplement react better to stressful situations, staying more alert and less anxious, and have fewer complaints about physical discomforts. Vitamin C, found in oranges, blackcurrants, and bell peppers, is a great stress reliever and boosts immunity, making you fitter and healthier.

Bell peppers

Pumpkin seeds, which contain high quantities of zinc, iron, and calcium, as well as B vitamins and proteins, which are necessary for brain function, will help you to deal with the effects of stress. Oats are vital for a healthy nervous system. In periods of stress, start the day with oatmeal, which will help to keep you calm, and prevent depression and general debility.

Pumpkin seeds

HERBAL REMEDIES FOR STRESS

Herbs that encourage relaxation and act as a tonic to the nervous system include lemon balm, lavender, chamomile, passiflora (*Passiflora incarnata*) and oats. These can be drunk as an infusion when in a stressful situation. Ginseng is an "adaptogenic" herb, which means that it lifts you when you are tired and relaxes you when you are stressed. It also works on the immune system and energizes. Some therapists recommend a daily dose at stressful times. It is not suitable for use during pregnancy or by those with high blood pressure.

Lemon balm

Chamomile

Ginseng

Passiflora

Lavender

RECOGNIZING FORMS OF STRESS

—

Each individual is able to cope with a different amount of stress in life, and while some seem to draw on endless reserves to keep going, others succumb. A certain amount of stress provides stimulation, but prolonged stress can cause mental and physical damage. Most of us think of tense situations and worries as being the cause of stress. In reality, stresses are wide-ranging. They include environmental stresses, such as pollution, noise, housing problems, cold, or overheating; physical stresses, such as illnesses, injuries, an inadequate diet; and mental stresses, such as relationship problems, financial strains, bereavement, and job difficulties.

All these factors affect the body, causing it to make a series of rapid physiological changes, called "adaptive responses," to deal with threatening or demanding situations. In the first stage of stress, hormones are poured into the bloodstream. The pulse quickens, the lungs take in more oxygen to fuel the muscles, blood sugar increases to supply added energy, digestion slows, and perspiration increases. In the second stage of stress, the body begins to repair the damage caused by the first stage. If the stressful situation is resolved, the stress symptoms vanish. If the situation continues, however, exhaustion sets in, and the body's energy gives out.

Anxiety is an element of many psychological disorders, including phobias, panic attacks, obsessive-compulsive disorders, and post-traumatic stress disorder. Anxiety is a state of fear or apprehension in the face of threat or danger. It is a natural, healthy response since it allows the body to prepare itself (through adrenaline) to cope with the danger.

Anxiety can, however, take a person over—a condition known as anxiety neurosis—and the person is then said to be in an anxiety state. This may be chronic anxiety, with a constant feeling of worry, associated with depression, or an acute anxiety attack, when the sufferer will be suddenly overwhelmed by fear and feelings of dread. When we are faced with a frightening or threatening situation, our body goes into a "fight or flight" response, when adrenaline pours into the system and the body prepares itself for action. When no action follows, and nervous energy is not discharged, there is physiological confusion, otherwise known as a panic attack. Symptoms may include dizziness, visual disturbance, clammy hands, racing heart, dry mouth, and overbreathing.

An obsession is a persistent, recurring thought or idea, while a compulsion is an overwhelming drive to perform a particular act. When a person becomes dominated by these intrusions, despite knowing that they are irrational, he or she is said to be suffering from an obsessive-compulsive disorder. This may take the form of a hand-washing ritual, for example, or repeated checking that doors and windows are locked. The problem is often triggered by a stressful life event, but can also be due to subtle brain damage (usually the result of illnesses affecting the brain), especially when due to encephalitis. Obsessive-compulsive disorder is rare, although minor obsessional symptoms probably occur in about 15 percent of the population. At least two-thirds of all people who have obsessive-compulsive disorder respond well to therapy. Symptoms may recur under stress but can usually be controlled.

RESCUE REMEDY

This herbal remedy can be bought as a liquid or as a cream. It is made from equal amounts of these five essences: cherry plum, for feelings of desperation; rock rose, to ease terror, fear, or panic; impatiens, to soothe irritability and agitation; clematis, to counteract the tendency to drift away from the present; and star of Bethlehem, to address the mental and physical symptoms of shock. Together, these flower essences make a safe mental sanctuary in which to recover. Carry Rescue Remedy with you for all emergencies, such as a shock, an accident, or an argument; or to take before a trying event, such as an examination, court appearance, or operation.

Make a treatment bottle of Rescue Remedy by adding 2 drops of each constituent flower remedy to a 1fl oz (30ml) bottle of brandy. A cream can be made at home by adding 4 drops of stock Rescue Remedy to a favorite skin cream or neutral base, then adding 2 drops of crab apple.

Rescue Remedy is the only Bach Flower Remedy that is usually taken neat, straight from the bottle. Put 4 drops directly onto or under the tongue. Repeat dosage as often as needed. Put 4 drops into a glass of water and sip throughout the day until you feel more settled.

CALMING MASSAGE OIL BLEND

Add 10 drops of geranium oil, 10 drops clary sage, and 10 drops bergamot to a bottle containing 1fl oz (30ml) or 6 teaspoons of vegetable oil and shake well. Put 6–8 drops in your bath or use a little as a body oil for a calming massage of your back, shoulders, and neck.

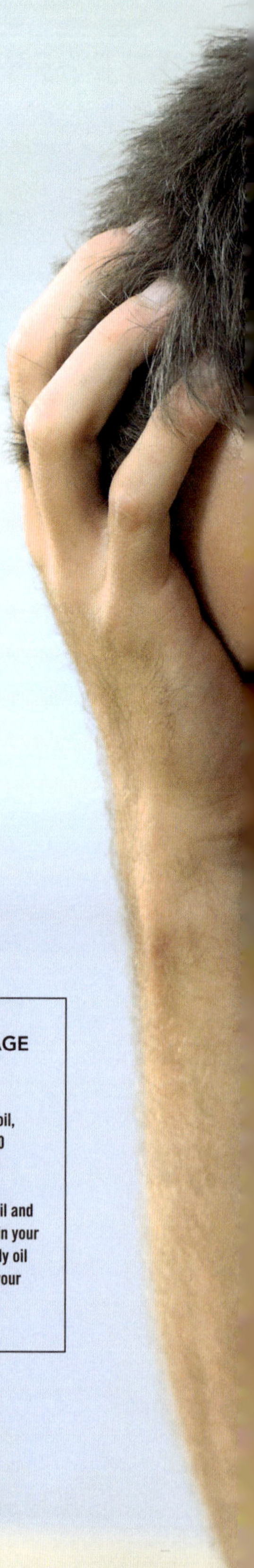

Recognizing what is causing you stress is part of the battle in eradicating it.

RELEASING STRESS THROUGH MEDITATION

—

When we use the word "stress" everyone immediately knows what it is we are talking about. Yet stress is a generic term that attempts to describe a multi-dimensional and complex experience. It is not just a static state of mind, but a process that describes the way we are interacting and interfacing with the world around us and within us. We can feel stressed by work pressures, by goals, the needs or expectations of others, and by time. We can feel stressed by the weight of our own thoughts, unfulfilled wants, conflicting emotions, and the quality of our bodies. Stress is what happens when an overburdened mind adversely impacts upon our bodies and incapacitates us in our ability to meet life calmly and wholeheartedly.

Stress is symptomatic of an underlying disharmony in ourselves and our lives. It is a messenger asking us to examine what we are neglecting or not giving attention to. Much of the stress we experience may be much more optional than we initially believe. We can all learn to attend to our life with greater wholeheartedness, to let go with more ease and to care for the moment we are in.

A meditation teacher was once asked about the right amount of time to give to meditation. His answer was that half an hour was fine except in times of exceptional busyness, then an hour was needed. Too often we misinterpret stress as a signal to do and accomplish more. Yet we need to listen to stress as an indicator of our need to slow down, attend to each moment with greater care, and release the haste that has come to govern our minds and lives. We cannot afford to ignore the signals that it is sending us—tension, agitation, and anxiety. Meditation is not a quick-fix solution for stress. Ease, clarity, effectiveness, and sensitivity in our lives will not arise from a mind and heart that are overburdened. Thoughts, choices, words, and actions born of an agitated mind will invariably be themselves agitated and anxious, and rarely bring the consequences or results we are seeking.

Our conditioned response to stress is to go faster or to hide. We try to do more, accomplish more, or simply flee. None of these responses are effective in teaching us to live a more easeful, creative, and sensitive life. In the midst of feeling stressed it rarely occurs to us that what is needed is for us to stop and be still, yet this is the most instrumental and effective way to heal our bodies, minds, and lives. The moments of greatest tension, anxiety, and agitation are the very moments to which we are asked to bring a mindful attention. Finding the willingness to stop and be still provides the opportunity to meet the internal and external dynamics that are creating havoc in our lives. We see that it is not just the factors of time, demands, people, or even our own thoughts that intrinsically possess the power to stress us. Stress and ease both lie within how we perceive and respond to everything that life brings to us. Stress is what happens when the multiplicity of events in our life and our reactions to them mass together into a form of inner gridlock. Eventually we find ourselves stuck in an inner paralysis—unable to respond well to even the smallest details. Life feels impossible—everything appears to be too much to respond to. We feel we are facing an impenetrable mass of need, demand, and pressure.

In the midst of chaos, it is so beneficial to take a moment out to find calm.

Feeling overwhelmed by demands is a state of mind that can be overturned for the better.

This is in truth a state of mind and not a description of reality. We need to learn to unpack the solidity of that perception. We can pay attention to one moment, one event and one impression at a time. We can learn to calm our bodies and explore with attention what it is we might be able to let go of in our minds. We can learn to pay attention to the beginnings and endings that are part of all our internal and external events. Stress is born of not feeling able to let go of events that have already passed or our thoughts and apprehensions of events that are yet to arise. We can learn to meet the moment we are in wholeheartedly and to let it go as it passes.

Learning to meet the moment and let it go can bring a sense of inner peace.

GUIDED MEDITATION

RELEASING STRESS

- Find a position for your body in which you feel deeply relaxed and at ease. Let your eyes gently close and for a few moments just focus on your breathing, noticing the beginning of each breath and the end of each breath.

- Follow each out-breath to its very end, sensing it dissolving into space. Let yourself rest in that momentary pause between the end of one breath and the beginning of another.

- Expand your attention and listen to what is happening in your body and mind in that moment. Notice how many of your thoughts are preoccupied with events, people, meetings, and experiences that are not actually present in that moment. Sense this without judgment or resistance and see whether it is possible for you to gently release those thoughts and return to an awareness of breathing.

- Notice the waves of agitation, tension, or anxiety that arise with the thoughts of the past and future and how they may be impacting on your body.

- Come back once more to an awareness of your breathing.

- Resting in calmness and ease, consciously invite into your mind an event, person, or experience that you have been preoccupied with or obsessing about. Surround that thought with a mindful attention. Look at it directly. Can you see it as just a thought, an event in the mind?

- Sense how that event in your mind is co-existing in this moment with countless other events—sounds, sensations in your body—and how they are all arising and passing together. Move your attention between the thought, the sounds, and the bodily sensations that are present in this moment. Notice how they all appear, last for a time, and then begin to fade or turn into something else.

- Sense the natural rhythm of this arising and passing. Notice how when any of these events are surrounded by aversion, agitation, or resistance, their lifespan is extended. When the surrounding reactions are released, the events find their place again in the natural rhythm of arising and passing.

- Attend mindfully not only to the events that appear in your mind and body, but also to those subtle pauses and places of stillness between events. Just as you are able to notice the momentary pause between an out-breath and the next in-breath, sense what is present after the fading away of a sound, a thought, or a bodily sensation.

- Allow yourself to rest in the pauses and sense the possibility of resting in all the events that arise in your mind and body. When you are ready, let your eyes open and move out of the posture.

Look past your thoughts so you may drink the pure nectar of this moment.

Rumi

EMOTIONAL RESILIENCE

The phrase emotional resilience refers to how you cope with and adapt to stressful or negative situations. If you have strong emotional resilience, you're likely to be able to cope easily, adapt to the changes that the situation brings, and sail on with your life. But if you have a low level of emotional resilience, you're likely to find life a lot harder, perhaps taking things to heart and finding the situation difficult to move on from.

Levels of emotional resilience can change over time and be affected by the situations you've experienced and the circumstances you've found yourself in. If someone has a higher level of emotional resilience than you, it doesn't make them any better than you, it just means you deal with things differently. Sometimes you can be your own worst inner critic and be far too hard on yourself.

The good news is that you can learn how to boost your emotional resilience, so you're better placed to deal with unexpected situations or sudden changes. To do so, you need to identify how you tend to react to things now, then focus on ways in which you could change this response to be more positive or keep things in perspective, rather than succumbing to being anxious. Plus, you can use practical techniques and meditations to help you develop a better sense of inner peace, feel more confident, and knock fear on its head.

INNER PEACE

Peace is not the absence of challenge or difficulty, but the release of judgment and fear. It begins in our own hearts, minds, and lives. We cannot control or govern the hearts and minds of another, but we can reclaim our own capacity to be at peace with all things, including ourselves. Learning to make peace with ourselves is the first step in understanding what it means to be at peace with all things. It is not difficult for us to see that our relationships with other people frequently mirror the kind of relationship we have with our own bodies, minds, and hearts. If we are prone to be judgmental or dismissive of others, it may be worthwhile to explore the ways in which we are judgmental or dismissive of ourselves. The impatience, frustration, expectancy, or blame that may sabotage our relationship with all those who are part of our lives will likely have their roots in the ways in which we relate to our own inner world.

Learning to make peace with ourselves is the first step in being at peace with all things.

Being content with ourselves will strengthen our relationships with others.

If we wish to nurture relationships of kindness, understanding, and intimacy in our lives it may be important to acknowledge that our relationship with ourselves is the classroom in which we learn the arts of generosity, tolerance, care, and tenderness. Wherever we go in this life, whether alone or with others, we can never divorce ourselves from our own hearts and minds. The longings we treasure for intimacy, oneness, and friendship with others rest upon our capacity to cross the abyss of distance and fear that can separate us from ourselves. Peace in our lives is not separate from our capacity to make peace with ourselves. Serenity in our lives rests upon our capacity to make peace with the inner struggles that devastate the calmness of our own hearts and minds. Peacemaking begins with our capacity to release ourselves from the conflicts and struggles we carry in our relationship to ourselves.

JASMINE MASSAGE FOR INNER STRENGTH

- Add 4 drops jasmine oil, 4 drops clary sage, and 2 drops lavender to 5 teaspoons (25ml.) sweet almond oil.
- Start the massage by sliding your hands from your hips across your abdomen.
- Gently stroke around the abdomen in a clockwise direction, sliding one hand after the other.
- Move gently over your chest.
- Stroke your hands up and around your hips, and around to the small of your back. Repeat..

Massage with aromatherapy oils will support inner strength in stressful times.

GUIDED MEDITATION

INNER PEACE

- Settle into a posture that is as relaxed and alert as possible.
- Allow your eyes to gently close.
- Take a few moments to be aware of your body, releasing any areas of tension.
- Let your shoulders, face, and hands relax and soften.
- For a few moments focus your attention on your breathing. Be particularly aware of your outgoing breath, following it with your attention until the very end of the breath.
- Rest your attention in the brief moment between the ending of an out-breath and the beginning of the next in-breath.
- Take a few moments to reflect on where you most repetitively battle with yourself. Sense the places you are most judgmental of yourself, the places where you extend to yourself the greatest unkindness or blame, the places that trigger feelings of shame or self-consciousness.
- You may be aware of carrying events or acts from the past in your heart and mind that are laden with guilt or regret. You may be aware of recurring patterns in your present, in speech, thought, or action, that cause pain or alienation and that you wish to be free from.
- As you reflect on these patterns or events, sense what happens in your body and mind.
- Sense how simply bringing these places of pain into your attention may trigger feelings of contraction, tension, or resistance in your body. You may be aware of the rhythm of your breathing changing, becoming shorter or tighter. If this happens, bring your attention to the part of your body that is registering distress or discomfort and let it soften and relax.
- Sense the aversion you have for these places in your own heart and mind. Sense your wish to be free from them. Be aware of how the aversion and resistance themselves are the energy of struggle and inner estrangement.
- Reflect on what you may need to cultivate or nurture to make peace with yourself.`
- Reflect on what difference it would make to those places of rejection and alienation to cultivate a greater kindness, acceptance, or compassion.
- Can you offer to yourself the forgiveness and generosity of heart to embrace the places of greatest difficulty and unease in your own heart and mind?
- Are you able to stay present with those places in yourself that you are most tempted to flee from? Reflect on what it might mean to befriend yourself, to offer to yourself the openness and understanding you would both wish to offer to others and to receive from others.
- Sense that your capacity to make peace with yourself may not depend upon denying anything.
- Your capacity to be at peace with yourself begins with your willingness to let go of prejudice and judgment. With a wholehearted and gentle attentiveness, explore those places in your heart and mind that are the source of the greatest struggle and pain.
- Sense how it may be possible to bring calmness, gentleness, and care to those places without any expectation.
- When you are ready, open your eyes and come out of the posture.

CULTIVATING FEARLESSNESS

Fear is one of the most debilitating and paralyzing emotions in our lives. It is often the root of a wide spectrum of other emotions in our lives. Fear appears in various forms, from twinges of anxiety to waves of terror and dread that obstruct our capacity to live with openness and receptivity. It appears in the forms of self-consciousness, mistrust, and doubt. Increasingly we begin to see that fear thrives in a lack of awareness.

Cultivating fearlessness does not presume that fear will never arise in our hearts and lives. Fearlessness is not living without fear, but turning directly toward the fears and anxieties that do arise. When we are willing to do this, we learn that it is possible to embrace fear with a gentle and loving attention rather than being governed by it. We learn to touch fear with compassion, to investigate and understand it.

Stepping outside your comfort zone will help you address the fears that hold you back.

GUIDED MEDITATION

EXPLORING FEAR

- Sit comfortably and allow your body to relax fully. Bring a gentle attention to any places in your body where there is tightness or discomfort. Gently and consciously soften those areas, allowing your whole body to relax.
- Close your eyes and for a few moments pay attention to your breathing. Give particular attention to your outgoing breath. With each out-breath, relax more deeply and consciously release any of the turmoil or busyness in your mind. Follow each out-breath with your attention until its very end. When you feel calmer, consciously invite into your attention and heart something that makes you afraid. Initially, don't focus upon anything you feel terrified or overwhelmed by, but upon a dimension of your life that you may habitually flinch from or avoid. It might be a fear of speaking honestly, a difficult person who is part of your life, making changes or relationships you tend to turn away from. It may be a fear of illness, aging, or death. It might be a fear of the dark or of loss.
- Let yourself feel the fear that arises in the face of the object, situation, or event you resist or feel anxious about.
- Sense where the fear is in your body and explore those sensations with your attention. Cultivate a curious attention, sensing how the sensations change and move. Allow yourself to rest within those sensations. If they become overwhelming, come back to your breathing for a few moments, connect deeply with each out-breath and allow your mind and body to calm once more.
- As you invite the object or situation of anxiety into your attention, be aware of the different emotions, memories, or images that arise. Let them rest in your attention without trying to get rid of them or becoming lost within them. They may be uncomfortable, but you may also begin to sense they are not intrinsically threatening.
- Sense that fear and all its associated images and reactions may be uncomfortable yet in itself need not be threatening or overwhelming.
- Move your attention back and forth between the fear and your breathing, cultivating a calm steadiness moment to moment.
- Sense the way that avoidance deepens and perpetuates fear. Sense, too, how fear diminishes in the light of calm attention.
- Throughout the meditation continue to check in with your body, relaxing and softening any tightness or tension that appears.
- When you are ready, open your eyes and come out of the posture.

FLOWER ESSENCES FOR FEAR

Mimulus may help with the everyday fears of known things, such as spiders, being late for work, flying, and being ill.

Aspen is for unknown fears, the vague and dark fears which hover and play on the imagination.

Rock rose should be added when the fear is turning into terror and perhaps even panic.

Cherry plum is for the fear that everything will fall apart.

Red chestnut is for fear for another's safety.

Cherry plum blossom

LETTING GO

Life continues to teach us the direct relationship between peace and our willingness to let go. No matter how tightly or fearfully we hold on to something, inwardly and outwardly, it will change and we will be asked to let it go. The art of being able to let go fully and freely in every moment of our lives is the art of finding balance and serenity.

Fear makes us hold tightly to countless things in our lives; trust and understanding teach us how to let go.

The openness and intimacy we long to find in all of our relationships are born of our capacity to let go of mistrust, anger, and alienation. Our capacity to be fully present in all of the moments of our lives, to be touched and taught by them, is born of our willingness to let go of our preoccupations with past and future.

Learning to let go will never be born of willpower, forcing, or striving. Commanding ourselves to let go will only set up new standards and judgments of success and failure that harm our well-being.

Letting go is born of calmness, compassion, and understanding. These are qualities we cultivate moment to moment in our meditation practice and our lives. Every time we sit in meditation may be when we are asked to let go a thousand times. Each day of our lives invites us to let go in countless moments and encounters. We learn to let go not in order to make ourselves suffer, feel deprived, or bereft, but to bring about an end to suffering, to feelings of deprivation and fear. Letting go is the art of happiness and contentment. Finding a greater simplicity in our lives has the inevitable companion of learning to let go.

As we become increasingly sensitive to our inner life we begin to see the ways in which we are imprisoned by whatever it is we are clinging to most tightly. The times when we feel least free, connected, and open in our lives are when we are desperately trying to make life conform to our wishes and expectations. At these times we are lost in identification and holding. The times of greatest freedom are when we can embrace each moment, person, and encounter in our lives just as it is, free of demand and expectation. Meditation practice invites us to bring a wholehearted attention to all the places where we struggle and suffer most deeply. We often discover that these are the places where we are holding on most tightly. Opinions, expectations, roles, identities, fears, objects, goals, and desires are all fertile ground for holding and clinging, so becoming the places of greatest distress in our lives. Yet it is in the places where we hold on most fiercely that we can also discover the greatest freedom as we learn to loosen the hold of clinging.

It is not always difficult for us to see the places in our lives that are inviting us to learn to let go, but there are many ways in which we learn to let go freely and wholeheartedly. Whatever way we learn is to be honored—it is in the service of peace. When our mind is calm and attentive, letting go is often effortless and easeful. And the more we are able to let go, the more generosity, compassion, simplicity, and freedom we discover in our lives.

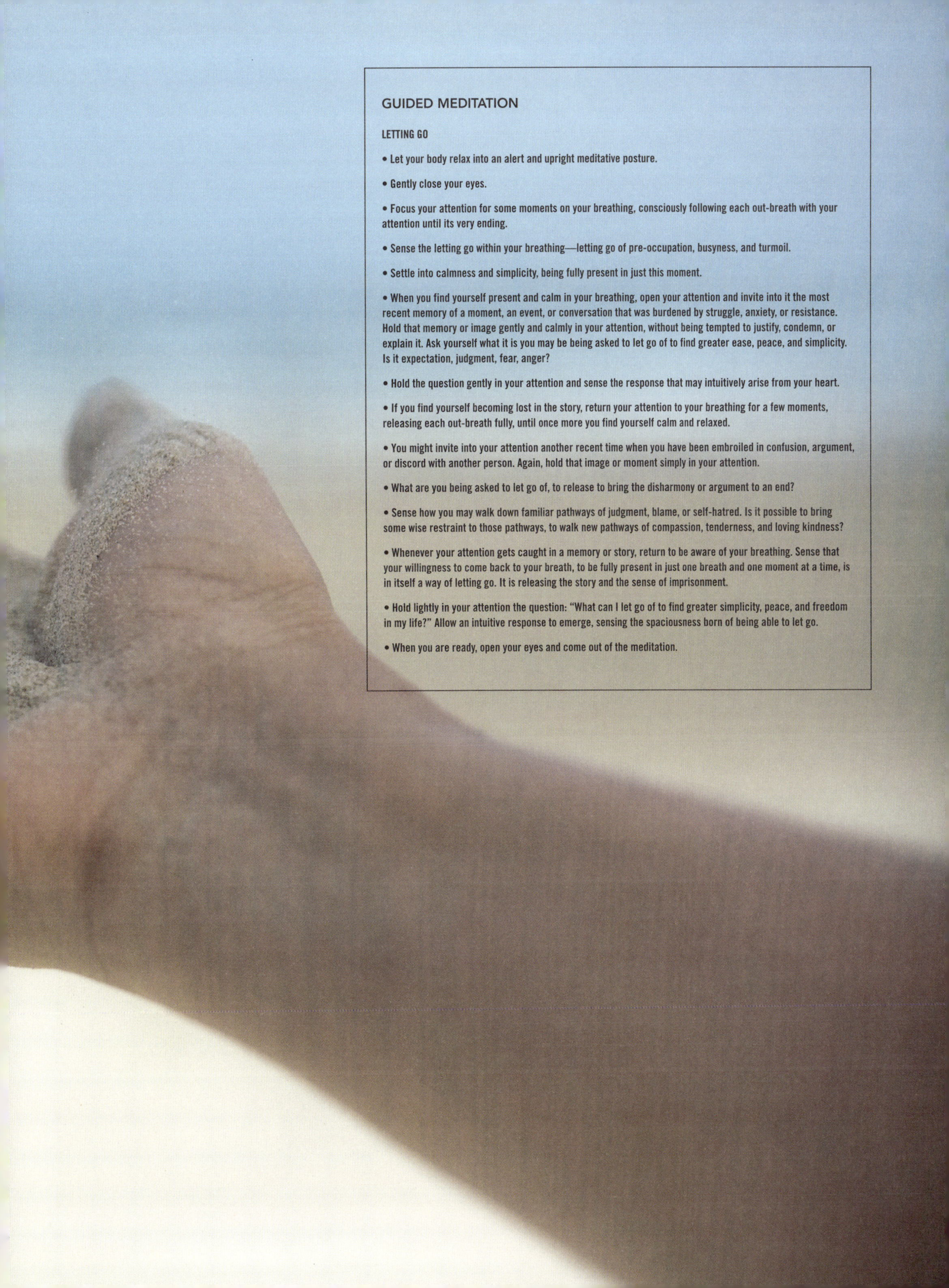

GUIDED MEDITATION

LETTING GO

- Let your body relax into an alert and upright meditative posture.

- Gently close your eyes.

- Focus your attention for some moments on your breathing, consciously following each out-breath with your attention until its very ending.

- Sense the letting go within your breathing—letting go of pre-occupation, busyness, and turmoil.

- Settle into calmness and simplicity, being fully present in just this moment.

- When you find yourself present and calm in your breathing, open your attention and invite into it the most recent memory of a moment, an event, or conversation that was burdened by struggle, anxiety, or resistance. Hold that memory or image gently and calmly in your attention, without being tempted to justify, condemn, or explain it. Ask yourself what it is you may be being asked to let go of to find greater ease, peace, and simplicity. Is it expectation, judgment, fear, anger?

- Hold the question gently in your attention and sense the response that may intuitively arise from your heart.

- If you find yourself becoming lost in the story, return your attention to your breathing for a few moments, releasing each out-breath fully, until once more you find yourself calm and relaxed.

- You might invite into your attention another recent time when you have been embroiled in confusion, argument, or discord with another person. Again, hold that image or moment simply in your attention.

- What are you being asked to let go of, to release to bring the disharmony or argument to an end?

- Sense how you may walk down familiar pathways of judgment, blame, or self-hatred. Is it possible to bring some wise restraint to those pathways, to walk new pathways of compassion, tenderness, and loving kindness?

- Whenever your attention gets caught in a memory or story, return to be aware of your breathing. Sense that your willingness to come back to your breath, to be fully present in just one breath and one moment at a time, is in itself a way of letting go. It is releasing the story and the sense of imprisonment.

- Hold lightly in your attention the question: "What can I let go of to find greater simplicity, peace, and freedom in my life?" Allow an intuitive response to emerge, sensing the spaciousness born of being able to let go.

- When you are ready, open your eyes and come out of the meditation.

Perfection of character is this: to live each day as if it were your last, without frenzy, without apathy, without pretence.

Marcus Aurelius

FORGIVENESS

Our hearts and minds can be tormented by storms of hatred, anger, resentment, and fear. They can equally be healed by the power of forgiveness. Our common bond as human beings is our capacity both to be hurt and to hurt others.

In our life we will face difficult situations in which we may be insulted, humiliated, dismissed, or rejected. These are all painful experiences that can fester in our hearts, poisoning our capacity to trust and care, and leaching joy from our lives. We can carry these moments of pain through the whole of our lives. Fearing and resenting those who have harmed us, in truth we often think more about them than the people we love. We can expend considerable energy planning strategies of retaliation or self-protection.

We can find ourselves obsessing about experiences that have long passed, while those who have harmed us may be oblivious to the impact they have had upon us. We can live our lives in regret and bitterness, which is often to forget to live at all. A wounded heart and all the fears and apprehensions born of that hurt can seem to create an eternal prison. And though the pain may have been inflicted upon us by another, we are perhaps the only ones who can release ourselves from that prison of resentment and fear. We may also encounter times in our lives when it feels deeply difficult to forgive not only others but also ourselves. We may have harmed another person through our words, actions, unconsciousness, or insensitivity, and we sense the divide of mistrust, fear, and anger that now separates us from that person. We cannot undo the acts that have been done, we cannot take back the words that have been spoken. So guilt, regret, and remorse become part of our lives. Storms of thought are born, beginning with the phrases "if only" and "I wish," and taking up space in our minds. Forgiveness does not condone or justify the unjust, harmful, or unacceptable.

WILLOW FOR FORGIVENESS

- **An infusion of willow encourages a more positive and mature attitude.**
- **Do not take willow bark when pregnant or breastfeeding.**
- **Add 2 heaped teaspoons of dried willow bark to 2 cups of water. Simmer for 10 minutes. Strain.**
- **Add honey to taste, then drink.**

But with wise forgiveness may come the resolve never to permit any past harm to be repeated in the present or future. It is not easy to forgive, but it is less painful than continuing to carry the burden of a painful past into all the remaining moments of our lives. So forgiveness is a way of releasing our own hearts from pain. It allows us to live a life in which we no longer carry the burdens of the past or endlessly replay the past in the present. We are released into a present that is no longer defined by the past. It is here that we find peace and the capacity to live with openness and trust. Forgiveness is built upon patience, tolerance, and acceptance—qualities we extend to both ourselves and others. In doing so, we do not erase the imprints of pain from our own hearts or the hearts of others. Forgiveness is often a long journey that asks us to meet the hurt of betrayal, loss, and anger over and over. In each of these meetings we see the choices we face: we can linger in what has gone by and suffer, or we can meet that pain with understanding, compassion, and courage, and find a heart of ease. The forgiving heart is also a free heart.

Forgiving ourselves and others can put a stop to the inner turmoil of guilt and anger.

FORGIVENESS FOR OURSELVES

In our lives we can harm and abandon ourselves in countless ways—physically, emotionally, and psychologically. Through feelings of worthlessness, habit, and self-judgment we forget how to care for ourselves. For many people it is easier to care for others than to care for themselves. But through being overly busy, needing the approval and affirmation of others, and judging ourselves we can sabotage our well-being. The trail of regret and anxiety burdens our hearts, undermining our capacity to hold our own body, mind, and heart in an embrace of sensitivity and compassion in the present. We need to forgive ourselves for all the harm or hurt we may have inflicted on ourselves. We must also learn to forgive ourselves for the harm we have done to others. Out of unconsciousness, fear, and anxiety we can speak, think, and act in ways that hurt others, that make others fear us. The words we have spoken and the actions we have engaged in cannot be undone. Yet we can do what is possible to reconcile ourselves with the person we have hurt and forgive ourselves for our past insensitivity. Forgiveness for ourselves rests upon our capacity to let go of what has already gone by and find a new beginning in the present. We can learn in our meditation to move from insensitivity and unconsciousness to a sensitivity and awareness that is both healing and freeing.

GUIDED MEDITATION

FORGIVENESS FOR OURSELVES

- Take some moments to find a posture of calmness and ease. Let your eyes close and consciously soften all the parts of your body that feel tight or contracted.
- Let your breathing relax and find its own natural rhythm.
- Let your attention rest in the center of your chest, in the area of your heart, and just sense the life of your body in that area.
- Cultivate an attentiveness of sensitivity and calm.
- Take some moments to reflect on the ways that you may harm or hurt yourself through thought, word, or action.
- Receive with kindness the images, memories, or bodily feelings that may arise, even if they are deeply painful.
- Sense how those images, memories, or feelings belong to actions, words, and thoughts that have already passed.
- In the present, let go of any form of self-judgment, guilt, or anxiety over what has in truth passed. Reflect on what forgiveness might mean in this moment, what it might mean to release the burden of the past and all that you regret.
- Let your attention rest in the heart center, at the center of your chest, without demand or expectation.
- Let these phrases rest softly in your attention and your heart:

"I forgive myself."

"I forgive myself for the words, actions,
or thoughts that caused harm to myself,
whether intentional or unintentional."

"I forgive myself for any way
that I have hurt myself through fear,
pain, or confusion."

"I forgive myself."

- Continue for some minutes to rest your attention in these phrases.
- Sense in your heart the possibility of letting go of the past, of learning new pathways of respect, kindness, and compassion for yourself.
- Memories and images laden with regret may arise. You can also allow them to pass and return to a forgiving heart.
- When you are ready, open your eyes and come out of the posture.

Forgiveness for ourselves rests on being able to let go of what has passed.

ASKING FORGIVENESS FROM OTHERS

Out of confusion, fear, and pain we can hurt others both through action and inaction. In fear and anger we can strike out at another as a way of trying to protect ourselves. Lost in confusion, we don't always appreciate the hurtful impact our words or actions have on the heart of another, except in retrospect. Then we can carry the legacy in our hearts throughout our lives. Regret and shame can dominate our inner story as we struggle with guilt and remorse. At times our inaction can cause as much pain as our actions. We remember the times when we failed to reach out to another in need, we recall the words of comfort we never said and the times when we turned away from a person in pain out of fear or a sense of inadequacy. Just as we need to forgive ourselves for the confusion and fear that guided us in those moments of neglect, so we can also ask forgiveness from another. Asking for forgiveness from others can be a powerful way of recommitting ourselves to sensitivity, integrity, and care in the present.

Take the time and strength to ask for forgiveness of others.

GUIDED MEDITATION

ASKING FORGIVENESS FROM OTHERS

- Let your body relax into a posture of ease and balance.
- Close your eyes if it enables you to focus more wholeheartedly.
- Spend some moments focusing on your breathing.
- With each out-breath, sense the release of any agitation or busyness within your mind.
- Let the memories, images, and emotions arise in your heart of the times when you may have wounded, hurt, or neglected another. They may be memories of hurtful words you have spoken or hurtful ways of relating to another person through rage, fear, or jealousy.
- Sense the heaviness of those images and feel your own sorrow and regret.
- Numerous people and situations of pain may arise. Make room for them, one by one. Sense the possibility of releasing this burden and healing these wounds.
- Silently forgive yourself, letting these phrases of forgiveness rest in your heart:

"I forgive myself."

"I forgive myself for any hurt or suffering I may have caused you by my words, actions, or thoughts."

"I forgive myself for neglecting to care for you when it was asked of me."

"I forgive myself."

- Let your attention rest in the phrases for a time and then turn your attention to those whom you would ask forgiveness of. Invite into your heart and attention anyone from the past or present you feel you have hurt through action or inaction, whether intentional or unintentional. Invite them to take a seat in your meditation and let your attention rest in these phrases:

"For any way I have caused you pain or hurt, I ask your forgiveness."

"For any way I have neglected you, I ask your forgiveness."

"For any way I have made you fear me, I ask your forgiveness."

- Let your attention rest within those phrases for a time, with sincerity bridging the gap that exists between you and the other person, a gap born of pain or neglect.
- As you rest your attention in the phrases, try not to become lost in the story of past pain and hurt. Come back to the present, come back to the sincerity and simplicity of the phrases.
- Let go of the guilt or regret as you recommit yourself to kindness and integrity in the present.
- When you are ready, open your eyes and come out of the posture.

FORGIVENESS FOR THOSE WHO HAVE CAUSED PAIN

—

It is not easy for us to forgive those who have caused hurt or suffering to us or to others. It is not easy for us to sense the anger, fear, and confusion that drive those acts and words that can so deeply damage. It is truly challenging to open our hearts to those whom we fear, despise, and judge for the pain they have caused. Yet forgiveness asks us to cultivate understanding; it is an invitation to intimacy rather than alienation.

Forgiveness is choosing a path of healing rather than abandonment and division. In the absence of forgiveness, people who have harmed us can govern our hearts and lives. We think about them, dwell upon the ways they have hurt us, and allow them to shape our present through fear and anger. The incidents, words, and acts that have wounded us deeply may belong to a distant past, yet they can continue to dominate our present. We can find ourselves endlessly replaying them. Forgiveness releases us from this prison of fear and anger. Forgiving those who cause pain is in truth a way of protecting and healing ourselves. Forgiving those who hurt us does not mean, however, that we should ever place ourselves in situations of danger or peril, nor does it mean justifying or condoning actions or words that are clearly harmful. We all need to find the courage and clarity to bring about the end of anything that violates and damages our world. We also need to find the mercy and compassion to embrace and understand those who cause pain. Then the wall of anger, hatred, and fear that can so powerfully divide us from one another can begin to melt in the light of forgiveness.

Forgiveness for those who have harmed us asks for a powerful generosity of heart. It is often helpful to begin with a case where the barriers of fear and anger do not feel so solid. We need to find deep inner resources of balance and courage to approach those who have most deeply wounded us. Sometimes we are simply not ready to reach out with forgiveness and understanding to a person who has hurt us deeply. But we can forgive ourselves for that reluctance and fear until a time comes when we feel more inwardly healed and renewed and we are able to forgive another.

Forgiving those who have harmed us is in fact a profound act of compassion for ourselves. It allows us to move on, unburdened by fear and anger, and embrace our present wholeheartedly. In forgiveness we are releasing ourselves from the tortured world of blame, anger, and hatred. As we forgive those who cause suffering, what we are in truth forgiving are the powerful forces of confusion, ignorance, fear, and anger that can blight any of our lives. In cultivating forgiveness we need to respect the limits of our own hearts. It may be too soon for us to forgive. We may still be too wounded to open our hearts to someone who has hurt us. At these times we can learn just to visit the places where our hearts feel most raw or painful, to acknowledge the need to heal these tender places of division and pain, and to learn the kindness and power of forgiveness for ourselves and for all those who, through ignorance and confusion, cause pain.

CALMING AND UPLIFTING MASSAGE BLEND

As you reach forgiveness, this aromatherapy blend will boost your mood.

- Add 4 drops rose essential oil, 2 drops frankincense, and 4 drops chamomile to 3 teaspoons (15ml) of sweet almond or grapeseed oil.
- This blend encourages positivity, acceptance of others, and joyfulness.
- Do not use rose essential oil during the first three months of pregnancy and not at all if there is a history of miscarriage.

GUIDED MEDITATION

FORGIVENESS FOR THOSE WHO HAVE CAUSED PAIN

- Find a position for your body that is relaxed and free from tension.
- Gently close your eyes.
- Bring your attention into your body, consciously softening any places that feel tight or contracted.
- Pay particular attention to your face and jaw, your neck, shoulders, and hands, letting them relax fully.
- Bring a gentle and calm attention to rest in your chest, in your heart area.
- Invite into your attention someone who has hurt you, whether in small or deep ways.
- Hold that person in your attention and sense the array of images and emotions that arise, without judging any of them. Let them rest in your heart and mind without grasping hold of any of them.
- Sense the ways in which you have felt harmed or abandoned, intentionally or unintentionally, by that person. Feel the pain you carry with you from this past and sense that it may be time to lay down this burden.
- Holding the difficult person in your attention, gently begin to offer the intention of forgiveness with the phrases:

"I forgive you for the pain you have caused."

"I forgive the anger, confusion, and ignorance at the heart of your harmfulness."

"To you who have hurt me, I offer forgiveness."

- As you rest your attention in the phrases and intentions of forgiveness, sense whether even the tiniest glimmers of release or opening may be possible.
- Sense the new beginnings that may be possible for you as you release the weight of the past.
- You may find it difficult to stay connected with the image or memory of someone who has hurt you deeply. Do not be harsh with demands on yourself. If you begin to flounder in the memories of pain, just return your attention to your body and breathing. Let your body relax and soften, and when you are ready, come back to the phrases, again offering forgiveness.
- When you are ready, open your eyes.

Forgiving others for the hurt they have caused is the first step toward healing.

SELF AND SELFLESSNESS

CHAPTER SIX

IDENTITY AND TRUE SELF

Our minds are the forerunners of our speech, actions, choices, and the way that we personally experience and interpret the world. They can be a cauldron of seething thoughts, worries, memories, and plans. They can also be pervaded by profound serenity, stillness, and clarity. The times of greatest confusion, obsession, turmoil, and preoccupation are all experienced within our minds. But our minds also have the capacity to be a landscape of clarity, simplicity, and peace.

Learning to care for our minds with sensitivity, understanding, and mindfulness, we learn to care for everything that is born of our minds. A mind rooted in calm clarity, understanding, and stillness finds its embodiment in every word, gesture, and choice in our lives. Learning to befriend our minds, we discover the possibility of finding ease in every area of our lives.

Rooting your mind in calm can help you face the world with the same intention.

When our minds are overly full, burdened with unnecessary thought and preoccupation, they propel us through our lives with haste and agitation. Learning to find spaciousness within our minds, we approach our world with a deepening care and calmness.

A central part of meditation practice is devoted to understanding the nature of our minds, simply because they play such a central role in our lives and our capacity to find well-being. It is possible to embrace our minds with awareness—to sense on a moment-to-moment level the arising and passing of thoughts, images, and mental states. Our minds are no obstacle to deep understanding and compassion—the obstacle lies in the unconsciousness or lack of awareness that leads us to be lost in clouds of confusion. In meditation we explore the possibility of bringing a sensitive and clear attentiveness to our minds, just as we learn to bring that quality of attention to every other dimension of our lives.

The first step to clarity of purpose is clearing our minds of everyday clutter.

KNOWING YOUR MIND

In the times of greatest inner chaos and turmoil in our lives we can regard our minds almost as enemies—untrustworthy and the source of pain. There are moments when our deepest and most noble intentions to cultivate loving kindness, generosity, and openness seem to be sabotaged by the compelling and habitual thoughts and fears that take root in our minds. Unpredictability appears to be part of our minds. Moments of calm and peace are overtaken by bursts of preoccupation and obsession. The wonderful moments of serenity and ease we nurture are suddenly ambushed by frantic bursts of anxiety or rehearsals of the future. The state and quality of our minds often seems to be beyond our control. We wish to be present, spacious, and clear, only to find ourselves floundering in dullness or clouds of confusion.

It is tempting to blame our minds for the turmoil and agitation we can all too easily find ourselves lost in. But the

first step in developing clarity of mind is to let go of the blame and begin to approach our minds with interest, investigation, and sensitivity.

Meditation is not anti-thought, nor is it a means to suppress the mind. Just as the mind can be the source of some of the most destructive acts and conflicts in our world, so too can it be the source of some of the greatest insights and creativity in our world. The divisions and separations that scar our world will also be healed through our ability and willingness to find peace and understanding within our own minds.

Acknowledging the power of the mind both for chaos and stillness, we learn to bring a meditative awareness directly to our own minds and all their activities. We learn we can find simplicity and cultivate the capacity of our minds for insight, investigation, and stillness. We discover we can see thought just as thought, held within the same rhythm of arising and passing as everything else in our lives. We can think with clarity, learn to investigate the places of confusion that beleaguer us, and nurture a mind of peace.

A calm mind is not intrinsically a mind that it is devoid of thought. If meditative depth were dependent upon the absence of thought, it would be irrelevant to our lives. Learning to investigate and understand our minds, we enhance our capacity to think and reflect with clarity. We discover the wisdom of releasing much of the identification and holding that agitates our minds. We learn to let go of many of the futile avenues of thinking, judgment, anxiety, and obsession that do not contribute to our well-being. A mind that is deeply rooted in calmness is an ally in our lives, the source of effective, clear action. Approaching our minds in a meditative way, on a moment-to-moment level, we see more clearly the impact of the mind upon our bodies, hearts, and all of the relationships we form in our lives. Too often we are so entangled in the stories we hold about ourselves and the world that we forget how to listen with openness and sensitivity. Meditation teaches us to listen to our minds, to reject nothing and to discover the freedom of not being entangled and lost in the world of interpretation and judgment.The first step in the cultivation of a mind of serenity and wisdom is to learn to be aware of our minds, moment to moment. Awareness is the forerunner of all transformation. It is what illuminates the mind, bringing clarity into a dimension of our lives that often seems to be shrouded in clouds of confusion and complexity. In meditation we bring a clear, sensitive attention directly to all of the activities of our minds.

Finding our own peace can help us address the divisions and separations in the world around us.

NOTING

The first step in cultivating a mind of calmness and clarity is to know the nature of our mind on a moment-to-moment level, to cultivate a mindful intimacy with it, exploring it in all its movements and activities.

We discover that our mind is not a static, uninterrupted entity. It is an ongoing process of arising and passing thoughts, images, memories, plans, moods, and responses. We receive the world, moment to moment, through our sensory doors, and our minds perceive and interpret those impressions. The inner world of association, memory, comparison, emotion, and evaluation is set in motion. It is helpful to see the changing nature of our mental processes, as it is the first step in forming a mindful relationship to our minds. As we learn to be increasingly present within those mental processes we discover we are not helpless, not sentenced to an eternal inner life of floundering, reactivity, and powerlessness before the force of our minds. We are able to introduce into the life of our minds the qualities of investigation, serenity, and simplicity. These are the qualities that teach us how to let go of confusion and complexity and realize the capacity of our minds for clarity, understanding, and creativity.

We discover, too, that the mind is not always constant—that the space and stillness between thoughts can learn to sense the arising of thoughts and be increasingly attuned to some of the states of mind that can, if unnoticed, govern our relationship to every moment in our life.

If our minds are at peace, we discover increasing depths of peace everywhere in our lives. If our minds are balanced and receptive, we are no longer prone to being lost in the multiplicity of events that are part of all of our lives. Being intimate with our own minds enhances our capacity to understand the nature of all minds. Learning to step out of the cycles of reactivity and confusion within ourselves, we discover the means to bring clarity and sensitivity to each moment.

When our minds are balanced, we can step out of confusion and find clarity.

Investigation, serenity, and simplicity teach us how to let go of confusion and complexity.

GUIDED MEDITATION

NOTING

- Find a posture in which your body can be relaxed and upright. Take a few moments to settle into that posture, finding a deep sense of ease within your body. Let your eyes gently close. Bring your attention to rest within your breathing, focusing your attention either on the area of your upper lip and nostrils or on the rising and falling of your abdomen with each breath. Let your attention rest lightly in that area of your body, cultivating a base of calm attentiveness.

- As you rest your attention in your breathing, begin to sense all the moments when your attention is drawn to whatever is occurring in your mind. Fantasy, memory, planning, judgment, daydreaming, rehearsing—make a simple note of whatever is occurring so you can see clearly where your attention is lingering in the world of thought. Note it calmly, clearly, and then return your attention to your breathing.

- You may find that you are present only with a single breath before your attention is attracted once more to activity in your mind. Just breathe that breath fully, sensing its beginning and its ending. If your attention is once more drawn to a thought or series of thoughts or images that have appeared in your mind, again just make a simple mental note of that activity. Thinking, daydreaming, planning, fantasy, memory—as far as you are able, just note each thought simply and clearly.

- Return once more to the next breath. Sense that each time you return your attention to your breathing that you are letting go of complexity and entanglement.

- There may be moments when you are not aware of the movement of your attention from your breath and into a thought pattern. Suddenly you wake up as if from a dream, realizing you have been lost in a thought or fantasy. Don't judge those moments, just make a simple mental note—"Thinking, thinking'—and return to the next breath. Don't be tempted to try to figure out where the thoughts are coming from or what underlies them. Just bring simplicity into the world of thought and imagery, cultivating calmness and clarity with that simplicity. Let your breath be an anchor and also be a mirror, reflecting all those moments when your attention leaves your breath and goes to your mind.

- Know when your attention is present within your breathing and when your attention is present within thought. Be equally attentive, with calmness and sensitivity, to each of those moments. You may discover that when you bring a conscious attention to a thought, the thought simply dissolves and disappears. This is fine—don't try to hold on to anything. Sense the disappearing of the thought and again bring a wholehearted attentiveness to your breathing.

- Sense the possibility of seeing a thought as a thought, arising and passing, appearing and fading away.

- Sense a breath as a breath, arising and passing, appearing and fading away.

- Let yourself rest in calm attentiveness, aware and clear within the life of your mind. As your attention deepens, you may discover that your thought processes begin to calm and slow down. You may sense a growing capacity to see thoughts more clearly and realize that you are closer to the moments when thought processes begin to appear in your mind. You may discover a growing stillness that does not rely upon the absence of thought but is tangible within the presence of thought.

- Patiently cultivate your capacity to be aware of the life of your mind. You may encounter many moments of becoming lost or entranced in thought. Always be willing to begin again, reconnecting with your breath and the moment you are in.

- Cultivate calmness and clarity of mind in each moment.

- When you are ready, open your eyes and come out of the posture.

WHO AM I?

There are a number of classical meditations that devote themselves to the simple question: "Who am I?" We can go through our lives carrying within us an array of assumptions and images about who we are.

We relate to the world from the perspective of these images and conclusions. As we begin to explore our sense of "self" we also begin to see that it is essentially formed by whatever we identify with—our bodies, thoughts, emotions, opinions, and experience. We are prone to describe ourselves by all that we identify with in the moment, saying or believing, "I am sad/happy/a failure/loveable/unworthy/etc." Many of these descriptions have a long history that becomes increasingly solid over time.

Just as we are prone to freeze our sense of "self" within the confines of these assumptions, so we tend to enact a similar process with others, identifying them by their bodies, minds, opinions, and appearances. We can feel ourselves to be just one "self" living in a world of many "selves" that we compete with, compare ourselves to, fear, envy, or love. There is a deep anxiety underlying many of these assumptions and images—the anxiety of feeling separate and apart from the world.

Our images of our "self" can deeply debilitate us, hindering creativity, growth, and our capacity to explore new horizons in our hearts and lives. With investigation we begin to see the sorrow and turmoil that follow in the wake of our identification with these images. Vast amounts of time and energy are expended in protecting, asserting, and proving ourselves or defending ourselves from threat. The divide between "self" and "other" is too often charged with mistrust and fear.

Openness of heart and depth of understanding are found through questioning the solidity of all of our images and assumptions about "self" and "other." With awareness we begin to understand that all of our notions about "I" and "you" are perhaps not so solid and immutable as they first appear to be. Our sense of who we are undergoes countless changes within a single day. The "I" that was so downcast at breakfast can be exhilarated by lunch; the "self" that glories in the success of achievement looks very different from the "self" that feels despondent in the face of failure.

Each time we hold on to or identify with any of the changing appearances of "self," we are inviting into our hearts the possibility of struggle and sorrow. Each time we are able to question and investigate those changing appearances we sow the seeds of inner balance and wisdom. There is a profound freedom in not holding any appearance to be the absolute truth of who we are. Meditation is not concerned with cultivating a more "perfect self," improving "self," or arriving at a final conclusion of who we are. It is concerned with liberating our hearts and minds from the confines and limitations born of identification and holding. In meditation we learn to bring a gentle and inquiring attention to all the changing faces of "self" as they appear and fade away in our day. Moment to moment, we learn to question and to let go. Inviting the question "Who am I?" into our lives and hearts, we learn the art of inner freedom.

GUIDED MEDITATION

WHO AM I?

- As you begin your meditation, settle into a posture of calm balance and allow your body to relax and be still.
- Gently close your eyes and for a few moments bring your attention to your breathing to steady and calm your mind.
- When you feel sufficiently calm and balanced inwardly, turn your attention to the thoughts, concepts, and images that arise, linger, and pass in your mind. Sense how many of those thoughts carry in subtle or glaring words the sense of "I" —"I want," "I like," "I need," "I am." Don't judge any of those thoughts or images, simply sense the way that the sense of "I" attaches itself to them. Be aware of a tendency to build a sense of "self" around a passing thought or image. Sense the way that a kind and investigating attention brought directly to any of those thoughts or images loosens the glue of the identification.
- Notice when particularly compelling thoughts, memories, or images arise how an equally strong sense of "self" appears with them and becomes defined by whatever has been taken hold of in the mind.
- Sense whether it is possible to see a thought as a thought and an image as an image, and not as an absolute description of yourself.
- If you sense the phrase "I am" appearing in relationship to any of those thoughts, turn the words around and ask yourself, "Am I?" Notice when there are strong emotions present in your mind and heart, feelings of anger, fear, anxiety, or resentment. Sense in those moments how strongly the sense of "I" appears, how you define yourself by the emotion. Again, in the face of "I am," ask yourself, "Am I?"
- Notice when your attention is drawn to a sensation in your body that may be painful or even slightly uncomfortable. Again sense the tendency to identify with that sensation—"my knee," "my back," "I am in pain" —and be aware of the fear or agitation that is born with the identification. Explore the possibility of probing beneath the concepts and seeing a sensation as a sensation rather than as a personal description.
- Sense how the sense of "I" never stands alone but is defined by whatever it is identified with. Sense how the identification solidifies everything we take hold of. Bring a willingness to question all of the descriptions and images. Be aware of how learning to question, investigate, and let go frees our hearts and minds from the confines of all the descriptions. Thoughts, feelings, and the sensations in our body will continue to appear, yet they will also pass with greater ease.
- Cultivate the willingness to question "Who am I?" in the face of everything that appears in your inner world, moment to moment. When you are ready, open your eyes and come out of the posture.

FRANKINCENSE FOR MEDITATION

Frankincense essential oil, also known as olibanum, is distilled from the resin produced by the bark of a small North African tree. Wonderfully calming and richly fragrant, it is considered a spiritual oil, used by many to encourage meditation. It slows the breathing and calms the nervous and digestive systems, relieving anxiety, depression, nervous tension, emotional upsets, and stress-related digestive problems. The gum resin used to make frankincense essential oil oozes out from the tree as a milky-white liquid and then solidifies into tear-shaped, amber to orange-brown lumps. Frankincense blends well with rose, lavender, geranium, neroli, orange, bergamot, mandarin, sandalwood, pine, black pepper, cinnamon, and other spice oils. Do not take frankincense internally and keep it out of children's reach.

Set the scene for your meditation with a calming space and conducive scents, such as frankincense.

AWAKENING OUR LIVES

An awakened life is one in which the confines of habit are challenged through interest and attention. Habit and wakefulness are rarely compatible. Habit leads us to see life through the eyes of images and assumptions. Awareness teaches us to see each moment, event, person, and ourselves anew. Habit binds us to the past, awareness awakens us to the present. Habit distances us from the moment-to-moment realities of our life.

Habit binds us to the past and the present, and restricts us from finding a new future.

Awareness is the cultivation of intimacy within each moment. Habit inclines us to dismiss many of the simple activities and events of our day as being insignificant or unworthy. Awareness is free of hierarchies of value, deeming every single moment and activity of our day as being worthy of our wholehearted attention. In all of the moments of our lives that are governed by habit we live only on the surface of existence, disconnected from its depth and richness. Lost in habit, we deny ourselves the capacity to approach each moment with a beginner's mind, the capacity to see anew and to be taught by life. Awareness dissolves habit and gives birth to openness and a deepening connection with all life. It teaches us to probe beneath the surface of all things—our conclusions, opinions, images, and assumptions—to take nothing for granted in this life. Rather than believing we "know" someone, ourselves, or all that we can learn from any moment in life, awareness teaches us to rest in a deeper "not knowing" and questioning. This is the home of wonder, learning, and mystery. Habit appears to relieve us of the need to be present, enabling us to attend to multiple tasks at the same time. We can wash the dishes while rehearsing our day. We can appear to listen to another while planning our next encounter. We can walk while entertaining our favorite fantasy. Habit equally appears to relieve us of the need to deepen our understanding of ourselves or of another person. If we conclude someone is boring, irritating, or obnoxious and freeze them into that assumption, we may feel no need to probe our own reactivity nor seek to find a greater tolerance, acceptance, or patience within ourselves. If we hold an image of ourselves as being a failure, inadequate, or always right in our opinions, we may also feel no urgency to probe our own conclusions and self-images and find inner transformation.

Awareness offers us a fresh approach to our lives, inviting new possibilities.

Habit disconnects us from the moment-to-moment realities of our lives and leads us to live in a world created by our thoughts and images. Awareness connects us, seeking to discover the possibilities of each moment.

With awareness and wisdom we come to understand that none of our images can ever describe the truth of ourselves, another person or anything we meet in our life.

Habit engenders dullness and sensitivity, and awareness engenders vitality and depth. In search of peace, completeness, and understanding we increasingly treasure vitality and depth, and learn to gently probe the areas of our lives, inwardly and outwardly, that are dulled by habit.

A DAILY PRACTICE

AWAKENING OUR LIVES

Reflect upon your life and all of the activities you frequently engage in, sensing where habit is most strongly present.

You might see habit being the governing force in some of the simple actions you undertake—how you wash your dishes, cook a meal, drive your car, or walk to work.

You might see that it is within the repetitive activities that are part of all of our lives that we are most prone to becoming habitual and mechanical.

Take just one or two activities and commit yourself to undertaking them as if for the first time.

As you wash your dishes, sense all of the sensations and movements involved—the touch of the water on your skin, your hand touching a glass, the movement of your arm. Have the intention of bringing a genuine depth of sensitivity to that moment. If there is a familiar path you walk many times in your life—up a flight of stairs, to your bus stop, or into your workplace—experiment with walking that path with a fullness of sensitivity and a commitment to being present in each step.

Sense if there are people in your life who have in some way been dismissed from your heart because of an image or assumption you hold about them. They may be the people you find yourself avoiding, the person in your neighborhood store who is hardly seen through lack of interest, or someone who has in some way offended you. Make a commitment to meeting that person, seeing and listening to them with a fullness of sensitivity and attention, as if they were your dearest friend or as if this was both the first and last time you would ever have the opportunity to know that person. Sense what happens when you are willing to probe beneath your images and conclusions.

Each day make a simple commitment to bring a fullness of sensitivity and interest to just one area of your life that you sense is governed by habit. Sense how the commitment to awareness has the power to dissolve habit in a moment, allowing a new depth and sensitivity to emerge.

CONNECTING WITH NATURE

The natural world is a powerful ally reminding us of the possibility of discovering richness, appreciation, and sensitivity in all the moments of our lives. Awake to the unfolding seasons, the buds and growth of spring, the abundance of summer, the fading in fall, and the dormancy of winter, we remember too the inevitable seasons of change within our own lives.

Birth and death, arising and passing are the rhythms of everything in our own lives inwardly and outwardly, reminding us to receive life with a fullness of appreciation and yet also to find the ease of being able to let go in all of the endings that are part of our lives.

When our hearts and minds are burdened, overfull, or contracted, forging a connection with the natural world is a way of finding a greater simplicity and ease. Learning to see fully, to appreciate the texture and color of a single leaf, to listen wholeheartedly to the song of a bird, we remember that life is vaster than just the current contents of our minds and hearts.

We sense our place in the natural rhythm of all things. When our minds feel most obsessed or preoccupied, in learning to open our eyes and hearts to the natural world around us we can discover a greater spaciousness and a sense of refuge within its simplicity.

New shoots remind us of the seasons and that everything changes.

The lessons we learn within nature are the same lessons we are asked to learn in our own lives. The daffodil does not demand to be a rose, the wilting flower does not argue with the natural rhythm of its ending. Everything arises and changes in nature according to conditions. The soil, a seed, rain, and sun combine for a flower to bloom. Everything in our life too grows from a combination of conditions that we cannot always control or govern. Control, expectation, demand, and argument destroy the ease possible for us in our lives.

Appreciation and sensitivity are integral to a life of joy and richness. None of these qualities are far away from us. Opening our eyes and hearts to the world around us in this moment, we cultivate the pathways of appreciation. Sensitive to the world around us, we are reminded to bring that same sensitivity to attending to our inner world. Learning to receive the natural world with appreciation and connectedness, we remember the possibility of receiving ourselves in the same spirit.

We can find tranquility in sensing our place in the natural rhythm of the world.

A DAILY PRACTICE

A PLACE OF CONNECTION

Experiment with taking a day to bring wholehearted attention to the sensory doors of seeing and listening.

When you wake in the morning, take a few moments to connect fully with the sights and sounds of your day. You may see the sun touching the ground outside your window. Look at both the ground illuminated by the light and the places of shadow. You may see the raindrops on your window. See fully their shape and movement.

Take a few moments to listen fully. Listen to the sounds of birds as they appear and fade away or the sound of the wind in the branches of the trees. Bring a total attention to just listening to the sounds of nature.

As you walk out of your house, take a few moments to pause and sense the natural world. Bring your attention to see fully a single blade of grass, a leaf on a tree, or the bare earth. Explore with your eyes all of the texture, color, and shape held within that moment. Notice the intricacy of a single leaf, holding it fully in your attention.

If you are able to walk in nature, explore the possibility of seeing and hearing fully, without expectation or preference, simply absorbing the world around you. See the birds in the sky and the spaciousness of the sky itself. Focus your attention upon a single cloud, absorbing its shape and color with your attention.

There are moments when your attention may get lost in judgment, concepts, and descriptions. Sense the possibility of coming back to just seeing and just listening, allowing all of the descriptions to be just a whisper in the mind.

Sense the deepening appreciation and sensitivity that are born of your wholehearted attention. Sense the deepening connectedness and richness that are born of your capacity to see and listen deeply and fully.

Take time to think about and connect with the natural world around you.

FINDING SIMPLICITY

On a daily basis we face an ongoing bombardment of messages that endeavor to convince us that having more, becoming more, doing more and possessing more are the pathways to happiness, fulfilment, and security. All of the great spiritual traditions deliver a somewhat different message, suggesting that genuine happiness lies within our own hearts and minds and can never be truly secured through the multiplicity of possessions, identities, and achievements we can gather in our lives. It is also suggested that none of what we can accumulate will ever effectively armor us against the rhythms of change that will ask us to meet loss, failure, and disappointment with grace. Fulfilment will be found through the authenticity of our hearts and lives, rather than resting upon the shaky foundations of possession and accumulation.

By not pursuing or gathering more than we need for our well-being we are letting go of the pathways of greed and exaggerated need that damage our world. Learning to find well-being in simplicity is a direct way of caring for ourselves and our world.

Simplicity is a multi-dimensional exploration. Cultivating greater simplicity in our lives does not demand that we forsake our homes and families, divorce ourselves from our careers, or abandon all of our possessions. Simplicity is also a direct expression and embodiment of understanding. We see that bottomless need and want are frequently driven by an inner sense of impoverishment that can never be satisfied by the multiplicity of things that we surround ourselves with. We begin to notice that the moments of desperate wanting, pursuit, and need that arise in our days are inextricably linked to an equally dire sense of anxiety. We fill our lives with distraction and busyness to divert ourselves from the painful sense of there being something amiss when we are not constantly occupied. Coming home from work, sitting on a train and in countless other situations when "doing" is not demanded of us, we are prone to immediately fill the silence and stillness with distraction.

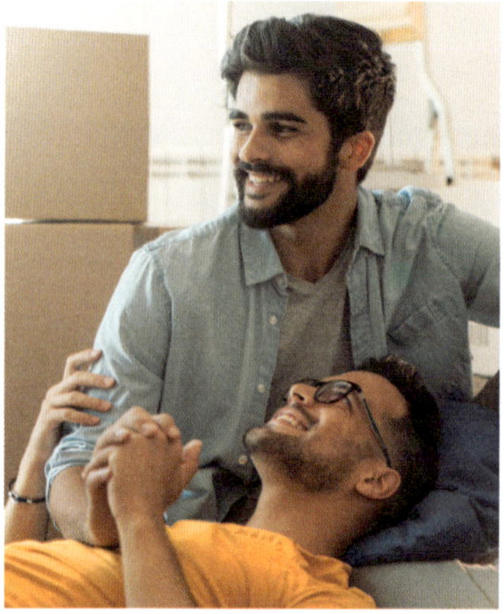

Genuine happiness lies within our own hearts and minds, not possessions.

As our minds are increasingly acclimatized to non-stop activity, sensory impressions, and distraction, it becomes increasingly difficult for us to "un-hook" and be still. We see times of simplicity and non-doing as wasted or uncomfortable moments. Thomas Merton, a great Christian mystic, described the habit of doing too much, answering to too many demands, taking on too many projects, as the most prevalent form of contemporary violence. Meditative paths do not judge the anxiety or sense of impoverishment that may drive us, but invite us to attend to them directly rather than endeavoring to camouflage them with busyness and obsession. At the heart of every meditative path lies the commitment to caring for our well-being with respect and sensitivity. It is the training ground for learning to bring that same respect and sensitivity to every moment and encounter in our lives.

Simplicity is not the pursuit of austerity but an ongoing life exploration that asks us to carefully examine what truly contributes to well-being and what undermines inner balance, happiness, and spaciousness. We can bring the exploration of simplicity into every area of our lives—the choices we make, the actions we engage in, the goals that can obsess us, our speech, the ways we use our time, and our relationship to the world of things, possessions, opinions, and roles. In doing so, we begin to see that simplicity is not a rejection of anything, but is in reality the most compassionate way of being in this world. We learn to treasure moments of stillness, finding within them a genuine sense of ease and spaciousness.

Through finding simplicity we learn to treasure moments of joy.

Meditation helps us to find moments of stillness beneath the camouflage of busyness.

A DAILY PRACTICE

SIMPLICITY

As you move into your day, take with you the intention to notice all the moments when no specific activity demands your attention. They might be moments traveling to or from work, breaks in your working day, or a lull at the end of the day in which nothing demands your engagement.

Sense what happens in your mind and body in those moments. Be aware if you are carrying an inclination to immediately fill that space with something to occupy your attention. There may be an inclination to pick up a book, turn on the radio, make a telephone call, or search for food.

See if it is possible to restrain the immediate impulse towards busyness or distraction and to simply rest in that moment. Initially you may find that these spaces of "nothing to do" feel moderately uncomfortable or carry with them a sense of there being something missing. Bring your attention to your body and mind to simply explore the landscape of that sense of unease, without judging it in any way.

Reflect on how you might feel at home in stillness, in "non-doing."Initially, the simplicity of stillness and "non-doing" may reveal the complexity and busyness of your mind. Pay attention to the thought streams that arise in those moments rather than being pushed by them into new cycles of busyness. You might experiment with adopting the lulls in your day as times when you commit yourself to stillness and simplicity. They can be moments in which you befriend your mind and body, learn to let go of some of the busyness that drives you, and discover the deep sense of ease and resting in the moment that may be available to you. Instead of focusing upon what appears to be missing, bring your attention to what is present. The capacity to connect with your mind, body, and present moment is available to you.

You may discover that your capacity to feel at ease in stillness and simplicity brings with it a greater sensitivity and awareness. Let stillness and simplicity be regular companions in each day, a source of renewal and creativity.

Take some moments to reflect upon your life and sense where it is cluttered by objects that no longer serve you well. What are you holding on to, out of anxiety, that you no longer need? Sense whether letting it go would create more spaciousness in your life.

Reflect on what your mind most frequently dwells on. Sense whether the spaciousness of your own mind has been undermined by preoccupations, fantasies, goals, or desires that do not contribute to your well-being. Is it possible to let them go? Reflect on your life and sense where it may be possible for you to create a greater simplicity. What would you be asked to let go of?

Sense how many of the richest and deepest moments of happiness in your life have been moments of great simplicity. Reflect on what it would mean for simplicity to be a dedicated theme in your life.

Being present in our activities allows us to really enjoy the moment.

SIMPLICITY IN ACTION

—

Genuine simplicity does not depend upon the absence of activity or engagement. In our lives we act, make choices, and move through a world that needs our attention. The activities we engage in, when undertaken with awareness, communicate and embody all that we value and respect. Our aspirations are realized through action and expression. Our choices and acts have the power to communicate a profound calmness, compassion, integrity, and connectedness. A meditative life does not depend upon retreating to the nearest monastery or cave, but learning to be present in all the activities of our lives with awareness and balance. The countless activities that make up our days are not obstacles to peace or stillness. Undertaken with mindfulness and sensitivity, they become the places in which we learn to deepen the calmness and peace we treasure. The wisest people, who have been central in bringing about the greatest social, political, and spiritual transformations, have been people of engagement and action. Moved by compassion, understanding, and care, they have been fully present in their communities, relationships, and world. Their inner core of balance and understanding has found its expression in the choices and activities they have dedicated themselves to. In a life that often seems overfull, with little ease or "non-doing," we may come to believe that we have to postpone a deep spiritual life until we reach a point where life asks less of us. Yet a meditative life doesn't demand that we forsake the world, but that we forsake postponement. We can bring simplicity and stillness to our lives in the midst of activity.

Stepping out of the demands and habits of everyday lives can bring simplicity to busy days.

Slowly slowly O mind...
Everything in own pace happens,
Gardner may water a hundred buckets...
Fruit arrives only in its season.

Kabir

COMMUNICATION

One of the most challenging dimensions of our lives to bring awareness into is the dimension of communication. Yet our words are powerful, holding within them the capacity to harm and to heal, to be a source of joy or sorrow. Through our speech we have the power to bridge the separations that divide us from others and find intimacy and understanding. Our words can also carry the power to create new rifts and further alienation.

Through our speech we communicate our thoughts, emotions, and states of mind. We also receive the inner landscape of others' minds and hearts through the ways in which they communicate with us. Anger, sadness, and fear all find form in our words, as do appreciation, generosity, and tenderness. Learning to be increasingly mindful of our communication is a way of becoming increasingly aware of the inner climate that lies beneath the words.

There are times when we feel uncomfortable and uncertain in silence, and filling that space with words becomes a way of distancing ourselves from that discomfort.

Our words become a means of finding reassurance and familiarity. There are also moments when our words are habitual and reactive. We may find ourselves uttering words of harshness and condemnation that we later regret, yet they fly from our mouths with an intensity and unconsciousness that sometimes frightens us. In the moments when we feel most governed by anxiety, agitation, or anger our speech tends to be the most impulsive, at times wounding ourselves or another person. In learning to be more awake and sensitive within our speech, we can appreciate the impact it has upon our own consciousness and upon the heart of another.

Through our speech we communicate our intentions and our thoughts.

Wise speech is a meditative practice. Are our words spoken in a tone and at a time when they can be truly listened to by another? Are we saying what is true and useful? What are the intentions in our speech—do we seek to harm or to heal?

Our relationships, families, communities, and world plead for greater understanding and communication. In our own lives and connections with others we can be a conscious participant in contributing to the ending of alienation and mistrust through our own commitment to mindful communication.

A DAILY PRACTICE

MINDFUL SPEECH

As you go into your day, take with you the intention to be mindful of all the different moments of communication.

Notice how your awareness of speech is different in different contexts.

Be aware of how you speak with the people you feel somewhat neutral towards—the person in the store, the coffee shop, the ticket seller.

Take a day when you approach those people differently. Look into their eyes as you request something or thank them. In even the few words you use in these contacts, experiment with speaking in a heartfelt way, making a genuine connection with that person.

Stay in contact with your speech in the moments when your are speaking to someone you care for and feel affection for. Be aware of the words you are speaking and what they are communicating. Sense whether you are comfortable in silence.

Be aware of your speech in the moments you are in contact with someone you dislike or feel threatened by, or in situations that are charged with anger or blame. In those moments, try to stay in touch with your own emotional landscape before you speak. Can your words be born of that awareness rather being purely reactive? Is it possible for you to stay connected with the person you feel angry towards or are receiving anger from rather than withdrawing and becoming lost in the anxiety or anger? Sense whether it is possible in those charged moments to speak with calmness and care or to be silent rather than uttering words that may wound.

An aid to being increasingly aware within your communication is to allow your attention to rest more fully in your throat, lips, and face. Sense what happens in those areas when you speak and before you speak.

It is important to cultivate an awareness in speaking that is free from judgment or condemnation. The right attitude is to be simply interested in exploring what happens in this powerful dimension of our lives. There may be a wisdom in cultivating restraint—in the times when we feel most compelled by anger or anxiety it can be helpful to learn to pause before speaking. Restraint is different from suppression: the primary motivation in restraint is to be aware and to understand. As you are increasingly aware of your speech throughout your day, sense its potential to be a source of intimacy and connectedness.

ENDSRECEPTIVE LISTENING

Communication is a twofold process, involving not only speaking with authenticity and awareness, but also listening with a deep receptivity.

There is a great art in learning to be mindful in listening. We can learn to listen to ourselves as we speak, allowing our words to rise from an inner stillness and calm. We can also learn to bring that same receptivity and stillness to listening to others, being wholehearted in our receptivity rather than formulating our responses and impatiently waiting for a moment to interject them.

Mindful communication is more than just an exchange of words—it is a time that holds the possibility of a genuine connection and bond of intimacy with another. When we listen to another, are we listening in a non-judgmental way? Are we able to offer a patient presence that is genuinely connected with the person speaking to us?

Carrying with us into our lives the commitment to conscious communication, we learn to value the bonds we form with all those who are part of our lives. We learn to cultivate intimacy and respect.

A DAILY PRACTICE

RECEPTIVE LISTENING

Bring with you into your day the commitment to listen whole-heartedly in all the moments when someone is asking for your attention and presence. In contact with a friend, listen with awareness and spaciousness.

Listen with your heart, sensing their reaching out to forge a connection with you and be fully present. Listen with patience, noticing the moments when with impatience or boredom you start to disconnect. See if you can bring your attention back to be fully present.

Listen with openness, instead of preparing your responses or waiting for a lull in their speech so you can say something you deem to be more interesting or important.

Notice if there are moments when you start to judge whatever they are recounting to you. Sense whether it is possible to let go of those judgments and renew your commitment to being fully present with the person in front of you.

Bring awareness into those moments in your day when you are listening to someone who is distressed or angry. Sense what happens in your own body, mind, and heart as you listen to distress or anger.

Notice how you may be prone to stop listening as you prepare your defenses or retorts. Sense if you feel hurt or helpless as you absorb the words of another.

When faced with someone who is enraged, it may be helpful to explore what it means to stay connected with that person without being lost in the barrage of their words. Are you able to sustain eye contact with them, sense the pain or frustration that underlies their anger, and listen without feeling attacked? Are you able to leave their anger with them rather than feeling you need to defend yourself or respond in kind? Listening to someone who is deeply distressed or in pain can be deeply challenging.

As you listen to someone recounting to you their heartache, notice if as a reaction to feeling helpless, you begin to search for formulas or prescriptions to 'fix' their pain. This may not be what is being asked of you. What is being asked for is a compassionate presence.

Faced with someone in distress, explore what it may mean simply to bring a compassionate, open stillness that can receive that sorrow.

Experiment with listening to yourself as you speak, sensing whether your speech is a genuine expression of care and sensitivity. Are you saying what you wish to say, communicating what you most need to communicate? Are you able to listen to your own heart and mind before the words are spoken?

Communication is a two-way process, of speaking and listening.

AGRIMONY FOR OPENNNESS

The agrimony flower remedy may be useful for those who hide their problems behind a cheerful face and laughter. They may be reluctant to burden others and dread arguments, pursuing peace at all costs. This can lead to an inner anguish that is masked by alcohol or drugs.

KINDNESS AND COMPASSION

Loving kindness embraces the qualities of acceptance, generosity, friendliness, and warmth we long to receive from others. It describes an unconditional warmth and care that we are able to extend to all those who are part of our lives—those we cherish and love, those we are indifferent to, those we feel most separate from, and our own selves. Cultivating loving kindness, we discover that the walls of mistrust and fear that can so painfully separate us from others can also begin to crumble. In developing our own capacities for fearlessness, tenderness, and benevolence, our lives are lived with greater ease and connectedness. The small gestures of love we receive from others nurture and heal us, while the gestures and words of love and kindness we are able to offer to others bring depth and intimacy to all of our relationships. Loving kindness awakens and gladdens our hearts.

We all know the power that ill will, anger, and fear have to damage and scar our lives and our world. Individuals, communities, and nations are divided by mistrust, fear, and rage. Our whole world cries out for greater generosity, tenderness, and love. Its divisions and conflicts will not be healed by yet more formulas, prescriptions, and strategies, but through a radical change in each of our hearts. We share with all living beings the longing to be happy and free from pain and fear. We share with all living beings the yearning to be accepted, loved, and cared for. In the face of anger our tendency is to withdraw, close down, or disconnect from the person before us. Gripped by the rage or hurt present in our own hearts, we are prone to strike out, to harm another or exile them from our lives. The division, mistrust, and alienation that follow scar our lives and relationships. Our own anger and fear will lead us to commit countless acts that are born of unconsciousness and reactivity and lead to sorrow and alienation. Loving kindness meditation teaches us how to find a refuge of calm openness within our own hearts. It is a refuge that protects us from fear, anger, and turmoil. With loving kindness meditation we learn to remember, honor, and cultivate the capacity each of us has to touch our world with warmth and friendliness. We nurture a sanctuary of balance and strength within ourselves that allows us to turn towards pain and adversity and heal division. In loving kindness meditation we cultivate, again and again, the intention to embrace all moments with generosity and warmth.

GUIDED MEDITATION

LOVING KINDNESS FOR A FRIEND

- **Once more relax into a calm and upright posture, closing your eyes gently.**
- **Again bring your attention to rest in the center of your chest, in the area of your heart. Be aware of your body expanding and relaxing with each breath.**
- **Begin your meditation once more by extending a genuine sense of loving kindness towards yourself, letting your attention rest easily within each phrase:**

"May I be free from fear and danger."
"May I be happy."
"May I be peaceful."

- **When you are ready, invite into your heart and your attention someone who is dear to you, a friend you treasure.**
- **Again, if possible, visualize their face or remember a contact you have had with them. As you bring them into your attention, sense the qualities of the friendship that bonds you with that person—the trust, acceptance, tenderness, and love that you cherish.**
- **As far as possible, sustain the connection, offering to that person your heartfelt wishes for their well-being:**

"May you be free from fear and danger."
"May you be happy."
"May you be peaceful."

- **Continue to rest your attention in the phrases, extending loving kindness, warmth, and care.**
- **If you wish you can alternate your attention between your friend and yourself, sensing your mutual wish to be free from pain and to be happy.**
- **Stay present with the phrases of intention, aware of the warmth, tenderness, and happiness that can begin to emerge in your heart and mind. Let them pervade the whole of your body and mind.**
- **If your attention wanders, come gently back to the phrases, nurturing your capacity for profound loving kindness and sensitivity.**
- **When you are ready, open your eyes and sense the calmness and happiness that might continue to pervade your body and mind.**

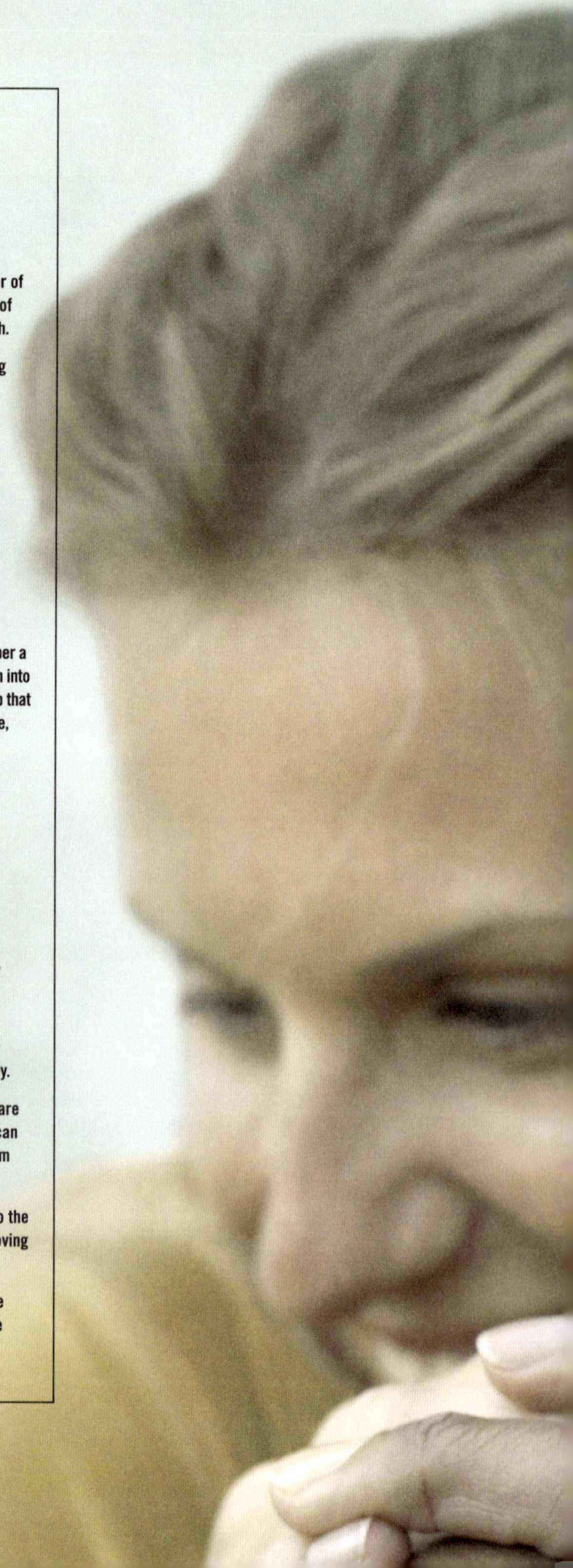

Practicing loving kindness with others brings happiness in a divided world.

Yet loving kindness is not sentimentality, or even a particular kind of feeling. Simply in each moment we nurture our capacity for intimacy and understanding. Loving kindness meditation is a practice of happiness.

KINDNESS FOR ONESELF

Traditionally, loving kindness meditation begins with ourselves. We learn to offer an unconditional warmth, acceptance, and tenderness to our own bodies, minds, and hearts. Many people find it easier to extend love and care to others than to receive it or to offer that same generosity of heart to themselves.

Historical feelings of worthlessness or inadequacy at times make us feel we are undeserving of love and tenderness. Loving kindness meditation can heal those historical wounds that impair our capacity to offer to ourselves the boundless generosity, acceptance, and tenderness that make our hearts sing. In learning to extend loving kindness to ourselves we discover the freedom of heart born of letting go of the painful judgments, expectations, and demands. Cultivating loving kindness for ourselves is also the training ground for learning the lessons of the patience, attentiveness, tolerance, and warmth that we would wish to pervade all of our relationships.

Cultivating loving kindness for ourselves allows us to extend it to others.

Classically, loving kindness is developed through establishing our attention in a few simple phrases that embody the intentions for the happiness and well-being we treasure. The phrases remind us of the possibility of making our inner home in a place of fearlessness, warmth, and balance instead of one of confusion or ill will. The practice is not a mechanical repetition of empty words, but a genuine offering of kindness and love in each moment. Loving kindness meditation can be developed in a dedicated posture and time; it can also be cultivated in all the moments and circumstances of our lives that ask for healing and connectedness and invite us to nurture a loving heart.

GUIDED MEDITATION

LOVING KINDNESS FOR ONESELF

• Find a position that is relaxed and comfortable. You can develop this practice in any posture, though you may find that sitting upright helps you to be more alert and attentive.

• Let your eyes close and take some moments to consciously relax your body, softening any areas of holding or tension.

• For a few minutes focus a gentle, alert attentiveness on your breathing, letting your mind and body calm with each out-breath. Bring your attention to rest in the center of your chest, in the area of your heart.

• Silently repeat the simple phrases of loving kindness, sensing the meaning of each one:

"May I be free from fear and danger."
"May I be happy."
"May I be peaceful."

• Let each phrase rest gently in your heart and mind, taking care not to hurry the words, simply offering to yourself your heartfelt wishes for your well-being and happiness.

• Don't expect that any particular feeling will arise. Simply allow the phrases and their meaning to fill your heart and mind.

• If you wish, you can alter the words so that you are using phrases that have a personal meaning for you.

• Expand your attention to be aware of your body, sensing all the pain and well-being your body can experience in this life. Youth, aging, health, illness, birth, and death are held within all of our bodies. Holding your body in your awareness, continue to rest your attention in the phrases:

"May I be free from fear and danger."
"May I be happy."
"May I be peaceful."

• Expand your awareness to sense the life of your mind, with the spectrum of experiences it can undergo—confusion, calm, agitation, serenity, contractedness, spaciousness, busyness, and stillness. With loving kindness befriending your mind, gently repeat the phrases:

"May I be free from fear and danger."
"May I be happy."
"May I be peaceful."

• Expand your awareness further to embrace the life of your heart, sensing all the joy and sorrow that can live in our hearts. Anger, love, fear, trust, anxiety, and happiness touch all of our lives. We can learn to befriend them all without exception; we can learn to embrace the world of our emotions without fear.

• Continue to rest your attention in the phrases. It is not unusual in this practice for buried feelings of confusion, pain, or anger to arise. Do not try to banish them, simply touch them with the intention to welcome them, accept them, and befriend them.

• Stay with the phrases for as long as you wish. If they become an empty repetition of words, let them go for a few moments and reflect upon what it is that brings meaning, richness, and depth to your life, and upon all the qualities of heart you long to bring to fruition. Then, on the foundation of that reflection, return your attention to rest in the area of your heart and begin once more to offer the phrases of intention to yourself.

• When you are ready, open your eyes and come out of your posture.

KINDNESS IN THE MIDST OF INDIFFERENCE

—

The people we love and the people we despise both evoke powerful emotional responses in us. It is often our histories and our stories about our friends and our enemies, as much as our present relationship, that bonds us to them. Yet as we move through our lives and our days we are surrounded by countless beings with whom we share no common story or history. We walk down a crowded street, sit on a train or stand in line in a store, and all around us are those who, like us, long to be happy and free from pain. Yet we often feel neutral towards these people; we feel separate and apart from them. We easily sink into feeling indifferent towards them. They become invisible to us.

Indifference is the first building block of passivity and disconnection. A homeless man once said that the greatest curse of homelessness was not the obvious lack of a home or security—it was that most people would not look him in the eye. No matter our history, identity, race, or circumstances, we are all connected in our longing for happiness, intimacy, safety, and peace. We share the common bonds of yearning to be free from pain, turmoil, confusion, and fear. No one wants to suffer. All of us wish to be happy. Loving kindness meditation roots itself in the mutuality of these longings—it is where we are all connected.

Loving kindness meditation can bring a renewed depth to our relationships of care and intimacy. It can heal the wounds of fractured and painful relationships. On a deeper level it can awaken our hearts so that no one is dismissed or felt to be separate from ourselves. Cultivating loving kindness, we learn to embrace everyone who comes into our life with respect, sensitivity, and friendliness.

In focusing loving kindness upon a neutral person, we learn to cultivate an unconditional friendliness that has no expectation of anything in return. We are nurturing a profound inner generosity that can freely offer warmth and care without investment in result or preference. We discover that our capacity to bring caring attention to all the people we encounter in our lives lifts our hearts and we form bonds of connection and care that are rooted in sensitivity and generosity.

Loving kindness meditation can bring depth to our relationships with others.

It is a fascinating exploration to go into each day of our life with the intention to receive each person we meet with unconditional warmth and friendliness. Cultivating the intention to ignore no one, to dismiss no one, awakens our hearts and brings only joy. When our words and actions are born of loving attention, our hearts become saturated with friendliness. There are countless opportunities for us to experiment with cultivating loving kindness for the neutral person, and a single word or gesture of care and friendliness can transform our day. Indifference turns to affection, distance turns to warmth, and separation turns to connection. Cultivating loving kindness is learning to smile upon our world.

Loving kindness meditation can be cultivated and deepened in formal meditation practice; it can also be nurtured in all the moments of our lives. Experiment with this practice in the situations and circumstances where you feel the most separate and isolated from others. Sense the aliveness and vitality it brings.

Cultivating loving kindness encourages us to see those who feel invisible.

GUIDED MEDITATION

KINDNESS IN THE MIDST OF INDIFFERENCE

• Settle your body into a posture of alertness and ease.

• Gently close your eyes and rest your attention in the center of your chest, in the area of your heart. Bring a sensitive attention to your breathing. Be aware of your body expanding and relaxing with each breath.

• With each out-breath consciously release anything that is pre-occupying your mind—thoughts of the past, the future, and anything you are anxious about in the present.

• Begin your meditation by inviting into your attention a person you feel affection and tenderness for—a good friend or loved one. Visualize their face or remember your last contact with them. Offer to that person your heartfelt wishes for their well-being, using the same phrases you previously used:

"May you be free from fear and danger."
"May you be happy."
"May you be peaceful."

• Sense the warmth and friendliness that may arise. Continue for some minutes to rest your attention in the phrases of intention. Now expand your attention and bring to mind a person you feel quite neutral towards. It may be someone you work with, the teller in your bank, the driver of your bus, a person in your neighborhood you frequently pass yet do not know. If possible remember their face or the last time you encountered them.

• Begin to offer to them the same warmth and friendliness you feel for the person you feel most affectionate towards, using the phrases:

"May you be free from fear and danger."
"May you be happy."
"May you be peaceful."

• Sustain your connection with the neutral person for as long as you are able, with your attention steadily rooted in the phrases of intention. Don't anticipate the arising of any particular emotional responses.

• If your attention begins to waver, return your focus to the person you feel more close to for a time. When you are ready once more, switch back to the neutral person, remembering the phrases:

"May you be free from fear and danger."
"May you be happy."
"May you be peaceful."

• Sense whether it is possible for you to offer the same depth of warmth and care to the neutral person as to the person who is dear to you.

• When you are ready, open your eyes and come out of the posture.

Through self-care we can release ourselves from any pain in our past.

KINDNESS IN THE FACE OF DIFFICULTY AND FEAR

—

The greatest challenge we face in our lives is learning to be present and receptive to those we fear or dislike. Yet the most direct way to transformation is to turn towards the moments and people in our lives we resist most strongly.

We can be deeply hurt and shattered by the words and actions of another. Even when that pain lies in a distant past we carry its scars and we can become a prisoner of it.

When we are hurt by or afraid of another person, our tendency is to strike out in anger or to disconnect through fear. But it is not difficult for us to see that anger is not healed by anger and that ever-deepening division and conflict are the children of fear.

We think a lot about the people we dislike and fear in our lives. They can govern our hearts and minds. Cultivating loving kindness for these people does not mean trying to force an artificial affection or tenderness. We do, however, discover that our capacity to turn toward the people from whom we habitually recoil begins to loosen the grip of aversion and fear. We may, through loving kindness meditation, begin to find a way to calm the turmoil and anxiety in our own hearts and minds. We may begin to discover the possibility of greater forgiveness, tolerance, and patience.

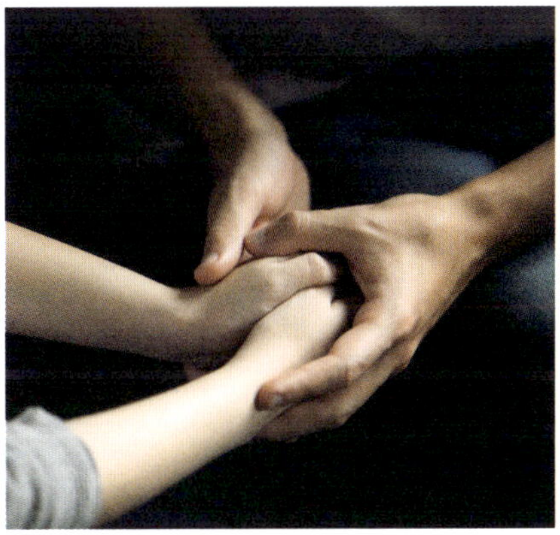

Through loving kindness we can find a way to forgive and embrace tolerance.

The difficult person sometimes lives within our own hearts and minds in our relationship to ourselves. We see inner tendencies of judgment, harshness, blame, or anger that damage our well-being and impair our capacity to live with happiness and peace. We can learn to approach those areas of inner struggle with care and sensitivity and heal that inner division. As you approach dimensions of your life where there is estrangement and struggle, whether inner or outer, take care not to expect some immediate transformation or inner emotional shift. Be patient—it is enough to find the willingness to embrace with kind attention any area of your life that has previously been banished from your heart.

As you open up to your own struggles, be kind and patient to yourself.

GUIDED MEDITATION

LOVING KINDNESS IN THE FACE OF DIFFICULTY AND FEAR

- Find a posture for your body that is as relaxed and tension free as possible.
- Gently close your eyes and bring your attention once more to rest in the center of your chest.
- Remain present with your breathing for a few moments to let your mind and body settle in the present.
- Begin to offer the phrases and intentions of loving kindness first to yourself:

"May I be free from fear and danger."
"May I be happy."
"May I be peaceful."

- Extend your attention and invite into your heart and mind the image or awareness of someone you have had difficulty with. Let them rest in the center of your attention.
- Offer them a genuine wish for their well-being and peace:

"May you too be free from fear and danger."
"May you too be happy."
"May you too be peaceful."

- If it is difficult to stay connected, bring your attention once more back to yourself for a time and then open again to the difficult person, using whatever phrases have meaning for you.
- You may wish to focus your phrases and intentions upon parts of your own emotional or psychological being that bring pain or harm to yourself.
- Find just a few phrases that embody your wish for healing and peace:

"May I find acceptance."
"May I find peace."
"May I find healing."

- After some time you may want to expand your attention to embrace all beings in our world—the people you are close to, those you struggle with, and those you feel indifferent towards.
- Open your attention even further to include all those in the world you don't know, all the animals and creatures on the Earth, in the seas and in the sky:

"May all beings be free from fear and danger."
"May all beings be happy."
"May all beings be peaceful."

- Let your attention rest for a time in that open, warm attentiveness.
- When you are ready, open your eyes and come out of the posture.

COMPASSION FOR BLAMELESS SORROWS

—

Sorrow, loss, and pain will be part of all of our lives and at some time we will all meet people in the midst of great physical, emotional, or mental pain and distress—a child with a terminal illness, a friend grieving in the midst of loss, a person whose world has been shattered by violence. We see, too, endless images of people caught in famine or desolation, or brutalized by wars they do not even understand. There is suffering in this world that is blameless.

Faced with situations of severe distress, our first response is often to feel stunned. We desperately search to find the "right" words or actions, yet often feel they are inadequate. Confronted with great pain and our own feelings of helplessness, we may be tempted to withdraw to protect ourselves. Alternatively, we may be tempted to throw ourselves into a frenzy of busyness, searching for solutions that can fix the suffering we see before us. Yet there is not always a solution for a broken heart, an illness, or the unexpected losses that touch our lives.

Compassion asks us to be still in the face of immeasurable pain, not to blame or judge, or try to control or fix. Blame and judgment can be mechanisms we use to console ourselves in our own despair and helplessness. The heart of compassion is willing to surrender both numbness and the desperate desire to try to control the world. With compassion we can learn to open to pain and in so doing find a deep inner steadiness that can embrace the anguish we face. We can find the empathy within ourselves to dissolve the separation between ourselves and another. We can discover a way of being awake and receptive in the face of pain without being shattered or overwhelmed.

Sometimes anguish feels bottomless. Compassion too can be bottomless. Our world and all those in it who live on a daily diet of deprivation, fear, and pain cry out for compassion. We do not need to hold grandiose thoughts of healing the world—we would break beneath the weight of that expectation—but we can commit to opening our hearts to the moments in each of our days when we meet sorrow and pain, whether in ourselves or in another. All of us have experienced times in our lives when compassion is our immediate and natural response to suffering. At such times the walls of distance melt and we see ourselves in the eyes and life of another person.

Compassion allows us to connect with others and heal.

These are powerful moments of connection and healing. Compassion meditation encourages us not to look upon that heartfelt response as a random accident. We can commit ourselves to finding compassion in all the moments of our lives.

BREATHING IN SORROW, BREATHING OUT COMPASSION

Sometimes it can be useful to use a visualization practice as a way of awakening compassion within our hearts.

When you are ready, open your eyes and come out of the posture.

GUIDED MEDITATION

COMPASSION FOR BLAMELESS SORROW

- **Find a posture that is relaxed and comfortable for your body.**
- **Let your eyes gently close.**
- **Take a few moments to be aware of your body, its stillness, and the life within it.**
- **Bring your attention to rest in the center of your chest, in the area of your heart, and for a few moments be aware of your breathing.**
- **Let your mind relax and calm.Invite into your heart and attention the image or awareness of a person who is in the midst of great physical, emotional, or mental pain. It might be someone close to you, but it can also be someone you don't know personally. Let the image settle in your attention. Sense the struggle and sorrow that person is living with. Reflect on their hardship, heartache, or pain.**
- **With an open heart filled with empathy and sensitivity, offer to that person your heartfelt wishes for their healing and well-being:**

"May you find healing."
"May you find peace."

- **Let these phrases rest in your heart and mind. If you find that you begin to become lost in despair, pity, or anxiety, just come back to your breathing for a few moments to steady your heart and mind. You may need to find words and phrases that are appropriate to the person you are connecting with. You might use:**

"May you find acceptance."
"May you find ease."

- **Stay with the phrases as long as you wish. Before coming out of the posture, extend the scope of your compassion to embrace all beings:**

"May all beings find healing."
"May all beings find peace."

COMPASSION FOR YOURSELF

—

Many people in this world find it easier to extend compassion to others than to receive it or to offer it to themselves. Aware of the dire and bottomless pain that pervades the lives of so many people, we may feel it is inappropriate to reflect on the pain or sorrow in our own life. We may even believe that it is self-indulgent to care for our own broken hearts, ailing bodies, or confused minds. Compassion does not measure the worth of suffering—it is a commitment to the healing of sorrow, no matter how small or large, wherever it arises. Compassion invites us to go beyond the concepts of "right" and "wrong," "good" and "bad," "worthy" and "unworthy," and explore what it means to receive all sorrow, pain, and heartache with a compassionate presence. If we are able to surrender our tendency to flee from pain, we discover an inner balance that is not shattered by change and loss. In our relationship to our own bodies, minds, and hearts we learn the lessons of patience, tolerance, equanimity, and receptivity. In the world of our body, mind, and heart we sense the world of all bodies, minds, and hearts—moments of joy and despair, health and illness, fear and trust. Compassion invites us to be intimate with this universal story and deeply acknowledge the essential interconnectedness and interdependence of all life. The lessons of healing we learn within our own story are the lessons we bring to our lives.

COMPASSION IN GRIEF AND LOSS

—

Our capacity to form bonds of intimacy with people in our lives inevitably means that all of us will experience the sorrow of loss and separation. Grief is our very human and heartfelt response to death and the endings of the relationships that have gladdened our hearts. In the midst of grieving it can feel that it will be endless, as if the fabric of our lives has been torn apart. In the pain of grief we may find ourselves lost in a cascade of memories, replaying the endless stories of our relationship with the person who has died. Our hearts can fill with an overwhelming sense of injustice, particularly when someone we care for deeply dies unexpectedly and unpredictably. Part of our grieving in those moments may be to shut out the world, to seek causes we may never be able to find or understand, or to blame ourselves for not preventing the death.

Times of grief are moments when being listened to and connecting with others is important for healing.

Grief is a territory in which we feel rootless and bereft. It can seem a time of such darkness, sorrow, and uncertainty that there is nowhere we can find a place of rest. Meditation practice is not a device to make grief disappear, but it can offer a way of discovering a sense of refuge and ease. We can learn to find a home for ourselves in the present, one moment at a time, rather than being lost in stories of the past or fears about the future. Grief has no predetermined timetable, but within it we can discover a way of caring for ourselves. The times of greatest sorrow in our lives are those that ask for the greatest compassion. Compassion has its roots in listening, the capacity to receive sorrow without fear or anxiety. In grief, being listened to by others is part of our healing. Our capacity to listen deeply to our own hearts and minds is equally part of the fabric of our healing.

GUIDED MEDITATION

COMPASSION IN GRIEF AND LOSS

- Take a few moments to settle into a posture that is as relaxed and comfortable as possible. Gently close your eyes and be aware of your whole body.
- Let your breathing relax. Consciously take a few slightly fuller breaths, and as you breathe out, be aware of releasing the out-breath fully.
- With each out-breath sense your body relaxing more and more deeply.
- Bring your attention to your heart area, the center of your chest, and sense what sensations or feelings are being held in that area of your body.
- Your heart may feel heavy, contracted, or painful. Let your attention rest gently there without demanding that it should feel different.
- Offer to yourself heartfelt compassion and care:

"May I find ease within this sorrow."
"May I find peace within this sorrow."
"May I find healing."

- Thoughts and memories may flood your mind, bringing their own waves of grief. Embrace them with the same compassionate attention. Discover that it is possible to be present with these thoughts and memories without becoming lost.
- Bring your attention gently back to the phrases of compassion:

"May I find ease within this sorrow."
"May I find peace within this sorrow."
"May I find healing."

- Stay with this practice as long as it is comfortable for you. In the moments of greatest heartache you may discover that it is possible for you to find some sense of refuge and ease within the phrases of compassion.

To be nobody-but-yourself—in a world which is doing its best, night and day, to make you everybody else—means to fight the hardest battle which any human being can fight, and never stop fighting.

e.e. cummings

TAKING CARE OF YOUR LIFE-BALANCE

SOCIAL WELLNESS

PART THREE

FRIENDS AND HOME

CHAPTER SEVEN

SUPPORT SYSTEMS

It's normal for life to have its ups and downs, and for you to experience times that are more challenging and difficult than others. To help you on this rollercoaster, it's beneficial to have support systems and friendships in place. Support systems consist of people you trust, who are good at listening, and to whom you can turn for help if you need it.

Good friendships bring meaning and connection to your life, and they help you gain a vital sense of belonging. Some friendships are long-lasting, with people you've known for years and are still in touch with, while other friends come and go. As you journey through life, it's only natural for friendships to change, as people grow, change, and move on.

The people you surround yourself with can have a huge impact on your well-being. Negative people can be toxic and bring you down, but people who share common interests and have similar values to you can benefit you in many ways. They can lift your mood when you're feeling down, know how to make you smile and laugh, and be the people with whom you celebrate your successes.

Good friendships can give you support and a sense of belonging.

While some people thrive on having a large network of friends and acquaintances, when you're looking to establish a solid support network, quality over quantity tends to work best.

You may have family that is supportive, but it's good to have people in your life beyond family whom you can call on. Support systems can involve friends, neighbors, mentors, colleagues, or other people you know and trust. It's good to have people in your support system that have different skills and strengths, so you don't rely on the same person all the time.

Support systems offer care, advice, and help when you need it, but they also provide joy, pleasure, and friendship. It's not just one way: support systems function and survive best when they're mutually beneficial, so make sure you help and support one another.

People who share common interests and passions can benefit your life in so many ways.

Nurture and maintain relationships by making the effort to keep in touch.

HOW TO CREATE SUPPORT SYSTEMS

Support systems don't just happen overnight; they develop with time. With the right skills, you can create valuable support systems.

GET TO KNOW PEOPLE

—

Make an effort to get to know people. Start with those you're already acquainted with, such as neighbors, people you see regularly at clubs or the gym, or who you say hello to while walking your dog, or work colleagues. Talk to them, take an interest in their views, skills, hobbies, and lives, and get to know them better. They will, in turn, do the same.

JOIN NEW GROUPS OR ACTIVITIES

—

Expand your friendships by joining new groups or activities. Find activity, hobby, or sporting groups where you'll share common interests and values. Or try volunteering for a cause that you're passionate about.

ORGANIZE SOCIAL GET-TOGETHERS

—

When you've made new friends, organize a social activity or get-together so that you can get to know them better. For example, meet for a coffee, have a drink together, or go for a walk. Sometimes individual friendships can deepen away from the wider shared group.

BE POSITIVE AND OPEN

—

Be positive and open and try to see the good in people. Be tolerant of others and don't get annoyed if their behavior or views are different from yours. Instead, ask them to explain why they think or act the way they do. This doesn't mean you have to put up with offensive behavior or views, though.

KEEP IN TOUCH

—

Make an effort to develop and nurture connections by staying in touch regularly, be it through phone calls, texts, emails, or seeing each other in person.

LEARN TO BE A GOOD LISTENER

—

Support systems thrive when you listen to each other. Dedicate time to listening to other people, whether they simply want a chat after a busy day, or they need to offload their worries and concerns.

CONFIDE IN OTHERS

—

Learn to open up and confide in the people you trust. No one will offer you help if they don't know that you need it. Confiding in each other builds and strengthens support systems.

SUPPORT OTHERS

—

Show you care by being there to support other people when they need help. Offer support in any way you can. Support systems are most successful when you help each other.

PERSEVERE AND GATHER THE RIGHT TRIBE

—

It's not always easy building up your support system, or your tribe of connections, but persevere. If you eventually find that someone you've got to know doesn't turn out to be who you thought they were, don't be afraid to let that friendship go. Negative and toxic people will only bring you down. Start again and look to meet other people, or strengthen the bonds you have with existing members of your support group.

Above all, persevere. We all need support systems and, however hard it may seem to build yours, it's well worth it in the long run.

Make time for friends, to listen, to talk, and share your concerns.

SETTING BOUNDARIES

All relationships, whether with friends, family, or even with work colleagues (see page 317), need to have boundaries. Boundaries are important for you and your self-care so that you can ensure you get the time to yourself that you need. They're also important for other people, so they respect you, know what is and isn't acceptable, and how best to interact with you.

When you don't have boundaries, there's the risk that problems can occur in relationships—such as one person demanding too much time, not respecting your feelings, or a so-called friend only contacting you when they want or need something.

Although it might seem tricky to establish boundaries, it's well worth persevering with it as it can make relationships a lot healthier, happier, and more fulfilled. Plus, it can highlight toxic relationships that are, dragging you down, and which are perhaps better left behind.

HOW TO SET BOUNDARIES

Use these practical steps to guide you with setting boundaries with your friends and family.

EVALUATE YOUR RELATIONSHIPS

—

Start by evaluating your relationships and think about how, where, and why you need to put boundaries in place. Is a particular person demanding too much of your time? Are you uncomfortable around certain people? Do you wish you had more time to spend with other people, those who make you feel happier? Or are you fed up with someone else being too "helpful" and trying to make your decisions for you?

Assess your relationships and decide whether you are happy with their balance.

THINK ABOUT WHAT IMPROVEMENTS YOU'D LIKE TO MAKE

—

So, what changes would you like to make to improve these issues? For example, would seeing a friend just once a week, rather than several times a week, make things easier for you? Do you need to remind a friend that while you appreciate their help, you are capable of making your own decisions? When you're thinking things through, it might help to jot down notes about what you're aiming for.

START AFRESH

—

Once you've established your new boundaries, start afresh and maintain the boundaries. Don't be tempted to give in and let your standards slide, as this will only encourage previous bad habits to rear their head. You've gone to the trouble of raising your concerns and discussing boundaries, so stick to them. If your friends "forget" the new boundaries, calmly remind them exactly why they were needed. If they are true and worthy friends, they'll understand.

BE FLEXIBLE

—

Be aware that boundaries can change over time, so make sure you don't get too caught up in being obsessive and rigid with the boundaries you set. Accept that people and situations can alter and be prepared to re-evaluate things in the future if needs be. Don't, however, let other people force you to adjust your boundaries if you're not happy to do so.

COMMUNICATE

—

Boundaries are only going to work if other people know about them, so communication is key. This is the part that can be the most difficult, as you may worry how others will feel about it—and that's a perfectly normal reaction. They may not know you've been struggling or feeling uncomfortable, and it can bring up difficult feelings to talk about it.

However, you need to discuss what's bothering you; expressing your needs and feelings makes your friendship honest and healthy. Talk to them calmly and openly and explain exactly what the issue is. Stick with it and remember you're doing this for a good reason and that, in the long run, the intention is good and it will help you both.

GIVE THEM TIME

—

If your boundary idea has come as a shock to the other person, be prepared to give them time to ponder on it. Some space from each other can help you both get

Communication is key to maintaining a healthy relationship.

things in perspective and provide a clean slate from which you can start afresh. Be there for them if they want to clarify things further, but avoid getting caught up in endless discussions where nothing gets resolved, as this will only add more stress.

ACCEPT A BREAK-UP

—

Setting boundaries can highlight problems in relationships that can't be be solved. If there are feelings of emotional manipulation or passive aggressiveness and the other person is not amenable to discussing boundaries, be prepared to accept that the friendship just might not be right for you. It's not unacceptable to break up and move on from friends—your self-esteem, self-worth, and happiness matters, and it could open the door for better things. Of course, it can be a lot trickier with family, but for your own well-being, you might need to accept that it's better for you if you don't see them so frequently.

Maintaining healthy boundaries can be challenging, but stay firm and stick to your decisions. If you have any doubts or niggling worries, remind yourself that your emotional health and wellbeing are important and that you feel happier and more in control with boundaries in place.

When a relationship doesn't go the way you want it to, be flexible and be positive.

Silence is sometimes the best answer.

The Dalai Lama

COMMUNICATION

Communication allows you to express yourself and listen to other people. In order to build social relationships, share your experiences, and enhance your support systems, clear communication is crucial.

Good communication is a skill that can be built on and developed. Being able to communicate more effectively can boost your self-confidence, improve your relationships, and help you feel better about yourself. It's a form of self-care, as sharing your true feelings can help release bottled-up feelings and emotions.

As well as just spoken words, good communication involves body language, facial expressions, and posture, from all parties involved.

HOW TO EXPRESS YOURSELF

It's not always easy or straightforward to express yourself, especially if you've not been used to talking about yourself. But when you've got someone on your team or in your support system who cares and will take time to listen to you, it's well worth trying. It can really help lift burdens and boost your emotional wellness.

Good communication is a skill that can be learned and developed.

Here are some tips to help you learn to express yourself effectively:

- Be assertive—be calm and relaxed and try to have positive body posture.
- Explain things as clearly as you can.
- Think before you speak—consider how someone else might take what you say.
- Express your emotions appropriately—don't get angry or confrontational.
- Don't get defensive if the other person expresses a view or opinion that's different to yours.

LISTENING TO OTHER PEOPLE

Communication is a two-way process—it involves talking and listening. In the same way that you'd like people to listen to you, other people in your support network will appreciate you listening to them too. Listening will help build and strengthen your relationship.

You can improve your listening skills by:

- Being patient—let someone else take their time speaking and don't interrupt them.
- Giving them 100 percent attention—turn off your cell phone and focus on the other person.
- Being neutral and open to listening—don't be judgmental about someone else's views or experiences, even if they differ from yours.

The strongest relationships are those where communication is two-way.

- Being prepared to just listen—sometimes a person might simply need someone else to listen to them, without having your advice or input.
- Showing empathy—show that you're listening, and you care, by using verbal and non-verbal acknowledgements.
- Acknowledging their feelings—if someone has strong feelings, acknowledge them so they know you're listening and taking them seriously.
- Being encouraging—if someone else is feeling low or down, be encouraging towards them; it's not always easy to open up and talk.

ONLINE COMMUNICATION

These days, a lot of communication is conducted online. Although some people find it easier to type emails or messages rather than talk to someone, this form of communication comes with its ups and downs.

When you're communicating online, you lose the ability to see each other's facial reactions, posture, and body language. This can sometimes make it tricky to convey a true picture of how you're feeling and the real meaning behind some words and sentences can be misread, misjudged, or lost completely.

Of course, emojis can go some way to express how words are intended, but they still don't replace the ability to actually see an individual's body language or reaction. It's important to bear such issues in mind when you're communicating online and try to be even clearer in the language you use and the way you express yourself with the written word. For example, if you're telling someone about how you feel, you may have to write this down more explicitly, explaining exactly how something or someone made you feel.

In a world of online communication, make time to talk face to face.

COPING WITH CONFLICT

If your communication breaks down and conflict occurs, it can trigger strong emotions, disappointment, and hurt feelings. If handled inappropriately, the conflict can rage on and cause ongoing resentment and fractured relationships. However, by learning to cope with conflict more effectively, you can help to resolve it.

Communication is key when you're dealing with conflict. As much as you may feel hurt, annoyed, or upset, try to remain as calm as possible. Being calm will help you to understand someone else's verbal and non-verbal communication more effectively. Being in control of your emotions also helps you communicate with the other person without intimidating or challenging them.

It's hard to remain calm in the face of conflict, but it's a very useful skill to learn. If necessary, you can save and offload your true emotions later, either to someone else that you trust or to yourself through techniques such as journaling.

Don't allow conflict to dominate a relationship, tackle it as it arises.

Sometimes conflict can also be eased by adding a degree of humor into the situation. It's important that you judge the situation first, though, as when used inappropriately this could escalate things.

Being able to resolve conflict provides an opportunity for growth. You can learn from your experiences, feel confident in your actions, and build a stronger relationship with the person concerned.

ASKING FOR HELP

Asking for help is not a sign of weakness or failure. On the contrary, reaching out is a sign of strength and means that you're taking control.

There's only so much that you can deal with on your own, and support from other people can make a world of difference. Your friends and family won't want you to be suffering alone—and if it was the other way around, you'd want to help them, rather than see them struggling on their own.

If you've already got a self-care support system in place, you'll have people around you that you know and trust and can reach out to when you need to. If you don't have anything like that yet, there are groups of people you can turn to for help, such as community support groups, neighbors, third-sector organizations, charities, religious leaders, or pastoral workers. If they aren't able to help you directly, the chances are they can signpost you in the direction of someone else, or an experienced organization, that could help.

HOW TO ASK FOR HELP

It's not always easy or straightforward to ask for help, especially if you're feeling out of sorts or in a difficult place emotionally. It's important to try to remember that you're not alone, that you deserve support, and it's not a sign of weakness to ask for it.

Remember that you are not alone; there is always somewhere you can get help.

Some ways that you could ask for help from friends or a member of your support network include:

- Phoning them.
- Meeting for a coffee and discussing your issues.
- Arranging to go for a walk with them and talking about it while you walk.
- Inviting them to your house to chat about it in private.
- Sending someone you really trust an email in which you write down your needs.
- Chatting to them online.
- Using an online instant messaging system with a trusted contact.

If you find it difficult to immediately open up and express your needs and concerns verbally, trying a method such as chatting online or emailing might be easier. Just be aware of how you express yourself through words—online communication can sometimes lose the intended context without body language. If necessary, you can always use an online or email method as the first port of call and an easier way to open up, then switch to meeting up with the other person or talking together on the phone.

It's important you feel comfortable when you're asking for help, so choose the approach that resonates most with you.

HOW TO KNOW WHEN TO ASK FOR HELP

Sometimes when you're in the midst of everything and in a dark place, it can be hard to know exactly when you need to ask for help.

However much you practice your own self-care routine and regularly manage to achieve your self-care goals, sometimes it's not enough. When you're leading a busy life, working hard, and socializing hard, burnout can occur. Burnout doesn't necessarily happen suddenly: it can slowly and steadily creep up on you and catch you unawares.

As a rough guide, if your self-care routine doesn't seem to be as effective as normal, you're feeling disconnected from yourself, you're struggling with things, or you're feeling like you can't cope in your usual way, it's time to ask for help.

Sometimes self-care isn't enough to solve your issues and you need expert guidance.

SEEKING PROFESSIONAL HELP

There are times when your self-care alone isn't enough and neither is asking for help from friends or family. If you feel that your mood has taken a serious dip, you're not coping well with life, or are suddenly very depressed, you need to seek advice from a medical practitioner.

It's by no means unusual for mental and emotional health problems to need the expertise of a healthcare professional. Seeking help isn't a bad thing and neither is it a sign that you're incapable of coping. It's brave and a sign that you care about your wellness and want to make positive changes to get better.

It can help to take someone else with you to a medical appointment, both in terms of support and as an additional listening ear. It can sometimes be tricky to take in all the advice and information that you're given if you're feeling unwell.

It may be that you need extra support in the form of medication, treatment, or therapy, or perhaps you may need to be looked after as an in-patient for a while. As the self-care continuum model demonstrates, pure medical care is necessary sometimes and plays a crucial part in health and wellness.

Medical care can help you move forward to a point where you can begin to add in self-care routines, too, and ultimately take over with pure self-care when you're feeling stronger.

SPATIAL WELLNESS

Taking care of your life balance and social wellness involves ensuring you feel happy, safe, stable, and secure at home.

Feeling happy in your mind is easier if you are happy in your environment.

Health and well-being involve more than just physical and emotional health—your sense of well-being can also be strongly affected by spatial elements. Studies have found that the surroundings you live in can enhance your well-being and have a positive impact on your mood and perception of happiness. So it makes sense to create a living environment that makes you feel good.

Your home is your personal domain and it's a place to which you should be able to retreat and where you can feel comfortable, nurtured, and relaxed. In many ways, your home is an extension of your identity—how you decorate it, the furniture you have, and the accessories on display all reflect your individual interests and traits.

There's a lot that you can do to influence and control your sense of spatial wellness and well-being at home, and it's definitely worth investing time and effort into making improvements if you feel a sense of imbalance in this area.

HOW TO IMPROVE SPATIAL WELLNESS AT HOME

Your social wellness can be helped by living in a place that you feel safe in. You may not be able to change the wider outside environment around you, but you can play an active part in ensuring that your home feels safe and nurturing when you're inside it.

If you currently don't feel safe at home, think about changes you could make that could improve this. For example, would changing the locks, adding window locks, having a burglar alarm fitted, adding a fire alarm and carbon monoxide alarm, or fitting a new, stronger front door improve your perception of safety and security?

Make a list of the changes you're keen to make, then rate them in order of priority. If you're short on funds you may need to pick out the most appropriate and affordable option, rather than trying to do everything at once.

If you live directly on a road or your front door opens straight in off the sidewalk, you might feel exposed or a bit vulnerable as people pass by. To make you feel safer, you could fit slatted blinds in your windows. These are a modern alternative to net curtains and are practical, as you can angle them in a way that ensures people can't look in, but you can still see out and still get a good level of light coming in.

If you have a garden, backyard, or small area of outdoor space at your home, having walls or fences marking out the boundaries of your space can increase feelings of safety and security. If your neighbors can see right into your property and you don't feel comfortable with this, consider putting up higher fences, adding panels of trellis to the top of existing fences, or planting trees, climbing plants, or shrubs to naturally fill in the gaps.

Before making structural changes, such as putting up higher fences or altering existing walls, do make sure that they are yours to alter—you don't want to find yourself dealing with neighbor disputes!

It can be tricky making improvements if you're in a rental property or house-share, when the changes aren't fully under your control. If you have strong concerns about lack of safety and security, such as apartments not having intercom systems or the locks not being as secure as they could be, speak to the landlord or rental agency and see if they would consider making or allowing you to make the improvements.

MOVING TO A NEW HOME

Uprooting yourself from a familiar living environment can understandably disturb your sense of stability. This is especially so if you move frequently due to work or study and keep having to get used to new properties and living arrangements.

Even though moving might be beyond your control, you can create a sense of stability by having familiar possessions and decor in your home. Although the building and location may be different, surrounding yourself with favorite items, photographs of loved ones, and memories of happy times, as well as artwork that makes you feel good, can help your feelings of positivity and aid your perception of stability.

Keeping communication channels open with friends and family and staying in touch regularly can increase your personal sense of well-being and keep you grounded even if your living arrangements feel shaky and unstable.

If you are moving, create a sense of stability with favorite possessions.

SPATIAL WELLNESS

Improving your spatial wellness at home also involves creating a healthy living environment.

Research studies have shown that homes that are untidy, unclean, and unkempt are more likely to be associated with physical and mental health issues, such as allergies, stress, and even depression. In contrast, if you live in a clean, tidy, and organized home, you're more likely to feel happy, healthier, and positive.

Think about how your home makes you feel. When you step through the front door, do you feel relaxed, calm, and happy to be back? Or does the sight of piles of ironing, dirty dishes, and untidiness make you want to leave again?

If it's the latter scenario, now's the time to rectify it. It's your home and you have the power to control what it looks like and ultimately how it makes you feel.

CLEANING YOUR HOME

If you're not a fan of housework, you're not alone! It's a task many people detest, but in order to have a clean home, doing some housework is essential.

Dust is renowned for building up in a seemingly neverending manner, and if you have children or pets, keeping floors and surfaces clean may seem like an endless task.

The key to preventing the idea of housework from becoming overwhelming is to break it down into smaller, manageable chunks. For example, tasks such as vacuuming the stairs, cleaning the kitchen, cleaning the bathroom, and dusting certain rooms can be done individually, rather than all in one long slog.

Cleaning may not be everyone's favorite pastime, but it's a necessary routine for self-care.

Some people find that tackling a little bit of cleaning every day works for them, while others favor doing it on certain days. However you choose to organize your time and fit chores into your week, write yourself a cleaning schedule to keep yourself on track. Building tasks into your regular schedule and doing them at set times means they're more likely to become a habit.

If you've got other family members or housemates on hand to help, delegating tasks to them will also help relieve the pressure! As the saying goes, "many hands make light work."

If you really don't like cleaning, or only have limited time available, consider hiring someone to do it for you. It doesn't have to be an expensive investment and it can help reduce any stress you have about getting it all done on your own. Find a local cleaner by asking around friends or neighbors—you may be surprised by how many people you know have their own cleaners!

A tidy, ordered home is more likely to make you feel positive about your life.

ORGANIZING YOUR HOME

In the same way that cleaning your home can have a positive impact on your well-being, so too can organizing it.

Clutter can have a damaging effect on your sense of well-being, mood, and even your relationships. It may affect your social life, too, if you're reluctant to invite people to your home when it looks untidy. With a bit of care and attention, a disorganized house can be transformed into a clutter-free haven.

Take time to examine your house and reflect on the good and bad points in each room. Look for particular areas of clutter and untidiness that need to be sorted. For example, are your kids' toys scattered all over the floor in your living room, do your kitchen cupboards need to be re-organized in a better way, or are your closets overflowing with clothes?

If you live in a shared house and aren't able to tidy or re-organize shared rooms, instead focus on any spaces that are purely yours, such as your bedroom or your food cupboards in the kitchen.

Devote time to tidying and re-organization. Don't try to do everything at once; tackle one task at a time. If you've got too much stuff that you just don't need anymore, be ruthless and donate it to charity or sell it at a yard sale.

In the case of items that are untidy but needed, such as kids' toys, look out for ways you could contain them better. Invest in storage containers, pieces of furniture that have hidden storage solutions (such as a blanket box or divan-style bed with drawers built into the base), and tidy items away out of sight.

An ordered space can help you keep an ordered mind.

Re-organized cupboards can make finding things much easier, so take out all the items and carefully decide what needs to go back in and what can be got rid of or put elsewhere. In the case of kitchen or bathroom cupboards, use storage pots to organize similar items, such as packets or boxes, so that you can find items more easily.

Once you've tackled your problem areas, work at keeping them tidy and encourage your partner or kids to do so too. Adopting a policy of "one item in, one item out" could help you control the items in your home and stop clutter getting out of hand.

FINANCES AND WORK

CHAPTER EIGHT

MONEY MANAGEMENT

One aspect of life that can sadly be the cause of much stress and despair is money. Of course, good management alone can't make up for lack of money or solve your financial problems, but in many cases this skill can really help ease your money woes. By learning a few practical money management skills, you can get a better handle on your income and expenses and reduce the amount of stress that financial issues cause you. It's great for your peace of mind as well as your self-care.

BUDGETING

Budgeting is a useful technique for managing your money. In essence, budgeting simply involves keeping track of what you have coming in each month and what goes out.

Creating a budget helps you become more clued up about your income and expenses and lets you see at a glance where your money goes. It can help you make better decisions about whether you have enough income to afford certain things and means you can be sure you've got enough money for everything that needs to be paid.

Start by making a list of all the expenses you have to pay each month, such as grocery bills, mortgage or rent, utilities (gas, electricity, water,) health insurance, car insurance. Use your check account statements to remind you of everything that goes out every month.

Then make a list of expenses that need to be paid more infrequently, such as subscriptions, car repairs, vet bills, clothing, toiletries. Next make a note of your monthly and annual income.

In an ideal scenario, your monthly bills and expenses will be less than your monthly income. Try to keep this extra set aside for unexpected bills or emergencies, or to save for future use.

If your income is less than your expenditure, you need to look at ways to cut back your spending. The longer you spend more than you have, the more debt you'll get into. Perhaps you can shop at a different store, buy unbranded groceries rather than brand names, cut out your gym subscription, or swap utility providers to save money? Once you know what your budget is, you can make better financial decisions and plans about what you're spending.

PAYING BILLS

When it comes to bills, ideally aim to pay them off completely each month. This is especially important in the case of credit cards, which will charge you interest on unpaid bills—and it can really add up. This prevents you from getting into unwanted debt and ensures you're living within your means.

You can use your budget to help you save money for bills and to have a bit aside for any unexpected costs that arise.

If you have existing debts, such as loans or credit cards, it's a good idea to plan how you could pay them off as quickly as

possible. It might mean forgoing a holiday this year or cutting back on buying new clothes, but it can be well worth the peace of mind to get debts paid off as soon as you can.

SAVING

It's always good to have a savings nest egg if you can, as you never know when you might need to dip into it. Having a separate savings account from your check account works well, so that the money is separated

Managing your income and expenditure is the best way to keep money worries at bay.

from your general income and doesn't get used accidentally. Even just saving a few dollars a week can add up considerably over the year. Try setting up a direct debit to make an automatic payment to your savings account each week or month.

You can also save money on utility bills, food shopping, or other expenses by

Every month, try to set aside a little money into your savings. It soon adds up.

regularly looking out for discount offers or coupons to use. In some instances, you may be able to stack multiple coupons together and use them in one purchase for an even better discount.

Look out for money saving deals online—online groups and forums often highlight the best deals available.

SPENDING

In terms of spending, the aim is to spend within your means and not go over your budget. It can, of course, be easier said than done, but for your emotional wellness, sticking to a spending budget does help.

Try allocating yourself some spending money each month as part of your budget. You can use it for meals out, trips to the movies, or for buying yourself a treat. Any of that spending money that you don't spend each month can form a rolling budget or be added to your savings account.

Some people find it beneficial to just stick to spending cash, rather than using a card, as it can make you more accountable and aware of your budget. It's all too easy to stick purchases on a credit card without thinking about what you're spending and whether you really need to do so!

WORKPLACE WELLNESS

Being aware of your self-care at work and taking action to boost it is important to create a better sense of wellness in the workplace.

You're likely to spend a considerable number of hours a week at work, perhaps under stress or working to strict deadlines and targets, and all this can take its toll on your health. The environment you work in, your seating or standing position, and the physical and mental effects of the work can all have an impact on your wellness.

Some employers have become aware of the important role that workplace wellness schemes can play and have begun to implement changes to help employees. Research has found that by looking after employee well-being, employers benefit from reduced sickness rates, better work productivity, and increased resilience.

Whether or not your employer has such a scheme in action, there are practical steps that you can take to ensure your personal well-being at work is a priority and that you're looking after yourself as best as possible.

OFFICE PLANTS

Having fresh, green, healthy plants in an office—whether small plants positioned on your desk, or larger plants in pots on the floor—could help you feel better at work. It brings an element of the outdoor natural world inside, and green can be a calming color to have around.

Research has shown that plants incorporated into the workplace design can even boost productivity levels. What's more, plants can create a cleaner environment by helping to remove indoor toxins, making a healthier space to work in. There's also evidence that plants positioned at strategic points may help absorb noise in the office, which is useful in an open-plan setting.

HYDRATION

For your physical health, drinking plenty of water throughout the day is essential. If your workplace has a water fountain, make use of it! Or take your own water bottle into work and refill it throughout the day. Some double-walled metal drinks bottles will help keep water cool.

If you get bored with drinking water and would like some more variety, bring some slices of fruit into work and put them inside a water bottle to add some natural fruity flavor. Aim to drink eight glasses of water daily for optimal hydration.

WORKPLACE POSTURE

How you sit can have a positive or negative effect on your body and affect your health and well-being. Your HR department should be aware of workplace ergonomics and any working equipment should be appropriately tailored. As a guide, if you're sitting at a desk your computer monitor should be positioned at eye level, so your head looks straight at it without you tilting your neck.

Office chairs supplied by your employer should support your back. If your back or shoulders tend to slouch while sitting, you may benefit from having a lumbar support on your chair to encourage your upper back to remain straight. For the best position, you should aim to keep your feet flat on the ground while you're sitting and pull your shoulders back so your back is flat against the chair.

MOVEMENT

If you spend a lot of your working day sitting at a desk, or being in the same position, taking time to move around will be beneficial. You could balance out all the sitting by walking to work in the morning, or by getting off the bus a stop early and incorporating a short walk into your morning routine. At work, consider taking the stairs instead of the elevator and, where possible, have short breaks in which you stretch, stand up, and walk around.

If your work situation allows it, you could swap a conventional desk for a standing desk, as this could help reduce postural issues and stiff joints.

BREAK REMINDERS

If you easily get absorbed in what you're doing and tend to forget when to take a break, try out a reminder app. Apps can be downloaded onto your work computer or onto your cell phone and can be set up to remind you to take a break at regular intervals. Ideally, try to get up and away from your desk every hour.

FRESH AIR

Being stuck inside working, especially in a busy office, can get stuffy and hot. Where possible, try to get some fresh air during the day, either by opening a window or taking a quick walk outside. Fresh air can help you clear your head and improve your productivity.

SNACKS

If sugary and fatty snacks are common in your workplace, avoid them by taking in your own healthy treats. A slice of cake every now and again is fine, but not every day! Healthier food will help prevent the sudden highs and lows of energy that are caused by a sugar rush.

Bring calm and color into your work environment with a plant or two.

If you find yourself at a desk or computer for much of the day, take breaks and check your posture.

TIME MANAGEMENT

Effective time management is crucial in a work environment where you're juggling multiple priorities and tasks. If you're going to get everything completed successfully without ending up stressed and exhausted, you need to know how to manage your time, prioritize responsibilities, and learn when to say no to unreasonable requests.

It can take time to find the best way for you to manage work responsibilities and balance your self-care needs, but it's worth persevering until you get it right. Good time management involves giving yourself realistic, achievable goals, setting boundaries, and knowing when to take breaks.

SETTING BOUNDARIES

Healthy work-related boundaries help define how you work and guide your relationships with colleagues, managers, and clients. Boundaries are crucial, as they determine physical and emotional limits for you. You can use boundaries to protect yourself from taking on too much work, dealing with unreasonable requests, or getting too involved in office politics. In order to be healthy, a work boundary needs to be flexible and open to change as situations and circumstances evolve. You need to be able to control your limits, but not obsess about them remaining rigid forever.

Setting healthy boundaries at work can sometimes seem tricky, as you don't want to upset your colleagues or how they view you. But if you communicate clearly and ensure your boundaries are mutually beneficial and supportive, everyone should be happy.

If you're not sure how or where you need to set boundaries, takes some time to think about the actions, situations, and people in your workplace that make you feel uncomfortable, irritated, or stressed. Then think about what changes could be made to make you feel better and more comfortable. Talk to any other people involved to get their point of view (they may well see the situation in a completely different way) and come to a mutually acceptable way of dealing with it. Good communication is essential in order for boundaries to work.

TAKING BREAKS

Taking breaks is vital for your health, well-being, and self-care. Your workplace should include set break times within the working day, as you are legally entitled to these. If you're self-employed and managing your schedule yourself, you'll need to be disciplined about setting your own breaks.

Studies have shown that if you don't take breaks, your productivity, mental well-being, and work performance all suffer, so doing so is good for both you and your employer.

Boundaries at work are crucial for life balance. Learn to say no to taking on too much.

Taking breaks and communicating with others makes working more productive.

It's also important to step away from the computer screen regularly, as too long spent in front of a screen can lead to eye strain or headaches. In fact, experts suggest it's beneficial to look away from your screen every 20 minutes. As you look away, fix your eye on something else approximately 20 feet away for at least 20 seconds. This simple act could help reduce the strain on your eyes.

Don't be tempted to stay sitting at your desk during your break—this doesn't count! Get up, stretch, move your body, and get a change of scene.

A proper time out away from your desk gives you the chance to incorporate healthy self-care habits into your daily routine. For example, eating a healthy lunch, having a walk outside in the fresh air or a jog around the block, having a 5-minute mindfulness or meditation session, or even fitting in a quick 10-minute power nap if you need one.

TIME MANAGEMENT TIPS

Use these practical time management tips to help you learn to organize your time more effectively and ensure you complete all the essential tasks you need to do.

BE ORGANIZED

—

Write lists so you're clear on what you need to do. Prioritize tasks so you get the most important things done first. Do them one at a time and enjoy ticking them off your list when they're completed!

ALLOCATE YOUR TIME

—

Manage your time effectively by allocating specific amounts of time to certain tasks or activities. For example, allow for working, socializing, spending time with family, exercising, taking part in hobbies, and relaxing.

SET DEADLINES

—

Set yourself deadlines for when things need to be completed. Make sure they're realistic—it's not helpful to put yourself under excess pressure.

BE FLEXIBLE

—

Accept that not everything goes to plan and interruptions do occur. Add some extra time in your schedule that allows you to be flexible if you don't get everything done as planned. Be kind to yourself!

DELEGATE

—

Don't try to do everything yourself. Where possible, delegate tasks to other people—whether that's work colleagues, friends, or family.

BE ASSERTIVE

—

Learn to say "no" to unreasonable requests—and mean it. You can't take everything on, whether that's work colleagues, friends, or family.

PLAN TIME FOR YOURSELF

—

Make sure you designate time in your schedule for yourself each day, so you can relax, look after your own needs, and enjoy doing the things you love.

SET FINISHING TIMES

—

Set yourself finishing times and stick to them. This is especially important if you're self-employed and don't have a specific end point to your day.

OPPORTUNITIES FOR LEARNING

The benefits of learning should never be overlooked. It's something that occurs throughout life and you're never too old to learn something new. In fact, as part of your self-care habit, it's worth actively seeking out opportunities for learning.

Studies have found that developing skills or knowledge can play a positive role in aiding well-being. Learning something new can boost social qualities such as confidence, self-esteem, optimism, and a sense of purpose.

It can also provide new directions to your life, unexpectedly open up new doors, and improve social connections, too—helping you meet new people, make new friends, and increase your social support network of like-minded people.

Learning doesn't have to be hard work, nor does it have to take place in a classroom. Learning can take many forms—including being vocational, artistic, physical, or musical.

Don't be afraid to learn something new and open new doors.

Some things can be learned on your own, through reading books, listening to podcasts, or watching videos, while other things are best learned in a group or on a one-to-one basis. Be open to, and look out for, new learning opportunities in your life; you never know where they'll take you.

LEARNING OPPORTUNITIES AT WORK

Learning new skills related to your work could broaden your horizons in the workplace. It could even help provide a way onto a new career pathway or a promotion.

If your employer offers work-related courses, consider signing up or ask if there's anything available that you could do. If your boss could do with a prompt, seek out relevant courses yourself, then propose something that you'd like to do. It will make you seem proactive and keen, as well as creating a great opportunity for you.

ADULT EDUCATION CLASSES

There are always plenty of evening and adult education classes available in local neighborhoods, often held at high schools or colleges. The courses frequently run parallel to school semesters, so look out for details being advertised near the start of each semester.

It's never too late to learn something new, and there are myriad courses on offer for adults.

Craft classes will offer something new and a mindful session, too.

Other good places to look out for learning opportunities include arts centers, theater groups, community centers, and via independent craftspeople.

Adult education classes can take numerous forms. Physical classes help hone your exercise skills and improve your fitness. Art classes help unleash your creativity and give you the chance to explore new forms of expression. Cookery classes help you improve your cooking skills, understand what makes a healthy diet, and discover new sweet and savory dishes to try. Technical classes can teach you new skills. Literary classes introduce you to new authors to read and deepen your connection with books. Health classes teach skills such as first aid or offer tips and insight into living a healthy lifestyle.

The list goes on and on—there really is something for everyone and plenty of opportunities to learn.

ONLINE COURSES

If your free time is limited due to work and family commitments, an alternative option is to do an online course.

Many of these are professionally run and offer just as good a learning experience as taking a course in person. Plus, they often have interactive elements, too, such as forums or online sessions with other learners, so you still gain the benefits of social interaction with the tutor and the other students.

Some online courses can be completed at your own pace, which might fit in better with a busy schedule, while others need to be completed during a set time period. Courses can be paid-for or free to participate in.

To find online courses that would suit your needs and interests, use an Internet search engine to look up what's on offer—search for ads on sites such as on social media or ask on online groups for ideas about what might be on offer. Ask friends or work colleagues if they've taken any courses online recently; getting a personal recommendation is always useful.

VOLUNTEERING

Another option that can provide valuable learning opportunities is volunteering.

There's always a variety of charitable groups and organizations looking for help from volunteers, either on a regular or occasional basis. Volunteering your time to get stuck in and help with a cause that means a lot to you can offer good social opportunities as well as a chance to grow and learn.

You can volunteer to help local, national, or even international organizations; volunteering abroad can double up as a vacation or educational trip, although you do need to take the cost of travel and accommodation into consideration.

Sometimes employers enable employees to take an occasional day to volunteer with a local cause—ask your HR department if there are any opportunities available at your place of work. If not, perhaps it's something you could suggest for the future?

Volunteering offers an opportunity to support a cause and feel a part of something.

SETTING GOALS

Setting goals is a great way of giving yourself a sense of meaning and purpose. Goals can be used in any area of your life, from physical well-being, such as challenging yourself to eat healthier food or exercise more regularly; to emotional well-being, such as learning to love yourself more or boost your confidence; and to social well-being, such as making a new friend or getting a new job.

By setting yourself goals, you give yourself something to aim for and achieve. Goals can keep you interested and engaged, especially if you have mini milestones along the way, and it's lovely to be able to celebrate when you eventually reach them. Studies have shown that if you want to make a change in your life, setting yourself a target will make you more likely to achieve it.

When you're setting yourself wellness-related goals, it's helpful to have a mix of different aims that are achievable at different points in time—for example, daily, weekly, monthly, or long-term goals. This will help to keep you on track and your sense of achievement will be boosted as you reach each milestone. It's good to have one or two long-term goals, but too many might seem too far away or out of your reach, and you don't want to end up feeling despondent about your chances of achieving them.

Planning and goal-setting can help you navigate a less stressful path to your goal.

HOW TO SET GOALS

When you're setting goals, first start by deciding exactly what it is you'd like to achieve. It needs to be something you really want, as well as something that you're excited by and will stick to. It doesn't have to be a huge goal; in fact, it's good to start small and then work up to something bigger.

Be realistic and take into account aspects such as your existing commitments and energy levels and ensure it's something you can currently see yourself being able to achieve.

Write down your goal. Describe exactly what it is you'd like to achieve and why you'd like to do it. Committing it to paper firms up your decision and increases your chances of sticking to it. Telling somebody else about it also helps to make you accountable.

Plan how you're going to achieve your goal. What steps do you need to take? If necessary, do some research into how best you could work towards your goal, or ask a friend for help. Depending on the nature of your goal, you may find it easier to break it down into several smaller steps or stages.

Think about what obstacles or issues might occur and consider ways in which you could deal with them. Planning in advance for potential problems can make it easier to deal with them if they do arise.

As you work towards your goal, maintain a positive attitude and tick off the smaller milestones as you reach them. If you need help along the way, ask your friends, family, or support network to help you.

If life throws you a curveball and your circumstances change, don't be hard on yourself or abandon your aims completely. Just reset your goal, adjust it as necessary, and resume working towards it.

When you reach your goals, celebrate your success! Feel proud of your achievements and your perseverance, and enjoy the moment with friends.

Once you've achieved your goal, you'll know how good it feels and how motivated having that target has kept you, so maybe you might want to consider setting yourself another goal?

CREATE A VISION BOARD

Some people find goals easier to aim for if they can visualize the end result. That's where creating a vision board can come in handy.

A vision board is literally a visual representation of your goals or aims. If your goal is to save enough money to go on holiday, your vision board could have pictures of the location where you'd like to go and images of the things you'd do while you're there—like swimming in a pool, visiting historic landmarks, or relaxing on a beach.

A vision board doesn't have to just be made up of images, you can also add words or sentences describing your goal and how you'll feel when you achieve it. You can create a board the old-school way—by cutting out images and sticking them on a board—or draw one up digitally.

However you choose to put together your vision board, the idea is to hang it up somewhere you'll see if frequently. That will help keep your goal visible and in your mind and motivate you to continue to strive for it. If it's something you feel awkward about other people seeing, or if you live in a shared house or apartment, you could always put it inside a cupboard or a drawer where only you will see it.

You don't have to get to your goal alone, enlist the support of those you trust.

And the day came when the risk to remain tight in a bud was more painful than the risk it took to blossom.

Anaïs Nin

REFERENCE AND RESOURCES

PART FOUR

SELF-CARE CHECKLIST

PHYSICAL WELLNESS	MONDAY	TUESDAY	WEDNESDAY	THURSDAY
Go to bed at the same time each night.	☐	☐	☐	☐
Drink eight glasses of water throughout the day.	☐	☐	☐	☐
Practice mindful eating.	☐	☐	☐	☐
Every day, do 10 minutes of an exercise you enjoy.	☐	☐	☐	☐
Cook a healthy meal.	☐	☐	☐	☐

EMOTIONAL WELLNESS				
Spend 10 minutes meditating each day.	☐	☐	☐	☐
Write down five things that make you happy.	☐	☐	☐	☐
Turn negative thoughts into positive ones.	☐	☐	☐	☐
Spend 30 minutes reading or being creative.	☐	☐	☐	☐
Focus on your breathing.	☐	☐	☐	☐

SOCIAL WELLNESS				
Take a five-minute break at work and go for a walk or have a stretch.	☐	☐	☐	☐
Phone, email, or text a friend with whom you've not connected recently.	☐	☐	☐	☐
Spend 10 minutes tidying and organizing your home.	☐	☐	☐	☐

ENJOY SPENDING TIME WITH FAMILY OR FRIENDS.				
Set yourself a goal and a plan to save money.	☐	☐	☐	☐

FRIDAY	SATURDAY	SUNDAY
☐	☐	☐
☐	☐	☐
☐	☐	☐
☐	☐	☐
☐	☐	☐
☐	☐	☐
☐	☐	☐
☐	☐	☐
☐	☐	☐
☐	☐	☐
☐	☐	☐
☐	☐	☐
☐	☐	☐
☐	☐	☐

IMPROVE YOUR SELF-CARE HABITS

Each week try to add a new self-care habit to your routine. It will provide you with more variation and help you develop new healthy habits.

- Walk or cycle to work instead of driving.
- Look at your monthly expenses and see what savings you can make.
- Get to know an acquaintance better—talk to them and listen to what they have to say.
- Start a gratitude journal and record the things that you're grateful for.
- Try cooking a meal with ingredients you wouldn't normally use.
- Give yourself a foot massage.
- Create an area of sacred space where you can be still and unwind.
- Try a new hobby or creative activity.
- Focus on being kinder and more compassionate to yourself and others.
- Discover new opportunities for learning.
- Pamper yourself with a new skincare product or a manicure.
- Make a cleaning playlist of your favorite songs so you can play it when you're doing the housework.
- Learn to say "no" to unreasonable requests.
- Make a list of happy and uplifting music to play if you're feeling down.

SETTING GOALS TEMPLATE

EVERY DAY

I will take care of my physical, emotional, and social wellness in these ways:

Physical wellness

Emotional wellness

Social wellness

WEEKLY GOALS

Each week I will look after my self-care needs in these ways:

Physical self-care

Emotional self-care

Social self-care

MONTHLY GOALS

Each month I will achieve these goals:

LONG-TERM GOALS

My self-care aims, long term, are:

"You are never too old to set another goal or to dream a new dream."

C. S. Lewis

TIPS FOR SETTING GOALS

Use these tips to set yourself achievable self-care goals:

- Start small, so you can feel accomplished when you achieve your targets.
- Make your goals practical and realistic, so you can act on them easily.
- Make your goals inspiring, to give you something to aim for.
- Keep a record of your past and present goals, so you can reflect on them.
- Celebrate your successes!

EXERCISE PLANNER

Exercise is a great way to tend to your physical wellness needs and it helps to get into regular habits.

Use this weekly exercise planner to create an achievable routine that you can follow each week. Incorporating a little bit of exercise into each day will gradually build up your fitness levels.

	MONDAY	TUESDAY	WEDNESDAY
WEEK 1			
WEEK 2			
WEEK 3			
WEEK 4			

Don't forget to include different types of exercises, such as aerobics, to give you a cardio workout, and yoga and Pilates to help stretch and strengthen your muscles.

THURSDAY	FRIDAY	SATURDAY	SUNDAY

HEALTHY EATING TEMPLATE

Develop a healthy eating habit by keeping a record of what you eat and drink each day. As well as being a good record of your diet, it could help identify problem areas that may benefit from changes.

WEEK 1	BREAKFAST	LUNCH	DINNER	SNACKS	DRINKS
MONDAY					
TUESDAY					
WEDNESDAY					
THURSDAY					
FRIDAY					
SATURDAY					
SUNDAY					

WEEK 2	BREAKFAST	LUNCH	DINNER	SNACKS	DRINKS
MONDAY					
TUESDAY					
WEDNESDAY					
THURSDAY					
FRIDAY					
SATURDAY					
SUNDAY					

WEEK 3	BREAKFAST	LUNCH	DINNER	SNACKS	DRINKS
MONDAY					
TUESDAY					
WEDNESDAY					
THURSDAY					
FRIDAY					
SATURDAY					
SUNDAY					

WEEK 4	BREAKFAST	LUNCH	DINNER	SNACKS	DRINKS
MONDAY					
TUESDAY					
WEDNESDAY					
THURSDAY					
FRIDAY					
SATURDAY					
SUNDAY					

	NEW HEALTHY FOODS TRIED	NEW HEALTHY FOODS TRIED
HEALTHY FOOD GOALS		

BUDGET TEMPLATE

Use these templates to keep a record of how much money you have coming in and going out each month.

MONTHLY INCOME

Keep a note of exactly how much income you have coming in each month and when it's typically paid in. It will help you plan your spending more effectively.

Don't forget to keep a record of any other income sources you have, beyond your employment, such as side hustles or selling on eBay. Every little bit helps!

For example:

INCOME SOURCE	AMOUNT	DATE PAID
Main employment		
Delivery round		
Selling on eBay		

MONTHLY EXPENDITURE

Get a clearer perspective of exactly how much you spend each month. If you live with a partner or in a shared household, use the middle column to record how much your share is each month.

Look for any ways by which you can reduce this expenditure.

For example:

INCOME SOURCE	BILL AMOUNT	MY SHARE	DATE DUE
Main employment			
Delivery round			
Selling on eBay			

OCCASIONAL EXPENDITURE

If you have bills that you need to pay only occasionally, such as seasonally or annually, make a note of them in the chart below so you can keep track of what they are and when they are payable. These are the kind of bills that can catch you off guard if you've forgotten they're due.

For example:

INCOME SOURCE	BILL AMOUNT	DATE DUE
Quarterly gym membership		
Vacation payment		
Birthday presents		

MONEY SAVING CHALLENGE

Keen to save money? It's amazing how small savings can add up over the course of a year.

Use this simple weekly savings challenge and you can accumulate $1,040 in one year, by saving just $20 per week. Add a tick as you make your saving each week, then enjoy planning what you'll spend your $1,040 on at the end of the challenge.

1	2	3	4	5	6	7
8	9	10	11	12	13	14
15	16	17	18	19	20	21
22	23	24	25	26	27	28
29	30	31	32	33	34	35
36	37	38	39	40	41	42
43	44	45	46	47	48	49
50	51	52				

USEFUL RESOURCES

AROMATHERAPY

—

North America

Alliance of International Aromatherapists (AIS)
www.alliance-aromatherapists.org
3758 E. 104th Ave #36
Thornton, CO 80233
USA

National Association of Holistic Aromatherapy (NAHA)
www.naha.org
6000 S. 5th Ave
Pocatello, ID 83204
USA

The Pacific Institute of Aromatherapy
www.pacificinstituteofaromatherapy.com
P.O. Box 6723
San Rafael, CA 94903
USA

United Kingdom

International Federation of Professional Aromatherapists
www.ifparoma.org
82 Ashby Rd
Hinckley
Leicestershire LE10 1SN
UK

MEDITATION

—

North America

American Meditation Society
www.americanmeditationsociety.org/
Heartfulness
www.heartfulnessinstitute.org/

United Kingdom

Headspace
www.headspace.com/meditation

The Meditation Trust
www.meditationtrust.com
11 Daryngton Ave
Birchington
Kent CT7 9PS
UK

MENTAL HEALTH & EMOTIONAL WELLBEING

—

North America

American Counseling Association
www.counseling.org/
6101 Stevenson Ave
Suite 600
Alexandria, VA 22304
USA

American Psychological Association (APA)
www.apa.org
750 First St, N.E.
Washington, D.C. 20002-4242
USA

American Psychotherapy Association
www.americanpsychotherapy.com
American Psychotherapy Association
2750 E. Sunshine St
Springfield, MO 65804
USA

United Kingdom

British Association for Counselling and Psychotherapy (BACP)
www.bacp.co.uk
BACP
15 St. John's Business Park
Lutterworth
Leicestershire LE17 4HB
UK

Royal College of Psychiatrists
www.rcpsych.ac.uk
21 Prescot St
London E1 8BB
UK

The British Psychological Society (BPS)
www.bps.org.uk
St. Andrews House
48 Princess Rd East
Leicester LE1 7DR
UK

NUTRITION

—

North America

American Nutrition Association
www.theana.org
211 West Chicago Ave
Suite 217
Hinsdale, IL 60521
USA

Academy of Nutrition and Dietetics
www.eatright.org
120 S. Riverside Plaza
Suite 2190
Chicago, IL 60606-6995
USA

Canadian Association of Natural Nutritional Practitioners
www.cannp.ca
335 St. Andrews St East
Fergus, ON N1M 1R3
Canada

Dietitians of Canada
www.dietitians.ca
99 Yorkville Ave
Second Floor
Toronto, ON M5R 1C1
Canada

United Kingdom

British Dietetic Association (BDA)
www.bda.uk.com
3rd Floor Interchange Place
151-165 Edmund St
Birmingham B3 2TA
UK

British Nutrition Foundation
www.nutrition.org.uk
New Derwent House
69-73 Theobalds Rd
London WC1X 8TA
UK

PILATES

North America

Pilates Method Alliance
www.pilatesmethodalliance.org
1666 John F. Kennedy Causeway
Suite 402
North Bay Village, FL 33141
USA

United States Pilates Association
www.unitedstatespilatesassociation.com
1500 East Broward Blvd
Suite 250
Ft. Lauderdale, FL 33301
USA

United Kingdom

Independent Pilates Teachers Association
www.iptauk.com

Pilates Teacher Association
www.pilatesteacherassociation.org
9 Church St
Troon KA10 6AU
UK

YOGA

North America

International Association of Yoga Therapists
www.iayt.org
P.O. Box 251563
Little Rock, AR 7222
USA

Yoga Alliance
www.yogaalliance.org
1560 Wilson Blvd
Suite 700
Arlington, VA 22209
USA

United Kingdom

British Wheel of Yoga
www.bwy.org.uk
25 Jermyn St
Sleaford
Lincolnshire NG34 7RU
UK

Yoga Alliance Professionals
www.yogaalliance.co.uk
10/2 Beaverhall Rd
Edinburgh EH7 4JE
Scotland
UK

FURTHER READING

Atomic Habits: An Easy and Proven Way to Build Good Habits and Break Bad Ones
James Clear
Avery, 2018

Everything is Figureoutable
Marie Forleo
Penguin, 2019

Getting Things Done: The Art of Stress-free Productivity
David Allen
Penguin Books, 2015

Good Vibes, Good Life: How Self-love is the Key to Unlocking Your Greatness
Vex King
Hay House, 2018

Happy: Finding Joy in Every Day and Letting Go of Perfect
Fearne Cotton
Orion Spring, 2017

How to Win Friends and Influence People
Dale Carnegie
Vermillion, 2006

Life-balance / Social Wellness
12 Rules for Life: An Antidote to Chaos
Jordan B. Peterson
Penguin, 2019

Mental Health and Wellbeing in the Workplace: A Practical Guide for Employers and Employees
Gill Hasson
Capstone, 2020

Mindfulness: An Eight-week Plan to Finding Peace in a Frantic World
Mark Williams, Dr. Danny Pearson
Rodale Books, 2012

Mindset: Changing the Way You Think to Fulfil Your Potential
Dr. Carol Dweck
Robinson, 2017

Money: A User's Guide
Laura Whateley
Fourth Estate, 2018

No Mud, No Lotus: The Art of Transforming Suffering
Thich Nhat Hanh
Parallax Press, 2014

Non-violent Communication: A Language of Life
Marshall B. Rosenberg
Puddle Dancer Press, 2015

One Zentangle a Day
Beckah Krahula
Quarry Books, 2012

Practicing Mindfulness: 75 Essential Meditations to Reduce Stress, Improve, Mental Health and Find Peace in the Everyday
Matthew Sockolov
Althea Press, 2018

Simply Living Well: A Guide to Creating a Natural, Low-waste Home
Julia Watkins
Hardie Grant Books, 2020

Switch: How to Change Things When Change Is Hard
Chip Heath, Dan Heath
Crown Business, 2010

Take a Moment: Activities to Refocus, Re-centre and Relax Wherever You Are
MIND
Michael O'Mara, 2018

The Book of Joy: Lasting Happiness in a Changing World
Dalai Lama, Desmond Tutu, Douglas Carlton Abrams
Avery, 2016

The Chimp Paradox
Dr. Steve Peters
Vermillion, 2012

The Holistic Home
Laura Benko
Skyhorse, 2016

The Lazy Genius Way: Embrace What Matters, Ditch What Doesn't and Get Stuff Done
Kendra Adachi
WaterBrook 2020

The Little Book of Mindfulness: 10 Minutes a Day to Less Stress
Patrizia Collard
Gaia Books, 2014

The One Thing
Gary Keller
John Murray Learning, 2014

When Things Fall Apart: Heart Advice for Difficult Times
Pema Chodron
Shambala, 2016

Why We Sleep
Matthew Walker
Penguin, 2018

You Are a Badass: How to Stop Doubting Your Greatness and Start Living an Awesome Life
Jen Sincero
John Murray Learning, 2016

INDEX